"ATM is taking the telecommunications world by storm. It promises to fundamentally reorganize the way we use networks and is being applied in every quarter of the telecommunications industry. There is a lot to learn so let Tim Kwok pilot you through this tornado. He takes off with multimedia applications and the Internet, two driving forces powering ATM. Next, he barnstorms deeply into ATM technology areas such as signalling and traffic management and then provides a smooth landing with ATM over xDSL and Hybrid Fiber Coax. This excellent book will expose you to ATM at its very best: solving problems for residential and business users. Kwok will reveal it to you in every aspect and in every detail. Read it and become a high-flying ATM expert!"

Dr. Stephen M. Walters
Past President and Chairman, The ATM Forum
Principal and Fellow, Bellcore
11 July 1997

"Tim Kwok is... one of the few people that have successfully bridged the gap between the science of network developments and the art of application requirements..."

Fred Sammartino
Founding President and Chairman, The ATM Forum

ATM:

The New Paradigm for Internet, Intranet, and Residential Broadband Services and Applications

Timothy Kwok

Microsoft Corporation
Redmond, Washington

To join a Prentice Hall PTR internet mailing list, point to
http://www.prenhall.com/mail_lists/

ISBN 0-13-107244-7

90000

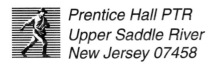

Prentice Hall PTR
Upper Saddle River
New Jersey 07458

9 780131 072442

Library of Congress Cataloging in Publication Data

Kwok, Timothy
    ATM: The New Paradigm for Internet, Intranet, and residential broadband services
and applications /Timothy Kwok.
        p.   cm
    Includes index.
    ISBN 0-13-107244-7
    1. Asynchronous transfer mode. 2. Internet (computer network). 3. Intranets
(computer networks) 4. Client/server computing. 5. broadband network. 6. multimedia
applications. I. Title.
TK5105.35.K86   1997
004.6'6—dc21   97-22878
                                                   CIP

Editorial/Production Supervision: *Joanne Anzalone*
Acquisitions Editor: *Mary Franz*
Cover Design Director: *Jerry Votta*
Cover Design: *Scott Weiss*
Manufacturing Manager: *Alexis R. Heydt*
Marketing Manager: *Miles Williams*
Editorial Assistant: *Noreen Regina*

© 1998 Prentice Hall PTR
Prentice-Hall, Inc.
A Simon & Schuster Company
Upper Saddle River, New Jersey 07458

Prentice Hall books are widely used by corporations and government agencies
for training, marketing, and resale.
The publisher offers discounts on this book when ordered in bulk quantities.
For more information, contact: Corporate Sales Department, Phone: 800-382-3419;
FAX: 201-236-7141; E-mail: corpsales@prenhall.com
Or write: Corp. Sales Dept., Prentice Hall PTR,
1 Lake Street, Upper Saddle River, NJ   07458

Printed in the United States of America
10 9 8 7 6 5 4 3 2

ISBN 0-13-107244-7

Prentice-Hall International (UK) Limited, *London*
Prentice-Hall of Australia Pty. Limited, *Sydney*
Prentice-Hall Canada Inc., *Toronto*
Prentice-Hall Hispanoamericana, S.A., *Mexico*
Prentice-Hall of India Private Limited, *New Delhi*
Prentice-Hall of Japan, Inc., *Tokyo*
Simon & Schuster Asia Pte. Ltd., *Singapore*
Editora Prentice-Hall do Brasil, Ltda., *Rio de Janeiro*

To my wife Janice, my father,
and in memory of my mother

Contents

Foreword,   xix

Preface,   xxiii

    Outline of this book,   xxvi

Acknowledgments,   xxix

Part I

Multimedia Applications Requirements,   1

Chapter 1

Multimedia Applications and ATM,   3

    1.1 Interactive Multimedia Applications,   3

        1.1.1 ATM,   4

        1.1.2 ATM and the Internet,   5

        1.1.3 ATM and the Intranets,   8

        1.1.4 ATM and Residential Broadband Networks,   8

    1.2 An Ideal Communications Network,   9

        1.2.1 Distance,   9

      1.2.2 Location, 9

      1.2.3 Time, 10

      1.2.4 Media, 10

   1.3 Summary and Outline of This Part, 12

   1.4 References, 12

Chapter 2
Network Architectures: The Telephone Network, the Internet and Intranets, 15

   2.1 Introduction, 15

   2.2 Networking Architectures, 16

      2.2.1 Fully Connected Point-to-point Networks, 16

      2.2.2 Switched Point-to-point Networks, 18

         2.2.2.1 Circuit Switching, 19

         2.2.2.2 Packet Switching, 22

         2.2.2.3 Permanent Connections, 27

      2.2.3 Broadcast Networks, 27

         2.2.3.1 One-way Broadcast, 27

         2.2.3.2 Two-way Communications, 28

         2.2.3.3 Circuit Switching on Shared Medium, 28

         2.2.3.4 Packet Switching on Shared Medium, 29

   2.3 Limitations of Today's Network Infrastructures, 30

      2.3.1 Telephone Networks, 30

         2.3.1.1 Characteristics, 30

         2.3.1.2 Limitations, 31

      2.3.2 The Internet and Intranets, 32

         2.3.2.1 Characteristics, 32

         2.3.2.2 Limitations, 37

   2.4 Summary, 39

   2.5 References, 40

Chapter 3
An Application Classification, 41

   3.1 Introduction, 41

   3.2 Communications Applications, 42

      3.2.1 Definition, 42

      3.2.2 Networking Attributes of an Application, 42

         3.2.2.1 Information Types, 42

         3.2.2.2 Delivery Requirements, 43

         3.2.2.3 Symmetry, 44

         3.2.2.4 Number of Parties, 46

         3.2.2.5 Wired or Wireless Access, 47

3.2.2.6 Mobility, 48

3.2.2.7 Human versus Non-Human, 49

3.3 A Classification of Applications, 50

3.3.1 Real-time Streaming Applications, 50

3.3.2 Real-time Block Transfer Applications, 52

3.3.2.1 Internet Applications, 53

3.3.2.2 Web Browsing, 53

3.3.2.3 Bandwidth- versus Latency-Limited, 55

3.3.3 Non-real-time Applications, 56

3.4 Summary, 58

3.5 References, 58

Chapter 4
Application Traffic Requirements, 59

4.1 Introduction, 59

4.1.1 Applications Requirements, 60

4.1.2 Traffic and QoS Requirements, 61

4.2 Traffic Generation Patterns, 61

4.2.1 Arrival Distribution: Continuous versus Bursty Traffic, 62

4.2.2 ADU Length Distribution, 62

4.2.3 Packet Length Distribution, 63

4.2.3.1 Packet Loss Probability, 64

4.2.3.2 MTU Size of Link Layer, 64

4.2.3.3 Default Packet Size Limit, 64

4.2.3.4 Packetization Delay, 65

4.2.3.5 Transmission Delay, 65

4.2.3.6 Effects of Loss Packets, 65

4.2.4 Self-similarity Traffic, 66

4.2.5 CBR versus VBR, 66

4.2.6 Traffic Shaping, 67

4.2.7 Adaptive Applications, 69

4.2.8 Traffic Asymmetry, 69

4.3 Bandwidth Requirements, 70

4.3.1 Bandwidth Parameters, 70

4.3.1.1 Peak Bandwidth, 70

4.3.1.2 Average Bandwidth, 71

4.3.2 Real-time Streaming Applications, 72

4.3.3 Real-time Block Transfer Applications, 73

4.3.4 Time-based Information Delivery Requirements, 75

4.3.5 User Level Behavior, 76

4.4 Summary,   77

4.5 References,   77

Chapter 5
Application QoS Requirements,   79

5.1 Introduction,   79

5.2 Delay Requirements,   81
  5.2.1 Delay Distribution,   81
  5.2.2 Delay Components,   81
  5.2.3 Absolute Delay Requirements,   86
    5.2.3.1 Real-time Streaming Applications,   87
    5.2.3.2 Real-time Block Transfer Applications,   89
  5.2.4 Delay Variation (Jitters) Requirements,   90
    5.2.4.1 Telephony,   92

5.3 Error Requirements,   92
  5.3.1 Error Tolerances,   93
    5.3.1.1 Information Types,   93
    5.3.1.2 Usage,   94
    5.3.1.3 Components,   94
    5.3.1.4 Compression Ratio,   94
  5.3.2 Error Characterization,   95
    5.3.2.1 Application Layer: ADU Loss Ratio,   95
    5.3.2.2 Network Layer: PDU Loss Ratio,   95
    5.3.2.3 Physical Layer: Bit Error Ratio,   95
  5.3.3 Error Requirements for Different Application Classes,   96
    5.3.3.1 Real-time Streaming Applications,   96
    5.3.3.2 Real-time Block Transfer Applications,   100
    5.3.3.3 Non-real-time Applications,   100

5.4 Summary,   101

5.5 References,   101

Part II
Fundamentals of ATM,   103

Chapter 6
Principles of ATM,   105

6.1 Introduction,   105

6.2 Principles of ATM,   107
  6.2.1 Switched Point-to-point Architecture,   107
  6.2.2 Packet Switching,   108
  6.2.3 Fast Packet Switching,   109

6.2.3.1 Problems of Classic Packet Switching,   109
6.2.3.2 Solution: Fast Packet Switching,   111
6.2.3.3 Techniques of Fast Packet Switching,   111
6.2.4 Resource Reservation and Admission Control,   117
6.2.5 Asynchronous Time Division Multiplexing,   118

6.3 Advantages of ATM,   119
6.3.1 Technical Advantages,   119
6.3.1.1 High Bandwidth,   119
6.3.1.2 Quality of Service Guarantee,   120
6.3.1.3 Flexibility,   120
6.3.1.4 Integration,   120
6.3.1.5 Scaleability,   121
6.3.1.6 Efficiency,   122
6.3.1.7 Operations,   122
6.3.2 Strategic Advantages,   122
6.3.2.1 One Networking Architecture,   122
6.3.2.2 Compatible Architectures,   123
6.3.2.3 True Multi-vendor Support,   123

6.4 Summary,   123

6.5 References,   124

Chapter 7
Overview of ATM,   125

7.1 Introduction,   125

7.2 Basic Elements of an ATM Network,   125

7.3 Standard ATM Interfaces,   127

7.4 ATM Layered Model,   129

7.5 Basic ATM Network Operations,   130
7.5.1 Call Establishment,   130
7.5.2 Cell Sequencing and VC Routes,   132

7.6 Call Negotiation and Renegotiation,   132

7.7 VC Number and Translation,   133

7.8 Virtual Channel and Virtual Channel Connection,   136

7.9 Virtual Path Connection,   136

7.10   VCC and VPC Usage,   138
7.10.1 One VCC for Multiple Applications,   139
7.10.2 One VCC for Each Application,   139
7.10.3 Multiple VCCs for an Application,   140
7.10.4 One VPC per Application,   140

        7.10.5 One VPC per Component,   140
        7.10.6 One VPC per Pair of Locations,   141
        7.10.7 One VCC per Pair of Locations,   141

    7.11   Summary,   141
    7.12   References,   141

Chapter 8
The Protocol Reference Model of ATM,   143

    8.1 Introduction,   143
    8.2 Layered Architecture,   144
        8.2.1 Physical Layer,   146
        8.2.2 The (Optional) MAC layer,   150
        8.2.3 ATM Layer,   152
            8.2.3.1 ATM Cell Format,   153
            8.2.3.2 ATM Layer Functions at the UNI,   157
        8.2.4 ATM Adaptation Layer (AAL),   159
        8.2.5 Higher Layer Protocols,   160
    8.3 The Hourglass Model,   160
    8.4 Multi-Plane Model,   161
        8.4.1 User Plane,   162
        8.4.2 Control Plane,   163
        8.4.3 Management Plane,   163
    8.5 B-ISDN PRM and ISO OSI Reference Model,   164
        8.5.1 Pure ATM Networks,   164
        8.5.2 Internetworking,   165
            8.5.2.1 Internetworking with Legacy LANs using IP,   165
    8.6 Summary,   167
    8.7 References,   167

Chapter 9
ATM Adaptation Layer,   169

    9.1 Introduction,   169
    9.2 End-to-end ATM Protocol Model,   170
    9.3 AAL Functions,   172
        9.3.1 Segmentation and Reassembly,   172
        9.3.2 Reduction of CPU Processing Overhead,   173
        9.3.3 Error Control Mechanisms,   174
        9.3.4 Synchronization and Clock Recovery,   175
        9.3.5 Maintenance of Traffic Patterns,   176

      9.3.6 Receive Buffer Allocation, 176

      9.3.7 Multiplexing of Multiple Data Streams, 177

   9.4 AAL Service Classes and AAL Types, 177

      9.4.1 Origin of AAL Types, 177

      9.4.2 Attributes of AAL Service Classes, 178

         9.4.2.1 Source Traffic Pattern, 178

         9.4.2.2 End-to-end Timing Relationship, 178

         9.4.2.3 Connection Mode, 178

      9.4.3 AAL Service Classes: An Overview, 179

         9.4.3.1 Class A, 179

         9.4.3.2 Class B, 179

         9.4.3.3 Class C, 179

         9.4.3.4 Class D, 179

         9.4.3.5 Class X, 180

      9.4.4 Service Model Evolution, 181

   9.5 AAL Types, 181

      9.5.1 AAL 1, 184

         9.5.1.1 Functions, 184

         9.5.1.2 Convergence Sublayer, 187

         9.5.1.3 SAR Sublayer, 188

         9.5.1.4 Applications, 190

      9.5.2 AAL 3/4, 190

         9.5.2.1 CS Sublayer, 191

         9.5.2.2 SAR Sublayer, 192

         9.5.2.3 Message and Streaming Modes, 194

      9.5.3 AAL 5, 194

         9.5.3.1 Functions, 195

         9.5.3.2 CS Sublayer, 196

         9.5.3.3 SAR, 197

         9.5.3.4 Comparison Between AAL 5 and AAL 3/4, 197

      9.5.4 Comparisons of AAL Types, 198

   9.6 Summary, 199

   9.7 References, 199

Chapter 10

ATM Access (UNI) Signaling, 201

     10.1 Introduction, 201

     10.2 ATM Signaling Concepts, 202

        10.2.1 Permanent and Switched VCs, 202

        10.2.2 Signaling Virtual Channel, 203

        10.2.3 VPI and VPCI, 204

10.2.3.1 Proxy Signaling Capability, 206
10.2.3.2 Virtual UNIs and ATM Multiplexer,   207
10.2.4 Signaling Protocol Model and SAAL, 209
10.2.5 ATM Addressing, 210
10.2.6 Address Registration, 212
10.2.7 Anycast and Group Address, 213

10.3 ATM Connection Types,   213
10.3.1 Type 1: Point-to-Point, 213
10.3.2 Type 2: Point-to-Multipoint, 214
10.3.3 Type 3: Multipoint-to-Point, 215
10.3.4 Type 4: Multipoint-to-Multipoint, 217
10.3.5 First Party Versus Third Party Control, 217

10.4 ATM UNI Signaling Protocol,   218
10.4.1 Signaling Messages, 218
10.4.1.1 Protocol Discriminator (1 octet),   219
10.4.1.2 Call Reference (4 octets),   219
10.4.1.3 Message Type (2 octets),   219
10.4.1.4 Message Length (2 octets),   219
10.4.2 Signaling Procedures, 226
10.4.2.1 Point-to-Point Connection,   226
10.4.3 ATM Call States, 232
10.4.4 Timers, 233
10.4.5 Point-to-Multipoint Connection Type, 234
10.4.5.1 Root Initiated,   234
10.4.5.2 Leaf Initiated Join Call,   235

10.5 Summary,   236

10.6 References,   236

Chapter 11
Traffic Management and ATM Service Categories,   237
11.1 Introduction,   237
11.2 Traffic Management,   237
11.2.1 Connection-based Traffic Management, 239
11.2.1.1 Connection Admission Control,   239
11.2.1.2 Network Resource Management,   240
11.2.2 Cell-by-Cell-Based Traffic Management, 240
11.2.2.1 Usage Parameter Control,   240
11.2.2.2 Traffic Shaping,   241
11.2.2.3 Scheduling,   241
11.2.2.4 Buffer Management,   244
11.2.2.5 CLP Control,   247

11.2.2.6 Feedback Control,   247

11.3 Traffic Contract,   248

    11.3.1 ATM Traffic Parameters and Source Traffic Descriptor,   248

        11.3.1.1 Peak Cell Rate,   248

        11.3.1.2 Sustainable Cell Rate,   249

        11.3.1.3 Maximum Burst Size,   249

        11.3.1.4 Minimum Cell Rate,   249

    11.3.2 Connection Traffic Descriptor,   250

        11.3.2.1 Cell Delay Variation Tolerance,   250

        11.3.2.2 Cell Conformance and Connection Compliance,   250

    11.3.3 ATM QoS Parameters,   251

        11.3.3.1 Maximum Cell Transfer Delay,   251

        11.3.3.2 Peak-to-Peak Cell Delay Variation,   251

        11.3.3.3 Cell Loss Ratio,   252

11.4 ATM Service Categories,   252

    11.4.1 CBR,   254

    11.4.2 rt-VBR,   254

    11.4.3 nrt-VBR,   254

    11.4.4 UBR,   254

    11.4.5 ABR,   255

11.5 ABR Service,   255

    11.5.1 Feedback Mechanisms,   256

    11.5.2 ABR Flow Control,   258

11.6 Summary,   259

11.7 References,   260

Part III

Residential Broadband Networks: ATM-to-the-Home,   261

Chapter 12

Residential Broadband Service and Network Architectures,   263

    12.1 Introduction,   263

    12.2 Legacy Residential Networks and Internet Access,   265

        12.2.1 Dial-up Internet Access,   267

    12.3 Residential Broadband Service Requirements,   269

        12.3.1 Connectivity,   269

            12.3.1.1 The Internet,   269

            12.3.1.2 Corporate Networks,   269

            12.3.1.3 Local Content,   270

            12.3.1.4 Peer-to-peer Communication,   270

12.3.2 *Functional Requirements, 271*
  12.3.2.1 Easy Migration from Existing ISP Access Infrastructure, 271
  12.3.2.2 Simultaneous Connectivity: Internet and Corporate Network, 271
  12.3.2.3 Multi-Protocol Support, 271
  12.3.2.4 Security, 271
  12.3.2.5 Multicast, 272
  12.3.2.6 Multiple Service Class Support, 272
  12.3.2.7 Quality of Service Support, 272
12.4 Residential Broadband Service Architecture, 272
  12.4.1 *Residential Access Network, 273*
    12.4.1.1 XDSL Modems, 274
    12.4.1.2 Cable Modems, 275
  12.4.2 *CO and Headend Networks, 276*
  12.4.3 *Broadband Internet Access, 277*
  12.4.4 *In-Home Network, 279*
    12.4.4.1 External Modem, 280
    12.4.4.2 Internal PC Modems, 281
  12.4.5 *End-to-end ATM Architecture, 282*
12.5 Summary, 283
12.6 References, 283

Chapter 13
ATM Over xDSL Network Architecture, 285
13.1 Introduction, 285
  13.1.1 *Interactive TV Market, 286*
  13.1.2 *Internet Opportunity and Cable Modem Threat, 286*
13.2 Subscriber Loop Architecture, 287
  13.2.1 *Subscriber Loop, 287*
  13.2.2 *Digital Transmissions in the Loop, 289*
    13.2.2.1 DLC Systems, 289
    13.2.2.2 CSA Guidelines, 290
    13.2.2.3 ISDN: First Digital Service to the Home, 290
13.3 xDSL Technologies, 291
  13.3.1 *History, 291*
  13.3.2 *xDSL Characteristics, 292*
    13.3.2.1 Bandwidth Improvement, 292
    13.3.2.2 Point-to-point, 294
    13.3.2.3 Always "Connected", 294
    13.3.2.4 Simultaneous POTS support, 295
    13.3.2.5 Rate Adaptive, 295
  13.3.3 *The xDSL Family, 295*

13.3.3.1 Symmetry in Bi-directional Bandwidth,   296

13.3.3.2 Bandwidth,   296

13.3.3.3 Maximum Loop Distance,   296

13.3.3.4 Lifeline POTS Support,   297

13.3.3.5 HDSL,   297

13.3.3.6 ADSL,   298

13.3.3.7 SDSL,   299

13.3.3.8 VDSL,   299

13.4 ADSL-based Broadband Service Architecture,   300

13.5 ADSL-based ATM-to-the-Home Architecture,   302

13.5.1 Architecture,   302

13.5.1.1 DSLAM,   302

13.5.1.2 Customer Premise,   305

13.5.2 Broadband Internet and Telecommuting Services,   305

13.5.2.1 Null Encapsulation and VC Multiplexing of PPP over ATM,   306

13.6 Summary,   307

13.7 References,   307

Chapter 14
Hybrid Fiber/Coax Network Architecture,   309

14.1 Introduction,   309

14.2 Legacy Cable Network Architecture,   310

14.2.1 History,   310

14.2.2 Topology,   310

14.2.3 Network Architecture: Passband and Broadcast,   312

14.2.4 Spectrum Allocation,   314

14.3 The Hybrid Fiber Coax Network Architecture,   315

14.3.1 Legacy Cable Network Problems,   315

14.3.1.1 Reliability,   315

14.3.1.2 Signal Quality,   315

14.3.1.3 Return Path,   315

14.3.2 The HFC Network Architecture,   317

14.3.2.1 Fiber Optics,   317

14.3.2.2 The HFC Topology: Node Architecture,   318

14.3.2.3 Digital Transmission,   319

14.3.2.4 Upstream Transmission,   320

14.3.2.5 Switched Two-Way HFC Architecture,   321

14.4 ATM-to-the-Home over HFC Network,   322

14.4.1 Interactive TV and the Internet,   322

14.4.2 ATM-to-the-Home Architecture,   323

14.4.2.1 ATM Node Switch,   323

14.4.2.2 Home Termination Unit, 326
14.4.2.3 Headend Network, 327
14.4.2.4 Headend Servers, 327
14.4.3 Operation, 327
14.4.4 End-to-end Protocol Architecture, 328
14.4.5 Hybrid Cable Modem: Analog Modem Dial-up Return, 330
14.5 Summary, 330
14.6 References, 331

Foreword

Networks are built for a reason. They are not an end onto themselves, as many modern proponents would lead you to believe. Network architectures are just foundations that connect large application bases. Any network that doesn't meet the evolving requirements of the current generation of applications will soon fade into obscurity. But what ARE the networking requirements of applications that are popular now, and even more intriguing, applications that will be popular in the future?

Over the last century humanity has built and re-built a massive communications network spanning the entire globe. This network has been flexible enough to not only span cultural and political barriers, but also to scale from tens to billions of users. While this is an impressive accomplishment, one should realize that this network is limited in that it was designed to handle a single application ñ transmitting voice traffic rapidly and without perceptible errors between any locations.

With the advent of new computer communication applications in the last two decades has been pulled into new services. One might think it is because the phone network was somehow flexible enough to handle this new data type, but that is really not the case ñ the voice network still switches voice connections. It is the ability of these new data types to transform themselves into voice, and NOT the ability of the voice network to efficiently handle new data types that has allowed our first generation of computer communications to successfully use the voice network. In fact, the whole purpose of modems and transmission interfaces built into faxes is to translate the 1's and 0's of computer communications into analog frequencies that trick the phone network into thinking it is simply handling a human voice call.

Different types of new networks need to be built to natively handle the high bandwidths and particular characteristics of computer communication applications. We've seen this so far on a relatively small scale with the advent of Local Area Networks (LANs) constrained to handle areas no larger than a single building or small campus. Also, we have recently seen the first generation buildout of the Internet, a new specialized network to service the current generation of computer applications. While this is impressive in the relatively short period over which this network was built, the Internet today can only handle a tiny fraction of a percent of the data load the is expected in the next decade. But the biggest problem is the current Internet is largely constrained to only handle *non-realtime* data like computer email, file transfers, and information downloading through web browsing.

We will certainly see a continued buildout of worldwide networking and an eventual merger of the worldwide voice network and current Internet. A single networking infrastructure that can handle multiple types of data, multiple applications, spanning the stringent real-time requirements of voice and interactive video and the massive bandwidths needed for many computer applications. To prepare ourselves for this expensive undertaking of building a communication network to last for the next century flexible enough to handle current and future generations of applications, we first must understand what the requirements are for these applications.

Tim Kwok has taken a forward-looking, top-down approach to networking in this book. He explains the services that need to be supported by these new networks in terms of the overlying application requirements. This approach helps you to understand the *why* and not just the *what* of multimedia networks. Interesting perspective necessary to understand the new architectures that will soon be deployed. Tim successfully frames an in-depth tutorial on ATM between an introduction on applications, and an update on emerging technologies for future home deployment.

Tim Kwok is one of the few people who have bridged the gap between the science of network developments and the art of application requirements, and also have first hand experience in applying them to the design of residential broadband services. Tim has truly *been into multimedia networks before multimedia networks were cool.* He started his career by obtaining a Ph.D. from Stanford University in high performance ATM switch architecture design, even before the ATM approach was formally adopted by the ITU in 1989. Tim has spent the last several years fully surrounded by broadband deployments at the worldwide hub of application development at Microsoft in Redmond, Washington. He has designed IP- and ATM-based residential broadband services over xDSL (Digital Subscriber Loop), FTTC (Fiber-To-The-Curb), FTTH (Fiber-To-The-Home) and HFC (Hybrid Fiber/Coaxial) networks. His work at Microsoft has lead to one of the first successful ADSL trial (in Redmond with GTE) and an FTTH trial (in Japan with NTT). More recently, he has spearheaded an industry effort to define an end-to-end interoperable broadband service architecture to accelerate xDSL deployment.

The information that Tim shares in this book is important for the reader to draw their own conclusions and make their own choices on technology. Instead of networking becoming simpler, it is becoming more complicated. Application interfaces have standardized on IP, but there has not yet been an analogous convergence in underlying supporting networking technology. Tim views ATM not as a monolithic network, but as a foundation with the flexibility to change to meet the changing demands of applications. But what are the real requirements? Which out of the hundreds of options are the few that will make the difference?

Will applications be constrained by limits of underlying network, or will the network be flexible enough to meet the application demands that don't even exist today? Only when application requirement needs are fully considered will we have the security to make the investment required to deploy the new generation of networks for the next century.

Fred Sammartino
Founding President and Chairman, The ATM Forum

Preface

Although multimedia applications appeared in the 1980s on standalone computing environments, such as on a personal computer (PC), multimedia *communication* applications did not become popular until recently. With advances in high-performance computing such as the ever more powerful PCs, and the increased awareness of digital communications because of the Internet, demand for interactive multimedia communication applications is growing rapidly. Even with today's Internet, multimedia communication applications like Web browsing and streaming audio and video have approached mainstream status. However, this is only the tip of the iceberg of what multimedia communication applications can be because the quality for such applications on the legacy network infrastructure (such as the current Internet implementation) is much lower than required or desired for many of today's applications. Ideally, such applications can be enabled anytime, anywhere, at the required quality demanded by a particular application. The problem with the legacy networks is that they were not designed for multimedia communication applications and that therefore they lack the bandwidth and Quality of Service (QoS) guarantees required for these applications.

Before we can design a network that can support multimedia communication applications, we need to understand their networking requirements in detail. Hence, one of the three main objectives of this book is to provide an in-depth discussion of multimedia applications and their networking requirements, which include both traffic (including bandwidth) and QoS requirements (delay and error constraints). Also provided is an introduction to fundamental networking paradigms such as packet switching versus circuit switching. The legacy network infrastructures—the telephone, cable, and the Internet—are shown as prime examples and the major limitations that make them unsuitable for multimedia applications are identified. These discussions provide the motivation for a new networking paradigm that can support multimedia communication applications, which in turn leads to the second objective of this book.

In the late 1980s, the International Telecommunications Union (ITU) selected a new networking paradigm known as Asynchronous Transfer Mode (ATM) for Broadband Integrated Service Digital Network (B-ISDN). The goal of B-ISDN was to provide an integrated public broadband network that was capable of a wide range of applications with diverse networking requirements, particularly multimedia communication applications. ATM is based on a fast packet-switching paradigm using the well-known fixed size 53-byte packet format called a cell. ATM can support a wide range of multimedia applications because it has been designed to scale to a very high bandwidth and to guarantee the quality of service of applications. Furthermore, ATM is designed to be physical-media independent; it can run a variety of physical media, from copper to fiber to wireless. This also implies that ATM can support a wide range of distances, from local- to wide-area networks (LAN to WAN). Hence, although ATM was originally designed for public networking, the computer and communications industries have also designed ATM for LANs.

The ATM Forum was created in 1991 to accelerate ATM deployment through the development of interoperability specifications. In less than five years, its member companies grew from four to over 900! The competition among the large number of networking vendors that have entered the public and private ATM network market has significantly reduced ATM equipment cost. For example, ATM 25 Mbps network adapters for PCs have reached the price range of about $100. Currently, most major public carriers are building ATM infrastructures. The second objective of this book is to provide a solid introduction to the ATM networking paradigm. Instead of explaining ATM starting from its formal specification, we will begin with its fundamental principles, followed by its core networking components such as signaling and traffic management. We explain how the ATM principles can support high-bandwidth integrated services and guarantee QoS of multimedia applications. This approach allows the reader to understand the principles behind multimedia networking in general, instead of just learning all the detailed facts about ATM. Furthermore, we will discuss the key ATM concepts that are necessary to understand the ATM specifications from the ITU and The ATM Forum.

In the early 1990s, there was a major drive to deploy residential broadband networks by public network operators (telephone and cable companies) around the world to deliver interactive television (ITV) services to the home. However, by the mid-1990s, the ITV networks had taken longer than expected to deploy and there was no obvious killer application. Even for the highly touted ITV application, video-on-demand, its projected revenues could not justify the billions of dollars of investment. Around 1995, while the ITV market was fading, the Internet "phenomenon" suddenly took many companies by surprise. Consumer interest in accessing the Internet for browsing the World Wide Web exploded. However, the current narrowband residential infrastructure using analog phone or ISDN dial-up (both circuit-switched-based) for Internet access was too slow, and led to the term "World Wide Wait." Also, using a circuit-switched infrastructure to access the Internet (a packet-switched network) is fundamentally misguided. It not only is inefficient, but also can tie up telephone circuits for hours, not uncommon for today's on-line access duration for a subscriber.

Deploying a residential broadband network based on packet switching for Internet access not only solves the bandwidth bottleneck problem at the residential access network, but also bypasses the circuit-switched infrastructure to avoid tying up telephone circuits. Furthermore, there is a clear pent-up demand for more efficient use of bandwidth from the user perspectives, as opposed to the illusive ITV market. Hence, high-speed Internet access has been viewed as the new killer application for residential broadband networks. Many public network operators are deploying residential broadband networks based on xDSL (various high-speed digital subscriber-line technologies) and cable modem over their copper loop and cable plant infrastructures, respectively. The final objective of this book is to present the residential broadband service requirements and explain how to design residential broadband network architectures based on the ATM-to-the-home architecture to satisfy these requirements. In particular, we will provide a detailed discussion of the local loop architecture and the legacy cable, and the emerging hybrid fiber coaxial (HFC) architectures. This is followed by an in-depth discussion of the residential broadband network architectures based on xDSL and cable modems.

Outline of this book

This book is divided into three parts following the sequence of the three objectives just discussed.

In Part I, we discuss multimedia applications requirements in detail and explain the limitations of the legacy network infrastructures such as the telephone, cable, and the Internet. Chapter 1 gives an overview of multimedia applications. In Chapter 2, we give an overview of the key networking paradigms such as circuit switching and packet switching. We use the legacy networks as key examples and explain their limitations in support of multimedia applications. We then provide a classification of applications in Chapter 3 and discuss the characteristics of each class. The three classes of applications are real-time streaming, real-time block transfer and non-real-time applications. Chapters 4 and 5 discuss the bandwidth and QoS requirements, respectively, of all three classes of applications in detail.

Part II of this book gives an in-depth discussion of the fundamentals of ATM. Chapter 6 explains the fundamental principles behind ATM. We also discuss both the technical and strategic advantages of ATM. Chapter 7 integrates these fundamental principles and gives a unified view of the end-to-end operations of an ATM network. In Chapter 8, we provide a more rigorous discussion of ATM by explaining the protocol reference model of ATM. Chapter 9 discusses the ATM adaptation layer, the key protocol layer for enabling the support of the wide range of applications and higher layer ATM protocols. Chapter 10 introduces the key concepts of ATM signaling, which is the core component of the ATM architecture that allows applications to dynamically request their bandwidth and QoS requirements. This chapter also provides a step-by-step example of how an ATM connection is established using the signaling messages and corresponding information elements. In Chapter 11, we discuss the other core component of ATM, its traffic management paradigm. Traffic management makes possible not only the efficient use of ATM network resources, but also, more importantly, the QoS guarantees that it can provide to real-time applications. We also discuss the new ATM service categories and the Available Bit Rate (ABR) service recently specified by The ATM Forum's traffic management 4.0 specification.

Finally, Part III provides a detailed discussion of residential broadband networks and how an ATM-to-the-home architecture can be designed to provide various residential broadband services and applications. Chapter 12 provides an overview of the legacy residential network developed by the telephone and cable companies. It further provides a discussion of the residential broadband service requirements, which are important to understand before we can design residential broadband networks. Also included is an overview of the in-home network architectures that support multiple devices. In Chapter 13 we discuss xDSL technologies in detail and explain how they enable high-speed communications over the existing copper loop. We then discuss how an end-to-end broadband service architecture can be designed over ADSL using the ATM-to-the-home and the PPP over ATM architecture. Finally, in Chapter 14, we discuss the legacy cable networks and explain how they can be upgraded to the hybrid fiber/coaxial (HFC) architecture to support residential broadband services. Then, we discuss how an ATM-to-the-home architecture can be designed over HFC networks.

Timothy Kwok
Microsoft Corporation
Redmond, Washington

Acknowledgments

This book would not have been possible without the assistance of many individuals. First, I must thank my wife, Janice, whose continual support was absolutely crucial for this book project, which took four years to complete. Also, I am very fortunate to have many experts as the reviewers. They have provided very useful feedback to this book. They include George Dobrowski (the past chair of the worldwide technical committee of The ATM Forum and its current president), Fred Sammartino (founding chairman and past president of The ATM Forum), Dr. Steve Walters (past chairman and past president of The ATM Forum and fellow of Bellcore), Tom Helstern (past chair of the signaling group of The ATM Forum), John Swenson (past chair of the AAL group in ANSI TIS1 committee and past board member of The ATM Forum) and Rhonda Hilton (CableLabs). Also, I would like to specifically thank my editor Mary Franz for her dedication, patience and contributions during the entire book project. I also would like to thank my production editor Joanne Anzalone for her tremendous assistance. Finally, I would like to thank Microsoft, and Craig Mundie in particular, for providing me with such an exciting opportunity to work in the residential broadband area, not to mention the excellent working environment that includes the most talented people I have ever worked with.

Multimedia Applications Requirements

Chapter **1**

Multimedia Applications and ATM

1.1 Interactive Multimedia Applications

Paul Sanders has just checked into his hotel in Hong Kong. He is alone on a business trip, and this is his first trip to the Orient. It's 8:30 at night, and Paul has a craving for authentic Italian food. He turns on the television in his hotel room. Using the remote control, Paul finds a listing of local Italian restaurants. After picking three restaurants with the highest ratings, Paul browsed through each of these three restaurants via video clips that show the restaurants' interior decorations, dinner menus and specials of the day. He selects a restaurant, and a reservation is made automatically. After a wonderful meal, Paul feels like watching a comedy movie. Returning to his hotel room, he turns on the television again. With the same remote control, he searches through a list of available movies using the movie guide by category, title, production date and stars. Two of the movies starring Tom Hanks seem interesting, so Paul plays the previews. He then picks one, and watches it with full controlling functions, pausing and rewinding at will, as if the movie is being played on a video cassette recorder. After the movie, Paul suddenly realizes that he did not bring enough copies of his market research report for a meeting the next morning. He pulls out his notebook computer, connects it to a wall outlet and enters a request to print five copies of his report. A few minutes later, a hotel attendant knocks on his door to deliver his reports, which have just been printed by the high-speed color printer at the hotel office center.

You are working on a very important project in your office. At the corporate auditorium in the next building, a seminar is just about to begin. You do not know if the seminar will be relevant to your project, and you really don't have time to make a trip to the auditorium just to see if the seminar would interest you or not. So, you make a video connection to the auditorium from your personal computer in your office. After watching the seminar for 10 minutes, you find it very useful for your current project. Then you notice that a video call is coming in from your boss. You quickly record the seminar on your computer, while you take the call from your boss. He is calling from a meeting at a conference room downstairs. The group in meeting has a question that requires your input immediately. A window on your high-resolution screen shows the conference room's whiteboard that illustrates the problem. You present the solution to the group on screen, and the video call ends. About five minutes of the seminar has been recorded during the call. You replay and quickly scan through the recording, and then switch back to the "live" seminar. Now, you can participate in discussions or ask questions by calling in through your computer's connection to the auditorium.

1.1.1 ATM

Although the above scenarios seem far-fetched, the networking technologies required to achieve them are all available today. Interactive multimedia applications, as alluded to in these scenarios, require networks that can handle a high volume of data flow while providing a guaranteed performance such as bandwidth guarantees and delay bound. Asynchronous transfer mode (ATM) technologies promise to satisfy all these networking requirements for multimedia applications. The main objective of this book is to detail how ATM protocols are designed to achieve these goals.

ATM was designed to support a wide variety of applications with diverse networking requirements, including bandwidth and quality of service guarantees. A key goal of ATM design is to allow a single ATM network to be used to support all applications, carrying data, voice and video, instead of delivering them in separate and incompatible networks in corporate networks and public networks today.

ATM is distance independent and can be deployed as local area networks (LANs) and wide area networks (WANs), unlike today's LAN technologies such as Ethernet (which is distance–limited). ATM can be applied to residential broadband networks to provide broadband services to the home and small office/home office (SOHO). Hence, for the first time, the same networking technologies can be applied to both private and public networks, LAN and WAN, to support voice, video and data simultaneously on the same network. ATM makes it possible to integrate a single unified management system, instead of the disparate and incompatible systems we have today.

In this book, we focus not only on ATM itself, but, more importantly, on how ATM can be applied to support the Internet, intranets and residential broadband networks. ATM can be applied to many other networks, including wireless (terrestrial and satellite) networks. Since their standards are less mature, they are beyond the scope of this book, though they are based on many of the ATM principles, as discussed in this book.

There are many industries that can benefit from ATM. Table 1-1 shows examples of applications that can be supported by ATM networks for different industries. They are discussed in more detail below.

1.1.2 ATM and the Internet

For WANs, ATM can be applied in three scenarios. First, ATM networks can be deployed as a corporation's private WAN to interconnect different corporate offices around the country or internationally. Second, ATM networks can be used by public network operators to provide broadband networking services to businesses and residences.

Last, but not the least, ATM can be used to upgrade the existing Internet infrastructure. In the mid-1990s, while the projected interactive TV market is not being realized as soon as expected, the "Internet phenomenon" is suddenly taking many people by surprise. Interest in accessing the Internet for browsing the World Wide Web has exploded.[1] Web browsing has emerged to be one of the most popular Internet applications beginning around 1994. According to the traffic statistics of the NSF Backbone[2] (which was the Internet backbone until 1995), the web traffic in terms of packet counts (using hypertext transfer protocol or HTTP) has jumped from a mere 1.5% in January 1994 to 21.4% in April 1995. Such traffic explosion on the Internet has resulted in frequent congestion because the Internet backbone is based on IP routers and they are reaching performance limits. Upgrading the Internet to an ATM backbone could help to solve the capacity problem. Furthermore, since ATM is designed to scale with increased bandwidth, an increase in traffic can be accommodated by higher capacity ATM switches and link capacity, without changing the underlying ATM protocols. This not only provides high capacity, but also quality of service on the Internet.

The Internet and public broadband networks based on ATM are very valuable to education. Schools, libraries and even individual homes with the proper computer facilities can provide students with access to shared video servers through networks of educational materials. Digital video encyclopedias, for example, allow students to explore subjects that are interesting to them. This will definitely increase their motivation for learning, because students can learn their favorite topics at their own pace. Education can be "tailored" to every student, regardless of age and learning ability, as opposed to the "cookie-cutter" lessons of today. They also can exchange ideas and collaborate in both video and image forms with one another, within one school and with other schools as well. These collaborations over educational networks can take place worldwide. College students can participate in class discussions with tutors and attend lectures given by professors who are hundreds of miles away. Geography is no longer a limitation. A wide variety of classes held by highly qualified teachers from around the world will be accessible to everyone over ATM networks.

The healthcare industry can utilize ATM-based Internet to improve healthcare services by interconnecting medical professionals and patients. Patients can "visit" doctors without leaving their homes (this is especially helpful to elderly patients), because homes can be connected to hospitals and clinics by public ATM networks. These networks allow video-based communications that include video conferencing and consultation by sharing live videos of patient test data. They also make image-based communications possible. For example, high-resolution images, such as X-rays and MRI scans, can be easily exchanged for consultation among doctors and medical specialists. Applications in this area will greatly benefit elderly and home-bound patients.

Table 1-1 *Interactive multimedia applications that can be supported by ATM networks*

User/Industry	Sample Applications
Corporate offices	Live video desktop seminar Multimedia collaboration Image-based document exchanges Web browsing on the intranet
Remote offices	Virtual corporation Video conferencing with headquarter office Synchronization to remote, central database
Hospitals	Remote consultation and diagnosis Sharing video- and image- (X-rays) based documents Multimedia conferencing and collaboration
University and schools	National interactive lectures and classes Multimedia rich Web browsing for learning and research Video- and image-based collaboration across the country
Real Estate	Home, rental browsing
Residential	High speed Internet access such as Web browsing Telecommuting Virtual corporation Video on demand Electronic yellow page Distance learning Home shopping
Hotels	Video on-demand Video-based tour guide Electronic yellow pages Internal and external video conferencing
Advertising	Access to image database Access to footage Video conferencing to clients
Stock broker	On-demand access to news conference (or stored) Access to companies' annual meetings footage
Engineering	Computation-intense applications Exchange CAD/CAM design images Multimedia conferencing and collaboration

The real estate industry can utilize ATM-based Internet to connect to video servers that give video tours of properties currently listed for sale. Buyers can search not only by quantitative information, such as price or square footage, or a single image clip, but can also have a video tour for inside and outside the property, from the neighborhood and structural appearance outside, to the floor plan and decorations inside. Buyers can use this service at their homes, through connections to a high-speed public network that has these video servers.

1.1.3 ATM and the Intranets

As LANs, ATM can replace existing corporate networks either entirely or incrementally as campus backbone or high-performance work groups. Since ATM is protocol independent, ATM-based LANs can support a wide variety of protocols used in today's LANs, such as IP, IPX and Appletalk protocols. This implies that ATM can become the high capacity and quality of service based infrastructure to support the intranets. Intranets are corporate networks running IP-based protocols.

With ATM networks, corporate offices can support in-house and external interactive multimedia collaboration with live video and audio sharing images, graphics and data using their desktop PCs or workstations. Office workers can send video mail of multi-Mbytes (100s or more), in addition to text-only electronic mail, through these networks just as easily as today's text-based email. Furthermore, these networks can interconnect facsimile machines, copiers and scanners, because they can handle the volume of data generated by these *image-based* document exchanges that involves multi-Mbytes.

1.1.4 ATM and Residential Broadband Networks

The current narrowband residential infrastructure using dial-up (e.g., POTS or ISDN) is too slow, which led to the complaint that WWW stands for "world wide wait." There is a clear pent-up demand for bandwidth to get much better user satisfaction. Since this is an existing market as opposed to the future ITV market, high-speed Internet access has been viewed as the killer application for residential broadband networks. This will spur the telephone companies and cable companies to deploy residential broadband Internet access networks based on xDSL (family of digital subscriber line technologies) modems and cable modems, respectively.[3] These residential broadband network architectures can be based on an ATM-to-the-home architecture.[4] The entire Part III of this book is devoted to residential broadband network architectures based on ATM and Internet access network architectures.

Residential broadband networks based on ATM have many different applications. Through a PC or a television (with a smart set-top box) that connects to a residential broadband network, broadband Internet access to the World Wide Web is possible with superior user experience because of the broadband infrastructure. Also, a home shopper can interactively select and purchase the exact items of interest, instead of passively watching an entire program on today's home shopping channels. Many new forms of entertainment services will become possible. Video-on-demand provides a wide variety of movies to home viewers instantly. An electronic yellow page at home will make restaurant selections fun and easy through video clips that show various restaurants' interior decor and menus. Surfing the Web does not have to be painfully slow anymore (no more "world wide wait"). Communication by full motion video will be readily available, in contrast to today's voice-only or low-quality video phones.

1.2 An Ideal Communications Network

We will now explore communications in a broader perspective and discuss an ideal communication network. The goal of an ideal communication network is to set people free from the constraints of distance, location, time and media of communications.

1.2.1 Distance

The constraint of distance refers to the physical separation among the communicating parties. For a developed country like the United States, the telephone network has evolved to a near-ubiquitous presence, primarily through a wired access infrastructure. For developing countries and for less populated areas, the provision of telephone service is mainly limited by financial constraints, rather than technical feasibility.

1.2.2 Location

The wired access infrastructure ties a person to a telephone at a fixed access point. To make outgoing calls, the caller has to find a location with a telephone connected to this infrastructure. Then, in order to reach the other party, the caller has to know the location of that party as well as the telephone number at that location (provided that the receiving location has a telephone). Only during the last decade has the constraint of location (for voice and limited message communications) been addressed effectively, with the development of the wireless "cellular" telephony and paging infrastructure. More recently, wireless data services are emerging, some of them through existing cellular technologies. These wireless technologies allow a person to communicate wherever he or she is, that is, independent of location. The personal communications services (PCS) under development promise to make such location-independent services widely available by significantly reducing the cost to a level acceptable to the general public while increasing the capacity (number of subscribers) for a given coverage area.[5]

1.2.3 Time

For many years, a telephone communication between two parties required both parties to be present at the same time. However, during the last decade, the proliferation of answering machines has removed the constraint of time for most users: The recipient of a voice message does not have to be present when the caller makes the call. (Before voice mail, another person taking messages provides a solution to remove this time constraint.) Simultaneously, the proliferation of personal computers (and workstations) has allowed many people to access computers, and the need to communicate through computers has spawned the era of electronic mail. Electronic mail effectively removes the constraint of time for data communications. Since electronic mail provides a level of detail that, in many instances, is difficult to achieve by voice conversation alone, it has become an indispensable tool for many businesses.

1.2.4 Media

Media refers to the types of information (e.g., voice, data, images, video, etc.) that can be communicated. For decades, the type of information communicated was primarily voice. More recently, data (electronic mail), image (fax and more recently high-resolution images through World Wide Web) and low-quality video (videoconferencing) communication services have also become more popular, as improvements in technologies drive down the cost of owning equipment. However, some of these new forms of communications are being supported by the telephone network and the cellular network infrastructure in a very inefficient manner, because the current infrastructure has been designed primarily for voice communication. (Such inefficiencies and limitations will be discussed in more detail in the next chapter). Ideally, a communications network should allow flexible exchanges of text, audio, image and video information, so as to support all forms of multimedia and collaborative applications easily. In addition to the networking constraint, the constraint of media is limited by the technologies available for providing the endpoint equipment at low cost. The reason is that to transfer different media over a network, not only does the network have to support the required quality of service, but so do the endpoints, which need to encode at the sender and decode at the receiver to complete the communications. Fortunately, the age of digitalization and a dramatic reduction in cost of personal computers and related products has facilitated the arrival of these endpoint devices to make possible the communications of different media (telephone for voice, fax for low-quality image, scanner for high-quality image, and low-cost camcorder for video).

In summary, to eliminate the constraints of distance, location, time and media is to enable people to communicate anywhere, anytime and in any media type. The goal of the ultimate communication network is to break the barrier of space and time so that any information can be communicated freely anytime and anywhere. Table 1-2 summarizes these four constraints and lists applications (with their current status) that can remove these constraints.

Table 1-2 *Summary of applications that address the various constraints on communications*

Media	Distance	Location	Time
Voice	Telephone	Cellular phone PCS	Voice Mail
Data	E-mail	Dial-up to Email	Email
Image	Fax (popular) World Wide Web	Dial-up to Fax Image-based Email Dial-up to Web	Fax Image-based Email Dial-up to Web

Table 1-2 *Summary of applications that address the various constraints on communications (Continued)*

Media	Distance	Location	Time
Video	Video conferencing Video Phone Video-on-demand	Satellite Broadcast TV	VCR Video Mail stored on Hard Drive

1.3 Summary and Outline of This Part

In this chapter, we described a vision of the interactive multimedia applications and the role of ATM to support these applications. We provided a high level perspective of an ideal communications network and its objectives.

Before explaining what ATM is, we need to understand the motivations for ATM, which is the focus of the Part I of this book. Motivations come from multimedia application requirements and a deficiency in existing networking technologies. In Chapter 2, we give an overview of the current networking technologies including the PSTN, the Internet and the intranets. We identify their current deficiencies that motivate the use of ATM. Since it is essential to first understand communications applications and why we need a high performance networking technology, Chapter 3 provides a basic understanding of communications applications in general and presents a classification scheme for all applications. This provides a framework to understand applications requirements in the following two chapters. Chapter 4 and 5 discuss the traffic and quality of service requirements, respectively.

1.4 References

[1]T. Berners-Lee, R. Cailliau, A. Luotonen, H. Nielsen, A. Secret, "The World-Wide Web," *Communications of the ACM*, Vol.37, No.8, Aug. 1994, pp. 76-82.

[2]W.R. Stevens, *TCP/IP Illustrated*, Volume 3, Addison-Wesley, 1996.

[3]T. Kwok, "Residential Broadband Internet Services and Network Architecture," *SCTE 1997 Conference on Emerging Technologies*, Jan 8-10, 1997, pp. 113-124.

[4]T. Kwok, "A Vision for Residential Broadband Services: ATM-to-the-Home," *IEEE Network*, Sept/Oct, 1995, pp. 14-28.

[5]D. Cox, "Personal Communications– A viewpoint," *IEEE Communications Magazine*, Nov. 1990, pp. 8-20, 1992.

Chapter 2

Network Architectures: The Telephone Network, the Internet and Intranets

2.1 Introduction

Ideally, we would like to support all types of communications applications in a single network. This simplifies management and significantly reduces the cost of operations. However, this has not been achieved by existing networking infrastructures. Although existing networks are sufficient to support the applications for which they are designed (such as supporting telephony in the public switched telephone network, or PSTN), they are usually unsuitable (either because they are inefficient or incapable) to support other kinds of applications. By exploring the limitations of existing networks to support different types of applications, we can identify the basic principles needed to design a broadband integrated service network to support all types of applications, especially multimedia applications. Since the motivation of the ATM protocols is to enable a single broadband integrated services network architecture to support all types of applications, these principles become the framework for the ATM protocol design (to be discussed in more detail in later chapters).

In this chapter, we give an overview of the key network architectures today. They form the underlying architecture of the current PSTN, the Internet and intranets. We explore in detail the primary limitations of these network architectures.

2.2 Networking Architectures

There are many ways to classify network architectures. Topologically, there are three types of network architectures: fully connected point-to-point networks, switched point-to-point networks and broadcast networks. Also, networks can be classified into switched and non-switched networks. Switched networks allow links within the network to be shared by multiple pairs of communicating parties simultaneously. There are two kinds of switching methodology: circuit-switched or packet-switched networks. All these network architectures are discussed in detail next.

2.2.1   Fully Connected Point-to-point Networks

The basic objective of networking is to interconnect a number of parties for the communication of one or more types of information. Full connectivity must be provided by the network, which means that there is at least one path to connect any pair of endpoints on the network. Conceptually, we can simply build a fully connected point-to-point network to connect N parties, as shown in Figure 2–1. Such a network has a point-to-point link between all possible pairs of endpoints in the network. If an endpoint (A) wants to communicate with another endpoint (B), A selects the link connected to B to communicate. The network does not participate in the path selection; there is no switching performed by the network. Each path across the network is always dedicated to a particular pair of communicating parties, without sharing with other parties. Hence, the fully connected point-to-point network is a nonswitched network.

Although this network architecture achieves full connectivity, it has a number of disadvantages. The main problem of this network architecture is the lack of scalability. The number of links required to connect every endpoint is equal to $N(N-1)/2$, which grows as N^2. Second, for each endpoint, the cost of the connectivity increases with N as new endpoints are added to the network, because a new link or interface must be added for

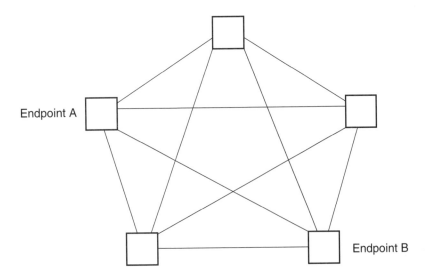

Figure 2–1 A fully connected point-to-point network

each new endpoint on the network. Third, this network architecture has very low bandwidth efficiency, because it provides dedicated links between all possible pairs regardless of whether those pairs would communicate or not. Even when an endpoint communicates, it is very likely that the endpoint uses only one link during a session; this makes the other N-2 links idle. Finally, it is also inefficient for multipoint communication because each piece of information must be replicated by the source endpoint to send on multiple links for their respective destination endpoints. Hence, the source cannot just send a single copy and have the network automatically replicate the information; it must perform the replication itself. This can contribute to additional traffic injected into the network, which could have been avoided if the network had been responsible for such replication and used a more efficient replication algorithm (such as replication as close to the destinations as possible).

Nevertheless, this architecture is sufficient for small N and is straightforward to implement. Hence, this architecture is used for interconnecting a small number of corporate locations through a public network infrastructure. In this case, each endpoint in Figure 2–1 can be an access point at each corporate location to the public network. Each access point has N - 1 interfaces connecting to the other N - 1 corporate locations. If the access point is actually an access switch, it determines the desired corporate location(s) of the information from one corporate location and sends it on the right link(s).

2.2.2 Switched Point-to-point Networks

Since fully connected point-to-point networks were not practical for connecting large number of endpoints, the switched point-to-point network was introduced. In the switched point-to-point network, each endpoint is connected to a switch by a single point-to-point link (see Figure 2–2). Each switch is connected with other switches by one or more point-to-point links to provide full connectivity among all endpoints on the network. The main function of the switch is to forward information received from each input port destined for a particular receiving endpoint(s) to the right path(s) (right output port(s) on the switch) across the network to reach that desired endpoint(s).

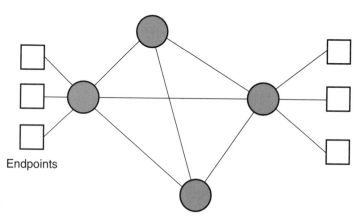

Figure 2–2   A Switched Point-to-point Network

Each link on the network can be shared by multiple pairs (sets) of communicating endpoints. Instead of dedicating networking resources for each pair of endpoints whether they are communicating or not, a switched point-to-point network provides a set of shared network resources for all endpoints to be allocated on demand. This sharing includes the connectivity between each endpoint and the network, which is a single physical link, as opposed to N-1 links in the fully connected point-to-point network architecture. The network bandwidth is allocated to pairs of communicating endpoints only. Hence, the switched point-to-point network is a form of switched network, as opposed to the non-switched, fully connected point-to-point network.

The physical links within the network are shared among different pairs of communicating endpoints using a multiplexing mechanism, such as time division or frequency division multiplexing. Hence, a switched network provides both switching and multiplexing mechanisms. These mechanisms are discussed in detail next.

There are two types of switching methodologies: circuit switching and packet switching. They were invented to support different types of applications — that is, voice and data applications, respectively. Circuit switching was invented first and used to support telephony. It was decades later before packet switching was introduced to support data communications.

2.2.2.1 Circuit Switching

A circuit switched network consists of a set of switches, called circuit switches, connected by point-to-point links, as shown in Figure 2–3. The circuit switched network has the switched point-to-point network architecture discussed above. Each endpoint is connected to a circuit switch by a point-to-point link. The circuit switches in the backbone are for connecting other circuit switches. The function of a circuit switch is to transfer (switch) information from an input port of the switch to the desired output port, to reach the desired link leading to the destined endpoint.

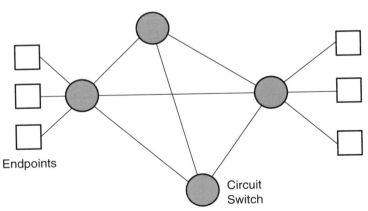

Endpoints

Circuit
Switch

Figure 2–3   A circuit switched network

The circuit switched network is a connection-oriented network. Before any two endpoints can start communicating across the network, a dedicated connection must be explicitly setup between two endpoints. Specifically, there are three phases of communications in the circuit switched network: connection setup phase, information transfer phase and connection tear-down phase. The connection setup phase is required for reserving the network resources (such as link and switch bandwidth) along a path between the communicating endpoints. The network resources are dedicated to these communicating endpoints for the duration of the information transfer phase. Hence, no other parties in the network can use these resources until either endpoint terminates the connection to release the network resources, which is the connection tear-down phase.

The key advantage of circuit switching is its guaranteed bandwidth, as network resources are reserved and dedicated to the communicating parties for the entire duration of the connection. Hence, both the bandwidth and delay are guaranteed for each connection once the connection has been established. Of course, network resources are limited. If there is no such resource available in the network, the network has to turn down the connection setup request and the endpoint has to retry later. For example, on Mother's Day, busy signals are common for international phone calls because the network runs out of capacity (instead of the endpoint being busy). More recently, the Internet access phenomenon (primarily via dial-up modem connections) has increased the load on telephone switches, increasing the blocking probability significantly.

Circuit switching is very appropriate for communications that involve sending information in a continuous fashion for a period of time, for which the information requires a guaranteed bandwidth and delay once the transfer begins. The reason is that it provides a mechanism to guarantee a fixed bandwidth and delay for each connection by dedicating bandwidth for each connection until the connection tear-down phase.

Telephony is such an application. It has an average connection duration of about 3 minutes and requires bandwidth and delay guarantee to achieve satisfactory performance. Hence, the PSTN is based on the circuit switching architecture and has been supporting telephony for about a century. The circuit switch that directly connects to a residence's telephone is located at the central office (CO) and is typically called the CO switch, which can support as many as 100,000 phones or more. The CO switches are either connected directly with each other for those serving in neighboring areas, or connected via another type of circuit switch called a tandem switch or toll switch. Toll switches are mainly for connecting to other toll switches in different areas (city or state).

However, circuit switching is very inefficient if the communication is very bursty, that is, for which the information is sent only once in a while and most of the time both parties are idle. Another disadvantage of circuit switching is the overhead in connection setup time. If only a very small amount of information is communicated which takes shorter than the connection setup time, then the overhead of the connection setup also makes circuit switching very inefficient. Since data communication is very bursty, circuit switching is not appropriate for supporting these applications. This lead to the invention of packet switching, as an alternative switching methodology.

Multiplexing mechanisms To carry multiple connections on a physical link between two circuit switches, a multiplexing mechanism must be used. Circuit switching was first implemented as space division multiplexing (SDM). Space refers to physical lines between two circuit switches and the paths within a circuit switch. Each connection takes up one line between two switches and a path within the switch. SDM refers to assigning the physical lines and paths to new connection requests. Blocking occurs when all lines or all paths are being used by existing connections and a new connection setup arrives. Such a new connection is blocked (busy signal) until one of the existing connections is torn down.

Later, frequency division multiplexing (FDM) was invented for circuit switching. FDM allows each physical line to be simultaneously used by multiple connections by dividing the frequency spectrum on the line into multiple frequency bands. Each such frequency band can be dedicated for a single connection. For the PSTN, the band is 4 KHz wide.

In the past two decades, the introduction of digital switching in telephony has provided a new multiplexing mechanism for the telephone network: time division multiplexing (TDM). In TDM, the transmission time on each line is divided into fixed size frames. Each frame is further divided into a fixed number of fixed size time slots. Each time slot in a frame represents a particular logical channel; an N-slot frame TDM system consists of N logical channels. In the other words, there is no explicit labeling on each time slot for each channel; they are implicitly associated with the corresponding channels by their positions in the frame. Before a connection can be set up, there must be an unused logical channel on all the links for a path between the communication parties. Hence, an end-to-end connection is a concatenation of logical channel along the path between the two communicating parties. The main function of the circuit switch in the TDM system is to translate the position of each time slot on each incoming line to its desired position (logical channel) in the output line for the next hop.

For digital telephony, each time slot carries a voice sample, which is 1-byte long. The 8 KHz sampling frequency (twice the 4 KHz voice band) determines the frame time to be 125 μs, which implies that each logical channel has a data rate of 64 Kbps.

2.2.2.2   Packet Switching

Packet switching was invented in the late 1960s for data communications. Data communications applications were mainly interactions between dumb terminals and a shared mainframe computer. These interactions were command traffic generated by humans and the corresponding responses from the mainframe. Such data transmissions occurred randomly and infrequently, and in bursts of arbitrary duration. Hence, data communications had (and still have) a very bursty traffic pattern. If circuit switching was used to support data communications, the dedicated resources for a connection would be idle most of the time — a very inefficient use of bandwidth. Therefore, packet switching was invented to achieve more efficiency to support the bursty traffic pattern of data communications.

The packet switched network can have the same architecture as the switched point-to-point network architecture, in which case the switch is called a packet switch (see Figure 2–4). The basic idea of packet switching is to not dedicate network resources statically as in circuit switching. Instead, packet switching allocates network resources to communicating parties on demand—only when they have information to send. This is sometimes referred to as bandwidth on demand. This allows more efficient sharing of network resources especially when the activity ratio of each source is low.

To provide such a fine level of network resource sharing, packet switching quantizes the network resource into small units of transmission bandwidth. The unit of bandwidth request is the amount of data to be

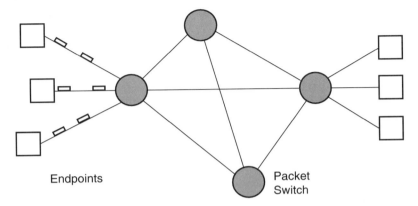

Figure 2–4 A packet switched network

transferred at a given instant. This is achieved by encoding user information in separate blocks. Data are sent in the form of packets; each consists of a header followed by a block of data as the payload (see Figure 2–5). Each packet represents the basic transmission unit and the quanta of communications bandwidth in the packet switched network.

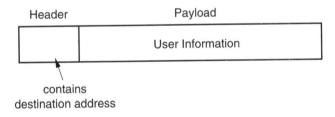

Figure 2–5 A packet

The packet header contains the address of the destination endpoint (plus other control information). The destination address is used by the packet switches for forwarding the packet along the path to its destination. Determining the right output of the packet switch for each packet is called packet routing. Each packet switch has a routing table that translates destination addresses into the outgoing ports of the switch. The routing table is set up via a routing protocol operated among packet switches. Packets can be sent to the network without first setting up a connection. Instead, the route of each packet is determined by the packet switches along the path using its destination address. The packet switched network essentially gives the resource to each communicating party on a per packet basis; no bandwidth is used by two communicating parties that are idle. In contrast, circuit switched networks dedicate network resources on a per connection (or circuit) basis and last for the entire connection, even if the communicating parties are idle.

The routing tables in packet switches can change dynamically by the routing protocol, as a result of topological or loading changes in the network, for example. Hence, different packets between two communicating parties may travel different paths. There is no guarantee that they will arrive in the same order they were sent.

The packet switch has four core functions: routing, switching, buffering and multiplexing. Again, routing determines the desired output port for the incoming packet. Then, the switching function delivers the packet from its input port to the desired output port. Since packet transmissions from different sources are not coordinated, multiple packets arriving simultaneously at the packet switch on different input ports can all be destined to the same output port (see Figure 2–6). Since only one of the packets can be transmitted on each output port, the other packets must be buffered for subsequent transmission. Hence, packet switches must provide buffering as its normal operation.[1]

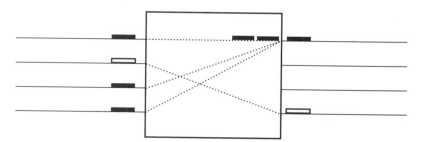

Figure 2–6   A packet switch

Although instantaneous overload is normal for packet switching, such an overload can be severe enough as to exceed the buffer capacity of the packet switch. In this case, packets will be dropped. Occasional packet drops due to buffer overflow (though these should be avoided) are normal for packet switched networks, because applications running over packet switched network are expected to handle lost packets. This can be achieved using various error control mechanisms, such as error detection with retransmission, if data integrity is important. However, if such packet losses become excessive for a long period of time, it means that there is network congestion and applications can have significant performance degradation in throughput and delay. Hence, congestion control algorithms must be provided for packet switched networks, to avoid congestion occurring in the first place, and to control congestion when it does occur.

The multiplexing methodology for packet switching is based on statistical multiplexing, a dynamic form of time division multiplexing (TDM). The packet switch is responsible for multiplexing packets from different sources arriving on different input ports destined to the same output port using time division.

The TDM mechanism used in packet switching is different from that in circuit switching. In packet switching, it requires an explicit label (destination address) on the header of each packet to associate it with its destination node, while the position of the packet in time does not correspond to any channel information. In fact, there is no concept of a frame to define position. No time slots are reserved and any time slots are ready for use by any packets arriving at that time. (Again, if more than one packet arrives or is buffered, only one is transmitted in the current time slot, while the rest is buffered for transmission in following time slots.) Hence, the transmission resources on each output link are only allocated to active communicating parties; no bandwidth is wasted for idle parties. In contrast, each time slot in TDM-based circuit switching belongs to a particular logical channel. Once a connection is accepted, a logical channel is assigned to it for the entire duration. If the connection is idle, it results in idle slots that cannot be used by other active parties. Therefore, packet switching is much more efficient in supporting bursty traffic than circuit switching.

Note that even for voice communications, circuit switching may not be that efficient. The reason is that a typical voice conversation is active for only 40% of the duration; the rest of the time the parties are silent and hence there is no need for sending any information. Therefore, voice over packet switched networks or packet voice communication has been explored extensively in the past two decades. In fact, voice over the Internet is intrinsically more efficient than over the PSTN. However, the problem is the lack of quality of service guarantees to ensure voice performance (delay) in the current Internet infrastructure, as discussed later.

In addition to using switched point-to-point architecture, packet switching can be implemented over a broadcast shared medium. A broadcast shared medium packet switched network does not need a packet switch, as switching is achieved in a distributed fashion among the endpoints. Packet switching over a broadcast network is discussed later in the chapter.

Connectionless and connection-oriented packet switching In the basic form of packet switching discussed above, no explicit connection setup is required before packet transmission. As a matter fact, there is no notion of a connection from the network point of view. Furthermore, there is no guarantee in bandwidth, delay or loss rate for any packet transfer, which means that there is no quality of service (QoS) guarantees. (In any case, there is no notion of a connection to associate a bandwidth to it.) This form of packet switching is known as connectionless packet switching. As discussed later, the Internet is based on this connectionless packet switching paradigm.[2]

However, there is another form of packet switching that requires an explicit connection setup and tear-down. This is called connection-oriented packet switching. In this case, the packet header contains a connection identifier for indicating the connection to which the packet belongs. The connection-oriented packet switch has a connection table that translates connection identifiers into output port numbers. The purpose of connection setup is to reserve network resources. The basic network resource is the support of a connection itself, because each packet switch can support a limited number of connections. The reason is that each connection requires memory space in the connection table to hold connection-related information. Hence, the number of connections that can be supported on a packet switch is memory-limited. In addition, the connection setup can reserve other network resources, such as bandwidth and buffer for guaranteeing performance of applications.

Connection-oriented packet switching still maintains the statistical multiplexing property of connectionless packet switching and corresponding efficiency in supporting bursty traffic. Hence, connections in packet switched network are known as virtual connections or VCs, to distinguish them from nailed up connections with dedicated resources in circuit switched networks. The VC paradigm allows the creation of a virtual private network across a public data network for corporations. VCs can be set up between different corporate locations to emulate a private network connectivity. X.25 and its follow on, frame relay, are examples of a connection-oriented packet switched network and are used exactly for the purpose of virtual private networking. As discussed in Part II, ATM also is based on connection-oriented packet switching.

Today, data communications applications are very different, as the centralized computing paradigm based on mainframes transformed into a distributed computing paradigm based on PCs and workstations. However, data traffic remains bursty because today's data applications (such as file transfer, printing and electronic mail) exhibit similar bursty behavior. Therefore, packet switching is still very important for data communications for both local area networks (LANs) and wide area networks (WANs).

2.2.2.3 Permanent Connections

Although both circuit switching and connection-oriented packet switching require connection setup before information transfer, the protocol for establishing such connection setup (known as a signaling protocol) might not be available at the endpoints or the network. Without signaling support to set up connections dynamically, the network has to provide connections on subscription basis (permanent connections), for which the connection is established by network management protocol at the beginning of the network service. Permanent (or non-switched) connections are common for circuit switched connections (leased line service) and packet switched connections (permanent virtual connections or PVCs in X.25, frame relay or ATM), either because they simplify network design, or there is no standard signaling protocol implementations. In fact, a fully connected point-to-point network can be logically constructed by these permanent connections over circuit switched and packet switched networks as if they were point-to-point links. Nevertheless, such fully connected permanent connections suffer from disadvantages similar to those of the fully connected point-to-point networks, such as scalability problems.

2.2.3 Broadcast Networks

The third class of network architecture is the broadcast network. Broadcast networks can provide one-way or two-way communications. To support two-way communications with full connectivity, the broadcast network also can use either circuit switching or packet switching. These architectures are discussed next.

2.2.3.1 One-way Broadcast

Not all communications applications require full connectivity. In fact, there are important communications applications that only require a one-way, one-to-many distribution of information. Broadcast TV service is such an application. It requires a one-way broadcast network to send information to all homes in a particular geographical region. As such, only a broadcast network is needed. This is achieved by taking advantage of the broadcast medium – over the air radio broadcast. Similarly, cable TV service distributes TV signals over a broadcast cable medium from a headend to the households in each neighborhood. Hence, neither a fully connected nor a switched network is needed for one-way broadcast applications.

2.2.3.2   Two-way Communications

A broadcast network can also provide two-way communications with full connectivity among all parties on the network. Two-way broadcast networks include both wireless networks (such as the cellular phone network) and wired networks (such as the Ethernet). However, using the broadcast medium to provide two-way communications for multiple pairs of endpoints introduces a network contention problem. A broadcast network is a shared medium that allows only a single data transmission to take place at any time. Otherwise, if multiple parties have overlapped transmissions, such transmissions will be corrupted. Hence, a way of coordinating the transmissions and multiplexing must be provided to support general two-way communications between any two parties over a broadcast network. This can be achieved by either circuit or packet switching.

2.2.3.3   Circuit Switching on Shared Medium

The cellular phone network is an example of using circuit switching on a broadcast shared medium (wireless) to provide two-way communications between multiple parties. The analog and digital cellular networks use FDM-based and TDM-based circuit switching, respectively. In a way the broadcast medium is similar to the link connected between circuit switches that must be shared by multiple communicating parties simultaneously. As such, the FDM and TDM used in circuit switching can be used to coordinate the transmission of multiple pairs of communicating parties. Specifically, the "link" (wireless medium) is logically divided into multiple channels (FDM or TDM). Access to each channel by any two parties must be granted through a connection setup process, which determines if there is a free channel available to the connection request. Hence, contention is prevented by this bandwidth allocation process on a per connection basis, as each logical channel is allocated to only one pair of communication parties.

2.2.3.4 Packet Switching on Shared Medium

In the 1970s, another form of packet switching emerged that did not require a packet switch. It is based on a passive coaxial cable that connects all endpoints. This is a broadcast shared medium. Any packet transmission from an endpoint is automatically broadcast to all other endpoints in the network (on the cable). It is a shared medium because at any given time, there can only be a single packet transmission on the network. Otherwise, there will be packet collisions, which means that multiple packet transmissions overlap in time and the packets involved in such a collision would become corrupted. Hence, endpoints must take turns for their packet transmissions. To avoid such collisions, a medium access control (MAC) protocol is required to coordinate the transmissions on the network. Another important property of broadcast shared medium networks is that each endpoint transmits on the network at the same bandwidth, which is equal to capacity of the broadcast shared medium.

In essence, a broadcast shared medium network combined with the MAC protocol used by the endstations together becomes a distributed packet switch. Hence, packet switching over a broadcast shared medium still provides the same benefits of statistical multiplexing. Another advantage of a shared medium broadcast network is the lack of an active switching device or a single point of failure. A third advantage is the ease of adding new stations by connecting directly on the cable.

However, there are quite a few disadvantages of the broadcast shared medium network compared with a packet switch. First, this network is not scalable. The more endpoints are added to the medium, the less per-endpoint bandwidth available for sharing. Second, every endpoint on the shared medium network is constrained to the same bandwidth for transmission. These limitations are discussed in more detail later. Third, the need for a MAC protocol introduces network overhead, leading to a less than 100% network utilization due to inefficiency of MAC protocols to coordinate transmissions. Although a broadcast shared medium network behaves like a distributed packet switch, there is no "buffer" in the network to handle simultaneous transmissions (contention), leading to packet losses (and wasted bandwidth). In contrast, a real packet switch has buffer to store multiple packets contending for the same output port.

2.3 Limitations of Today's Network Infrastructures

The PSTN, the Internet and the cable networks are today's key public network infrastructures for sending voice, data and video information, respectively. A common characteristic of these network infrastructures is that they were all designed (and optimized) for a particular application. As such, they are typically unsuitable for supporting applications other than the one for which they were designed. Nevertheless, by understanding their limitations we can learn to design a truly integrated network that supports all types of applications.

We focus on the PSTN, the Internet and the intranets below. The cable networks and their limitations are discussed in detail in the last part of this book.

2.3.1 Telephone Networks

2.3.1.1   Characteristics

The PSTN has been providing the public infrastructure for voice communications for both residences and businesses for a century. It is based on circuit switching, with each connection carrying a single voice conversation. As the PSTN moves from analog to digital *within* the network (between circuit switches), the basic connection transforms from a 4 KHz voice frequency band channel (using FDM) to a 64 Kbps digital channel (using TDM). Hence, the PSTN consists of circuit switches based on switching 64 Kbps connections, while a trunk of N x 64 Kbps (carrying N voice channels) is switched as a unit at the backbone switch (also called crossconnect) of the PSTN.

Although communication between circuit switches has become almost entirely digital in the United States and in many developed countries, the connection from an endpoint to the PSTN is still primarily analog plain old telephone service (POTS). Hence, the CO switches are required to provide analog to digital conversion. With ISDN service, this last link to the customer becomes digital. Therefore, ISDN service provides the first end-to-end digital connectivity over the PSTN.

Within businesses, voice communications are typically supported by PBX (private branch exchange), which is essentially a private version of a CO switch, with enhanced call features for businesses.

The PSTN has a number of key advantages. First, it is ubiquitous (at least in developed countries). Second, it provides full connectivity; anyone who is near a telephone can potentially be connected to almost every other telephone in the world (given the called party phone number and access privilege). Third, since the PSTN is based on circuit switching, it provides guaranteed bandwidth and delay once the connection is setup. Due to these advantages, many other applications have been designed to run over the PSTN, even though it has been designed for voice communications only. These include data applications using modem, (low quality) image communications based on facsimile, and even low bit rate video communications. It is interesting to note that more than half of today's PSTN connections across the Pacific Ocean are for facsimile transmission. Video conferencing uses p x 64 Kbps (p = 1 to 24) over switched fractional T1 or switched T1 (1.5 Mbps), which have been available in the past decade for transmitting real-time compressed video. Domestic and international video conferencing are also growing rapidly as the video conferencing equipment price dropped dramatically in the past few years. Desktop video conferencing has also arrived and is expected to spur the growth further.

2.3.1.2   Limitations

The main problem with today's PSTN is that it is based on circuit switching and was optimized for one application, that is, telephony. Although it serves this application extremely well, it has a number of problems that make it unsuitable for providing integrated services for a wide variety of applications.

Inflexible   Applications supported on this network must be encoded to fit the 64 Kbps channels, which have been designed to carry (PCM encoded) voice. There are many applications that require more than 64 Kbps. Even if we can combine multiple 64 Kbps channels (which is done for the p x 64 video conferencing standard), it is not a flexible architecture for which one can build applications that require arbitrary bandwidth that is exactly a multiple of 64 Kbps. Furthermore, switched (not permanent) p x 64 connections are still far from ubiquitous.

Inefficient   Since circuit switching is not efficient to support bursty applications, the PSTN does not support data applications efficiently. Furthermore, it is not even efficient to carry voice, the application for which it was originally designed, because an average voice conversations is only 40% active and so 60% of the bandwidth is wasted. The PSTN offers a fixed bandwidth, many applications, including voice and video, can be encoded at variable bit rate and it becomes very inefficient for this network to support.

Bandwidth limitations   Many applications require much higher than 2 Mbps, the typical upper limit of today's p x 64 Kbps switched connections. For example, MPEG 2 broadcast quality video requires 3-4 Mbps, while interactive image browsing requires on the order of 10 Mbps (such as transferring a 1 Mbytes image in less than 100ms). Furthermore, dynamic allocation of an arbitrary number of 64 Kbps connections on a call-by-call basis is still far from reality, because circuit switches today (supporting a single rate at 64 kbps) have to be redesigned to support multi-rate circuit switching.

2.3.2   The Internet and Intranets

2.3.2.1   Characteristics

The two key data network infrastructures today are the Internet and the intranets. The Internet is the interconnection of an increasing number of both private and public data networks based on the TCP/IP protocol suite. The term intranets has recently been used to refer to the set of corporate data networks that run the Internet protocol suite, which has become an ever-increasing proportion of today's corporate networks. We discuss both in more detail below.

The Internet   The Internet has evolved into the de facto worldwide public data network infrastructure, which originated from a US research network in the late 1960s. The Internet is based on connectionless packet switching using the TCP/IP protocol suite. The packet switches in the Internet that forward and route packets are commonly known as routers (used to be called gateways).

The packet in the Internet is called an IP (Internet Protocol) packet. The IP packet header contains both its destination and source IP address. The router uses the destination IP address to select the route and forward each IP packet to the next hop that would lead to its final destination. IP routers in general provide the same level of service to all packets – best-effort service. Hence, there is no guarantee for bandwidth, delay or loss rates in the Internet. Furthermore, since it is a connectionless packet switched network, packets between two communication parties of the same session can travel along different paths in general. Therefore, packets can arrive out-of-order.

To be exact, IP is an internetworking technology for connecting multiple networks of different technologies. Networks of different technologies are connected via a router. The IP packet is the common packet format being preserved from network to network. (The IP packet is typically encapsulated as the payload of the packet format, referred to as a frame, of local networking technologies. If the IP packet exceeds the local frame format length limit, it is fragmented into multiple fragments and encapsulated correspondingly.) Hence, the connectivity between adjacent routers can be a network such as the Ethernet in addition to being just a point-to-point link. Typically, for the Internet, the routers are connected via point-to-point links. For intranets, routers are connected by LAN (local area network) technologies such as Ethernet, Token Ring and FDDI, as discussed next.

The Intranets   After more than a decade since their introduction to the corporate environment in the early 1980s, the LANs have become the basic data communications infrastructure for corporations of different sizes. Intranets are the corporate data networks based on the TCP/IP protocol suite. The term was coined only recently to mirror the corporate data network equivalent to the Internet. However, we generalize intranets to include all corporate data networks that use protocols other than IP, unless otherwise stated.

As discussed below, intranets have evolved significantly in the last ten years from basic shared medium LANs to an internetwork of different LANs of higher bandwidth and non-shared bandwidth, as shown in the following architecture evolution. Some of these evolution steps have occurred in parallel.

- Basic LAN deployment: Shared medium LANs (such as Ethernet, Token Ring, FDDI)
- Internetworking: Bridged and Routed LANs
- From bus or ring-based topology to Hub-based
- From shared hub to switched hub
- From 10 Mbps to 100 Mbps Ethernet (and possibly Gigabit Ethernet)

Shared medium LANs   A LAN interconnects desktop personal computers (PCs), workstations, servers, and printers. LANs are used for both data communications and sharing of expensive devices (printers and servers). Typical LAN applications include electronic mail, file sharing, printing and file backup. Due to the burstiness of computer communications applications, LANs are based on packet switching. The LAN technology that has gained the widest acceptance is the Ethernet. Tens of millions of Ethernet endpoints (adapters) have been deployed since the early 1980s. Ethernet is based on broadcast shared medium packet switching using a broadcast coaxial bus of 10 Mbps capacity, as shown in Figure 2–7. Hence, the transmission capacity on the link between each station and the Ethernet is the same as the network capacity (10 Mbps). The MAC protocol is called CSMA/CD (carrier sense multiple access with collision detection).[3]

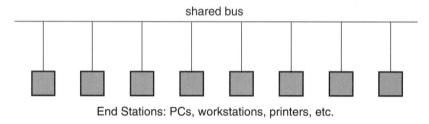

End Stations: PCs, workstations, printers, etc.

Figure 2–7   Ethernet

The MAC protocols used in LANs such as Ethernet and Token Ring provide only a best-effort service for packet delivery. It provides connectionless packet switching without bandwidth reservation. This means that neither the success of packet delivery nor the arrival time of packets is guaranteed by these LANs. Hence, packets might be lost, corrupted when they arrive or arrive late. In the other words, both the error and delay performance are unpredictable and are not guaranteed in these LANs.

Nevertheless, this simple delivery service is sufficient for many data applications such as file transfer, email and printing, because of two reasons. First, the error introduced by packet loss or corruption can be handled by both link layer (using error detection) and higher layer (transport) protocol (such as TCP[2] for TCP/IP) by re-transmitting lost or corrupted packets. Therefore, the end effect for such errors experienced by user is additional delay (longer response time) for the application, but not corruption of data. Second, since these LAN applications have been primarily non-real-time applications, they are delay tolerant. Furthermore, the delay introduced by the LAN is comparable to that incurred in processing at the endpoint devices (such as printers, mail servers and workstations). Therefore, the delay introduced by best-effort service does not significantly degrade user experience for LAN applications to make LANs unusable.

From disjoint LANs to internetworks   Today's large intranets typically consist of LANs (Ethernet, Token Ring and FDDI) interconnected with one another. There are two main motivations for this architecture. First, as independent LANs get installed in different departments of a company, it becomes necessary to communicate among these departmental LANs. Bridges and routers are used to interconnect these LANs to form a campus-wide internetwork or intranet.[2, 4] Bridges are active internetworking devices that operate in layer 2 (link layer) for forwarding link layer packets (frames) between interconnected LANs. Bridges are popular because of their ease of installation and maintenance. However, their disadvantages include the lack of scalability (broadcast IP packets to all bridged LANs) and the difficulty in providing security based on network layer addresses. Network layer addresses (such as IP) can be configured by network administrators as opposed to link layer physical addresses (Ethernet addresses), which are fixed by the adapters. Hence, this leads to the use of routers especially for large internetworks or intranets that demand scalability and management flexibility.

Routers are layer 3 (network layer) internetworking devices that forward network layer packets (such as IP) between two or more LANs that can be of different link layer technologies. They route packets depending on the protocol family that the packet belongs to, because routing is based on the protocol family address on the packet header. Managing layer 3 (IP layer) is much more flexible than layer 2, as network administrators can assign IP addresses (structured), but not Ethernet addresses (unstructured). However, management of routers also turns out to be a significant endeavor compared to configuring bridges. Also, routers typically cost significantly more than bridges.

In addition to providing full connectivity, there is another reason for creating an intranet. As both the number of workstations or PCs to be connected by a LAN increase and the processing power of these stations increase (faster microprocessors), the traffic load offered to the LAN will also increase significantly. To alleviate the load on the LAN, the LAN is segmented into separate segments (or subnetworks) at the link layer (or network layer) by bridges (or routers). This essentially increases the concurrency of communication and helps limit the offered load to each segment or subnetwork by limiting the number of devices connecting to the LAN.

From bus to hub-based LANs   Since the late 1980s, the wiring configuration of the Ethernet has evolved from a bus to a star configuration to take advantage of the existing wiring configuration of voice grade unshielded twisted pairs (or Category-3 UTP) from offices to a central wiring closet (see Figure 2-8). This is known as 10-baseT Ethernet. A hub is installed at the wiring closet for interconnecting twisted pairs from an individual office's Ethernet station. The hub becomes the point of sharing or broadcast for the CSMA/CD protocols. It is important to note that the hub is not a packet switch and there is no active switching (or buffering) inside the hub. Hence, the hub is only a physical layer device. This new implementation has two key advantages. Since it reuses existing wiring, it saves the costs of additional wiring. Second, it makes trouble shooting much easier because identification of individual stations or wiring causing the network problem is straightforward due to the point-to-point topology.

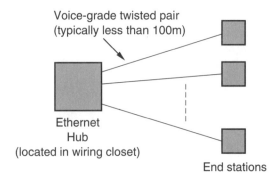

Figure 2–8   A Hub-based (star topology) Ethernet Configuration

From shared to switching hubs   As stations on the same shared medium LAN share the same bandwidth, such LANs create a major bandwidth bottleneck. This is especially the case when bandwidth demand of individual endpoints increase or when more endpoints are added to the LAN. A simple solution to this is to transform a shared medium LAN into a switched point-to-point LAN. A switched Ethernet allows each node to have full access to the 10 Mbps to the network. Furthermore, it provides scalability to support a large number of Ethernet endpoints, as the switching capacity is N x 10 Mbps, where N is the number of ports on the switch. Functionally, an Ethernet switch is the same as an Ethernet bridge, except with more ports and high switching capacity.

The switched Ethernet has become extremely popular in the past few years because it represents a very simple change in the physical network, yet results in significant performance improvements. Architecturally, this is a logical next step after transforming to a shared hub configuration (from a bus configuration), by replacing the shared hub with a switching hub.

From 10 Mbps to 100 Mbps Ethernet Another improvement that has occurred in the past few years is the development and rapid standardization of 100 Mbps Ethernet, also known as the Fast Ethernet. There are actually two flavors of Fast Ethernet: 100 base-T and 100 VG. 100 base-T essentially increases the speed of the 10 base-T from 10 to 100 Mbps, while maintaining the same MAC protocol (CSMA/CD). In contrast, 100VG uses a new MAC protocol that provides priority to time sensitive traffic to enhance the quality of service to support real-time applications. Due to the similarity between 10 base-T and 100 base-T, many 100 base-T adapters (and hubs) are designed to be dual mode 10/100 base-T using essentially the same processing logic that can run at the two different speeds. Installing a dual mode 10/100 base-T hub allows graceful migration of 10 base-T LANs into 100 base-T by allowing the upgrade of 10 base-T to 100 base-T stations one at a time, instead of requiring a wholesale upgrade. Furthermore, the commoditization of the 100 base-T makes their price amazingly close to its 10 base-T brother, which greatly facilitates their rapid adoption in the near future. Currently, 100 base-T is a much more popular version of fast Ethernet than 100 VG. More recently, Gigabit Ethernet has been proposed and is expected to be deployed in the near future. However, other than sharing the same name for marketing purpose, it does not use the same Ethernet protocols.

2.3.2.2 Limitations

We examine a number of problems of the legacy Internet and intranets and the approaches of addressing them.

Best-effort service A major limitation of most shared medium LANs arises from their MAC protocols; they provide only best-effort service. Real-time multimedia applications require guaranteed bandwidth and delay, and the delay and unpredictable service of existing LANs may not be acceptable. For instance, real-time video communications requires video frames to be delivered within a maximum delay constraint, after which the video frame becomes useless and is treated as lost. The communications requirements of these multimedia applications are discussed in more detail in the following chapters.

More recently, an overlay IP layer architecture has been proposed to provide bandwidth reservation for shared medium and switched LANs to guarantee QoS. However, this is still under development and standardization at the IETF's (Internet Engineering Task Force, the standard body for Internet protocols) ISSLL (Integrated Services over Specific Link Layers) working group.

Broadcast shared medium architecture   As discussed above, the sharing of a common broadcast channel in LANs imposes a limitation on sustained bandwidth available to each node. If k stations on the same LAN send data in a sustained fashion, the average throughput for each station will be limited to C/k, where C is the capacity of the LAN. Therefore, the average bandwidth available to a node decreases with an increasing number of nodes on a shared medium LAN (or active nodes during peak hours). (One can also argue that there is an intrinsic inefficiency in this design from the node's point of view. Even though each node can transmit at the full link capacity C all the time, it is limited to a duty cycle of $1/k$ on average.) Even with the recent hub implementation of these LANs, the above bandwidth reduction problem is the same, because the shared medium property remains. This problem can be solved by replacing the shared hubs with switching hubs. Nevertheless, the majority of Ethernet stations today are still on shared medium LANs.

Real-time delivery of time-based information such as video requires sustained bandwidth for a certain duration (much longer than packet transmission time). Video compression standards such as MPEG 1 require about 1.2 Mbps for sub-VCR quality, while MPEG 2 requires at least 3 to 4 Mbps for laser disc quality video. This means that there is a very limited number of video streams that can be supported over 10 Mbps shared LANs. Hence, Fast Ethernet has been developed to address the bandwidth bottleneck. More recently, Gigabit Ethernet, which has a capacity of a few hundred Mbps and a non-CSMA/CD protocol, has been proposed. Nevertheless, the majority of current LANs are still shared 10 Mbps Ethernets.

Internetworking   The characteristics of internetworks are similar to those of a LAN in that both offer best-effort delivery service. The reason is that the packet processing at a bridge or a router is typically based on a first-come-first-serve algorithm, without any notion of bandwidth or delay guarantees. Moreover, the end-to-end path still has to go through the same LANs that provide best-effort service. Hence, neither the intranets nor the Internet guarantees QoS. Hence, the IETF has been developing and standardizing an IP-based bandwidth reservation protocol known as RSVP (Resource ReSerVation Protocol).[5, 6] To guarantee quality of service across the Internet or intranets, two conditions must be met. First, the RSVP protocol must be supported by the routers along the path (at least those with congested links) and the endpoints. Second, the networks in between the routers must also provide quality of service guarantees (not just best-effort service), such as supporting subnet bandwidth manager over LANs, or they are point-to-point links between routers.

2.4 Summary

In this chapter, we gave an overview on today's networking architectures and how they evolved from one to another due to problems in the previous paradigms. We also discussed today's key networking infrastructures, the PSTN and the Internet and intranets and their limitations.

The basic network architectures are fully connected point-to-point networks, switched point-to-point networks and broadcast networks. The second and third network architectures are switched networks. There are two switching methodologies: circuit and packet switching. Circuit switching provides bandwidth on demand for endpoints that require a new connection. However, it dedicates network resources for each new connection and prevents others from using them even if the communicating endpoints are idle. Packet switching provides an additional (finer) level of bandwidth on demand by quantizing the bandwidth into units of bandwidth by using packets as basic unit of transmission, instead of the entire session.

Since the PSTN is based on circuit switching, it is unsuitable to support bursty applications and many emerging multimedia applications. However, even though the Internet and intranets are based on packet switching, they have problems of their own. To support future multimedia applications, they need to scale to very high bandwidth and to guarantee QoS. However, the shared medium LANs make it difficult to grow the bandwidth available to each node on the intranets, which lead to the deployment of switched Ethernet and Fast Ethernet (and emerging Gigabit Ethernet). Also, the best-effort delivery provided both by the Internet and the intranets cannot guarantee the QoS required by real-time multimedia applications. Nevertheless, there are efforts such as RSVP are underway to provide QoS guarantees on the Internet and intranets.

2.5 References

[1] T. Kwok, *Tandem Banyan Switching Fabric: A New Fast Packet Switching Architecture and its Performance Evaluation,* Ph.D. thesis, Stamford University, 1990.

[2] D. Comer, *Internetworking with TCP/IP,* Vol.1, Prentice Hall, Third Edition, 1996.

[3] R. Metcalfe, "Ethernet: Distributed Packet Switching for Local Area Networks," *Communications of the ACM,* vol. 19, pp. 395-404, July 1976.

[4] R. Perlman, *Interconnections: Bridges and Routers,* Addison Wesley, 1992.

[5] Zhang, L., Deering, S., Estrin, D., Shenker, S., and D. Zappala, "RSVP: A New Resource ReSerVation Protocol," *IEEE Network,* September 1993.

[6] R. Braden, Ed., L. Zhang, S. Berson, S. Herzog, S. Jamin, "Resource ReSerVation Protocol (RSVP)—Version 1 Functional Specification," draft-ietf-rsvp-spec-16.txt, IETF draft, June, 1997.

Chapter **3**

An Application Classification

3.1 Introduction

Before we understand the requirements of all types of multimedia applications, we need to have a framework of understanding applications in general. We need to first understand what is a communications application and what are the basic attributes of applications. To simplify the characterization of applications requirements, we need to have a way to classify all applications based on their networking requirements.

In this chapter, we first provide a definition of a communications application and identify its basic attributes. Then, we provide a classification scheme for all applications to provide a common framework for discussion later. This classification of applications is based on their real-time and quality of service (QoS) requirements.[1, 2] This will provide a framework for understanding applications requirements in general, with special emphasis on Internet applications such as Web browsing. Networking requirements of applications are discussed in detail in the next two chapters.

41

3.2 Communications Applications

3.2.1 Definition

A communications application is defined as a task that requires sending one or more flows of information between two or more locations. In this book, a communications application is simply referred to as an application.

3.2.2 Networking Attributes of an Application

An application can be characterized by the following networking attributes. Each of these attributes has significant implications to the networking requirements.

3.2.2.1 Information Types

Information communicated by an application can be classified into two types: **time-based** or **non-time-based**.[1, 2] Time-based information is a sequential set of information units, referred to as application data units (ADUs), ordered according to an associated set of timing information. Each ADU of the time-based information has an associated (explicit or implicit) timing component, relative to the rest of the ADUs of the time-based information. Time-based information for human consumption must be displayed or played back according to that timing information to convey its meaning.

For example, video is time-based information because video consists of a sequence of video frames (segments) that are displayed at regular time intervals. Similarly, audio is time-based information because it consists of a sequence of audio samples (segments of digitized information describing its amplitude as a function of time) played at a fixed rate. Other time-based information for human consumption includes voice and animation. In addition, there are types of time-based information that are for non-human consumption. These include carrying time division multiplexed (TDM) data stream such as T1 (1.544 Mbps). Such TDM data must be delivered at a specific constant rate to avoid receiver overflow or underflow. Carrying TDM data over a packet switched network is also known as circuit emulation, for which the sender and the receiver require a delivery service that is the same as a TDM circuit.

On the other hand, still images, graphics and text are non-time-based information because none of them have a time component as part of the information. In general, an application can include both time-based and non-time-based information. For example, a desktop application for stock brokers may require delivery of both TV news coverage (time-based) and real-time stock (non-time-based) information. Synchronization among multiple flows of information (possibly from multiple sources) can become an important issue. For example, an illustrated audio presentation application requires delivery of slides (non-time-based) synchronized with the speech (time-based) of the presenter.

3.2.2.2 Delivery Requirements

The information delivered by an application can have two types of delivery requirements: **real-time** or **non-real-time**. A real-time application requires the information delivered for immediate consumption, such as a telephone conversation or Web browsing. Since the information (both time-based and non-time-based) delivered is time sensitive, the real-time application requires guaranteed bandwidth, delay and loss rate to accomplish the delivery on time.

In contrast, for a non-real-time application, the information is transferred and stored at the receiving party for later consumption. Non-real-time applications are useful because the receiving party is not required to be present at the time the sending party is transferring the information. Most likely, the consumption of the information occurs some time after the sender transmits all the information. This implies that non-real-time applications require sufficient storage at the destination. Electronic mail is an example of a non-real-time application. The receiver of the email may not be available to read the email right away and so instant delivery is not required.

Information type and delivery requirements—orthogonal relationship It is important to understand the orthogonal relationship between the delivery requirement (real-time or non-real-time) of an application and the intrinsic time dependency of the information to be communicated (the content information can be time-based or non-time-based). In other words, the information type and the delivery requirement are independent attributes of an application. Table 3-1 shows the applications with different combinations of these two attributes. Video conferencing is a real-time application transferring time-based information (similar to telephony) as the communicating parties are present and consume the information in real-time. In general, real-time transfer of time-based information generates a continuous traffic pattern.

Table 3–1   *Examples of applications with different delivery requirements and information types*

DELIVERY REQUIREMENTS	INFORMATION TYPES	
	Time-based	**Non-time-based**
Real-time	Telephony Video conferencing	Web browsing Time sensitive Email, including video mail Time sensitive File Transfer
Non-real-time	Non-time sensitive video mail and voice mail	Non-time-sensitive Email and File Transfer

For image browsing applications such as Web browsing, even though each image is a piece of non-time-based information, to ensure interactive response for the user, they must be delivered within a maximum response time constraint to satisfy this application; so it is considered as a real-time application. Similarly, time-sensitive delivery of email and file transfer also can be considered real-time applications, if they need to consume a significant portion of the network bandwidth to satisfy their delay constraints.

On the other hand, the transfer of digitized movies is a non-real-time application if the delivery time constraint is so loose or the movie files so small that they do not consume a significant portion of network bandwidth. For downloading a digitized movie, even though the information content is time-based, the entire movie can be treated as a single file transfer (similar to electronic mail), because the movie is not being displayed in real-time at the receiver. However, movie downloads are considered real-time if they consume significant network bandwidth to meet the delay constraint.

3.2.2.3   Symmetry

In general, an application is a two-way information transfer between communicating parties. A one-way communication is a special case of a two-way communication with only one direction sending. Bi-directional applications can be classified as either symmetric or asymmetric. A symmetric application is one that involves the transfer of information of similar traffic characteristics in both directions; otherwise, it is called an asymmetric application. A voice call is an example of a symmetric application, as shown in Figure 3-1(a). The video on demand application is an asymmetric application, because it involves sending control messages in one direction and video transfer in the other direction. The broadcast TV application, an extreme case of an asymmetric application, involves one-way communication of video, as shown in Figure 3-1(b).

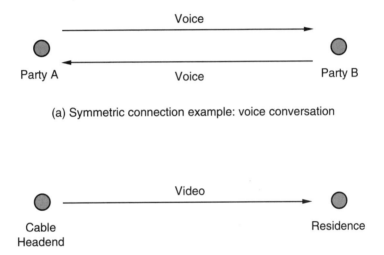

(a) Symmetric connection example: voice conversation

(b) Asymmetric connection example: cable TV distribution

Figure 3–1   Symmetry of an Application

Obviously, the communications requirements of an application depend on the symmetry of its connections. Many networks are designed to take advantage of the symmetry or asymmetry of the applications they intend to support. For example, the telephone network is designed as a symmetric two-way switched network (with same bandwidth in each direction) because it is designed for the telephony application (Figure 3-2). Traditional cable TV networks have been designed as a one-way broadcast type network, from the headend broadcasting downstream to the homes (Figure 3-3). To support video on demand applications or high-speed Internet access, a cable TV network has to be upgraded to a two-way switched network capable of providing interactive applications to a large number of homes (which is discussed in detail in Part III).

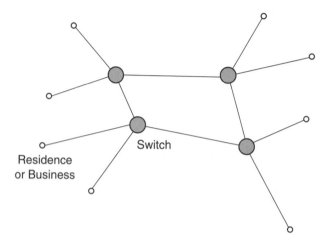

Figure 3–2   Topology of a telephone network

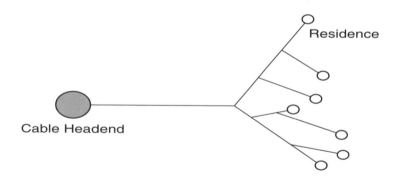

Figure 3–3   Topology of the cable TV network

3.2.2.4   Number of Parties

An application can be **point-to-point** or **multipoint** depending on the number of parties involved in the communication. An application involving only two parties is called a point-to-point application, while those involving more than two parties are called multipoint applications. Traditional phone conversations are point-to-point applications, whereas teleconferences that involve three or more parties are multipoint applications. Broadcast TV, an extreme case of a multipoint application, involves a single source sending information to all the other parties of the network.

Again, since communications requirements are very dependent on the number of parties involved, many networks that are designed for specific applications have been optimized for the number of parties involved in those applications. The telephone and the cable TV networks are both examples of such an optimized design. The telephone network has been optimized for point-to-point connections by using a switch-based, point-to-point network architecture, so that each endpoint is able to access all possible endpoints (Figure 3-2). On the other hand, the cable TV network is based on a broadcast non-switch-based architecture, allowing each user to communicate with only one particular endpoint, namely, the cable headend where the video source is located (Figure 3-3). Since everyone is going to select from the same (limited) number of channels, there is no need for a switch-based network for cable broadcast TV distribution. Traditional and emerging cable network designs are discussed in detail in Part III.

Both the symmetry and the number of parties are attributes which describe the nature of the connection for a communications application. Table 3-2 shows examples of the applications with different combinations of these two attributes.

Table 3–2 *Applications with different combinations of symmetry and number of party attributes*

Number of Parties	Symmetry of Connection	
	Symmetric	**Asymmetric**
Point-to-point	Voice call	Video on demand
Multipoint	Multi-party conference voice call	Broadcast TV

3.2.2.5 Wired or Wireless Access

A communications network can be designed with both wired and wireless access. Traditional access to the telephone network has been through a wired infrastructure. The need for wireless access stems from the need of communication independent of the location of the communicating parties; the parties are not limited to the fixed locations where the wired access network terminates. An example of a wireless access network is a cellular telephone network.

There are two types of wireless access networks: with or without base stations. The main functions of a base station include (local) bandwidth management, routing between communicating devices and relaying to other base stations if necessary. Without a base station, an ad hoc network[3] can be set up among wireless devices, in which these devices communicate directly with each other. This implies the devices have to resolve the contention for the same spectrum themselves. Ad hoc networking is very convenient for users in close proximity (such as in the same meeting room), because they can start communication with each other anywhere without restricting to places that have a base station. However, it is still limited to local communication because, without a base station, connection cannot be set up with remote devices.

Currently, there are various types of wired and wireless access available for personal and business uses from public network or private networks, as shown in Table 3-3.

Table 3–3   *Wired and wireless access networks for personal and business communications*

	Public network		Private network	
User	**wired**	**wireless**	**wired**	**wireless**
Personal	Public phone network	Cellular	Intercom in home	cordless telephone
Business	Business phone	Cellular	PBX, LAN	wireless LANs

3.2.2.6   Mobility

To reach an individual over a network, one has to first determine the location of the individual within the network and also the network address of the individual's closest network access point (such as his home or work number). This essentially ties the individual to a particular network access point from which he receives his calls. To reach the branch of a multi-location organization closest to the caller, one has to determine which branch is closest as well as its network address (which differs from those of other branches).

Mobility is a concept for simplifying the connection process with any desired entity. Mobility can be described as the ability to use a single logical label by any user (wherever he or she is) to access an entity (human or non-human) wherever the latter is within the network. With mobility, the caller does not need to determine where that entity is and the corresponding network address. In general, mobility requires an intelligent cooperation between the network and the endpoints to determine the location of the destination entity. Today, the primitive version is paging for the person before setting up the call.

The mobility concept can be applied to a person, a terminal or a service.[4] Personal mobility allows connection to a person through the network independent of the location of that person. Although personal mobility is usually associated with wireless networks such as the cellular telephone network, personal mobility can also be implemented in wired networks. For instance, the wired network can route the calls for a person to an office or home depending on the time of day, or to the person or a secretary depending on the calling party. Terminal mobility allows the same capability for the physical terminal; in addition, more than one person can be assigned to the same terminal. Service mobility allows communication to a service, which can be provided at multiple locations, that is closest to the caller. Service mobility exists today in the wired network, such as the 911 number service, where calls are automatically routed to the emergency service center closest to the calling party. Such service has been extended to pizza delivery service to allow a caller to be automatically connected to the closest pizza outlet by dialing the same number nationwide.[5]

3.2.2.7 Human versus Non-Human

In general, the parties involved in an application may either be a human user (through a PC or other intelligent terminal) or an information processing device (without human interpretation). For instance, a voice call is a user-user application, while a user accessing a remote database or an interactive voice response system is a user-device application, and two supercomputing devices performing parallel computations to solve the same problem by communicating intermediate results is considered as a device-device application. It is important to distinguish between a human endpoint and a device endpoint, because they have different information processing characteristics that translate into different communications requirements. For example, when a human interacts with a terminal to process information that may originate from the network, this requires acceptable response time for his/her interaction (such as accessing the database) and certain quality of the delivery (viewing a movie). On the other hand, a computing device may have larger tolerance with respect to response times in many cases (computing devices 'patiently' wait for user inputs).

Collaboration[6] is a class of applications between human users who share an electronic space for communication. Collaboration can occur between two individuals present at the same time (real-time) or at different times (non-real-time). Real-time collaboration is a user-user application, such as video conferencing and shared white board. Non-real-time collaboration is a user-device application. Electronic mail can be a non-real-time collaboration application, which involves a user sending a message to the other user's communication device (such as a PC). The message will eventually be viewed by a human, but not necessarily in real-time.

ITU provides taxonomy to classify communications modes based on human and non-human interactions.[7] Communications (any information types) between two humans are called conversational or interactive applications. A person sending information to a machine is called messaging. A person initiating information delivery from a machine is called retrieval. Distribution is a machine sending to humans or machines, which listen passively. Machine-to-machine interactions are considered computer communications.

3.3 A Classification of Applications

Communications applications can be classified according to their quality of service (QoS) requirements into three classes: real-time streaming, real-time block transfer, and non-real-time applications. Again, real-time refers to the time sensitivity of the information delivered by the application. These three classes are discussed in detail below.

3.3.1 Real-time Streaming Applications

As discussed earlier, information can be classified into time-based or non-time-based. Time-based information is user data that has an intrinsic time component. Video, audio, and animation are time-based information, because they generate a continuous sequence of data blocks that must be displayed or played back consecutively at predetermined time instants. On the other hand, text and images are non-time-based information. A real-time streaming application is one that delivers time-based information in real-time.

When time-based information is delivered in real-time over the network, such a display rate must be preserved to the remote user for transparency. Hence, real-time streaming applications are characterized as having a continuous traffic pattern. Delivering time-based information over the network at the same rate as its intended display rate is referred to as a real-time streaming application. This implies a certain QoS requirements (delay, jitter and error) must be satisfied for this class of applications, which is discussed in more detail in a later chapter.

A list of popular Internet applications is shown in Table 3-4. Real-time streaming on the Internet include playing audio and video from a Web site (one-way streaming) without first downloading the entire file. This represents a pull model of content delivery on a one-to-one basis. Alternatively, real-time streaming can be one-to-many audio and video deliveries using IP multicast over the Mbone (multicast backbone) on the Internet. The multicast model of content delivery represents a push model of content delivery. Two-way real-time streaming applications include Internet telephony and multimedia conferencing between two or more parties. Another example is multi-player interactive network games that include animation and live audio or video delivered to the game players.

Table 3–4   *A classification of internet applications*

Internet Applications Example	Real-time Streaming	Real-time Block Transfer	Non-real-time
Web browsing	Web page has streaming audio or video	Web page has only non-time-based information	
Email		Reading mail from a server	Mail delivery to destination email server
Internet telephony	Yes		

Table 3–4   *A classification of internet applications (continued)*

Internet Applications Example	Real-time Streaming	Real-time Block Transfer	Non-real-time
Interactive games	Yes	Yes	
Radio over the Internet	Streaming audio	Radio can be downloaded as a file	
Multicast Applications	Audio and video multicast	Live data multicast	Overnight download
News on demand with images, streaming audio and video	Yes	Yes	Yes
Application sharing		Yes	
Shared white board		Yes	
Chatting		Yes	
File Transfer		Yes	Yes

Table 3-4 shows that an application can belong to more than one application class. One reason is that the application can consist of multiple components, each delivering a different type of information, and they can belong to a different class of applications. Another reason is that the application can support more than one delivery mechanism for a given information type.

3.3.2   Real-time Block Transfer Applications

A real-time block transfer application delivers one or more blocks of data (ADUs), each of which must be delivered within a deadline. Each ADU can be time-based or non-time-based information. There is no intrinsic timing relationship between consecutive data blocks, which is a key difference relative to a real-time streaming application. Since each ADU delivery is time sensitive, it is considered a real-time application.

The networking requirements for a real-time block transfer application is independent of whether each ADU is itself time-based or non-time-based information. In either case, they are both delivered as a block of data by the network, which has no knowledge of the meaning of the data. Only the application layer at the receiving end can and should distinguish between them, for different presentations to the users.

An ADU can be a text character, a command, or an audio, image or video file. A large ADU can be segmented into multiple packets; very small ADUs can be accumulated into a single packet. In other words, the block size from the application layer can be converted into very different packet sizes at the network layer.

3.3.2.1 Internet Applications

It is very important to understand the networking requirements of real-time block transfer applications for the Internet, because many Internet-based applications, such as Web browsing, belong to this application class (Table 3-4). We discuss a number of important Internet-based applications below.

3.3.2.2 Web Browsing

Web browsing is a real-time block transfer application. Whenever a user clicks on a hyperlink to a new Web site (URL, or universal resource locator), the Web browser makes a TCP connection to the new Web site to deliver the Web page.[8] HTTP/1.0[9] (hypertext transfer protocol version 1.0) requires a new TCP connection for each HTTP request of a new object, when TCP is used for the underlying reliable transport (the most common case). If the first Web page contains a number of associated objects (such as graphics and images), subsequent TCP connection(s) are made to the HTTP server to deliver to the user these associated objects embedded in the Web page. HTTP/1.1[10] supports persistent connections to allow multiple Web objects being delivered over the same TCP connection, and avoids the overhead of additional TCP connections.

From the user point of view, the response time of clicking on a link (going to a Web site) must be short. This short response time is also very important for the Web site designer or owner. Ideally, response time should be instantaneous, as if the Web page were stored locally. This translates into a response time of about 100ms to make this transparent to the user.[1] The block delay requirement (D_b) for delivering each of the objects constituting the Web page (or the visible part) depends on the interest level of the user to justify its wait for each object. (Of course, progressive display of image objects and other user interface "tricks" would help the user experience.) When the user wants to go to the next Web site, another set of blocks of data must be delivered within a certain time. In addition, account must be made of the TCP overhead, which includes connection setup and tear down, and slow start algorithm.

Multimedia conferencing Multimedia conferencing applications include not only real-time transfers of audio and video (which are real-time streaming applications), but also deliveries of image, graphics, text and control information (which are real-time block transfer applications). These real-time block transfer applications include application sharing, shared white board and chat, as shown in Table 3–4.

Application sharing means that a user can share (over the Internet) a software application running on the local PC with another user. The remote user can not only view the local application on the remote PC (without having a copy of the software application resident), but can also control the application remotely. The information being transferred are control messages to drive the remote PC's display and commands to drive the application on the local PC. All these messages must be delivered in real-time within a certain deadline to achieve transparency to the remote user. Application sharing is a very important application because it is a big step towards true collaboration. It enables, among many key applications, sharing contract revisions with a lawyer and providing remote product support on software products.

Shared white board is a simpler form of collaboration, with the exchange of text and graphics information among users over the network. Chat is even simpler as only text exchange is involved. While application sharing and shared white board are peer-to-peer applications (client-to-client), chat is a client/server applications because each user is actually communicating with a chat server.

Network multi-player games Network multi-player games are also real-time block transfer applications. Such games require very fast delivery of commands and images across the network to update the actions taken by various players. They represent some of the most stringent networking requirements among real-time block transfer applications, because the delay acceptable is much lower to allow the players realistic responses. These games can be either client-server-based games (players connect to a game server) or peer-to-peer games.

File transfer   File transfer applications are typically associated with non-real-time applications. However, in many scenarios, a file transfer is actually a real-time block transfer application because the user is usually waiting the file transfer to finish before the file can be used immediately. The longer the wait, the less satisfied is the user. For example, if the wait is too long for downloading a piece of software, this will prompt the user to abort the transfer, which is not desirable for content providers over the Internet.

3.3.2.3   Bandwidth- versus Latency-Limited

Real-time block transfer applications can be further categorized as either bandwidth-limited or latency-limited. This classification depends on the relative ratio of the end-to-end available network bandwidth (C), the end-to-end propagation delay (D_p), the size of each data block (B) and the delay requirement of a block of data (D_b). If $D_p > D_b$, the application will not be satisfied, no matter how much bandwidth is available. Hence, we assume $D_p < D_b$ for the following discussion.

Depending on how bandwidth is shared among different applications across the network (or explicitly allocated if bandwidth reservation is possible), let C is the bandwidth available to the application (C can be variable), which is a fraction of the minimum end-to-end link bandwidth. Let C_l be the minimum of all link capacity along the path. Hence, $C_l > C > 0$.

If $B/C_l \gg D_p$, then the real-time block transfer application is bandwidth-limited. The reason is that an increase in bandwidth available to this application will help meet its delay requirement D_b. The key to satisfying this requirement is not only in delivering a single packet or the delay incurred by a single packet. Rather, all the packets that together constitute the block arrive within D_b. For bandwidth-limited real-time block transfer applications, there is a minimum bandwidth requirement (C_{min}) for satisfying the block delay requirement D_b of the application: C_{min} is equal to B/D_b. Hence, $C > C_{min} = B/D_b$ must be satisfied. This assumes that $C_l > B/D_b$. Most large transfers (such as Web browsing to image intensive sites) over low-speed links are bandwidth-limited, which explains why the increasing access line speed can improve user experience significantly by deploying residential broadband network, as the local access speed is the first bottleneck. The next network bottleneck is probably the Internet backbone, which can be alleviated by a regional or local caching solution.[11]

On the other hand, if $B/C_l << D_p$, then the application is latency-limited. This can be the case for many Internet-based applications, because packet latency across the Internet can be on the order of 100ms or more, especially for inter-continental communications. Such Internet latency depends not only on physical distance, but also on the path taken by the packet (number of router hops). This is even more important for short transactions (small B), where the transmission delay (B/C) is negligible compared with the propagation delay. The total delay incurred by each block would not be alleviated significantly by increasing bandwidth C. Hence, this type of real-time block transfer is called latency-limited.

3.3.3 Non-real-time Applications

A non-real-time application does not carry any time sensitive ADUs (can be time-based or non-time-based information), as shown in Table 3–4. In other words, the information being transferred by non-real-time applications has no strict time constraint. Non-real-time applications are similar to real-time block transfer applications in that they both deliver one or more blocks of data (ADUs) and both are opaque to the content of each ADUs (which can be time-based or non-time-based information).

Another way to define a non-real-time application is to use its relationship to the network bandwidth. The bandwidth that is required to support such an application is a very small fraction of the network bandwidth. In other words, bandwidth is not an issue for a non-real-time application. In fact, the ADUs to be transferred by the non-real-time application can be sent at a very low rate compared to the bandwidth of the network and still satisfy its requirements. Non-real-time applications are neither bandwidth-limited nor latency-limited. For example, an electronic mail is a block of data that needs to be delivered to the receiver at some later time, which can be hours later. This is acceptable in many situations because the recipient is typically not available to read the email anyway (either not physically present or busy on other tasks). Each mail is delivered in a store-and-forward manner across multiple mail servers or gateways along the path to the recipient. (Note that the email can contain video files, which can still be considered a non-real-time application.)

A file transfer also can be considered a non-real-time application in many situations, while it can be a real-time block transfer application in other situations, as discussed earlier. File transfer is a non-real-time application when the user does not care exactly how long it takes to finish the file transfer. For example, the user can be doing other tasks or not even present after the file transfer is initiated. Alternatively, the file transfer can happen in the background and the user can work on other tasks simultaneously.

Strictly speaking, there is still a time constraint requirement for non-real-time applications. After all, the data block is useless if it takes ten years to be delivered. Hence, the time constraint exists, but it is very loosely defined such that bandwidth is typically not an issue for such an application. One way to distinguish non-real-time from real-time block transfer is as follows: If the C_{min} required to satisfy the time constraint for each block is very small compared with the networking bandwidth available ($C_{min} << C$), then it is a non-real-time application. Hence, there is a lot of freedom to deliver this block of data. For example, we can wait until the network load is low (such as midnight) to deliver the data. In other words, we can use many adaptive schemes to deliver the data block according to the network loading conditions. In fact, TCP takes advantage of this fact to support file transfer applications.

Although non-real-time applications are not delay sensitive, they do have another strict QoS requirement—error requirements; many such applications must be loss-free at the application level, such as electronic mail. Unfortunately, many networking technologies, such as legacy LAN technologies (such as Ethernet and Token Ring) and the Internet do not guarantee error free delivery (in addition to not guaranteeing timely delivery). Legacy LANs and the Internet provide only best-effort service, which means that the network does its best to deliver the packets given its current network loading conditions and commitment to other applications. In other words, it is a "send-and-pray" delivery service. To support this class of applications over best-effort service (at the network level), the applications must rely on the transport layer—such as TCP—to provide reliable delivery over best-effort type networks. Therefore, there are very distinct error requirements at the application level and network level because of functionality that can be provided at the transport layer.

3.4 Summary

In this chapter, we first provide a definition of a communications applications and identify its basic attributes. Then, we provide a classification scheme for all applications based on networking requirements to provide a common framework of discussion in the next two chapters.

3.5 References

[1]T. Kwok, "A Vision for Residential Broadband Services; ATM-to the Home," *IEEE Network,* Sept./Oct, 1995, pp. 14-28.

[2]T. Kwok, "Communications Requirements of Multimedia applications: A preliminary study," *Proc. Int'l Conf. On Selected Topics in Wireless Commun.,* Vancouver, 1992, pp.138-142.

[3]J. Lovette, "Data-PCS", Petition for Rulemaking to FCC for Amendment of Section 2.106, Jan 28, 1991.

[4]R. Wolff, S. Parlamas, D. Hakim, M. Beller, "A Functional Model and Analysis of Personal Communications Services," to be published.

[5]A. Ramirez, "The Pizza Version of Dialing 911," *The New York Times,* C1, Sept. 9, 1991.

[6]M. Schrage, *Shared Minds: The New Technologies of Collaboration,* Random House, New York, 1990.

[7]ITU-T Recommendation I.211 [Rev. 1], "B-ISDN Service Aspects," ITU Study Group 13, Geneva, Switzerland, Nov. 1993.

[8]W.R. Stevens, *TCP/IP Illustrated,* Volume 1, Addison-Wesley, 1994.

[9]T. Berners-Lee, R. Fielding, H. Frystyk, "Hypertext Transfer Protocol — HTTP/1.0," *IETF Request for Comments: 1945,* May 1996.

[10]R. Fielding, J. Gettys, J. Mogul, H. Frystyk, T. Berners-Lee, "Hypertext Transfer Protocol — HTTP/1.0," *IETF Request for Comments: 2068,* January 1997.

[11]T. Kwok, "Residential Broadband Internet Services and Network Architecture," *SCTE Emerging Technologies Conference Proceeding*, Nashville, Tennessee, January 1997, pp. 113-126.

Chapter 4

Application Traffic Requirements

4.1 Introduction

Ideally, a communication network is designed to support the requirements of targeted applications. For example, the public switched telephone network (PSTN) was designed to support voice communications. However, the converse has been true for supporting emerging multimedia applications. Many multimedia applications have to be designed to run over existing networks such as the PSTN, the Internet and intranets. The reason is that these legacy networks have been deployed extensively already. To ensure the widest customer base for such applications, these applications must be optimized for these networks, and hence constrained by them. For example, most home users need to dial up through the PSTN network to access the Internet, even though the PSTN was not designed for data communications, leading to high inefficiency and high call blocking probability as a result of the long holding time.

The goal of ATM is to support all types of applications, including interactive multimedia applications, in the same network. Hence, to understand the design criteria of ATM, we need to understand the networking requirements of applications in general, including multimedia applications in particular.

4.1.1 Applications Requirements

ITU has classified networking functions into three main categories: user, control and management planes. The networking requirements of applications can be classified accordingly. User plane functions are those that enable the data transfer of the application in a satisfactory fashion in terms of delay and reliability. User plane application requirements are specified by the traffic and the quality of service (QoS) requirements of the application.

The control plane specifies the call or connection control functions for enabling an application, which includes connection setup, maintenance and tear-down. Control plane requirements are specified in terms of both functionality and performance. Functional requirements include enabling a certain connection configuration to support the required number of parties and the direction of information flow. The performance requirements of control plane include call setup delay and call throughput (number of call setup per sec). Management plane deals with the management of the user and control planes functions.

We will mainly focus on the user plane requirements in this book, because they have direct impact to the performance as perceived for the application. We will briefly discuss control plane requirements. Management plane requirements are beyond the scope of this book.

An application's networking requirements can have very distinct characteristics and requirements in each direction (that is, data that the application sends to the network and the data that the application receives from the network). (Also, there can be more than one endpoint in each direction for a multipoint application.) The following discussion of networking requirements applies to each direction independently. An application can belong to a different class with respect to each direction. Applications with distinct characteristics in each direction are referred to as asymmetric applications. Such application asymmetry should be distinguished from asymmetric networks, which have different characteristics (bandwidth or QoS) in each direction (such as most residential broadband networks,[1] which is discussed in detail in Part III).

In this chapter, we will discuss in detail the traffic requirements for each class of applications, based on the classification from the last chapter. We will discuss the QoS requirements for different application classes in the next chapter.

4.1.2 Traffic and QoS Requirements

The user plane networking requirements of an application consist of *traffic* and *QoS* requirements. The traffic requirement of an application is a function of the traffic generation patterns of all the senders for the application. For example, a point-to-point two-way communication application has two senders. The traffic generation pattern for each sender can be modeled as a sequence of data blocks generated by the application layer. (Unless indicated otherwise, we use layering terminology of the ISO's OSI 7-layer model.[2]) Again, we call each block of data an application data unit (ADU). Each ADU can be destined to one or multiple parties. An ADU can be of arbitrary length and generated at arbitrary instants of time. For example, an ADU can be a video frame, an audio sample, a Web object, or an RPC (remote procedure call) command.

This model of traffic generation at the application layer is network independent and applies to both circuit-switched and packet-switched networks. In packet switched networks, a large ADU (such as a video frame) can be fragmented into smaller packets (or protocol data units, PDUs) for transmission over the particular networking technologies. For example, Ethernet can carry a maximum packet size of about 1500 bytes. Alternatively, multiple small ADUs (such as voice samples) can be accumulated into a single packet for transmission. The pattern at which packets are generated at the network layer (as a result of the ADUs generated at the application layer) defines the traffic requirements of the application. The QoS requirements of an application are specified by its delay and error requirements of the delivering each packet.

4.2 Traffic Generation Patterns

Traffic generation patterns at the application layer are characterized the ADU arrival distribution and the ADU length distribution. The ADU arrival distribution specifies the probability distribution of the instants at which ADUs are generated. The ADU size distribution specifies the probability distribution of the length of an ADU. The traffic requirements are specified by the resulting PDU arrival and length distributions at the network layer. Together, these two network layer distributions contribute to the instantaneous variation of data rate of the application. Such data rate variation can also be affected by adding a feedback loop from the network to adapt the application's traffic generation rate at the application or network layer.

4.2.1 Arrival Distribution: Continuous versus Bursty Traffic

Traffic generation patterns can be broadly classified into continuous versus bursty traffic. Continuous traffic patterns mean that the ADU/PDUs are periodically generated for a period of time, depending on the duration of interactions. In general, real-time streaming applications generate continuous traffic pattern. For example, a video application has continuous traffic because a video frame can be generated once every $1/30^{th}$ second. On the other hand, if ADU/PDUs are generated at random instants and separated with a long silence period (compared with transmission period), the traffic pattern is bursty. Real-time block transfer and non-real-time applications, such as web browsing, file transfer and electronic mail, typically generate bursty traffic.

4.2.2 ADU Length Distribution

ADU sizes vary significantly not only among different applications, but also within a particular application. For real-time streaming applications, the ADU is a unit of the time-based information being delivered, such as a voice or audio sample, or an animation or video frame. A PCM voice sample is 1 byte. For a 30 frame/s MPEG compressed movie at a constant bit rate of 2 Mbps, it has an average frame size of 8.3 Kbytes, though the actual frame size can vary significantly. MPEG compression generates three types of compressed frames: I-frames (Intra-coded), P-frames (Predictive-coded) and B-frames (Bi-directionally predictive-coded).[3] Intraframe compressed frames (I-frames) are usually much larger than the interframe compressed frames (P- and B-frames) because the former only use spatial compression (without any temporal compression), which results in lower compression ratios.

For real-time block transfer applications such as Web browsing, each ADU being delivered is a Web object. A Web object can be a HTML (hypertext markup language) page, text file, image, or audio and video clips. (In addition, there is control information, such as HTTP requests, which are also ADUs.)

It is well-known that as a result of diverse content, Web objects vary significantly in size. There are three key characteristics of Web object size distribution on the Internet. First, the distribution of Web object size requests depends heavily on the particular Web site. Since each site can serve a very different purpose, the degree of multimedia content can be very diverse. For example, a text-based Web site would have a very different Web object size distribution from that of a Web site for delivering multimedia content from a movie studio. Second, the distribution typically consists of a long tail.[4] There are usually a few large files on the Web site that might skew the average of the distribution significantly. Hence, very often the median of the Web object size distribution is a more representative Web object size being requested from the site. For example, for the server at National Center for Supercomputing Applications (NCSA),[5] the Web object size requested distribution has a median of about 3 Kbytes but a mean of 17 Kbytes. On the other hand, Mogul[6] measured another Web site to have a median object size of about 1.7 Kbytes and a mean of about 13 Kbytes. Third, since the Web is a very dynamic publishing medium and Web technologies are evolving very quickly, Web object size distributions are also changing very quickly. For example, both the emerging Java-based applets and the recent "push" technologies will change the object distribution significantly.

Due to the diverse Web object distributions across Web sites, it is more informative to understand the Web object request distribution from a client point of view. Cunha, Bestavros and Crovella[7] measured a client-based Web object request distribution involving 591 users to find a mean of 11.5 Kbytes (no median was reported). More than 66% of the documents are image files; less than 10% are HTML pages and sound; video, text, and formatted documents each constitute less than 1%.

4.2.3 Packet Length Distribution

To determine the networking requirement, it is the traffic pattern at the network layer (packet level) that is important. Hence, the ADU length distribution must be translated into the packet length distribution. However, there are many other factors that affect packet distribution other than the ADU distribution. As discussed earlier, large ADUs can be segmented into smaller packets, or small ADUs can be accumulated into a single packet.

There is a lower bound to the packet length for each link layer because of the overhead (packet header and trailer) and the networking technologies themselves (such as the MAC protocol). For Ethernet, CSMA/CD requires a minimum packet length (64 bytes) to ensure collision detection take place. Obviously, the longer the packet, the higher the transmission efficiency as there are fewer overhead bytes per data bytes. However, there are many factors that limit the maximum length of packets, as discussed below.

4.2.3.1 Packet Loss Probability

The longer the packet transmitted on a given transmission medium, the higher the likelihood of introducing one or more bit errors in the pac. Since the receiving end usually drops a packet with any bit errors, bit errors can translate into packet loss. Hence, the packet length should be limited, especially when bit error rates (BER) are not negligible. That's why, IP packets, which have a theoretical limit of 64 Kbytes long, very seldom use such a large packet, even if it does not violate the other limits discussed here.

4.2.3.2 MTU Size of Link Layer

Each (link layer) networking technology dictates a maximum payload of the frame, known as the maximum transfer unit (MTU) of the link technology. As discussed above, Ethernet has an MTU size of about 1500 bytes. Since fragmentation to fit the MTU size at each hop is very expensive, ideally the minimum MTU along the path should be used for the IP packet length by the endpoints. Hence, IP stations are encouraged to use the path MTU discovery protocol[8] before sending IP packets to a destination.

4.2.3.3 Default Packet Size Limit

Nevertheless, the majority of Internet Web browser clients do not use path MTU discovery as reported by Stevens.[4] Most Internet hosts still do not have such a capability. To avoid fragmentation, many Internet hosts use the default MTU size of 576 bytes recommended by the IETF standard for non-local computer communications.[9]

This popular default MTU size, used for Internet hosts, explains the observed average FTP/TCP/IP packet length of 310 bytes on the Internet backbone (NSFnet).[10] Since it is typical to have a maximum packet length followed by an acknowledgment (40 bytes) for this traffic, if the maximum packet length is 576 bytes, it gives an average packet length of 308 bytes, which matches almost exactly what is observed.[11] The average IP packet length of the all Internet backbone traffic is actually much lower at about 220 bytes, because of the significant percentage of control traffic, such as DNS (domain name service) queries, which contribute to about 5% of overall packet count on the Internet backbone in 1994-5.[4]

4.2.3.4   Packetization Delay

For the IP telephony application (a real-time streaming application), the packet length used has significant effects on the delay incurred by filling up the packet payload with voice samples. The larger the packet, the longer the delay to accumulate sufficient voice samples. This can result in a very long delay for very low bit rate codecs. For example, if a 6.4 Kbps codec (such as G.723.1[12]) is used for IP telephony, a 1500-byte packet will incur a packetization delay of 1.875 sec (3.75 sec round-trip)! This is not acceptable because the end-to-end round-trip delay for telephone conversation should be limited to about 500 ms,[13] even if echo is not a problem.

4.2.3.5   Transmission Delay

Another reason to limit packet length is for transmission on slow links, as with a 28.8 Kbps analog modem, which is a very popular way of accessing the Internet today. Since all traffic generated by the same client share the same low speed link, a long packet can introduce significant delay for other packets during the multiplexing process. This is especially important if the other packets are time sensitive, such as voice conversation (IP telephony) being multiplexed on the same link. Another example is delivering a voice annotated slide show. The voice packets must be interleaved between the slide show packets, which must be limited in size.

4.2.3.6   Effects of Loss Packets

For real-time streaming applications, since the information being delivered is time sensitive, it is usually too late to retransmit corrupted or lost packets. Late packets are useless and are also considered lost. Since packet loss is unavoidable in a packet switched network, especially the Internet, the effect of lost packets on the quality of the applications must be minimized. As the packets get larger, more data would be lost as a result of a lost packet. The packet length must be limited for real-time streaming applications. For example, for packetized voice, Weinstein and Forgie recommended that the packet should contain less than 50 ms worth of voice samples to minimize the quality impact of a lost packet to the end user.[14]

4.2.4 Self-similarity Traffic

Recently, it was shown both LAN[15] and WAN[16] exhibit a traffic behavior called self-similarity. Self-similarity means that the traffic is bursty in many different time scales. This is in contrast to the popular model of a Poisson process, for which the burstiness would smooth out over a long enough process. The same has also been shown of WWW traffic behavior.[17] This implies that the traffic has long range dependence and the distributions of transfer time and document sizes can be modeled by very long tail distribution. This also explains why the mean object size is skewed by large Web objects to have much larger value than the median.

4.2.5 CBR versus VBR

The traffic generation pattern can be characterized by the rate at which data are generated over time. If the data rate is constant over time, it is called constant bit rate (CBR). Otherwise, it is called variable bit rate (VBR). CBR or VBR can be applied to both the application and the network layers. Since there may be a transport layer in between, the instantaneous traffic generation rate may differ significantly, as discussed in more detail below.

The rate at which traffic is generated is due to a combination of the ADU/PDU generation distribution and size distributions. The data rate of a continuous traffic application can be either CBR or VBR, depending on the ADU/PDU size distribution. Since ADU/PDU generation occurs at regular intervals for continuous traffic, if the ADU/PDU size is fixed (such as PCM telephony with 1-byte ADU size), the application is a CBR application. Otherwise, if ADU/PDU size is variable, then the continuous traffic application generates a VBR.

The *instantaneous* rate at which the PDUs are sent to the network layer can be different from the application traffic generation rate from the application layer. The application layer data rate variation depends not only on the application class, but also on the nature of the application. Real-time streaming applications can generate either CBR or VBR traffic at the application layer, while the other two classes (real-time block transfer and non-real-time traffic) are usually VBR traffic. For example, PCM telephony produces a CBR stream at the application layer, while Web browsing is a VBR application.

On the other hand, the instantaneous traffic generation rate to the network layer is limited by the network technologies (network layer capacity) and the network conditions (such as loading). For the file transfer application, the application layer can pass a 1 Mbyte file to the transport protocol layer (to transmit on the network) by using a single procedure call—which can take less than 1 ms. This means the instantaneous rate of the application traffic generation is more than 8 gigabits per second (Gbps)! If the network layer has a link speed of only 10 Mbps (such as Ethernet), the high application generation rate cannot be matched by the network layer. Hence, it is the responsibility of the protocol layer to buffer and schedule data delivery to the network according to the network technologies. In other words, the transport layer may exert back pressure to the application layer to limit the maximum transmission rate that the application layer uses. For example, the protocol layer may not provide a buffer so that the application layer cannot pass more data until the protocol layer finishes transmission of all its currently buffered data.

Another reason the transmission rate to the network is altered is due to the end-to-end flow control function of the transport layer. Such flow control is to ensure no receiver buffer overflow occurs as a result of the sender transmitting faster than the receiver can process it. In the case of TCP/IP,[18] it may reduce the window size (the number of packets that can be sent without receiving an acknowledgment) used for transmission.

Nevertheless, the protocol layer can be null, in which case the application traffic generation process is the same as the network traffic generation process. For example, telephony has a null protocol layer. In a telephone network, 1-byte voice samples (ADU) generated at 8 kilohertz (kHz) frequency are sent at 64 Kbps on the circuit switched network (TDM).

4.2.6 Traffic Shaping

Even though an application may not generate traffic periodically, the transport or network layers can use traffic shaping to send periodically the application data blocks or ADUs (in the form of packets). For example, an application may have a contract with the network for a CBR service (at the network layer). The network layer performs traffic shaping on the packet transmission to conform to the CBR service, such as sending a file at a CBR of 1 Mbps. If the PDU size is fixed at 1 Kbytes, then packets must be generated at intervals of 8 ms or longer to conform to the service. Therefore, real-time block transfer and non-real-time applications also can generate continuous traffic at the network layer (during their active transmission period).

A continuous traffic pattern at the network layer can also be the result of traffic shaping at the application layer. This is the case for real-time streaming applications sending compressed information. For compressed video, such as that generated by the MPEG algorithm,[3] a video frame is still created at regular intervals of 1/30th second, except that the amount of information generated is variable at each instant, depending on the degree of compression for each frame. This implies that compressed video intrinsically generates VBR traffic at the application layer, as opposed to the CBR traffic generated by uncompressed video. With traffic shaping at the application using a smoothing buffer at the output of the MPEG decoder, a CBR MPEG stream can be created. The compressed frame boundaries actually occur in irregular boundaries (non-periodic) because each frame is compressed with a different ratio; the interval between consecutive frames can be more or less than 1/30 second (see Figure 4-1).

Hence, with traffic shaping, applications can be made CBR at the application layer and the network layer. Similarly, a very bursty (VBR) application can be traffic shaped to be much less bursty (with less data rate variation by reducing the peak bandwidth), even though it can still be VBR.

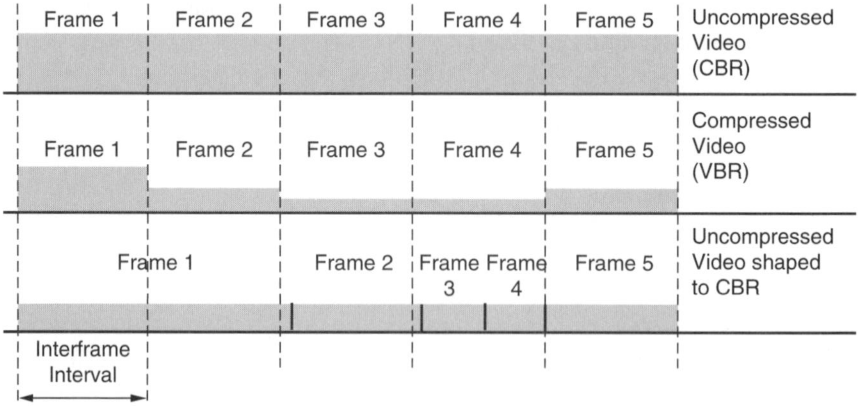

Figure 4–1 Application layer traffic-shapes a VBR source into a CBR stream

4.2.7 Adaptive Applications

Up to now, we have assumed that the data generation rate at the application layer only depends on the application itself and is not affected by the network load. There are two ways that the network traffic generated by the application can be made adaptive to the current network load. First, if the application is not delay sensitive (such as non-real-time applications), the transport layer, such as TCP/IP, can adjust the transmission rate according to the current network load. This means that it will take longer to finish delivery of all the application's data. However, even in such adaptive behavior, the total traffic (number of bytes) generated by the application to the network is still the same, except that they have been traffic-shaped by the transport layer. And the application itself does not actively participate in the adaptive behavior; only the transport layer does.

For a truly adaptive application, the traffic generated by the application is reduced as the network load increases. Such feedback is made possible by the transport layer to the application layer to actually reduce their generation rate (and total number of bytes generated.) Hence, such adaptive applications can truly reduce their load on the network under heavy load, instead of accumulating bytes until bandwidth is available again on the network. Real-time streaming applications can be implemented as true rate adaptive applications if they use an encoder that can vary its compression ratio. The transport protocol can feedback data rate information to the application to slow down or speed up (by increasing or decreasing the compression ratio, respectively) according to the loading conditions of the network. Hence, the user experience would decrease gracefully, instead of abruptly, as the network load increases. If there is not such an adaptive behavior, the applications might break immediately below a certain high threshold.

4.2.8 Traffic Asymmetry

Understanding packet length distribution is especially important in residential broadband network design because many of these architectures have asymmetric link bandwidth. The relative ratio of packet length distribution in each direction affects the throughput on an application, because they can be correlated.[11] For example, TCP requires acknowledgment traffic in the opposite direction to user data delivery. This means that, theoretically, transferring data using TCP can have an asymmetry ratio of 1500 bytes to 64 bytes using Ethernet frames, or a traffic asymmetry of about 23 to 1 for networking bandwidth. However, in reality, the default MTU in many existing hosts of 576 bytes might reduce it to a ratio of about 9 to 1. This implies that the downstream throughput can be limited to 9 times the upstream link bandwidth. This means that a cable modem using analog modem of 28.8 Kbps as return channel can potentially be limited to less than 270 Kbps downstream TCP throughput, even though the downstream bandwidth can be 10 Mbps or higher on cable networks (see Part III). (There are ways to alleviate this problem, such as acknowledgment traffic suppression or delayed acknowledgments, but they are beyond the scope of this book.)

4.3 Bandwidth Requirements

Since traffic characteristics of different application classes vary significantly, the approach of evaluating their bandwidth requirements is dependent on the applications class. Also, the nature of bandwidth guarantees are different for each class, which means that the required bandwidth allocation mechanism is also different. As discussed before, only real-time applications (streaming and block transfer) have stringent bandwidth requirements. The bandwidth requirements for non-real-time applications are by definition negligible compared with the bandwidth available on the network.

4.3.1 Bandwidth Parameters

The bandwidth requirements of an application are characterized by two main parameters: peak and average bandwidth.

4.3.1.1 Peak Bandwidth

Although the peak bandwidth concept is fairly straightforward to understand, defining the peak bandwidth parameter in a measurable way is nontrivial. For example, assume a transmission system uses fixed-size time slots, with each time slot carrying exactly one packet. At first glance, one can define the peak bandwidth of an application as the inverse of the inter-packet arrival time, because the packet is fixed size. There are certain ranges of peak bandwidth values which cannot be specified by this method, such as a bandwidth range between 50 percent and 100 percent of the link bandwidth. The reason is that inter-packet intervals can be 1 or 2 time slots, but cannot be anything between 1 and 2, such as 1.5.

The solution to defining measurable peak bandwidth is to define peak bandwidth not by using just two packets, but a sequence of packets over a period of time. This allows specification of arbitrary peak bandwidth values, as well as accounting for the duration. This can be achieved by introducing the concept of the *leaky bucket.*

Imagine a bucket that is constantly leaking at the rate of the peak bandwidth. Whenever a packet is sent on to the network, a packet-length amount of liquid is put into that bucket. The liquid, however, is leaking at the peak bandwidth. No new packets can be sent on the network until the bucket is empty again. Note that this leaky bucket model can be applied to peak bandwidth specifications of applications with variable size ADU/PDU. The leaky bucket model also can be used to traffic shape an application to a particular peak bandwidth.

Moreover, if an application's traffic generation pattern satisfies this leaky bucket model at a particular leaking rate, then this becomes peak bandwidth of the application. The value of this peak bandwidth can be used to communicate the peak bandwidth requirement of the application.

4.3.1.2   Average Bandwidth

Similar to the peak bandwidth concept, it is easier to understand the average bandwidth concept than to specify the average bandwidth parameter. The difficulty of specifying the average bandwidth parameter arises from the selection of the duration over which the average bandwidth should be calculated. For CBR traffic, selecting the duration to measure is simple because the average bandwidth value is independent of the duration used to calculate it (as long as it is more than a few packet intervals). Furthermore, for CBR traffic, the average bandwidth is equal to the peak bandwidth. For real-time streaming applications, the average bandwidth is relatively easy to measure because of the predictability (periodic traffic pattern) of the traffic pattern. Even if it is VBR, the average bandwidth can be calculated be sufficiently long duration, as they should not vary significantly beyond a certain time interval.

However, for both the real-time block transfer and non-real-time applications, calculating average bandwidth is much more difficult. These two classes of applications generate bursty traffic, for which the average bandwidth varies significantly depending on the duration used to calculate the average bandwidth. Bursty traffic means that the traffic generation instants, the number of ADUs generated and their size distribution are all indeterministic (and strongly user behavior dependent). Hence, for real-time block transfer applications, the applications do not know the average bandwidth requirements and they are typically left unspecified. A non-real-time application has negligible bandwidth requirements by definition. Nevertheless, a set of non-real-time applications can generate sufficient load on the network to result in congestion.

4.3.2   Real-time Streaming Applications

The bandwidth requirements for real-time streaming applications are very straightforward to evaluate since they are the direct result of the natural data generation rates of the time-based information. They are characterized by continuous traffic generated at either CBR or VBR.

To guarantee the QoS of these applications, the packet delay and jitters must be bounded below an application-dependent value. This implies that the bandwidth given to an application must match or exceed the natural data rate of the application. Furthermore, to guarantee such bandwidth is available to the application, the network must reserve bandwidth for it. Table 4-1 shows the bandwidth requirements for a number of key real-time streaming applications that deliver audio and video information. G.723.1 audio codec and H.263 video codec are particularly suitable for mass market Internet applications because they can be carried over 28.8 Kbps modem access to the Internet service providers. In fact, a PC implementing the ITU-T H.323 videoconferencing standard[19] can use these audio and video codecs for communications over the Internet. On the other hand, MPEG video delivery requires higher speed residential access networks, such as those based on xDSL or cable modems, or corporate LANs.

Table 4–1   *Bandwidth requirements of real-time streaming applications*

Real-time Streaming Applications	Bandwidth requirements (after compression)	
	Downstream	Upstream
Audio		
CD Quality Stereo: 10Hz–20KHz	256 Kbps[20]	
Broadcast quality (G.722): 50Hz–7KHz	64/56/48 Kbps[21]	
POTS (PCM, G.711): 0.2–3.4KHz	64 Kbps[22]	64 Kbps
Low bit rate POTS (G.723.1)	6.4 / 5.3 Kbps[12]	6.4 / 5.3 Kbps
Video		
HDTV	~ 20 Mbps[23]	
Video on demand MPEG 2	~ 4–6 Mbps[1]	
Video on demand MPEG 1	1–2 Mbps[3]	
ISDN p x 64 video conferencing (H.261)	64 Kbps–2 Mbps [24]	64 Kbps–2 Mbps
Low rate video conferencing (H.263)	Optimized for < 28.8 Kbps [25] (can be used for ISDN rates)	< 28.8 Kbps

4.3.3   Real-time Block Transfer Applications

The bandwidth requirement of a real-time block transfer application arises from meeting the application level QoS requirement in ADU delay. As mentioned before, this applies only to bandwidth-limited real-time block transfer applications. To satisfy the delay requirement (D_b) for an ADU, a minimum bandwidth $B_{min} = S/D_b$ can be calculated, assuming that the application can continuously send at the rate B_{min} to deliver the

ADU (size S in bits) at a CBR. Hence, the traffic requirements for this class of applications are determined by the ADU size and ADU delay requirements.

This is not the only way to satisfy the networking requirement; we can send this block at a VBR provided that the ADU can be delivered by the deadline or the average bandwidth is higher than or equal to B_{min}, with the peak bandwidth higher than B_{min}. In fact, all that is required is that the last packet of the ADU must arrive before D_b, independent of how long before the deadline the rest of the packets of the ADU arrive. However, any deviation from the CBR transmission results in a higher peak bandwidth requirement.

To provide bandwidth guarantees efficiently to real-time block transfer applications is one of the most challenging and unsolved problems[1] because the instant of the ADU generation, the frequency of ADU transmissions, and the ADU size are unpredictable. Theoretically, one can reserve bandwidth immediately before the transmission of an ADU to guarantee its bandwidth. However, this introduces significant overhead for reservation and releasing of bandwidth, especially for small block transfers or high frequency of block transfers. Alternatively, one can reserve the maximum bandwidth required to transfer the largest block possible for any individual application at the beginning of the application, and leave it on until the user explicitly leaves the application. Although this can provide a hard bandwidth guarantee, it is very inefficient because it ties up the bandwidth when the user is idle and oversubscribes bandwidth for block transfers smaller than the largest block (the same effect of circuit switching).

For a Web browsing application, the ADU size corresponds to that of each Web object requested, which can be text, image, audio, video, and software application files, with size ranging from less than 1 Kbytes for text to more than 10 Mbytes for large software application files. The ADU delay is the interactive response time requirement. Table 4-2 shows a number of real-time block transfer applications and their suggested block delay requirements and representative ADU lengths. Again, the 100 ms[1] requirement is the typical human response time below which delay is not noticeable. For network twitch games, there are more stringent requirements. Since this bandwidth calculation has not taken into account network propagation and buffering delay, the actual bandwidth requirements are higher.

Table 4–2 *Examples of bandwidth requirements of real-time block transfer applications*

Applications	ADU Delay (D_b)	ADU	ADU size (S)	B_{min}
Web browsing	100 ms	typical Web object	3 Kbytes	240 Kbps
	100 ms	large Web object	20 Kbytes	1.6 Mbps
File Transfer	1 min	large software application	10 Mbytes	1.3 Mbps
Network games	50 ms	commands	500 bytes	80 Kbps
Chat	1 sec	words	100 bytes	0.8 Kbps

For applications that generate more than one block of data, such as a Web browsing application, the number of blocks and the interval between block generation are also important parameters. Unfortunately, neither of these parameters can be accurately specified because they both vary widely depending on the particular Web page being viewed and the behavior of the user.

4.3.4 Time-based Information Delivery Requirements

Time-based information can be delivered in real time in two ways: real-time streaming and real-time block transfer. The bandwidth requirement for real-time streaming is the natural encoded rate of the time-based information. For real-time block transfer of the time-based information, the time-based information is treated as a data block—that is, it treats the information as it would for non-time-based information. Both apply to current Web browsing scenarios, for which a video or audio clip can have options of either immediate playback (real-time streaming) or download for delayed local playback (real-time block transfer).

Real-time block transfer of time-based information can occur at a rate higher or lower than the natural data generation rate of the time-based information (real-time streaming), depending on the delay constraints or network capacity limitations. This results in shorter or longer delivery time than the natural playing time of the time-based information, respectively. For example, one can send a two-hour, 4 Mbps-encoded movie at 80 Mbps. This requires 6 minutes to complete delivery, instead of 2 hours for real-time streaming. However, the receiver must have 3.6 GB of storage to receive the movie. Faster-than-real-time delivery can be used for replicating movies from a content provider's server through a nation wide high-speed ATM/backbone network (OC-3 or OC-12) to video servers at central offices or cable headends across the country. These movies can then be streamed (real-time playback) to subscribers. Alternatively, if a network has limited capacity and the bandwidth available is less than the natural data rate of the time-based content, the delivery time will be longer than the natural playing time of the information.

4.3.5 User Level Behavior

So far we have examined the microscopic traffic behavior and their requirements for an individual application, given a user initiate such an application. Nevertheless, the traffic requirements also depend on the user behavior. Hence, we need to understand how often the user initiates an application and the user behavior once the application has started.

Currently, Internet access has been very slow because of both the limited access bandwidth (using 28.8 Kbps modem) and Internet backbone capacity. Moreover, the dial-up access through the PSTN and the limited capacity of modem banks at the ISP (Internet service provider) have resulted in high blocking probability. Hence, once people pass the novelty stage, such low-speed and high blocking probability lead to an unsatisfactory experience with the World Wide Web. This has discouraged the frequency and duration of Internet access. In other words, limitations in bandwidth can alter the user behavior significantly. To avoid the wait, user tends to avoid downloading large files, unless the perceived utility of the file exceeds the pain for waiting for the download.

As we add bandwidth to the Internet backbone and deploy packet-switched-based residential broadband networks, the sudden increase in bandwidth and the "always-connected" (nonblocking access) will encourage the user to access the Internet and use many multimedia intensive applications. Hence, the usage pattern is not static; it changes with user experience. This implies that it is very difficult to accurately extrapolate from current traffic and usage behavior with low-speed access. Hence, although it is very tempting to extrapolate the current networking load to project the traffic load as we add more bandwidth to the network to support additional users, this feedback loop between the user behavior and the bandwidth available makes such a projection unrealistic and too optimistic.

4.4 Summary

Integrated service network design requires understanding of the networking requirements of all applications requirements. Networking requirements of an application include both traffic and QoS requirements. In this chapter, we discussed in detail the traffic requirements of all three classes of applications, based on the application classification framework from the last chapter: real-time streaming, real-time block transfer and non-real-time applications. We focused on special requirements for Internet applications such as Web browsing. In the next chapter, we will discuss the QoS requirements of all these three classes of applications in detail.

4.5 References

[1] T. Kwok, "A Vision for Residential Broadband Services: ATM-to-the-Home," *IEEE Network,* Sept./Oct, 1995, pp. 14-28.

[2] A. Tennanbaum, *Computer Networks*, Third Edition, Prentice Hall, 1996.

[3] D. Le Gall, "MPEG: A Video Compression Standard for Multimedia Applications," *Communications of the ACM*, vol. 34, no. 4, April 1991, pp. 46-58.

[4] W. R. Stevens, *TCP/IP Illustrated*, Volume 3, Addison-Wesley, 1996.

[5] H-W Braun, K.C. Claffy, "Web Traffic Characterization: An Assessment of the Impact of Caching Documents from NCSA's Web Server," *Proceedings of the Second World Wide Web Conference '94: Mosaic and the Web*, pp. 1007-1027, Chicago, Ill., October 1994.

[6] J. Mogul, "The Case for Persistent-Connection HTTP," *Computer Communication Review*, vol. 25, no.4, October 1995, pp.299-313.

[7] Cunha, C.R., Bestavros, A., and Crovella, M.E., "Characteristics of WWW Client-based Traces," BU-CS-95-010, Computer Science Department, Boston University, July 1995.

[8] J. Mogul, S. Steering, "Path MTU Discovery," *IETF Request for Comments 1191*, April, 1990.

[9] R. Braden, Editor, "Requirements for Internet Hosts — Communication Layers," *IETF Request for Comments 1122*, October 1989.

[10]http://www.merit.net.

[11]S. Deng, D. Veeneman, "Asymmetry Ratio for Internet Access: Revisited," ADSL Forum Contribution 96-044, June 18, 1996.

[12]ITU-T, Recommendation G.723.1, "Dual rate speech coder for multimedia communications transmitting at 5.3 and 6.3 kbit/s," 1996.

[13]N. Kitawaki, K. Itoh, "Pure Delay Effects on Speech Quality Telecommunications," *IEEE Journal on Selected Areas in Communications*, Vol.9, No. 4, May 1991, pp. 586-593.

[14]C. J. Weinstein, J. Forgie, "Experience with Speech Communication in Packet Networks," *IEEE Journal of Selected Areas on Communications*, Vol. SAC-1, No. 6, pp. 963-980, Dec. 1983.

[15]W. Leland, M. Taqqu. W. Willinger, D. Wilson, "On the Self-similar Nature of Ethernet Traffic (extended version)," *IEEE/ACM Transactions on Networking*, 2: 1-15, 1994.

[16]V. Paxson, S. Floyd, "Wide-area traffic: The failure of Poisson modeling," Proceedings of SIGCOMM'94, 1994.

[17]M. Crovella, A. Bestavros, "Explaining World Wide Web Traffic Self-Similarity," Technical Report TR-95-015, Computer Science Department, Boston University, October 12, 1995.

[18]W. R. Stevens, *TCP/IP Illustrated*, Volume 1, Addison-Wesley, 1994.

[19]ITU-T, Recommendation H.323, "Visual Telephone Systems and Terminal Equipment for Local Area Networks which Provide a Non-Guaranteed Quality of Service," 1996.

[20]H. Musmann, "The ISO Audio Coding Standard," *IEEE Globecom 1990*, pp. 511-517.

[21]ITU-T, Recommendation G.722, "7 kHz audio-coding within 64 kbit/s," 1988.

[22]ITU-T, Recommendation G.711, "Pulse code modulation (PCM) of voice frequencies," 1988.

[23]E. Petajan, "The HDTV Grand Alliance System," *IEEE Communications Magazine*, June 1996, pp. 126-132.

[24]ITU-T, Recommendation H.261, "Video codec for audiovisual services at p x 64 kbit/s," 1993.

[25]ITU-T, Recommendation H.263, "Video coding for low bit rate communication," 1996.

Chapter **5**

Application QoS Requirements

5.1 Introduction

The networking requirements of an application are specified in terms of its traffic and quality of service (QoS) requirements. In the last chapter, we discussed in detail the traffic requirements for each application class. Traffic requirements specify how data are sent over the network and the resources needed to support the traffic behavior of the application. Each packet sent by the application over the network will incur various delay and potential error (corruption or loss) probabilities, which must be constrained to different degrees depending on the application requirements. These delay and error requirements are called QoS requirements. The QoS offered by the network affects the performance received by the data being sent over the network. In this chapter, we discuss in detail the QoS requirements of all the application classes.

Similar to the traffic requirements for an application, we can discuss the QoS requirements at both the application and network layers. QoS requirements at these two layers are specified in terms of the delay and error incurred by ADUs and PDUs, respectively.

By definition, delay requirements only apply to real-time applications (streaming and block transfer). Delay requirements are specified in terms of absolute delay (latency) and delay variation. Although QoS requirements are typically associated with real-time applications, strictly speaking, all applications have QoS requirements, because even non-real-time applications have loss requirements. The factors affecting the QoS requirements of different application classes at the application and network layers are summarized in Table 5-1. They are explained in more detail next.

Table 5–1   *The QoS requirements of different classes of applications and their driving factors*

Application Class/ Layer	Absolute Delay (Latency)	Delay Variation	Error Tolerance
Real-time Streaming			
Application layer (ADU)	User response time	Application layer receive buffer size	Can be nonzero
Network layer (PDU)	User response time	Network layer receive buffer size	Can be nonzero
Real-time Block Transfer			
Application layer (ADU)	User response time	Not applicable	Usually zero
Network layer (PDU)	User response time	Not applicable	Nonzero
Non-real-time			
Application layer (ADU)	Not applicable	Not applicable	Usually zero
Network layer (PDU)	Not applicable	Not applicable	Nonzero

5.2 Delay Requirements

5.2.1 Delay Distribution

The delay incurred by an ADU/PDU can be described by its delay distribution function. Figure 5-1 shows a generic delay distribution function that can be experienced in a packet switched network (delay is fixed in the circuit switched network for a given path). The distribution function specifies the probability of an ADU/PDU to incur a certain delay. For example, the delay incurred by IP packets across the Internet can exceed 100ms and is highly variable. There is a nonzero minimum fixed delay (due to propagation delay, for example, as discussed below). The delay can vary upwards, depending on the amount of additional variable delay components up to the maximum delay. The true maximum delay may not be well defined, especially if the PDU is lost in the network, which can be considered at infinite delay. Nevertheless, we can define maximum delay statistically as the value for which all except a very small fraction (say 10^{-6}) of the packets incur a higher delay.

The delay incurred by each ADU/PDU for an application can be anywhere between the minimum and maximum delay for the given distribution. The maximum delay variation that can be incurred is the difference between the maximum and minimum delay. However, real-time applications have constraints in the maximum end-to-end ADU/PDU delay (absolute delay) and the amount of variations of delay between ADUs/PDUs (delay variation). These delay requirements will be discussed in detail after we understand the delay components that contribute to the delay distribution.

5.2.2 Delay Components

We now discuss the various delay components when generating and delivering PDUs across the network. The total end-to-end delay incurred by a PDU is the sum of the following delay components: packetization delay, transmission delay, propagation delay, queuing delay and processing delay. Table 5-2 shows the values of different delay components for different networks and indicates whether they are fixed or variable. These delay components are discussed in detail below.

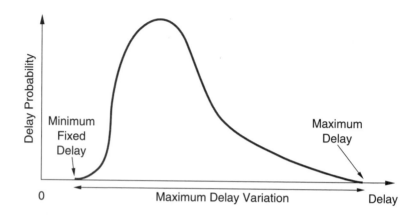

Figure 5–1   A generic delay distribution function of an ADU or PDU

Packetization delay   The packetization delay is only incurred for delivering live encoded source for real-time streaming applications. This delay is a result of waiting for enough data samples to fill up the payload of the PDU before beginning the transmission of the PDU on the network. In other words, this delay occurs at the source end stations.

The packetization delay is equal to the packet payload size divided by the application encoding rate. Hence, the packetization delay is large for low bit rate encoders. For example, a low bit rate voice encoder for Internet telephony at 4.8 Kbps can incur an 80-ms packetization delay using a 48-byte payload IP packet. As discussed later, such a large delay can have significant impact for telephony applications, especially when communicating with someone on a residential POTS line.

For a given CBR encoded stream, the packetization delay is fixed for a fixed PDU payload size. For a VBR source, the packetization delay is variable, unless the payload size chosen varies accordingly to maintain a constant packetization delay.

Transmission delay   The transmission delay of a PDU is the time it takes to complete the transmission of a PDU on the local link, or the interval between the first and last bit of the PDU leaving the source onto the network. Hence, the transmission delay is dependent on both the PDU size and the transmission rate of the local link. Specifically, the

Table 5–2   *Components of end-to-end delay (absolute delay) and examples*

Delay Components		Delay and its variability
Packetization Delay		Fixed for fixed size PDU & encoding rate; Varies depending on encoding rate and PDU size used
IP telephony using 4.8 Kbps codec		80 milliseconds with 48 byte payload
Transmission Delay of 500-byte PDU at		Fixed for given PDU size on a particular link
28.8 Kbps	Modem	140 milliseconds
128 Kbps	ISDN	31 milliseconds
10 Mbps	Ethernet	0.4 milliseconds
155 Mbps	OC-3c	26 microseconds
Propagation Delay		Fixed for a given path, but varies depending on path taken by the PDUs (e.g., Internet)
200 m	workgroup LAN	1 microsecond
10 km	MAN	50 microseconds
4000 km	WAN	20 milliseconds
72,000km	Satellite	260 milliseconds
Queuing Delay (per packet)		Varies depending on network load
1.5Kbytes at 10 Mbps	Ethernet	1.2 milliseconds per packet
200 bytes at T1	Internet with 10 hops	106 milliseconds for average 10 packet queue lengths
Processing Delay		Varies depending on processing load
Typical PBX		~ 2 milliseconds[1]
Typical ATM switch		~ 10 microseconds
MPEG decoding		~ 66–100 milliseconds

transmission delay is equal to the PDU length divided by the data rate of the local link. For a low-speed link, the transmission delay can be a significant delay component. For example, it takes more than a quarter of a second to send a 1-Kbyte PDU for an analog modem speed at 28.8 Kbps (see Table 5-2). This can become a real problem for dialup access to the Internet to transfer real-time applications, such as IP telephony, if the PDU size of other applications is not limited.

There can be multiple transmission delays incurred by a PDU as it is delivered across the network, if it is being stored and forwarded at each switch within the network (such as routers on the Internet). Each time the PDU is buffered and retransmitted on the next hop, another transmission delay is incurred. Again, each transmission delay is dependent on the link speed of each hop it is retransmitted on. At the minimum, there is one transmission delay incurred at the sender, even if it is not stored and forwarded at any intermediate stage.

Propagation Delay   The propagation delay is the delay due to the propagation time on the transmission medium over distance. This is limited by the speed at which the signal can traverse the medium. For fiber optics links, it is limited by the speed of light over the glass medium. The propagation delay over a link can be defined as the time it takes for the first bit (or any particular bit) of a PDU to traverse a link. The end-to-end propagation delay is the sum of the propagation delay on each link.

Obviously, the propagation time increases linearly with distance. For LAN or MAN (metropolitan area networks) communications, the propagation delay is typically not a major delay component. As shown in Table 5-2, it is only about 1 microsecond for a workgroup LAN distance of 200 m (100 m to the wiring closet for 10 Base-T Ethernet). Even for a MAN of about 10 Km wide, the propagation delay is still only about 50 microseconds.

The propagation delay becomes important for WAN communications. Survey data for North American terrestrial connections indicated one-way absolute delays of up to 30 ms for the backbone (circuit switched) telephone network.[2] For the Internet communications within the continental United States, the propagation delay component alone can exceed 30 ms, because the IP packets might traverse a convoluted path (instead of the shortest physical path). The propagation delay becomes worse for satellite communications. The one-way propagation delay between two endpoints through a geosynchronous satellite is about 260 milliseconds.

Queuing delay The queuing delay is a key delay component for packet switched networks. The queuing delay is the aggregate buffering delay incurred at every packet switch along the path of the packet (PDU). (Again, the queuing delay only applies to packet switched networks and not circuit switched networks.) If the packet switch is temporarily overloaded, there can be many other packets queued up at the same output port to which the PDU is destined. For each packet queued ahead of the packet being delivered, there is an additional queuing delay that is equal to the transmission delay of the queued packet on the output link. For a switch with a first-in-first-out queuing mechanism, the queuing delay incurred by a newly arrived packet is the sum of all the transmission time (delay) of all the packets currently queued up at that output port. Hence, queuing delay depends not only on the number packets currently buffered ahead (which is a function of the current network load), but also the transmission speed of the outgoing link for which the PDU is destined.

Since the queuing delay is the main delay component that depends on the instantaneous load on the network, it contributes to the majority of the delay variations incurred in the packet switched network. For example, most of the delay across the Internet can be attributed to the queuing delay, because of the congestion across the Internet backbone with large number of IP packets queued up at the routers. This can be understood by considering a path with T1 links only (in reality it ranges from below 28.8 kbps to 155 Mbps or higher) and 10 router hops (not uncommon on the Internet today). Let there be an average of 10 packets queue length on each router, with an average packet size of 200 bytes (typical for Internet backbone traffic). The total queuing delay on this path is 107 ms. This illustrates why we can typically observe over 100 ms total delay across the Internet, which also includes propagation delay (which can be more than 30 ms) and processing delay.

Processing delay This is the sum of all the processing time needed at each switch along the path and at the endpoints (source and destination), excluding the queuing delay above. For packet switching, this is typically the smallest delay component and is negligible compared to the queuing delay. However, the processing delay at the endpoints can become significant compared to the rest of the delay components. This is especially true for data that requires significant processing before displaying to the end users, such as video decoding (decompression). For example, an MPEG decoder might need to pre-buffer a number of compressed video frames before beginning the decoding process. The reason is that some of the compressed MPEG frames (B frames) must be decoded together with frames that arrive afterwards. Since on average a frame is separated by approximately 33 ms for a 30 frames/sec stream, close to 100 ms can easily be introduced by the decoder alone.

Now that we understand what causes the network delay to applications, we can next examine the delay requirements of the two classes of real-time applications.

5.2.3 Absolute Delay Requirements

At the application layer, the absolute delay requirement arises from the human response time requirements for different real-time applications (see Table 5-1). It is measured from the time an ADU is generated by the application to the instant at which the entire ADU is presented to the remote user.

The absolute delay requirement of an ADU translates into the absolute delay requirement of the PDU at the network layer. Since the ADU absolute delay refers to the delay on the delivery of the entire data block (ADU), this is equivalent to the absolute delay incurred by the last PDU (generated by that ADU) arriving at the receiver. If the PDUs are delivered out of order, such as over the Internet, the last PDU of the ADU arriving at the receiver may not be the last PDU of the ADU originally sent by the source.

More specifically, the absolute delay of a PDU is the end-to-end delay incurred PDU from the instant the first bit of the PDU is sent onto the network to the instant the last bit of the packet arrives at the destination. This relationship of the absolute delay between the ADU and corresponding PDUs is shown in the space-time diagram in Figure 5-2. The space-time diagram describes the behavior of three PDUs (all belong to a single ADU) over time as they are delivered across the network between the source and destination. Since the space-time diagram describes the delay incurred within the network (excluding the endpoints), it includes the propagation delay, transmission delay, queuing delay and network processing delay but not packetization delay (if relevant to the application) and processing delay at the endpoints.

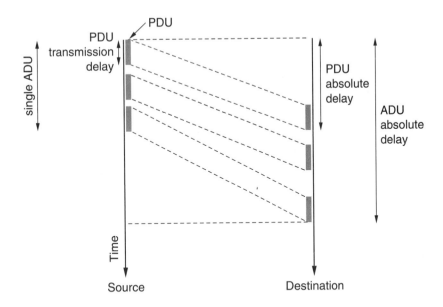

Figure 5–2 Space-time diagram: Relationship between the absolute delay of an ADU and its PDUs

5.2.3.1 Real-time Streaming Applications

The latency requirements for real-time streaming applications typically originate from human requirements at the application layer. People have well-understood response times for one-way and two-way real-time streaming applications. For example, for video-on-demand application, there is an expected latency constraint (say one second) from the time a user issues the play command to the instant that the movie actually begins. Telephony is one of the most important real-time streaming applications and has begun to play an important role on the Internet. We examine telephony's the absolute delay requirements below.

Telephony The absolute delay requirements for supporting telephony have two components: pure delay constraint in conversation and echo constraint in the PSTN to achieve acceptable quality.

    Pure Delay Constraints: Although the exact value of the maximum tolerable two-way (round trip) absolute delay is subject to debate, it is generally accepted to be in the range of 100 to 600ms.[3] While people today adjust to the 520 ms round trip delay for satellite transmission (through the satellite twice), this does not mean that such delay is acceptable for future network design. Of course, people can change their behavior to adapt to delay, for example, by limiting interruptions. It has been observed that a speaker is interrupted more than three times as frequently in a conversation over a satellite link as opposed to a terrestrial link. In general, the total round-trip time should not exceed about 500 ms[4] (one-way is 250 ms average) to achieve acceptable quality for a telephone conversation.

Echo Constraints: The most significant absolute delay constraint in existing PSTN arises from the echo problem in the local loop infrastructure, rather than from the pure delay considerations for human conversations above. Existing local loops (primarily analog) have a 4-wire to 2-wire conversion point called a *hybrid* (between the central office and each subscriber) that unfortunately also acts as a reflection point for electrical signals; it introduces significant echo along the return path to the far end. Echo with long delays (for example, greater than 35 ms) can annoy the speaker, and this annoyance generally increases with increasing echo delay and echo level. (Note that echo returning with negligible delay at levels comparable to those normally received by the listener are called *side-tone* and are essential to prevent the circuit from sounding dead.[5]) Hence, ITU has specified that the maximum one-way delay in the echo path must be less than 25 ms to avoid using any echo control device.[6]

In North America, echo control mechanisms are used for source-destination, one-way delay exceeding 17.5 ms[5] in telephone networks. Delays up to 35 ms can be accommodated by a full echo suppressor, which is needed for one end only. Delays up to 50 ms are handled by a split echo suppressor at both ends. Larger delays require echo cancellation. The average echo control limit for one-way, end-to-end delay is about 400 ms.[5] With more advanced echo control, above 600ms is acceptable.

Echoes are caused by analog signals that reflect off the imperfections in copper loop. Even if only one party to the telephone conversation is on such an analog loop, the echo problem still exists. Echo would not be a problem in a network consisting only of digital links connecting both end users. Hence, echo is not a problem for end-to-end ISDN and the emerging Internet telephony between two PC users. However, since the majority of telephone subscribers are going to be served by analog POTS line for quite some time, the problems of echoes must still be considered in general. For example, if one end is using Internet telephony through a PC, while the other end is using analog POTS (through an Internet to PSTN bridge), echo is still a problem to the PC user end. This requires an echo control mechanism be implemented, such as at the PC.

5.2.3.2   Real-time Block Transfer Applications

As discussed in the last chapter, real-time block transfer applications generate one or more ADUs, each with a specific deadline or ADU latency requirement. ADU latency requirements for real-time block transfer applications also typically originate from human response-time requirements. The response time should be about 1 sec or less for satisfactory human interactions with computers,[8] while below about 100 ms is perceived as "instantaneous." This means all the PDUs corresponding to a given ADU must all arrive within these constraints.

However, this does not imply the PDUs' absolute delay requirement is 100ms. The reason is that the last PDU might be sent at the 99th ms. This can be the case bandwidth limited real-time block transfer applications, and the last PDU must wait for the transmission of the previous PDUs (see Figure 5-2). This implies that the last PDU cannot incur an absolute delay of more than 1 ms.

However, as discussed before, the latency on the Internet can be much longer than 100 ms, because it is still a best-effort service-based packet switched network (high queuing delay). In fact, most of the delay components contributing to the Internet latency can be quite high. For communications across wide area, high propagation delay will be incurred that can be more than 30 ms. Also, the limited capacity both at the Internet backbone and at the access link speeds (which are still primarily 28.8 Kbps or less) lead to high transmission delay.

In general, it is impossible to satisfy the 100 ms delay requirements all the time because of transmission delay alone, due to the large variations of ADU size (such as Web object size), unless we have infinite bandwidth to play with. If a user is running preemptive multitasking operation systems, the user can switch to other tasks. Otherwise, the user might drop the particular request and surf to another site, or quit the Web browsing application entirely because of the generally slow response. In this case, it means the network fails to support such an application because the customer does not use the application.

On the other hand, the 100 ms and 1 second requirements might be relaxed in reality. In general, the response time requirements depend on many factors. For each application, the response time can vary according to the content, the user, and previous experience. For example, many users are accustomed to long delay on the Internet access via 28.8 Kbps modem. Also, the human factor requirement is alleviated by improved user interface design; for example, indicating the percentage of data delivered (left to deliver) during the transfer.

5.2.4 Delay Variation (Jitters) Requirements

The delay variation requirement only applies to real-time streaming applications. This QoS requirement arises from the continuous traffic characteristics of this class of application and the requirement of the receiver to receive at the traffic generation rate. An ADU is generated at regular instants in a continuous fashion. For example, video frames can be generated at 15 or 30 frames/s, while a PCM voice sample is generated every 125 microseconds.

Each ADU must arrive within a bounded interval to avoid being too late or too early. There is a receiver buffer to dejitter the delay variations of the ADU/PDU arrivals. Late ADU arrivals make the ADU useless, resulting in receiver buffer underflow. Early arrivals can lead to receiver buffer overflow, because the receiver has not played out earlier ADUs that are still in the buffer. Hence, high delay variations introduced to real-time streaming applications can lead to high loss to the applications.

Another constraint of delay variation arises from multimedia content delivery and the need to synchronize between different media streams. For example, video conferencing might require a video stream and audio stream to be within a certain time intervals of each other, Karlsson and Vetterli suggest that video should lag voice by at most -90 ms to 120 ms.[9] In addition, the receiver might use the packet arrival process as a way to synchronize the receiver time clock, putting more stringent delay variation requirements on the packet arrivals. For example, some MPEG decoders require a packet delay variation of about 1 ms for this reason.

To adapt to the delay variation from the network, real-time applications typically rely on a large dejitter buffer and prebuffer a certain amount of data before beginning the play back. Obviously, the higher the delay variation, the larger the buffer and the more expensive the receiver design due to additional memory requirements. Ideally, if we know the peak-to-peak delay variation (maximum minus minimum delay in Figure 5-1) that is possible over the network, we can design the buffer to be twice the size of the peak-to-peak delay variation times the data rate of the application. We can then prebuffer half the buffer size worth of data before playing back. This would avoid dejitter buffer overflow or underflow problems.

However, there are three potential problems with this approach. First, the buffer requirements may be too expensive to implement. Second, there might not be a known maximum delay variation on the network, which makes sizing the buffer difficult. Third, the prebuffer delay introduced may not be acceptable to certain applications. These problems imply that we need to understand a more realistic model of delay variation exceeding the receiver buffer constraints to avoid under- or overflow. This can be shown in Figure 5-3. This shows that the maximum delay can exceed the delay variation constrained by the application (such as buffer limitations). Hence, data that arrived beyond that limit is considered lost. The corresponding PDU loss probability can be calculated from the delay distribution by using the area beyond the maximum delay tolerable to the application.

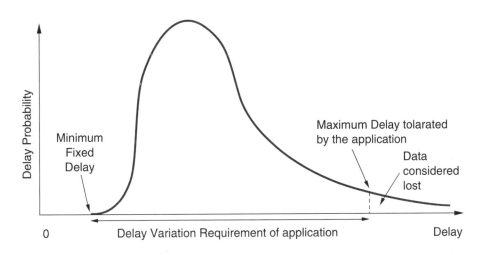

Figure 5–3   A model for handling delay variation for real-time streaming applications

5.2.4.1   Telephony

We have discussed that the ADU for telephony is a voice sample of 1 byte. With packetized voice using a speech activity detector (SAD), there can be another quanta known as the talk spurt. A talk spurt is the duration at which the SAD considers that there is voice activity. This talk spurt is established by the SAD by using a hangover for differentiating the presence of voice activity. Hangover is the period of time used by the SAD to determine the end of a talk spurt. If the total speech activity during the hangover period is below a certain threshold value, the talk spurt is considered to be ending. The longer the hangover period, the longer the average talk spurt will result from a SAD because consecutive talk spurts that are close in time will be treated as a single talk spurt. Hence, the sequence of talk spurts generated by a packetized voice system may resemble bursty traffic generation.

The average talk spurt is equal to 4.1 second according to experiments done by Bell Labs[10] for a set of conversations. This implies that each talk spurt is typically encoded into multiple speech packets. Otherwise, a single packet would introduce a packetization delay equal to the talk spurt duration, which is unacceptable for voice conversation. Furthermore, for 64 Kbps voice, the corresponding average packet size would need to hold 32,800 bytes voice samples for PCM (Pulse Code Modulation)! Hence, the talk spurt should not be confused with the ADU of telephony, which is a voice sample.

In addition to the delay variation requirement on a per packet basis which is limited by the dejitter buffer size at the receiver, there is another delay variation requirement. Since the delay variation of a PDU is absorbed into a single delay per talk spurt through the speech re-assembly and speech reconstitution processes, the delay variation of a talk spurt is important.[11] The delay variation effects of a talk spurt depend on the *hangover* parameter of the SAD. For a hangover interval of 200 ms, the delay variation requirements on talk spurts were shown to be between 200 and 300 ms.

5.3 Error Requirements

Since the purpose of a communications application is to deliver user information, any data loss or corruption is going to affect the application. Any data lost means that such data delivery will not be achieved completely. Hence, all classes of applications must have a set of error requirements, albeit to different degrees.

In general, real-time streaming applications might tolerate a limited amount of data loss, depending on the error resiliency of the decoder and the type of applications. On the other hand, the real-time block transfer and non-real-time applications typically do not tolerate any data error (at the application layer). This means that any data lost at the network layer must be recovered, such as by the transport layer (e.g., TCP).

In this section, we discuss the error requirements in detail. We first understand the different factors that might affect the error tolerance of an application. Then we discuss how error can be characterized at different levels. Finally, we explore the error requirements of all three classes of applications.

5.3.1 Error Tolerances

There are a number of factors that affect error requirements of different applications; they are discussed as follows.

5.3.1.1 Information Types

Data communication applications such as electronic mail, file transfer and transactions applications present the most stringent requirement—they must be error free. However, the physical media of a communication network is error prone and there are packet losses in packet switched networks. Packet losses occur in packet switched networks primarily because of buffer overflow in packet switches, or misrouting to a wrong destination (due to a corrupted header).

The transport layer can be used to achieve error-free communication for data, by providing error detection with retransmission. Data communication is typically achieved by packetizing data before transmission and encapsulating blocks of data with a framing structure that contains a error detection sequence and a sequence number. When the error detection mechanism determines that a received packet is corrupted, the transport layer manages the retransmission. Similarly, if the sequence numbers of received packets indicates that a packet is lost, the transport layer of the receiver requests retransmission of the lost packet, or the sender automatically retransmits when there is no acknowledgment within a particular time-out period.

However, the error recovery by retransmissions is not suitable for real-time applications (especially streaming) because of the latency involved. Fortunately, time-based information for human consumption are usually more tolerant of error because human perception is not perfect. This type of information includes video, voice, and image information.

5.3.1.2　Usage

Even for the same information type, the error requirements can vary significantly. Although image communications can tolerate a certain amount of error, there are diverse error requirements for different image communications applications. Facsimile communications is an image application that can tolerate a significant amount of error for document transfers. On the other hand, X-ray transfer cannot tolerate any error and should be treated as data communication because of the serious consequence of misrepresentation.

5.3.1.3　Components

Digitized versions of time-based information have different error requirements for different components of their information streams. For example, the framing control information within a video stream is more important than the information of a video frame. The reason is that the loss of the former may result in loss of multiple frames of video information (because such control information may not occurs frequently), or even termination of the video communications in the worst case.

Also, for the video telephony application, the audio component is usually more important and is less tolerant of loss than the video component. The reason is that people can communicate by falling back on voice conversation, but the video component alone might not be satisfactory in many situations.

5.3.1.4　Compression Ratio

For compressed video streams, different compressed frames may have different error requirements because certain frames are required for decoding other frames, making the former more important than those that are not required for decoding other frames. In addition, the higher the compression ratio, the lower the tolerance in error. The reason is that more information is being carried per compressed bit of information for highly compressed information (as most of the redundancy has been removed by compression).

5.3.2   Error Characterization

The error requirements can be specified at the application, network and physical layers, in terms of ADU, PDU or bit error rates, respectively.

5.3.2.1   Application Layer: ADU Loss Ratio

Ultimately, what is important is the error perceived by the application. Hence, even if the network is prone to loss, if there is a protocol layer such as transport that can handle packet losses or packet corruption, such an error can be transparent to the application. From the application's point of view, the error requirement on the ADU is most important.

5.3.2.2   Network Layer: PDU Loss Ratio

The packet level error requirements are measured in a number of ways. First, the packet loss ratio measures the probability that a packet is lost in the network. Packet loss is typically a result of a packet dropping within the network due to buffer overflow in switches, or a corrupted packet header. Packet loss also can be a result of misrouting due to packet header corruption, which can be measured as a separate parameter, known as the *packet misrouting ratio*. Finally, packet error can be caused by bit errors within the packet, especially the payload. If the network level detects such an error, it may drop the packet; this is equivalent to packet loss within the network. However, if a higher-layer protocol, such as the application layer, can tolerate bit errors, such a corrupted packet still can be passed to the higher layer. In general, if the network layer can locate the bit error within the packet, it will be much easier for the higher-layer protocol to handle bit errors. For example, if a video decoder knows where a detected bit error is located, the decoder can avoid or conceal the particular segment containing the bit error.

5.3.2.3   Physical Layer: Bit Error Ratio

At the physical layer, the error requirement is specified by the bit error ratio (BER). This is determined by the nature of the physical medium. The BER can be improved in an error-prone environment such as wireless and coaxial cables, by using forward error correction (FEC) techniques. FEC is best implemented at the physical layer so that it is transparent to the higher layer protocols.

The BER affects higher layer error requirements. For example, a bit error within a packet can mean that the packet is useless and is equivalent to a packet loss because the network layer may drop a packet that has a bit error detected. Similarly, a bit error in an ADU may mean the loss of the entire ADU.

Since the BER is an average value calculated over a long period of time, there is no guarantee that the bit error distribution is totally random. The BER cannot distinguish between bit errors that occur in bursts versus those that are random. Hence, a more detailed bit level error characterization is needed. Since it is difficult to characterize the full bit error distribution function, we can specify certain parameters that help understand the burst error requirements. For example, we can specify a interval such that the BER within that interval would not exceed a certain BER value with a particular probability. This BER can be higher than the average BER value in order to limit burst errors within the interval. Also, we can specify the BER to be zero for a particular interval to guarantee a percentage of error free intervals. These additional error parameters are discussed in more detail later in the discussion of telephony error requirements.

5.3.3 Error Requirements for Different Application Classes

We discuss the error requirements for each application class next.

5.3.3.1   Real-time Streaming Applications

As discussed above, real-time streaming applications are typically tolerant to some error, because they are typically for human consumption. Due to the limitations of humans to perceive certain error conditions, the applications can be designed to take advantage of this to allow for limited errors introduced by the network. We examine two real-time streaming applications below: telephony and video delivery.

Telephony

Network Layer: The packet loss ratio that can be tolerated for packetized voice depends not only on the encoding algorithm, but also on the packet length used, which affects the amount of voice samples carried. For PCM coded voice at 64 Kbps, Wasem et al[12] uses 128 bytes packet size (carrying 16 ms of voice) and shows that 2 percent packet loss ratio can be tolerated before degradation becomes noticeable. This is equivalent to packet loss caused by a BER of 2×10^{-5}, which is very close to the NTT's study[13] that shows an average BER of 3×10^{-5} will be perceptible on PCM (see Table 5-3). By using a simple packet repetition method, Wasen et al show that the acceptable ratio of missing packets to be 5 percent (equivalent to the effect of an average BER of 5×10^{-5}). The most effective estimation technique (although not the most complex) is pitch waveform replication, which extends the acceptable ratio of missing packets to 10 percent (similar to average BER of 10^{-4}).

Table 5–3 *Average BER requirements from an NTT study in the PSTN[13]*

Service Type	Acceptable Long Term Average BER Value	Average Error Free Interval	Note
Voice			
Log-PCM (64Kbps)	3×10^{-5}	5 sec	Perceptible threshold
ADPCM (32Kbps)	10^{-4}	0.3 sec	Perceptible, but not annoying
Data			
(bearer rate, 64Kbps, 16Kbps)	3×10^{-6}	5.2–21 sec	95 percent efficiency
(bearer rate, 384Kbps-6.1Mbps)	10^{-7}	1.6–26 sec	95 percent efficiency
Facsimile (Group IV)	3×10^{-6}	5.2 sec	95 percent efficiency
Video			
(4MHz) DPCM (32Mbps)	10^{-7}	0.3 sec	Perceptible, but not annoying
Inter-frame coding (1.5Mbps)	10^{-9}–10^{-10}	11 min–18 hrs	Perceptible, but not annoying

Separately, Jayant and Christensen[14] show that the tolerable average (random) packet loss rate (which is strictly input-speech-dependent) with packet lengths of 16 ms and 32 ms can be as high as 2 to 5 percent. With interpolation, the tolerable packet loss rate can be increased to 5 to 10 percent. These observations are based on computer simulation with three sentence-length speech inputs, and on informal listening tests.

For 32 Kbps ADPCM using a packet length of 32 bytes (8 ms of speech), Suzuki and Taka[15] show that packet loss rate should not be much greater than 0.1 percent to insure reasonable quality. This is equivalent to packet loss generated by average BER of 4×10^{-6}. Voice quality is significantly degraded with a loss rate of 0.5 percent (BER of 2×10^{-5}). The low packet loss tolerance should not be surprising given a higher compression ratio encoding algorithm.

If different packets within the same voice packet stream can be assigned different loss probabilities depending on the type of information they carry, greater loss can be tolerated without any increase in bandwidth requirements. For example, the embedded encoding scheme in which low bit rate encoding is embedded in a higher bit rate encoding can tolerate higher packet loss rate for higher frequency voice samples.[16] Yin and Stern[17] find that a loss rate up to 20 percent can be tolerated with this technique on selected packets.

DaSilva et al[18] suggest classifying packets based on the types of sounds they carry; that is, fricative, voiced speech, background, or other. It was found that the loss rates that can be tolerated in these four classes are 8 percent, 5 percent, 47 percent, and 4 percent, respectively, yielding a tolerable average loss rate of 16 percent.

Optimal packet length: To minimize both the packetization delay at the transmitter and the perceptual effect of lost packet anomalies at the receiver, packets should be as short as possible. Weinstein and Forgie[19] also note that experience with lost packet anomalies indicates that individual packets should ideally contain no more than approximately 50 ms of speech. It also has been observed that a 50 ms clipping of voice information is the maximum before speech loss is detectable. On the other hand, to maintain high utilization, the number of speech bits per packet should be as high as possible relative to the overhead per packet. This tradeoff is particularly difficult for low bit rate speech, as 50 ms of 2.4 Kbps encoded speech is only 120 bits. For higher bit rates, this is less of a problem. Also, longer packets reduce the frequency of packet processing and, therefore, lower the processing overhead (although at a low speed rate, this may not be important). Studies have shown the range of 8 to 32 ms is an appropriate choice for voice packet size in view of network delay, throughput, and perceptual effects of lost packets.[12, 14, 19]

Physical layer: The BER requirements shown in Table 5-3 assume the bit errors occur randomly and are evenly distributed. It shows that an average BER of 3 x 10^{-5} can be tolerated without being perceptible for 64 Kbps PCM voice.

ITU also recognizes the effects of unevenly distributed bit clippings. For this reason, Recommendation G.821[18] specifies a hypothetical performance reference connection of 27,000 km length at the 64 Kbps level for the percentage of time periods, T_O, during which the error ratio exceeds a threshold value. The percentage is assessed over a much longer time interval, T_L. G.821 defines the following three parameters and associated objectives:

- *Degraded minutes.* Fewer than 10 percent of 1-minute intervals can have a BER worse than 10^{-6} (that is, 4 bit errors/minute).
- *Severely errored seconds.* Fewer than 0.2 percent of 1-second intervals can have a BER worse than 10^{-3} (that is, 64 bit errors per second).
- *Errored seconds.* Fewer than 8 percent of 1-second intervals can have any error (the probability of an error-free second is 92 percent).

The objective of the first parameter (degraded minutes) is to specify the overall long-term average BER. Since this does not specify whether losses can bunch up within that minute, the severely errored seconds parameter is required to specify maximum burst error in the short interval (1 second, which is short compared to the connection duration). The errored seconds parameter guarantees the minimum percentage of time that will be error-free during connection.

Video   The error effects on video depend on the location of the error and the error rate. Errors can affect video quality in two different ways:

- *Impairing the picture quality without loss of video synchronization.* This is the case when the bit errors hit the content and not the header used for decoding. Such error may or may not be visible, depending on the BER and the location of the bit errors.
- *Causing failure of the multiplexing of the video signal with the accompanying audio and data signals, with possible loss of video line and field synchronization.* This is the case when the error hits the control data or headers of the video that are responsible for synchronization or identification of the data that follows it.

Error control strategies Two key error control strategies for video encoding are error concealment and hierarchical encoding.

Error concealment: A popular video encoding to minimize packet loss effects is error concealment during the decoding process using layered coding.[21] Error concealment is a technique of hiding the lost or the corrupted portion of images from a viewer's perception by using the redundancy left in the received video signal. This concealment is usually done by spatial or temporal interpolation from the adjacent areas of the same frame or previous frame. Packet loss and bit error detection are essential for locating the damaged areas of the image before applying any error concealment techniques. Although error concealment cannot hide the information loss completely, it is useful in many applications for avoiding the breakdown of service.

Hierarchical encoding: Layered coding schemes employ a hierarchy of resolutions based on decomposing the video signal into a number of components, with individual components having largely non-overlapping frequencies. If the coding and packetization are done separately for each component, the reconstruction is fairly tolerant to the loss of packets carrying the higher frequency components. However, the reconstruction quality is very sensitive to packet loss in the lowest frequency component; therefore, these packets require a high degree of protection from packet loss and bit errors.

5.3.3.2   Real-time Block Transfer Applications

Real-time block transfer applications typically can have a range of error requirements. As mentioned before, for image transfer, the error requirements depends on the nature of the image. For X-rays, no error should be tolerated. But for a fax-quality image, a certain amount of error can be tolerated. Due the time constraint of this class of applications, to achieve zero error using reliable transport protocol, sufficient bandwidth must be provided to allow for the additional overhead of possible retransmission of lost or corrupted packets.

5.3.3.3   Non-real-time Applications

Non-real-time applications can also have different error requirements, although most non-real-time applications require error free delivery. Since non-real-time applications do not have tight time constraints, such error requirements can be achieved by using reliable transport protocol, as the additional delay due to retransmission is not an issue for this class of applications.

5.4 Summary

In the last chapter, we discussed the traffic requirements of applications. In this chapter, we discuss the QoS requirements of all classes of applications in detail. Together, these two chapters complete the discussion of networking requirements of applications.

The QoS requirements for applications include both delay and error requirements. Again, we discussed QoS requirements both at the application and network layers. QoS requirements are specified in terms of the delay and error incurred by the individual ADU and PDU, respectively.

Each class of applications has QoS requirements, including non-real-time applications. Delay requirements only apply to real-time applications (streaming and block transfer) by definition. The loss requirements affect all three classes of applications.

5.5 References

[1] T. Gonsalves, et al., "Comparative Performance of Voice/Data Local Area Networks," *IEEE Journal of Selected Areas in Communications,* Vol. 7, No. 5, June 1989, pp. 657-669.

[2] F. Duffy, G. McNees, J. Nasell, and T. Thatcher, "Echo performance of toll telephone connections in the United States," *Bell System Technical Journal,* Vol. 54, pp. 209-243, Feb. 1975.

[3] T. Chen, J. Walrand, D. Messerschmitt, "Dynamic priority protocols for packet voice," *IEEE Journal of Selected Areas in Communications,* Vol. 7, No. 5, June 1989, pp. 632-643.

[4] N. Kitawaki, K. Itoh, "Pare Delay Effects on Speech Quality Telecommunications," *IEEE Journal of Selected Areas in Communications*, Vol. 7, No. 5, June 1989, pp. 632-643.

[5] M. Sondhi, DiBerkeley, "Silencing Echoes on the Telephone Network," *Proceedings of IEEE,* Vol. 68, No. 8, August 1980, pp. 948-963.

[6] ITU-T, Recommendation G.131, "Control of talker echo," 1996.

[7] Rec. G.114, "Mean one-way propagation time," CCITT fascicle III.1, Melbourne, Australia, pp. 84-93, 1988.

[8] B. Shneiderman, "Response Time and Display rate in Human Performance with Computers," *Computing Surveys*, Vol.16, No.3, Sept. 1984, pp. 265-285.

[9]K. Karlsson and M. Vetterli, "Packet video and its integration into the Network Architecture," *IEEE Journal of Selected Areas in Communications,* vol. 7, No. 5, June 1989, pp. 739-751.

[10]A. Norwine, and O. Murphy, "Characteristics Time Intervals in Telephonic Conversation, *Bell Telephone Systems Journal,* 17, April, 1938, pp. 281-291.

[11]Gruber, J. G., and Strawczynski, L., "Subjective Effects of Variable Delay and Speech Clipping in Dynamically Managed Voiced Systems," *IEEE Transactions on Communications,* Vol. 33, No. 8, pp. 801-808, August 1985

[12]O. J.Wasem, D. Goodman, C. Dvorak, H. G. Page, "The Effect of Waveform Substitution on the Quality of PCM Packet Communication," *IEEE Transactions on Acoustic Speech, and Signal Processing,* Vol. 34, No. 3, March 1988.

[13]Y. Yamamoto, T. Wright, "Error Performance in Evolving Digital Networks including ISDNs," *IEEE Communications Magazine,* Vol. 27, No. 4, pp. 12-18, Apr., 1989.

[14]N. Jayant, S. Christensen, "Effects of Packet losses in waveform coded speech and improvements due to an odd-even sample-interpolation procedure," *IEEE Transactions on Communications,* Vol. COM-29, No. 2, Feb. 1981.

[15]J. Suzuki, M. Taka, "Missing packet Recovery Techniques for Low-bit-rate Coded Speech," *IEEE Journal on Selected Areas in Communications,* Vol. 7, No. 5, pp. 707-717, June 1989.

[16]T. Bially, B. Gold, S. Seneff, "A technique for adaptive voice flow control in integrated packet networks," *IEEE Trans. Commun.,* vol. COM-28, pp. 324-333, Mar. 1980.

[17]N. Yin, S. Li, T. Stern, "Congestion Control for Packet Voice by selective Packet Discarding," *IEEE Transactions on Communications,* Vol. 38, No. 5, pp. 674-683, May 1990.

[18]L. DaSilva, D. Petr, V. Frost, "A Class-Oriented Replacement Technique for Lost Speech Packets," *Proceedings of IEEE Infocom 1989,* Ottawa, Canada, pp. 1098-1105, April 1989.

[19]C. J. Weinstein, J. Forgie, "Experience with speech communication in packet networks," *IEEE Journal of Selected Areas on Communications,* Vol. SAC-1, No. 6, pp. 963-980, Dec. 1983.

[20]CCITT Blue Book, Recommendation G.821, "Error performance of an international digital connection forming part of an Integrated Services Digital Networks," 1989.

[21]S. Lee and P. Lee, "Cell loss and error recovery in variable rate video," *Journal of Visual Communication and Image Representation,* vol.3, No. 3, Sept. 1992.

PART II

Fundamentals
of ATM

Chapter 6

Principles of ATM

6.1 Introduction

In Part I of this book, we discussed the key motivations for designing a new networking paradigm to support integrated services on a single network enabling all classes of applications, including but not limited to emerging multimedia applications. The objective of Part II is to introduce asynchronous transfer mode, or ATM, the new networking paradigm that achieves these purposes. We will give an overview of the ATM architecture and its foundation protocols.

ATM was formally proposed to the ITU-T (then CCITT) in the late 1980s as the solution for Broadband Integrated Service Digital Network (B-ISDN). ATM was adopted in 1989 over the alternate proposal of synchronous transfer mode (STM), a multi-rate circuit switching approach, as the technology for B-ISDN. ATM was then quickly embraced by the computer and data communication industry as the long-term networking solution. In late 1991, *The ATM Forum* was established by vendors to expedite the development of interoperability agreements to facilitate getting ATM products to the market. Since then, the ATM Forum has grown to include computer software and hardware vendors, in addition to networking vendors, as well as the user community. It has grown from 4 members to over 900 members in the first 5 years. Though the Forum is not a true standards organization, the interoperability specifications issued by the Forum have become de facto industry standards due to the support of a large number of member companies and the user community.

Before we discuss ATM as the new solution for supporting integrated services, it is useful to understand the evolution of thinking for supporting integrated services in the telecommunications industry. Before B-ISDN, ISDN was designed in the early 1980s to support voice and data integration based on the same circuit switching used for POTS (plain old telephone service). The major improvement of ISDN over POTS is that it is digital end-to-end all the way to the terminals (or phones), while the classic PSTN was digital within the networks (between switches) only. However, with ISDN, the PSTN continues to be circuit switched based.

On the other hand, B-ISDN is based on an entirely new networking technology, ATM, that requires a fundamental change from PSTN. ATM is based on packet switching as one of its key principles, as opposed to circuit switching. That's why it has been suggested that ISDN is a new name for an old network, while B-ISDN is an old name for a new network. Some even suggested that B-ISDN should be renamed to emphasize its distinguished networking technologies and avoid the confusion with the old baggage that comes with the term ISDN. Nevertheless, since the formation of The ATM Forum, the term ATM is more commonly used instead of B-ISDN, partly because of the extension of ATM to support LANs. In fact, the use of ATM in LANs has received comparable, if not more, attention to its use in public networks.

Understanding the basic principles behind ATM is the easiest way to learn the new networking paradigm. Hence, we first discuss in this chapter the basic principles behind ATM that are key to addressing the problems of existing networks to support integrated services for a wide range of applications. We conclude by summarizing the advantages of ATM. In the next chapter, we present an overview of the ATM architecture and discuss the functions and protocols of ATM endpoints and switches, which incorporate all the principles of ATM. Given a general understanding of ATM, we then proceed to a formal discussion of ATM using the Protocol Reference Model (PRM) in the following chapter. We round up the discussion of the fundamentals of ATM by discussing the three key components of the ATM architecture in the last three chapters of this Part: ATM adaptation layer, signaling and traffic management.

6.2 Principles of ATM

The key principles of ATM are: a switched point-to-point architecture, packet switching, fast packet switching, resource reservation and asynchronous time division multiplexing. It is interesting to note that although ATM was proposed only as recently as the late 1980s for adoption as the solution for B-ISDN, a number of ideas behind these principles of ATM are dated as far back as the late 1960s and 1970s. Of these principles, the last three principles form the most distinguishing properties of ATM from classic networking architectures, such as the Internet and LANs. It was the last principle that contributed to the name asynchronous transfer mode. They are discussed in detail next.

6.2.1 Switched Point-to-point Architecture

The first ATM principle is to use a switched point-to-point architecture (as discussed in Part I, Chapter 2), as shown in Figure 6-1. The switched point-to-point architecture includes both meshed point-to-point and hierarchical point-to-point architectures. This architecture provides the basis for flexibility in supporting different bandwidth for different links, and allows independent improvement in link bandwidth for different links.

Although this principle is not new in public network architectures (it's the same as the circuit switched based PSTN used for almost a century), this principle makes ATM based LANs much more scalable than legacy LANs based on shared medium architecture introduced in the 1980s. A switched-based network provides much higher concurrency or switched bandwidth per user than a shared medium network. In a shared medium network such as the Ethernet, all stations (say N) on the network share the same bandwidth, C (or 10 Mbps in the case of the original Ethernet). Hence, on average, each station can send at most C/N bandwidth. On the other hand, in a point-to-point switched network, the total bandwidth is equal to NxC (C is the link bandwidth) and grows linearly with the number of users on the network, as shown in Figure 6-1. Hence, a point-to-point switched network is more scalable in bandwidth as new users are added.

This principle assumes that we start from scratch to build an ATM network, or it is possible to create switched point-to-point architecture using existing physical topology. However, it might be prohibitively expensive to rewire the existing topology, especially if this is a residential access network (such as the shared cable network) supporting millions of homes that are extremely costly to rewire. Nevertheless, ATM can be applied in the shared network because there are many advantages adopting the ATM architecture as discussed in Part III, as a result of the following principles.

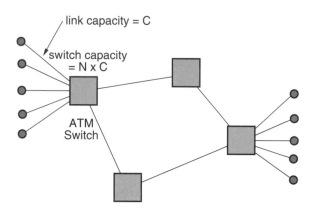

Figure 6–1   Switched point-to-point architecture of an ATM network.

6.2.2 Packet Switching

The second principle of ATM is to use packet switching as the switching and multiplexing methodology. As discussed in Part I, packet switching is very flexible in supporting applications with diverse traffic characteristics such as both streaming and bursty traffic. Furthermore, the statistical multiplexing mechanism provided by packet switching allows efficient simultaneous support of many different applications, especially bursty traffic. In contrast, circuit switching is very inefficient in supporting bursty traffic, because it dedicates bandwidth statically to a connection even if the communicating parties are idle. Again, packet switching is not new and has been used since the 1960s, first by the Internet (previously known as the ARPANET) and then by public data networks based on X.25.

However, there are still problems with the classic packet switched networks that make them unsuitable for providing integrated services and to scale to high bandwidth. Hence, the following three principles are added to improve upon the classic packet switching to achieve these objectives. These three principles of ATM are the fundamental building blocks of the ATM design.

6.2.3 Fast Packet Switching

6.2.3.1 Problems of Classic Packet Switching

The problems of applying classic packet switching techniques to support B-ISDN come from the fundamental differences in design assumptions in the target transmission technologies used and applications supported. The design assumptions for B-ISDN of using high-speed fiber optic links makes the design tradeoff adopted for the classic packet switching paradigm on low-speed noisy links unsuitable. Furthermore, B-ISDN is designed to support all classes of applications, especially those with QoS requirements, while classic packet switching was designed to support bursty data applications that have no QoS requirements. As explained below, the classic packet switching paradigm leads to performance bottleneck in packet switches and makes it unsuitable to support high-speed communications.

Classic packet switched network design was motivated by two basic limitations of the transmission links technologies used in the 1960s and 1970s (such as coaxial cable and copper): slow and unreliable. Typical transmission link speed was only 56 kbps or less, while having bit error rates as high as 10^{-6} or worse for coaxial cable, and 10^{-4} or 10^{-5} for copper. Hence, the links, not the packet switches, were the performance bottleneck. Therefore, in classic packet switched network design, transmission bandwidth was viewed as the scarce resource, not packet switching capacity. Packet switched networks are link-bandwidth limited instead of switching-bandwidth limited. This lead to the use of sophisticated protocol processing (such as link-by-link flow and error control) at the packet switches to alleviate the link bandwidth bottlenecks and error problems.

The high bit error rates on the transmission links made link-by-link error control techniques more suitable than end-to-end error control. A high link error rate means that a packet is easily corrupted in one or more of the transmission links across the network. By using link-by-link error control, such as error detection with retransmission on each link, corrupted packets only need to be retransmitted across one link, instead of over the entire network (which has a higher probability of repeated packet corruption). Furthermore, retransmission of lost packets is expensive across the entire network because transmission bandwidth is a scarce resource in such a network.

In packet switched networks (classic or ATM), congestion can occur at packet switches due to overload of their capacity (bandwidth and buffer) and result in significant packet losses (due to buffer overflow). Since, in classic packet switched networks, transmission link bandwidth was a scarce resource compared to packet switch processing, retransmission of lost packets was expensive even over one link. A typical solution in classic packet switched networks was to use a link-by-link flow control scheme to prevent packet loss due to switch buffer overflow. In general, flow control schemes control the amount of data that the sender can transmit to the receiver so that the sender will not swamp the receiver so as to make the receiver buffer overflow. In link-by-link flow control, sender and receiver are at either end of each link. Hence, packet switches can both be senders and receivers on the corresponding links. A link-by-link flow control scheme allows faster response time to congestion than an end-to-end flow control scheme. Also, any packet loss requires only retransmission over a single link.

Since the transmission links were the bottleneck in classic packet switched networks, the packet switches had very low switching capacity requirement (due to the low speed links to which they connect). Another reason for not requiring high-speed classic packet switches was that the endpoints were not capable of transmitting and processing at high speed in the first place. Hence, optimizing packet switch design was not the high priority and the tendency was to use software-based packet switch design. In software-based packet switch design, packets are queued by a shared memory in the switch and processed (or switched) one at a time by the CPU (central processing unit) on the switch. If multiple packets arrive simultaneously from different links, they are buffered and served sequentially, typically in a first-come-first-serve manner. Hence, the classic packet switched network is also known as the store and forward network, because complete packets are stored and processed individually before forwarding to the next hop. [The exception are packet switches that implement cut-through routing, for which only part of the packet is buffered (sufficient to process the packet) before forwarding to the next hop to avoid a complete packet transmission time delay.] Since software-based packet switching allows flexible packet processing, it also can accommodate variable size packets, which reduces the processing needed at the end points to preprocess packets if they are required to be one size. This increases the complexity to the network to solve the networking problems, as opposed to requiring computing power at the end systems.

On the other hand, the B-ISDN is a high-speed network targeted to run on fiber optic links, which have become very cost effective especially for long distance transmission links. This invalidates the classic packet network design assumptions and a totally different set of system tradeoffs must be made. Such high-speed fiber optic links have much higher transmission rates (multi-Gbps or more than four orders of magnitude speed improvement) and much lower error rates (from 10^{-9} to as low as 10^{-13}). Since the classic packet switching approach requires significant processing at the software-based packet switches (link-by-link error control, flow control and supporting variable size packet processing), the performance bottleneck for B-ISDN (based on packet switching) is shifted from transmission link bandwidth to the switching capacity of packet switches. This prompted the use of a fast packet switching paradigm, which can be considered as the most important principle behind ATM.

6.2.3.2   Solution: Fast Packet Switching

As transmission bandwidth increases by four or more orders of magnitude (from 10s kbps to multi-Gbps) since the days of classic packet switching, the central issue in designing B-ISDN is how to build a fast packet switch.[1] This has lead to the design of the following fast packet switching techniques.

6.2.3.3   Techniques of Fast Packet Switching

The goal of the fast packet switching principle is to simplify packet switch protocol processing and push the complexity to the edge of the network; that is, to the end systems. This makes sense because the end systems have also become increasingly more capable with ever increasing processing power available. In particular, the following techniques form the cornerstones of the fast packet switching principle, which collectively make the fast packet switch capacity significantly higher than that of the classic packet switch.

Hardware-based design and use of parallel processing   In a classic packet switch, all packets arriving from different input ports are processed and switched by a single CPU in software. All these packets are buffered at a central memory and processed on a first-come-first-serve basis. The CPU needs to process complex protocols such as error control, flow control and routing on a per packet basis. Hence, classic packet switches only had switching capacity on the order of Mbps.

Switching packets at multi-Gbps rates requires hardware-based switching and parallel switching architectures. Both in turn require simplifications of packet switch protocol processing by pushing the protocol processing to the edge of the network, that is, the endpoints.[2, 3, 4] They facilitate ATM switches (packet switches used in ATM networks) to concentrate on their principle task, namely, switching of packets (forwarding of packets from each input to the desired output ports), which must be performed at much higher speeds. As significant advances are being made to CPU speed at the endpoints with ever decreasing cost, this approach of shifting processing to outside the network makes perfect sense. Furthermore, this allows hardware-based packet switch designs to implement fewer functions and lend themselves to massively parallel design. As discussed in more detail below, such packet processing simplifications include supporting only fixed size packets, performing routing on a per connection basis, and removing link-by-link error and flow controls.

Short fixed size packet   An important way to simplify hardware design for packet switches is to use only fixed size packets instead of variable size packets. Using fixed size packets simplifies the design of parallel switching fabric as packets from different input links can be aligned and switched in parallel. Hence, in an ATM network, all packets are of a fixed size.

It was decided in 1989 to use fixed size small packets of 53 octets long for ATM, which have a 5-octet header and 48-octet payload. Such a fixed size packet used in ATM networks is referred to as an ATM cell. The choice of such a short size packet was based on a number of motivations. First, using short size packets avoids the problem of excessive delay incurred by short packets destined to an output port while the switch is transmitting a long packet on the same output port. Second, short packets allow fine grain multiplexing at the ATM switch and therefore support finer specification of data rates. Third, short packets reduce the queuing delay of each packet. For example, for a 155 Mbps (OC-3c) link, an ATM cell incurring a single cell buffering delay only suffers 2.7 microsecond delay. Fourth, short packets reduce packetization delay for real-time applications. This is especially important for real-time streaming applications at low data rates, such as telephony (as discussed in the Part I). At 64 Kbps, each ATM cell incurs

6 ms of packetization delay. In fact, it was the packetization delay requirement to support telephony that affected on the value of payload length of ATM to be about 48 octets.

In fact, the choice of a 48-byte payload was a political decision in the ITU-T standards process.[5] The European community preferred a 32-octet payload to avoid adding echo control equipment to support telephony as this packet length has only 4 ms packetization delay. However, as echo control mechanism was already in place in the United States' voice network, this was not a concern for the United States community. Instead, the United States was focused on using B-ISDN to support data communications and preferred a larger 64-octet payload to make data communications more efficient (since large payload leads to a lower per payload byte overhead). At the end, to settle the hot debate, it was decided to take the middle between 32- and 64-octet. Hence, the 48-octet payload was determined.

On the other hand, short packet size has the disadvantage of increasing the number of packets switched per second required to transfer a given amount of data. Nevertheless, this disadvantage is more than offset by the minimal processing needed to switch each ATM cell because routing is done only once due to the connection-oriented technique below.

Connection-oriented packet switching   To support high packet switching capacity, the processing on each packet must be minimized. One of the key functions that require substantial processing is the routing function. In connectionless packet switching, there are two key functions performed by the packet switch: packet routing and packet forwarding. Each packet carries its complete destination address to indicate its final destination. When a packet arrives at the packet switch, the routing function computes or looks up the next hop (the output port leading to the next packet switch or final destination) based on the destination address. After the packet switch knows which output port to forward the packet, it forwards the packet through its switching fabric to reach the destined output port. If that output port is busy transmitting another packet, it queues the packet at the corresponding output port's buffer for transmission. This is referred to as packet forwarding. A per packet routing function is expensive and can significantly reduce packet switching capacity. Hence, the fast packet switching principle uses the connection-oriented model of packet switching.

Based on the connection-oriented model, communications in the ATM network have three distinct phases. The first phase is connection establishment. It precedes any user data transfer. A virtual connection (VC) is setup by the originating party to the destination party by sending a connection setup message that contains the address of the destination party, among other control information. It is only during this phase that routing occurs. The connection establishment process determines the end-to-end physical path along which the user data will flow. The route of the established connection will be stored in routing tables in the ATM switches along the path. The fact that routing is determined only once during the entire connection means that all ATM cells of a VC follow the same path, as discussed in the following.

An ATM connection is called a *virtual* connection because if the connection becomes idle or transfers less information than it requested bandwidth for, the networking resources will be available to other users. This is opposed to the nailed up connection in circuit switching for which resources will be wasted if this connection becomes idle, because no other connections can use such resources.

After a VC has been established in phase one, the second phase is for actual user data transfer. Since the VC has a fixed physical path between the communicating parties, there is no need for carrying the destination on a per ATM cell basis during this data transfer phase. Instead, each cell only needs to carry a VC number in the header to identify for each ATM switch the VC to which the cell belongs. More importantly, there is no need for the routing function because it has been achieved during the connection setup phase. When a cell arrives at an ATM switch, only a simple table lookup is required that translates the VC number into the output port(s) of the ATM switch for the ATM packets (which can be implemented in hardware). As a result, the cells can be switched much faster with simplified header processing (VC number translation, which will be discussed in detail in Chapter 7), without processing the entire destination address and performing per packet routing. Another way of looking at ATM switching is that routing of user data at each switch is based on the relative information available in the local table lookup to determine the output link for the packet, instead of absolute addressing of the final destination. Hence, the ATM network can achieve higher switching capacity than a connectionless packet switched network. This also means that in the ATM network, the connection control function (which includes routing) is separated from the user data transfer function. (This is explained in more detail later in the protocol reference model of ATM.)

Finally, the third phase is connection tear down, after either party decides to terminate the connection by sending a tear down message.

Another very important characteristic for VC-based packet network relates to the order of packet arrivals. VC-based packet networks guarantee the arrival of packets to the destination to be in order. When a connection is set up for two parties, the physical route which all cells will follow during the information phase becomes fixed. In other words, all packets belonging to a particular virtual connection in the ATM network will follow the same physical route. (The only exception is when one of the links that this connection transverses fails and rerouting to a new link is required.) By further requiring the ATM switch to perform switching in order for packets belonging to the same connection, ATM then guarantees packet arrival in order. Hence, the receiving endpoints do not need to resequence the packets to reconstruct the original information, which significantly reduces endpoint processing requirements.

This is in contrast to the connectionless packet switched networks (also known as the datagram model) such as the Internet or the intranets within corporations. In connectionless packet networks, packets sent between two parties may not arrive in sequence because they usually take different routes for different packets, depending on the loading and availability of different paths (links and routers).

There are a number of advantages for the connection-oriented approach. First, multimedia applications based on images and video are characterized by transferring large amounts of information. Connection-oriented packet switching allows efficient transfer of such information because once a VC has been established, a large amount of information can be transferred efficiently without per packet routing overhead. Second, the connection-oriented approach guarantees in-sequence packet delivery, which significantly simplifies the end point processing (higher layer protocols) as they can rely on in-sequence delivery. Third, the fact that each packet carrying user information does not need to carry a destination address reduces the packet overhead, resulting in more efficient packet delivery. Finally, a VC can be setup with the associated network resources to support QoS guarantees, as discussed in more detail in the following.

However, there are also disadvantages to the connection-oriented approach. First, it is inefficient for applications that require only a short single packet (or small number of packets) transfer, because it requires a connection setup phase, only to tear down the connection after a single packet transfer. Second, there is a connection setup delay for each data transfer, if no connection has been established a priori. Third, for networks that support exclusively short data transactions, the connection-oriented model can result in high frequency of connection setup and tear down requests, which can become a capacity bottleneck. These problems can be reduced by leaving the connection up for a number of transactions or setting up permanent virtual connections. Since the maintaining idle VC does not consume switching capacity or bandwidth, this is acceptable in many scenarios. In any case, none of the disadvantages outweigh all the advantages of the virtual connection-based approach for fast packet switching.

Note that connection-oriented based packet switching is not new; it has been used in X.25 networks since the 1970s. However, the fast packet switching principle does not use the entire classic connection-oriented packet switching paradigm because, as discussed next, it has no link-by-link flow and error control. It is up to the endpoints to add end-to-end error and flow control mechanisms. Hence, one can refer to fast packet switching as a light-weight connection-oriented approach.

No link-by-link error control on payload Since fiber optic links have much lower error rates than those used in classic packet switched networks, link-by-link error control becomes unnecessary. By removing these error control functions, the processing at each packet switch is significantly reduced. Therefore, in the ATM network, error recovery becomes the responsibility of the endpoints; that is, it becomes an end-to-end function.

There is another advantage to this approach. Since ATM is designed to support all types of applications, it should be up to the endpoint to determine whether additional reliability is required on an application-by-application basis. As not all applications require such error recovery, it is best to leave to the endpoints (which have ever improving processing power) to choose the appropriate error control mechanisms depending on the applications. Although ATM does define a number of common error control mechanisms for end-to-end error control, it is an optional function for the applications. As discussed in Part I on applications requirements, video applications may tolerate a certain amount of information loss without perceivable loss of quality. Furthermore, retransmission of corrupted or lost video data is useless because of the time sensitivity of the information.

Note that there is still an error control field on the ATM cell header to protect the integrity of the ATM cell header (not the payload). It was decided that this is a reasonable tradeoff to avoid the consequence of header corruption as this can be performed in hardware. Hence, this does not lead to a significant performance degradation as compared to error control on the payload in classic packet switched networks.

No link-by-link flow control   The last simplification of packet switch functionality employed by the fast packet switching principle is the removal of the link-by-link flow control mechanism used in classic packet switching. It is up to the endpoints (higher layer protocols) to implement flow control on an end-to-end basis. In ATM design, congestion avoidance is achieved by explicit resource allocation using a combination of admission control, traffic shaping and policing mechanisms, as discussed in more detail in the chapter on traffic management.

6.2.4 Resource Reservation and Admission Control

Although classic packet switching supports diverse traffic classes, it does not guarantee QoS for different application classes, such as real-time streaming and real-time block transfer applications. The reason is that classic packet switching treats all packets equally without taking into account the time (and loss) sensitivity of certain data. This is addressed by another fundamental principle of ATM: resource reservation.

To ensure guaranteed quality of service to support multimedia and collaborative applications, reservation of networking resources is required. In addition, call admission control (CAC) is required to turn down new connection requests when the network becomes heavily loaded, so as to maintain the QoS of existing applications on the network. Note that resource reservation and CAC are actually two separate principles for guaranteeing QoS. Since they are closely related, we combine the discussion of them here.

The connection-oriented approach (as part of the fast packet switching principle above) is essential in providing a mechanism for resource reservation and admission control to guarantee QoS. This is achieved by including additional information such as bandwidth and QoS requirements in the call setup message during the connection setup phase. The network is then required to determine if sufficient network resources are available to handle this new connection. Such networking resources include switching, transmission bandwidth and buffer capacity available in the ATM switches along a route. If such resources are available, then the network will reserve those resources and send a confirmation message to the parties that the connection is being setup. If such resources are not available, the network can either turn down the connection request, or propose a lower quality or bandwidth connection given the available network resources. This mechanism ensures sufficient resources are available before accepting the call; it is known as CAC. (Since all cells of a VC will follow the same route, resources are reserved only along this route.) This resource reservation approach ensures network resources are not over allocated so that a new request will not jeopardize current connections. Admission control is a fundamental mechanism to prevent congestion in ATM networks and to guarantee QoS of existing connections. The details of the mechanisms to achieve these resource reservations will be discussed in the chapter on signaling. Hence, the ability to achieve resource reservation and admission control to guarantee QoS is yet another advantage of the connection-oriented approach.

However, resource reservation and CAC, though necessary, are not sufficient to guarantee QoS for each real-time application. They deal with the QoS guarantee during the call setup process. Another mechanism is needed to guarantee QoS during the data transfer phase. This is purpose of the next principle.

6.2.5 Asynchronous Time Division Multiplexing

ATM includes both a switching and a multiplexing methodology. Closely related to fast packet switching is the concept of asynchronous time division (ATD) multiplexing. Again, because of this principle, the term "asynchronous transfer mode" was coined to contrast it with synchronous transfer mode (STM). ATD is a methodology of multiplexing (or sharing the bandwidth for) different applications on a transmission link that guarantees their respective QoS. This, of course, assumes that the link is not overloaded, as guaranteed by the admission control and resource reservation mechanisms discussed above.

ATD is based on a time slotted transmission scheme by which data from different applications are multiplexed according to their bandwidth, delay and loss requirements. In ATM, each time slot carries exactly one ATM cell. Obviously, the higher the bandwidth required by an application, the greater the number of time slots required in a given period of time by the application. Time slots are first allocated to those connections to satisfy their QoS requirement, while the rest can be shared by connections without QoS requirements. This differs from the classic statistical multiplexing in packet switched networks, which are typically based on first-come-first-serve queuing or random statistical multiplexing. Since such statistical multiplexing treats all packets equally, there is no way of guaranteeing QoS for each application.

For the ATM network, ATD is implemented at each output port of the ATM switch. ATD decides how each application, identified by a connection identifier on each cell, multiplexes and shares the output link bandwidth with other applications. A bandwidth allocation scheme or a scheduling algorithm is needed to determine how time slots are allocated. One way to guarantee bandwidth is to use a weighted-round-robin algorithm according to the bandwidth reserved for each connections. These various traffic management mechanisms are discussed in the traffic management chapter.

In contrast, STM, the competing proposal for the solution to B-ISDN before ATM was adopted, uses TDM. In TDM, time is again divided into slots, but a fixed number of slots, say k, are grouped together to form a frame, which repeats in time. All the slots that are located at the same relative position in each frame belong to a particular TDM channel; the total system consists of k channels of equal bandwidth. More than one TDM channel can be associated with the same connection. This essentially creates a multi-rate circuit switched network. Hence, STM has all the inefficiencies associated with circuit switching, as discussed in Part I.

6.3 Advantages of ATM

Given an understanding of the principles of ATM, we will summarize the advantages of ATM in this section. ATM networks have many advantages over existing networking technologies. We can classify them into technical and strategic advantages.

6.3.1 Technical Advantages

6.3.1.1 High Bandwidth
Since ATM is based on a point-to-point switching topology with dedicated link bandwidth to each end station, much higher concurrent bandwidth is available than under shared medium type packet switching technologies,

such as the Ethernet. (Recently, the data communications industry also realizes this problem of Ethernet and has introduced point-to-point switched Ethernets.) Furthermore, an ATM switch can support much higher switching capacity than classic packet switches (Gbps or above switching) due to the fast packet switching principle. This much higher bandwidth not only makes high bandwidth applications possible (such as high quality video on demand, HDTV delivery, and Web browsing of image intensive applications), but also allows many more applications to be supported simultaneously for each user and for the entire network.

6.3.1.2   Quality of Service Guarantee

One of the key advantages of an ATM network is that it can provide QoS guarantees to applications. Such QoS guarantees are achieved by a combination of resource reservation, admission control and ATD mechanisms. This is very important because it is clear networked multimedia applications will become very important and many multimedia applications require guaranteed QoS.

6.3.1.3   Flexibility

Another advantage of ATM is its flexibility in supporting all types of applications (of course, provided there is sufficient link bandwidth). Applications can have very diverse traffic characteristics and communications requirements, which include bandwidth, delay constraints and error sensitivity. The switching and multiplexing methodologies of ATM (packet switching and ATD, respectively) provide support for diverse traffic types as well as QoS guarantees for diverse performance requirements. In addition, the ATM call setup procedure allows each application to request specific traffic and QoS requirements for each connection to tailor to its needs.

This kind of flexibility comes from the decoupling of the relationship of link bandwidth and application requirements. ATM allows the link bandwidth to be divided arbitrarily into a number of virtual connections with different bandwidths and QoS using fast packet switching and ATD. This compares to circuit switching (STM approach) for which the bandwidth is available at a fixed multiple of 64 kbps (or some fixed rate) at constant bit rate.

6.3.1.4   Integration

As a corollary to ATM's flexibility in supporting all types of applications, one can build a single networking platform based on ATM to support all types of applications. There is no need to design a special purpose network for each individual application, such as separate data and voice networks. ATM's ability to integrate all application support is one of the most significant advantages of ATM. This simplifies network management because only a single network is needed. Furthermore, it becomes unnecessary to train different groups of people to manage different types of networks. For public network operators, this can amount to big savings in maintenance and billing operations, as a single physical link to the customers can support all the applications.

6.3.1.5   Scalability

ATM is scalable in a number of dimensions: bandwidth, physical media, number of endpoints and geography. They are discussed below.

Bandwidth   An ATM network can scale to arbitrarily high bandwidth because it is bandwidth independent. The point-to-point switched architecture provides unified switching based on the common ATM cell format of arriving packets, independent of the bandwidth on each individual link of the ATM switch. This is very important not only because transmission bandwidth is always improving, but also because it allows ATM to be implemented in different speeds to adapt to the environment (such as twisted pair for LANs and fiber for wide area public networks). Furthermore, an ATM switch can support widely different speeds on its ports, supporting very different ATM endpoints.

Physical media   Not only can ATM be implemented in different transmission speeds, but also it can be implemented in different transmission media (for the same or different speed). For example, ATM can be designed to be carried at SONET OC-3c rate (155 Mbps) on both fiber (single or multimode) and twisted pair (shielded or unshielded). As discussed in Chapter 8, there is a layer in the ATM protocol that is responsible to map the ATM cells into different physical media, which is known as the transmission convergence sublayer (the upper sublayer of the physical layer of ATM).

Number of endpoints   Since ATM is based on a point-to-point switched architecture, the bandwidth available to each endpoint does not decrease with additional endpoints, because the switching capacity of an ATM switch is N x C, where N is the number of endpoints attached to an ATM switch, while C is the link bandwidth.

Geography ATM also can scale geographically because it can be implemented as a LAN as well as a WAN. It does not have the distance limitations of other LAN technologies such as Ethernet. The reason is that ATM is based on a point-to-point switched architecture and is media independent. So ATM can run over twisted pair for LANs and over fiber optics for WANs.

6.3.1.6 Efficiency

Since ATM employs statistical multiplexing for sharing transmission bandwidth, significant statistical gain can be achieved when applications with high peak to average bandwidth ratio (bursty traffic) are multiplexed together, especially legacy data applications. Furthermore, ATD provides QoS guarantee for real-time applications and allows the left over bandwidth to be efficiently shared by non-real-time applications. The resulting statistical gain implies very efficient sharing of transmission costs.

However, ATM is sometimes considered as inefficient when one focuses on the transmission overhead of 5 octets for every 48-octet payload (more than 10 percent overhead). This is important especially in low bandwidth link for which bandwidth is precious. Nevertheless, this does not outweigh all the advantages discussed in this section.

6.3.1.7 Operations

With the ability of an ATM network to support a multiservice environment on one common infrastructure, rather than application-specific parallel or overlay networks, common network management tools, systems and operational staff result in significant economies of scale. These reduced operational savings can be passed on to users via lower rates.

6.3.2 Strategic Advantages

6.3.2.1 One Networking Architecture

Currently, ATM is the only networking technology that has received worldwide recognition as the networking technology for both LANs and WANs in the future to support all applications (especially multimedia applications). ATM has been adopted by the ITU as the public networking technology and all public network operators and vendors are focusing on this technology. Also, ATM is being deployed in the Internet backbone to support the exponential increase in the bandwidth requirements, which cannot be matched by the classic IP router-based backbone. ATM is being deployed in the corporate LAN environment. Furthermore,

ATM can become the corporate backbone as the long term solution to the router bottlenecks. ATM-to-the-desktop provides a very simple way to support QoS to the desktop applications. However, it is not clear that ATM would replace the majority of Ethernets to the desktop (especially given the recent success of Fast Ethernet and switched Ethernet to the desktops).

6.3.2.2   Compatible Architectures

For the first time in networking history, telecommunications, computer and data communications industry can all use ATM as the platform to deploy future applications as the long term strategy. This certainly allows both public and private networking industry to leverage on the economy of scale achieved by wider deployment.

6.3.2.3   True Multi-vendor Support

Given the support for ATM in both the public and private networking industries, there were over 900 member companies at the ATM Forum in 1996 (from 4 members on late 1991) and literally over a hundred ATM companies deploying products today. This true multi-vendor environment ensure that ATM will become very low cost and widely deployed in the long term.

6.4 Summary

In this chapter, we have discussed the fundamental principles of ATM to satisfy the goal of supporting all applications classes with diverse networking requirements in a single integrated network and to be able to scale to Gbps link speeds or higher. These principles are

- switched point-to-point architecture;
- packet switching;
- fast packet switching: hardware based switch design, fixed size short packets, connection-oriented paradigm, no link-by-link flow and error control;
- resource reservation and call admission control;
- asynchronous time division multiplexing.

Also, we summarized the technical and strategic advantages of ATM. With this background, we can discuss the operations of an ATM network in the next chapter.

6.5 References

[1]T. Kwok, *Tandem Banyan Switching Fabric: A New Fast Packet Switching Architecture and its Performance Evaluation,* Ph.D thesis, Stanford University, 1990.

[2]J. Kulzer, W. Montgomery, "Statistical Switching Architectures for Future Services," *Proc. of the International Switching Symposium,* May 1984.

[3]J. Turner, L. Wyatt, "A Packet Network Architecture for Integrated Services," *Globecom 1983,* San Diego, Nov. 1983, pp. 45-50.

[4]J. Turner, "New Directions in Communications (or Which Way to the Information Age)," *IEEE Communications Magazine,* Oct, 1986, Vol. 24, No. 10, pp. 8-15.

[5]M. D. Prycker, *Asynchronous Transfer Mode, Solution for Broadband ISDN,* Third Edition, Prentice Hall, 1995.

Chapter 7

Overview of ATM

7.1 Introduction

In the last chapter, we learned the basic principles of ATM. The ATM network is a connection-oriented packet switched network based on fast packet switching principle, which is critical to increasing switching performance for high-speed networks. ATM uses fixed size 53-octet cells to carry all applications and there is no link-by-link error control (user data) or flow control. ATM uses admission control and resource reservation at call setup to provide bandwidth and QoS guarantees. It uses ATD to provide QoS guarantees at the ATM switches. In this chapter, we will put all the ATM principles together to understand the basic operations of the ATM network.

7.2 Basic Elements of an ATM Network

An ATM network consists of two types of network elements: ATM switches and ATM endpoints. The topology of an ATM network is composed of ATM switches interconnecting ATM endpoints via point-to-point transmission links, as shown in Figure 7-1. In the simplest case, the ATM network consists of a single ATM switch, which directly connects all ATM endpoints. For a small ATM network with a small number of ATM switches, they can be interconnected in a meshed configuration. For a large ATM network with a large number of ATM switches, they are typically interconnected in a hierarchical topology. Otherwise, to mesh together hundreds or thousands of switches would require too many ports on each switch just to connect with one another, making the network prohibitively expensive.

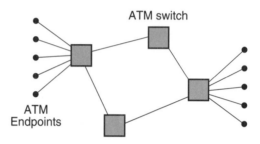

Figure 7–1   An ATM network

ATM switches are the packet switches used in the ATM network. They provide the basic packet switch functions of routing, switching and buffering. Buffering is required to resolve output port contention when multiple cells arrive simultaneously at the ATM switch and desire to go to the same output port. Output contention is a natural consequence of packet switching because cell arrivals from different sources are not coordinated a priori.

ATM endpoints are devices that originate and terminate ATM cells as source or destination points of user data in the ATM network. In a pure ATM network (such as the one in Figure 7-1), the ATM endpoints are computers (PCs, workstations, supercomputers), cable or xDSL modems (see Part III), home terminals (set-top-boxes or residential gateways), other information sources (such as cameras) or receivers (such as video decoders). In an internetwork that interconnects both ATM networks and non-ATM networks (see Figure 7-2), an ATM endpoint also can be an internetworking device (which connects two different physical networks that may or may not be of the same technology) such as a router. In general, all ATM endpoints are both sources and receivers in the ATM network. As sources, they are responsible for encoding all the information of various lengths into the 48-octet payload of ATM cells for transmission. As receivers, they are required to recover the original information from the 48-octet payload of the arriving ATM cells.

For a pure ATM network, the endpoints are the actual source and destination of the ATM cells. For an ATM internetwork that consists of non-ATM endpoints, some of the ATM endpoints are internetwork devices, which are *virtual* sources and destinations of *user* information because the actual sources and destinations can be in the non-ATM network.

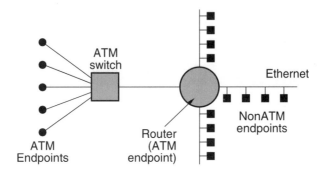

Figure 7–2 An internetwork consisting of both an ATM network and a non-ATM network connected by a router

Two ATM networks can be connected directly together through links between ATM switches from the networks. Hence, two interconnecting ATM switches can belong to two different ATM networks (owned by different organizations).

Other functions of the ATM switches and ATM endpoints are discussed next as we understand how ATM networks operate.

7.3 Standard ATM Interfaces

To design the protocols for an ATM network, it is important to identify the key interfaces where such protocols are communicated. More importantly, the motivation for networking standards is to define the protocols that will be communicated across these interfaces to guarantee interoperability for a multi-vendor environment. This is fundamental to the success of any networking protocol in the marketplace.

There are two classes of ATM interfaces: user-network interfaces (UNI) and network-node interfaces (NNI), as shown in Figure 7-3. The UNI is the interface between an ATM endpoint (the user of the ATM network) and an ATM switch. The NNI is the interface between two ATM networks as well as between two ATM switches (nodes within an ATM network), which explains the term *network-node interface* (instead of network-network interface).

The UNIs and the NNIs serve distinct networking functions. The UNI is mainly for ATM endpoints to communicate call setup and related control information to the ATM network and for the network to accept, reject or negotiate the call setup request. It is important to understand that the UNI protocols are exchanged only between an ATM endpoint and its attached ATM switch; there is no *direct* communication of UNI protocols between the ATM endpoint and other ATM switches in the network, or between two ATM endpoints through the ATM network. The NNI is used between directly attached switches (or ATM networks) for communicating routing information and call control information. These are discussed in more detail below when we discuss the operations of an ATM network.

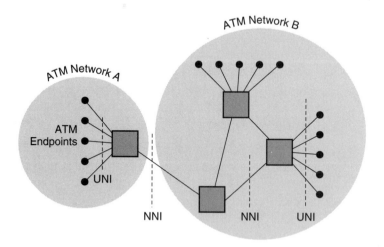

Figure 7–3   The UNI and NNI of ATM networks

In addition to distinguishing between the UNI and the NNI, there is a further classification of interfaces based on the ownership of the ATM network (public or private), as shown in Figure 7-4. For a private ATM network (such as one owned by a corporation), the corresponding UNI and NNI are referred to as Private UNI and Private NNI, respectively. For a public ATM network, all private endpoints are connected to the public network through public UNIs. This includes the interface between a private ATM switch (in addition to an ATM endpoint) that connects to the public network. The reason is that, from a public network point of view, both private ATM switches and ATM endpoints are all private endpoints. This simplifies connectivity to the public ATM network to a single type of interface. The interface between the public networks is called B-ICI (Broadband Inter-Carrier Interface).

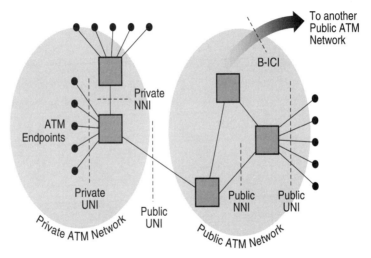

Figure 7–4   Private and Public ATM Interfaces

7.4 ATM Layered Model

The ATM protocols can be described using a layered model, as shown in Figure 7-5. There are four layers in the ATM protocol model. The ATM layer is the key layer that specifies how ATM cells are communicated across the ATM network. It is processed by all network elements in the ATM network (both switches and endpoints). The ATM layer is directly above the physical layer, which is why the ATM layer is sometimes referred to as a layer two protocol. The ATM adaptation layer (AAL) is responsible for mapping all information (which can be of different packet size) into the 48-

octet payload of the ATM cells for transferring over the ATM network. For user information transfer, the AAL is only processed at the ATM endpoints, as shown in Figure 7-6. Above the AAL is the collection of other higher layer ATM and non-ATM protocols, as well as applications. The ATM layered model is discussed in much greater detail in the next chapter.

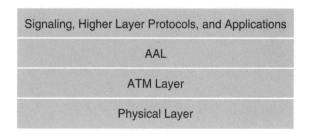

Figure 7–5   The ATM layered model

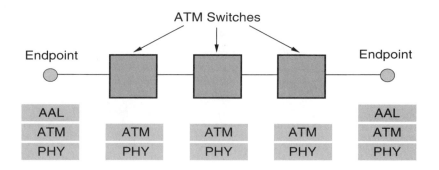

Figure 7–6   The ATM end-to-end layered model for user data transfer

7.5 Basic ATM Network Operations

The operation of an ATM network can be understood by considering the process by which user information from an ATM endpoint can be communicated to another endpoint over the ATM network (see Figure 7-7).

7.5.1 Call Establishment

Let us assume endpoint A would like to establish a video conferencing session to endpoint B over the ATM network. Before any video information can be communicated over the ATM network, an ATM virtual connection (VC) between A and B must first be established. A has to send a message to the ATM network to request a bi-directional connection to station B with sufficient bandwidth and QoS guarantees to support the video conferencing application. The messages used for call control (setup, tear down, modify connections) are called signaling messages. Signaling messages are communicated at both the UNIs and the NNIs in the ATM network which belong to UNI signaling and NNI signaling protocols, respectively.

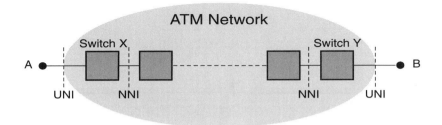

Figure 7–7   Setting up a connection across an ATM network between two endpoints

Since all information, including signaling messages, is communicated through a virtual connection over the ATM network, a VC to carry signaling messages must be setup a priori. Such a virtual connection is known as the signaling VC. This signaling VC is usually set up when endpoint A was physically connected to the ATM network as part of the initialization process. This signaling message is segmented into ATM cells payload by the AAL of endpoint A, with the signaling VC identifier in the ATM cell header. The message includes B's ATM address, the bandwidth and QoS required in each direction. (For a unidirectional connection, it is indicated by a zero bandwidth in one direction.) The ATM switch that is physically attached to A, referred to as switch X in Figure 7-7, will process this signaling information (as part of the UNI signaling protocol) and perform the call admission control (CAC) function. Switch X, working with other switches in the ATM network using a NNI signaling protocol, determines if the network has the available bandwidth and other networking resources to support this new connection.

If such network resources are available in the ATM network, a physical route will be determined between A and B for the connection. This results in the switch connected directly to B (switch Y) sending a call setup message (in ATM cell formats) to B as a call setup request from A, as part of the UNI protocols between switch Y and endpoint B. If B is interested in accepting the call and has sufficient resources to handle the call, B will reply with a call acceptance message. After switch Y receives this message, it forwards the reply across the network to switch X. Switch X then replies to endpoint A that its call setup is successful. As a result, the connection between A and B is established and they are ready to start the video conferencing application. A more detailed discussion of the call setup procedure will be provided in the chapter on ATM signaling.

7.5.2 Cell Sequencing and VC Routes

In ATM networks, the ATM cells for a connection are guaranteed to arrive in sequence. ATM cells of a given connection always follow the same physical path, as part of the virtual connection paradigm discussed in the previous chapter. Also, the ATM switches guarantee the cells in sequence for each connection during the switching process. Furthermore, data flow in each direction of a bi-directional virtual connection follows the same physical path (i.e., goes through the same set of ATM switches).

Routing, or finding a desirable route, may occur simultaneously with determining whether there are sufficient network resources to handle this connection. Using the above example, each switch determines whether it has sufficient resources to handle the connection through itself and if so, which outgoing link should be used based on routing and network resource information. Then, the switch at the next hop repeats the process until the next hop is the final destination (that is, endpoint B).

7.6 Call Negotiation and Renegotiation

Negotiation of bandwidth and QoS guarantees is possible between the ATM network and the ATM endpoints, as well as between two ATM endpoints. For example, endpoint A can specify a desired bandwidth B_d and a minimum acceptable bandwidth B_m. If the network cannot support the desired bandwidth B_d, but it can support a bandwidth B_a ($> B_m$), the network can offer B_a to A and B. The connection is established when both A and B accept the connection. Such negotiation can occur for other traffic or QoS parameters. For negotiation for multiple traffic and QoS parameters simultaneously in this way, the desired set of parameters collectively must have a strict order relationship. Furthermore, this negotiation approach can occur not only in traffic and QoS parameters, but also in service categories (one with guaranteed QoS and one without QoS guarantees, such as best effort service).

Negotiation can still occur for two sets of parameters that do not have strict ordering between them. This can be achieved by presenting two alternative sets of traffic and QoS parameters for the network to choose: one as primary and the other as the alternative.[1] The alternative set is used only if the primary set fails the connection setup, while the alternative set is acceptable to the network.

Similar negotiation can occur between two ATM endpoints. Since this kind of negotiation is on an end-to-end basis, only parameters that have end-to-end significance can be negotiated. For example, endpoint A would like to use a particular value for an end-to-end parameter (such as AAL PDU size) that cannot be supported by B. B can reply with a different value on the call acceptance message. The connection will not be established unless A also accepts with such a value. Since this is an end-to-end parameter, the network does not care about such negotiation and it is transparent to the network (except for carrying such a parameter between A and B).

Theoretically, the traffic and QoS parameters can be renegotiated after the connection has been setup. This is more difficult to support because the new set of parameters may exceed the network resources available, or require rerouting to get a better network utilization, because the network conditions have changed since the VC was set up. Such renegotiation support is expected to be standardized in the future.

7.7 VC Number and Translation

Since a VC must be set up before any ATM cells can be transmitted along the ATM network, each ATM cell transferred in the ATM network must belong to a particular VC. Otherwise, it will be dropped by the first ATM switch it encounters. Hence, the header of each ATM cell contains a VC number that uniquely identifies which VC it belongs. An ATM switch is required to drop any ATM cell that has a VC number not associated with any VC that the ATM switch knows.

How does one assign a VC number to a new VC? This might seem to be a simple question at first glance, but it requires a less obvious solution. To initiate a VC from endpoint A to endpoint B, A can assign a VC number that A has not been using for this new VC. However, problems occur when the same VC number has been used by an existing connection to endpoint B. In this case, B has no way to distinguish between ATM cells that arrives from the existing connection and those from the new connection originated from A. Similar problems can be envisioned for VC number conflicts at intermediate ATM switches along the path between A and B with other active VCs. Hence, the VC number assigned to each VC must be unique to avoid such VC number conflicts at every multiplexing point along the path (switches and endpoints).

One way to solve this is to require endpoint A to know all of the VC numbers that have been assigned in the ATM network before making its own assignment for new VCs. But this solution does not scale. It requires each endpoint in the ATM network to have access to global information about all current VC number assignments, which can change at any time as VCs get established and torn down continuously in the network. Furthermore, the number of VC numbers available decreases as more endpoints are added to the network using up more virtual connection numbers.

The solution to the VC number assignment problem is the realization that VC numbers do not need to be globally unique. In fact, we only need to make VC number unique locally on each physical link (multiplexing point). Furthermore, the VC number of a VC does not need to be same for on every physical link it passes through.

The solution can be shown using the example illustrated in Figure 7-8. When endpoint A wants to set up a new VC to endpoint B, an unused VC number on the link between A and the first switch (X) is assigned to the VC (say VC_1 = 16). For the link between switch X and the second switch along the VC route, another unused VC number (say VC_2 = 34) is chosen for the VC. Since the two VC numbers, VC_1 and VC_2, are not the same in general, a VC number translation table (or VC table) is required at switch X. The VC table maps incoming ATM cells with VC_1 = 16 (arriving on the input port connected to A) to VC_2 = 34 (and forward on the outgoing link to switch Y). In general, the VC table consists of an entry for each VC that passes through the ATM switch. Each entry consists of four parameters: incoming link (switch port), incoming VC number, outgoing link (switch port) and outgoing VC number. Every ATM switch has such a VC table for translating VC numbers for each connection through the switch. Furthermore, since the VC table also stores the outgoing link information for each VC from each incoming link, it is used by the switch to determine in real-time the outgoing link to which each ATM cell is destined; the VC table stores the routing information of *established* VCs. However, this routing information should not be confused with those for setting up *new* VCs, which is determined on a call-by-call basis by the routing function according to the traffic and QoS requirements and requires topological information about the ATM network.

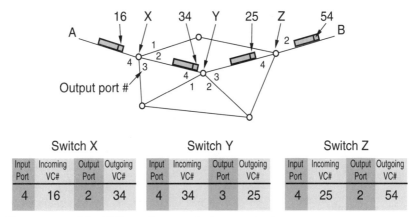

Switch X				Switch Y				Switch Z			
Input Port	Incoming VC#	Output Port	Outgoing VC#	Input Port	Incoming VC#	Output Port	Outgoing VC#	Input Port	Incoming VC#	Output Port	Outgoing VC#
4	16	2	34	4	34	3	25	4	25	2	54

Figure 7–8   The VC number translation approach.

This approach to VC number assignment and translation has two advantages. First, it solves the scalability problem because there is no need for global information before assigning a VC number on each link. Each entity only needs to guarantee uniqueness about the VC number used on its directly attached link. Second, by making the VC number with only local significance, it tremendously increases the number of VC number available for assignment. Otherwise, the total space of VC numbers available for assignment per endpoint will decrease as a function of number of attached endpoints in an ATM network. This VC translation approach is similar to the frequency reuse concept used in cellular phone network.

There is an interesting question about the VC number translation approach. If the VC numbers of a given VC are different at the two endpoints, A and B, how does B know the ATM cell containing the VC number it receives corresponds to the desired virtual connection from A? The truth is neither A nor B knows they are using different virtual connection numbers for the same VC. In fact, neither A nor B cares if they are different. All they care about is that the respective VC number is fixed at the beginning of the connection and does not change during the entire connection period. The reason is that when B receives the call setup from

A, B also gets assigned a VC number for the connection to be used on that link between B and its attached switch. B just keeps on using this VC number and it does not know that it is different from the one used by A. Similarly, A does not know B is using a different VC number either. Only the switches between A and B know that these VC numbers are different and they are responsible for the translation. Hence, VC numbers are of local significance only.

7.8 Virtual Channel and Virtual Channel Connection

We have discussed the notion of a VC used in ATM networks. We now are going to define a number of concepts and terms associated with the VC idea.

Each physical link in the ATM network is conceptually divided into a number of virtual channels. A virtual channel is a local concept for a particular link. Each virtual channel is identified by a *virtual channel identifier* (VCI). Any communication across a physical link must be assigned a virtual channel before any data (user or control) can be communicated over it. A virtual connection between two communicating parties is a concatenation of a sequence of virtual channels on the links along the physical route of the connection between the two parties. Hence, in ATM, a virtual connection is known as a *virtual channel connection* or VCC. A VCC is identified by a particular VCI on each link along the path and can change from link to link as discussed in the virtual connection number above.

As discussed before, the two directions of data flow of each connection follow the same physical path. Furthermore, the VCI assigned to a connection is the same for each direction. This simplifies the management of VCIs at each switch.

7.9 Virtual Path Connection

Consider an ATM switch at the backbone of a large ATM network. There can be thousands of VCs passing through the ATM switch, feeding from other ATM switches in the network. Since there is an entry for every VC in the VC table, this imposes significant requirements on memory and processing to add and remove every virtual connection. Actually, this problem is not unique to VC-based packet switched network like ATM, but is similar to any connection-oriented network including circuit switched networks.

In circuit switched networks such as the current telephone network, the switches at the center of the network also have thousands of voice connections passing through them. Managing so many connections independently requires tremendous resources. The solution in the PSTN is the introduction of crossconnect switches. Crossconnect switches differ from ordinary telephone switches in local central offices in that the former does not operate on individual connections, but on groups of connections. The idea is to group connections that have similar characteristics, especially those that have pairs of endpoints originating and terminating in the same two central offices (or switches). For example, let us consider a telephone switch (in reality, there is more than one) serving San Francisco and another switch serving New York. During normal hours, there must be many calls between San Francisco and New York. For a national backbone switch that connects these two cities, it can treat the group of calls between these two cities as a single group of connections. The crossconnect switch in the national backbone can be designed to operate on T1 (24 voice channels, or 1.544 Mbps) or DS-3 (28 T1 circuits, or 45 Mbsp) circuits. Calls between these two cities are grouped into T1 or DS-3 trunks. Whenever there are sufficient calls that exceed the current trunk (T1 or DS-3), a new trunk is assigned between these two cities. Hence, connection management problems are reduced by a factor of 24 (T1 trunks) or 672 (DS-3) for backbone using crossconnect switches.

Extending this basic concept of trunking connections to simplify backbone switching, ATM designers took the concept of the virtual connection one step further than that in the classic connection-oriented packet switched networks (such as X.25). In the telephone network, since all connections have identical traffic and QoS characteristics by definition (64 kbps circuits), the only characteristics that distinguish them are source and destination locations. In ATM networks, connections have much richer variety or traffic and QoS characteristics. The grouping of connections can be based on these characteristics as well. Hence, the notion of a virtual path (VP) is introduced in ATM to refer to a group of virtual channels that can have certain characteristics in common. The VP concept increases the flexibility and facilitates connection management in the ATM network. In parallel to the notion of VCC, a virtual path connection (VPC) consists of a concatenation of virtual paths in the physical links along the route.

Each VP on a link consists of a number of virtual channels and is identified by a unique identifier known as virtual path identifier (VPI). For the same reason as in VCC, VPI is translated at every ATM switch along its path. Hence, a virtual connection in the ATM is identified by two levels of identifiers: VPI and VCI. The VPI identifies which VP it belongs to, while the VCI identifies which virtual channel among the VP it actually represents. Note that VCI by itself no longer represents a VC uniquely, because the VP to which it belongs must be identified as well. Therefore, VPI/VCI pairs are part of the ATM cell header. The cell header is discussed in more detail in the next chapter.

Whereas VCCs are typically terminated at ATM endpoint, VPC are typically (but not always) terminated between ATM switches. This can be understood using the crossconnect example in telephone switches. T1 trunks originate and terminate at local phone switches and not at telephone customers because the telephone endpoints only operate at 64 kbps level. Similarly, VPCs are typically terminated at the ATM switches. However, VPCs can also terminate at ATM endpoints, because the ATM endpoints typically have much more capability than telephone endpoints and may need to have a VPC terminated (see discussion below on VPC usage).

An example of VPI translation of a VPC is shown in Figure 7-9, for which switch Y is a VP switch. It is important to note that since it is for a VPC, it treats all the VCCs within the VPC together as a single unit; so there is no need for VCI translation within the VPC for switch Y. As a result, the VP translation table is much smaller; it consists only of a VPI translation. This is similar to the simplification in crossconnect switches for the telephone network.

7.10 VCC and VPC Usage

Consider two ATM endpoints, A and B, in an ATM network that have an existing VCC between them. A would like to start another communications application with B. There are a number of choices for A, such as setting up a new VCC or using the existing VCC. The choice depends to a large extent on the traffic and QoS characteristics of the existing connection and those of the new application. To make these kind of decisions, we need to understand the usage of VCC and VPC in ATM networks in general. We discuss various applications of VCC and VPC in different scenarios below.

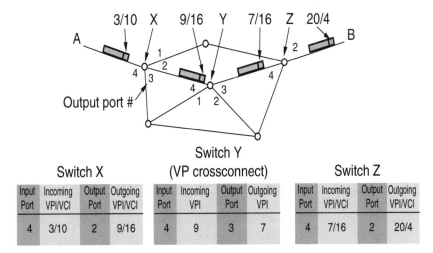

Figure 7–9   An example of VPI translation in ATM network.

7.10.1 One VCC for Multiple Applications

For non-real-time (best effort) applications that have the same two end-points, they can all share the same VCC between them. In the above example, there is no need for A to set up a new VCC; A can use the existing VCC to B for the new best effort application by multiplexing the two applications into the same VCC. (One needs a mechanism for demultiplexing multiple applications over the same VCCs, such as the IEEE LLC/SNAP mechanism discussed in RFC 1483.)[2] This kind of VCC usage is typical for supporting existing LAN traffic by multiplexing multiple protocols and applications into a single VCC. In this case, the ATM endpoints can be internetworking devices such as routers.

7.10.2 One VCC for Each Application

Theoretically, even for real-time applications, a single VCC can still be used as long as the VCC already takes into account the aggregate traffic and QoS requirements. However, evaluating the aggregate traffic and QoS requirements of multiple applications that have distinct requirements is a nontrivial problem. For example, one application might require a maximum delay of 1 ms and a cell delay variation of 100 microseconds, while the another might require only maximum delay of 100 microseconds and has no constraints in cell delay variation. There is no obvious way of specifying the combined requirements in an efficient way in general. Furthermore, there may not be a single physical path that can support both applications simultaneously, while there might be separate paths that satisfy them individually. Therefore, it might not be appropriate to force applications with different quality of service requirements to share the same VCC. For applications that have specific traffic and QoS requirements, a separate VCC typically is setup for each application.

7.10.3 Multiple VCCs for an Application

For an application that has multiple components, each with very distinct traffic and QoS requirements, the application can be supported by multiple VCCs, one for each component. An example is the video-conference application that involves audio and video components, which have different traffic and QoS requirements. Also, participants on the video conference might give distinct priority to the audio component over the video component. Two VCCs, one for each component, might be more suitable for this example. This is similar to the motivation for supporting multiple applications with different QoS requirements on separate VCCs.

7.10.4 One VPC per Application

Another way to support an application with multiple components with distinct QoS requirements is to set up a VPC for the application. Then, a VCC within this VPC is assigned to each component of the application. This forces all the VCCs (and hence all the components) to follow the same physical path. It is desirable for an application with synchronization requirements between different components to minimize differential delay between them. By forcing them to follow the same physical path, it removes the differential propagation delay (one of the key delay components) among the different components.

7.10.5 One VPC per Component

In an ATM network, one might want to manage connections with similar traffic and QoS requirements by grouping them into VCCs within the same VPC for the shared physical links. This is an extension to the cross-connect concept of grouping connections with similar sources and destinations geographically.

7.10.6 One VPC per Pair of Locations

The idea of traffic aggregation to simplify connection management is very important for the public network. As ATM is deployed both for public and private networks, there will be many VCCs requested from private ATM networks to public networks that go to similar destinations (such as other corporate locations across the country). We can assign VPCs among all corporate locations across the country for each corporation over the public ATM network. Furthermore, we can create virtual private networks by assigning VPCs between pairs of locations for each corporation. In this case, there are multiple VCCs within each VPC to support multiple simultaneous connections between two locations.

7.10.7 One VCC per Pair of Locations

For corporations that support only legacy data applications, best effort service is sufficient between corporation locations. Hence, instead of the VPC between each pair of locations, we can set up a VCC (that provides best effort service) between each pair of locations. Each VCC is responsible to support all the applications between the two locations. This is sufficient for applications with only best effort service requirements.[2] This is a generalization of the first usage above.

7.11 Summary

In this chapter, we gave an overview of how an ATM network operates, based on the principles of ATM discussed in the last chapter. We have discussed the standard interfaces within the ATM network: the UNIs and NNIs for private and public ATM networks. We also discussed how VPI and VCI are assigned and the VC and VP translation table operation. Finally, we discussed the concepts of virtual channel and virtual path connections and how they are be applied in various scenarios.

7.12 References

[1] The ATM Forum, *ATM User-Network Interface (UNI) Signaling Specification*, Version 4.0, 1996.

[2] J. Heinanen, "Multiprotocol Encapsulation over ATM Adaptation Layer 5," *IETF Request for Comments: 1483*, July 1993.

Chapter 8

The Protocol Reference Model of ATM

8.1 Introduction

In the last two chapters, we discussed the fundamental principles of ATM and presented an overview of ATM network operations. In this chapter, we proceed to a more formal discussion of ATM protocols using the Protocol Reference Model (PRM) introduced by ITU's B-ISDN standardization effort. The PRM provides an architectural framework for understanding how various functions of ATM protocols fit together. Such a framework is important for designing new protocols to support new services and applications based on ATM protocols.

Similar to the ISO's (International Standards Organization) OSI (Open System Interconnection) seven-layer model, ATM protocols also can be described by a layered architecture. We will first discuss the functions of each layer in detail. The key characteristic of the ATM layered model is a special unifying layer for both higher and lower layer protocols—the ATM layer. The ATM layer is shared among all protocols and applications above and different physical layer technologies below. Hence, the ATM protocol can be viewed as an hourglass model. We also discuss a new concept that distinguishes the PRM from the OSI model and is central to the ATM PRM model – the multi-plane model. Finally, we discuss the relationship of the PRM with the ISO's OSI model in both pure ATM networks and internetworking (with non-ATM networks) environments.

8.2 Layered Architecture

Conceptually, the ATM protocols can be divided into four layers: the physical layer, the ATM layer, the ATM adaptation layer (AAL) and higher layer protocols, as shown in Figure 8-1. The higher layer protocols include both ATM (such as ATM signaling protocols) and non-ATM protocols (such as TCP/IP).

However, the model in Figure 8-1 assumes that the ATM network is based on a switched point-to-point network. If ATM protocols are running over a shared medium such as the cable network, a MAC (media access control) protocol is required to support the ATM layer, as shown in Figure 8-2. Since ATM has been designed primarily for switched point-to-point networks, we assume in this book that there is no MAC layer unless we are explicitly discussing running ATM protocols over a shared medium type network (such as cable networks in Part III). However, we will briefly discuss the MAC layer later in this chapter. The functions of each layer are summarized in Table 8-1 and discussed in more detail next.

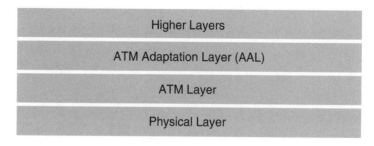

Figure 8–1   The ATM layered protocol model

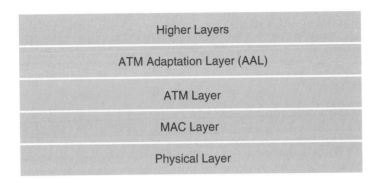

Figure 8–2   The ATM layered protocol model (for shared medium)

Table 8–1   *Functions provided by the different layers of the ATM layered protocol model[4, 10]*

Layer	Sublayers	Functions
Higher Layers		Applications (such as video on demand) Transport protocols (such as TCP) Internetworking protocols (such as IP) ATM protocols (such as signaling protocol)
AAL	Convergence sublayer	Mapping of higher layer PDUs to SAR sublayer Higher layer PDU delineation Other AAL services (depending on AAL types) to higher layer
	SAR sublayer	Segmentation and reassembly
ATM Layer		Cell header generation and extraction Cell VPI/VCI translation Cell multiplex and demultiplex Cell rate decoupling using unassigned cells (ATM Forum model)
MAC Layer*		Medium access control Generic flow control (GFC)

*optional

Table 8–1 *Functions provided by the different layers of the ATM layered protocol model[4,10] (continued)*

Layer	Sublayers	Functions
Physical Layer	Transmission convergence sublayer	Cell rate decoupling using idle cells (ITU model)
		HEC generation and verification
		Cell delineation
		Transmission frame adaptation
		Transmission frame generation and recovery
	PMD sublayer	Bit transmission capability: bit timing/ alignment, line coding, opto-electronic conversion
		Physical medium (such as copper, coaxial cable, fiber)

*The MAC layer is typically not explicitly discussed in ATM protocol model discussion and the MAC layer functions including the GFC are usually assumed to be part of the ATM layer, even though this is not strictly accurate.

8.2.1 Physical Layer

The physical layer of ATM protocols consists of two sublayers: the lower physical media dependent (PMD) sublayer and the higher transmission convergence (TC) sublayer, as shown in Figure 8-3.

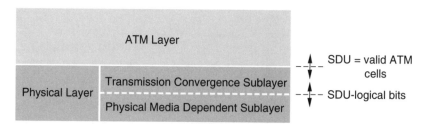

Figure 8–3 The physical layer model of ATM

The PMD sublayer provides the bit transmission capability on a physical medium and includes the physical medium itself. The physical medium can be copper (shielded and unshielded twisted pair, or UTP and STP), coaxial cable, fiber (single mode and multimode), or even wireless. The bit transmission capability includes bit transfer and bit alignment. It also may include line coding, opto-electronic conversion, modulation and demodulation functions to transfer bits on a particular medium. Since all these functions depend on the physical medium characteristics, they differ from medium to medium. Hence, this sublayer is the physical media dependent sublayer. Note that the PMD sublayer is responsible for only carrying raw bit information; all bits are identical for the PMD sublayer and any framing or overhead information belongs to the TC sublayer above. Hence, the information flow between the PMD and the higher TC sublayer are logical bits, as shown in Figure 8-3.

Since the PMD sublayer provides a logical bit interface to the TC sublayer, the TC sublayer is shielded from the characteristics of the physical medium. Hence, the TC sublayer can be defined independent of the underlying physical medium; the same TC sublayer can operate over different physical media.

The main function of the TC sublayer is to carry ATM cells from the ATM layer on the physical medium, given the bit transmission capability provided by the PMD sublayer. Since the TC sublayer is responsible for adapting the ATM layer into the particular physical medium, *it is the TC sublayer that enables the ATM layer to be truly media independent.*

The TC sublayer is responsible for creating a framing format using the basic bit streams provided by the PMD sublayer below. Such a framing format includes both overhead bytes and a payload envelope to carry the ATM cells. In addition, the TC sublayer provides a cell delineation function by preparing the cell flow at the transmitter to enable the receivers to recover the cell boundaries.

The Service Data Units or SDUs are the basic units of exchange between two adjacent layers, using the terminology from OSI's layered model. The SDUs exchanged at the boundary between the TC and ATM layers are valid ATM cells. Valid ATM cells are ATM cells that have no cell header errors. As discussed later in the chapter, the ATM cell header has a field known as a header error check (HEC) used to protect the cell header (see Figure 8-6). The TC sublayer is responsible for generating the HEC for each ATM cell at the transmitting side, while verifying any header errors based the HEC in the receiving side. Invalid ATM cells (those that have header errors according to the HEC verification) are dropped by the TC without passing to the ATM layer. Hence, HEC belongs to the physical layer (TC), not the ATM layer (see Figure 8-7).

In the ITU's B-ISDN model,[10] the physical layer also can provide cell rate decoupling function in the physical layer by inserting and extracting idle cells (physical layer) in order to adapt the cell rate at the boundary between the ATM layer and the physical layer to the available payload capacity of the transmission system used. This can apply to E3 and E4 physical interfaces used in Europe.

SONET is an example of a TC sublayer. It provides a number of functions: scrambling and descrambling, multiplexing and demultiplexing, and transmission frame generation and recovery. In addition, when used for carrying ATM cells, SONET also includes header error check (HEC) generation and verification for the ATM cell header, cell scrambling and descrambling and cell delineation.[4]

Although the physical layer for ATM has the classic meaning of a transmission link's physical properties and their ability to carry bits and framing, it has a significant implication for ATM. Unlike many other networking technologies that were designed on one particular physical interface, ATM is designed to run over many different media and at a variety of speeds. Many physical interfaces have been specified both for private and public ATM networks. They include a wide range of speed, physical media, framing formats and operating distances. The currently specified physical media are summarized in Table 8-2, including those under study. Table 8-2 also shows the physical media independence of the TC sublayer, as indicated by the same TC sublayer supported over different physical media. New physical layer interfaces are being defined at the standardization bodies for new environments for ATM.

There is a misconception that such a proliferation of physical media for ATM is a problem, as this implies a lack of a single standard for the ATM physical layer. However, to the contrary, the large number of physical interfaces available for ATM is actually one of its greatest strengths, because it allows the same ATM protocols to run over different environments such as LANs and WANs. Most environments have legacy wiring that is expensive to change and it is very desirable to define new physical layer interfaces based on those legacy wiring systems to simplify ATM deployment.

Table 8–2   *The ATM physical layer private and public UNI interfaces specified by the ATM forum*

UNI Physical Layer Interfaces

* Under study
** Depending on the region of the world, the distinction between private and public networks may not apply.

Private Network**				
Bit Rate	PMD: Physical Media	Distance	TC Sublayer (Framing)	Comments
25.6 Mbps / 32 Mbaud[1]	UTP-Category 3 (voice grade)	100m	Cell Stream	NRZI, 4B/5B encoding
51.84 Mbps[2]	UTP-Category 3	100m	STS-1	CAP modulation
51.84 Mbps[3]	Single Mode Fiber Multimode Fiber Coaxial pair	2 km 2 km 900 ft.	STS-1	
100 Mbps / 125 Mbaud[4]	Multimode Fiber	2 km	FDDI	NRZI, 4B/5B encoding
155.52 Mbps[5]	UTP-Category 5 (data grade)	100m	STS-3c	NRZ
155.52 Mbps[4]	Single Mode Fiber Multimode Fiber Coaxial pair	2 km 2 km 900 ft.	STS-3c	
155.52 Mbps/194.4 Mbaud[4]	Multimode Fiber STP	2 km 100m	cell stream	8B/10B encoding
155.52 Mbps*	UTP-Category 3	100m	STS-3c	
622.08 Mbps*	Multimode Fiber	300m	STS-12	

© 1996 The ATM Forum

Table 8–2 *The ATM physical layer private and public UNI interfaces specified by the ATM forum (continued)*

UNI Physical Layer Interfaces				
* Under study				
** Depending on the region of the world, the distinction between private and public networks may not apply.				
622.08 Mbps*	Single Mode Fiber	2 km	STS-12	
Public Network**				
1.544 Mbps[6]	Twisted Pair	3000 ft.	DS1	can also be used for Private UNI
2.048 Mbps*	Twisted Pair Coaxial pair	No distance specified	E1	
n x 1.544 Mbps*	Twisted Pair	under study	n x T1	
6.312 Mbps[7]	Coaxial pair	No distance specified	J2	Japanese Market
34.368 Mbps*	Coaxial pair	No distance specified	E3	
44.736 Mbps[4]	Coaxial pair	900 ft.	DS3	Can also be used as private UNI
51.840 Mbps[3]	Single Mode Fiber	15 km	STS-1	
155.520 Mbps[3]	Single Mode Fiber	15 km	STS-3c	
622.08 Mbps[3]	Single Mode Fiber	15 km	STS-12	

© 1996 The ATM Forum

8.2.2 The (Optional) MAC layer

The MAC layer of the layered protocol model of ATM is for supporting shared medium topology. This might seem to contradict one of the main ATM principles that states the use of a point-to-point meshed physical topology to provide high concurrent bandwidth availability. So why do we consider a shared medium topology for supporting ATM?

The reason is simple. There are legacy networks that have shared medium physical topologies, and they are not economically feasible to change to a point-to-point topology. An important example is the cable TV network's tree and branch architecture, which is a shared medium topology shared among many homes. (Supporting ATM over cable networks is discussed in detail in the Part III of this book). It is very expensive to rewire every home to a point-to-point topology in order to support ATM. Hence, to support ATM in such an environment, a MAC protocol layer is required. Note that the issue of supporting a shared medium topology usually occurs for the access network, because the backbone networks typically have a switched point-to-point topology.

Having said that, if it is economically possible to use a point-to-point topology, ATM should always be used as a point-to-point topology, without using a MAC protocol. Since ATM is assumed to be running over a point-to-point network, the MAC layer is typically not explicitly shown in the ATM protocol layer reference model.

The MAC layer is responsible for providing coordinated access to the shared medium for transferring ATM cells by the ATM endstations. The MAC layer shields the ATM layer from understanding the details of the shared medium; in fact, the ATM should not know that it is running over a shared medium. The SDUs communicated between the MAC layer and the physical layer are valid ATM cells (possibly encapsulated with additional MAC layer control information), as shown in Figure 8-4. The SDUs communicated between the MAC layer and ATM layer are ATM cells. From the ATM layer point of view, they are communicated to the physical layer, as the MAC layer acts as an emulated physical layer.

The MAC can consider the ATM cells stream offered by the ATM layer as a homogeneous cell stream; the MAC layer does not distinguish the ATM cells of different service classes or VCs. This is the same service that would have been offered by the physical layer to the ATM layer. It is up to the ATM layer to schedule the ATM cells of different VCs or service requirements before offering them to the MAC layer. Because of the shared medium, only a fraction of the bandwidth of the medium is available to the endpoint. Hence, the key effect of adding the MAC layer is offering a set of cell transmission opportunities at variable cell rate (a fraction of the cell rate at the physical layer) to the ATM layer, as opposed to

a fixed rate offered by the physical layer in a point-to-point switched network environment. (Alternatively, the slots provided by the MAC layer to
the endpoint's ATM layer are catergorized into different service classes. In
this case, the MAC layer distinguishes the cells submitted by the ATM
layer into different service categories, identified by their VPI/VCI values.
The MAC provides the scheduling needed to support the corresponding
service categories.)

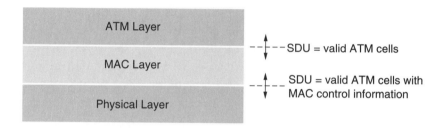

Figure 8–4   The MAC layer for ATM and relationship with adjacent layers at
an ATM endpoint

8.2.3 ATM Layer

Again, we assume in the following discussion that ATM is running over a
point-to-point network, unless stated otherwise. As shown in Figure 8-1,
the ATM layer is the second layer in the ATM layered protocol model.
The ATM layer is responsible for transferring all types of information:
user, control and management. User information includes higher layer
protocols and applications. All information is carried in the common 53-
octet ATM cell format in the ATM network, with a 5-octet header and a
48-octet payload. The ATM layer is responsible for transparently carrying
the 48-octet payload between two or more communicating entities over a
virtual connection across the ATM network. Such 48-octet payloads are
known as ATM service data units or ATM SDUs. They are passed
between the ATM layer and the AAL, as shown in Figure 8-5. Again, the
SDUs between the ATM and the physical layers are valid ATM cells.
Since the TC sublayer below the ATM layer is responsible for mapping
the ATM cells into different physical media, the ATM layer is physical
media independent.

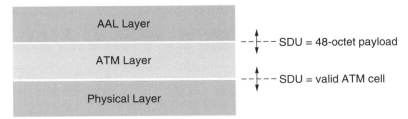

Figure 8–5   The ATM layer and its relationship with adjacent layers at an ATM endpoint

Next, we discuss the ATM cell format and the functions of the ATM layer in detail.

8.2.3.1   ATM Cell Format

The ATM cell format consists of a 5-octet header and a 48-octet payload. All information communicated across the ATM network is required to be encoded into the 48-octet payload of the ATM cell. It is the responsibility of the AAL to map different applications and protocols into the 48-octet payload. In general, the ATM layer functions are responsible for processing the header information, while the higher layer (AAL) is responsible for processing the ATM cell payload information. However, as we discuss next, some fields in the ATM cell header are actually processed by the physical and the MAC layers.

There are two different ATM cell formats. They are used at the UNIs and NNIs of the ATM network, as shown in Figure 8-6. They differ

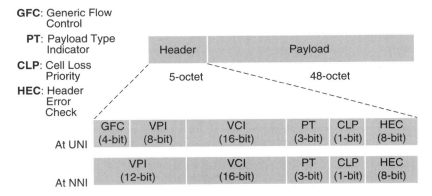

Figure 8–6   The ATM cell format at the UNI and NNI

only by the presence of a field in the header, the GFC field (generic flow control) in the UNI format, which reduces the size of VPI field accordingly.

At the UNI, the first field of the ATM cell format is the 4-bit GFC field. It is reserved for using ATM in shared medium networks as part of the MAC protocol. Hence, the GFC field actually belongs to the MAC layer. Since the NNI, which is between ATM switches, only applies to a point-to-point link, there is no MAC protocol. Hence, the ATM cell format for the NNI does not have the GFC field. For the UNI, the GFC field is only of local significance (at the UNI) and will be overwritten by the switches for the NNI.

The GFC field is currently undefined and is set to zero. According to the ITU standards, there are two modes of operations associated with the GFC field: controlled and uncontrolled access. Uncontrolled access is used for current ATM implementation of a point-to-point link between an ATM endpoint and an ATM switch, for which the GFC field is not used and set to zero. Controlled access is what the GFC field was designed for: flow control access to a shared medium using the GFC to communicate the states of the MAC protocol used on the shared medium. In this case, the GFC field is generally nonzero. However, controlled access is currently unspecified.

The two fields after the GFC field are the 8-bit VPI and 16-bit VCI fields, which identify the virtual path and virtual channel of the ATM cells, respectively. To reduce implementation costs at the user and network sides, not all bits in the VPI and VCI are required to be supported by the user and network sides. However, the user and network sides must agree during initial configuration to the minimum subsets of the VPI and VCI fields that they can both support. Such subsets for VPI and VCI must be contiguous bits and begin from the least significant bits. All other unassigned bits must be set to zero. Table 8-3 shows the specific VPI and VCI preassigned for specific uses.[4] For the NNI, there is a 12-bit VPI field instead of a VCI field, as there is no 4-bit GFC field. This provides more VPI space to support more VPs within the ATM network, which needs to support more VPs than at the UNI. Hence, the 4-bit GFC field becomes part of the larger VPI field.

Table 8–3 *VPI and VCI values dedicated for specific functions*

Usage	VPI values	VCI values
Unassigned cell indication	0	0
Meta-signaling (default)	0	1
Meta-signaling	1–255	1
General Broadcast Signaling (default)	0	2
General Broadcast Signaling	1–255	2
Point-to-point and point-to-multipoint signaling (default)	0	5
Point-to-point and point-to-multipoint signaling	1–255	5
Segment OAM F4 flow cell	appropriate VP	3
End-to-end OAM F4 flow cell	appropriate VP	4
Interim Local Management Interface (ILMI) (default)	0	16
Interim Local Management Interface (ILMI)	1–255	16

The ATM layer can be viewed as comprising two sublayers—the lower VP sublayer and the upper VC sublayer. They correspond to the concepts of virtual path (VPCs) and virtual channel connections (VCCs), respectively. We can describe the physical link on which the ATM cells flow as carrying multiple VPCs. Each VPC in turn carries multiple VCCs across the ATM network. Hence, from the VCC point of view, it is being carried over a virtual network of VPCs. This interpretation of VPCs and VCCs is useful not only for conceptual understanding, but also for real applications. In a public ATM network, one can create many virtual private networks for individual corporations. As discussed in the last chapter, each private virtual network is made up of VPCs connecting different corporate locations of a company. Within each VPC, applications requiring QoS guarantees can be carried in different VCCs with the VPC. For supporting legacy data applications, one can even build a virtual private network by using VCCs instead of VPCs for the connection of multiple locations. In this case, each VCC is used for multiplexing all the applications carried between the locations.

The next field in the ATM cell header is the 3-bit PT (payload type indicator). The PT is primarily used to distinguish between user and non-user ATM cells. Non-user ATM cells include those for OAM (operations, administration and management) and traffic management. As shown in Table 8-4,[4] code points 0 to 3 are for user cells, which are further distinguished by the SDU-type of the cell and whether the congestion state was experienced for the VC. SDU-type can be used by the higher layer (i.e., AAL) to indicate the location of the cell within the AAL-PDU. As discussed later in the AAL chapter, SDU-type 0 indicates the ATM cell is not the last cell for the AAL type 5 PDU, while SDU type 1 refers to the last cell of such a PDU. For each SDU type, the PT can further be used to indicate whether the ATM cell experiences any congestion along the path (see the traffic management chapter). PT = 4 and 5 are for OAM (operation, administration and management) cells. PT = 6 is for traffic management cells. PT = 7 is reserved for future use.

Table 8–4   *Payload type indicator encoding*

Payload Type Coding	Interpretation		
	Payload type		
000	User data cell	Congestion not experienced	SDU-type = 0
001			SDU-type = 1
010		Congestion experienced	SDU-type = 0
011			SDU-type = 1
100	OAM cell	Segment F5 flow related	
101	OAM cell	End-to-end F5 flow related	
110	Traffic management cell	Resource management (RM) cell	
111	Reserved		

The Cell Loss Priority (CLP) bit is used to explicitly indicate the cell loss priority of the cell for a particular VCC, which can be used to selectively cell discard in the ATM switch or endpoint. CLP = 0 indicates a high priority cell, while CLP = 1 indicates a low priority cell. A CLP = 1 cell is subject to discard by an ATM switch under heavy load or network congestion at the switch. The ATM endpoints can assign the value of the CLP to indicate the relative priority of the data. The network can change the CLP from 0 to 1 for ATM cells that exceed their traffic contract. The traffic contract is the network resource (such as peak and average bandwidth) that the ATM network has agreed to provide to the connection when it was set up and acknowledged by the users. Changing the CLP from 0 to 1 as a result of the user violating the traffic contract is called cell tagging. Tagged cells are typically dropped when there is congestion in the network. However, CLP = 1 cells in general must be carried in order with the rest of the cells of the connection because they must guarantee sequential delivery of all ATM cells for each connection. This implies that CLP = 1 cells are queued in the same queue of the CLP = 0 in the same connection.

The 8-bit header error check (HEC) is for detecting and correcting (optional) a single bit error in the ATM cell header (excluding ATM payload). Cell header error control is important to prevent misrouting and minimize the cell loss due to cell header errors (which can lead to cell dropping or misrouting).

It is interesting to note that even though the 8-bit HEC belongs to the ATM cell header, it is the responsibility of the physical layer to process (generate and check) it. In fact, not all the fields of the ATM cell header belong to the ATM layer (processed by ATM layer protocols). We have seen that the GFC field is processed by the MAC layer for running over a shared medium network. The rest of the fields of the ATM cell header belong to the ATM layer (see Figure 8-7).

8.2.3.2   ATM Layer Functions at the UNI

According to ATM Forum UNI 3.1,[4] there are a number of ATM layer functions at the UNI:

Multiplexing ATM connections   Different ATM connections (VPCs and VCCs) are multiplexed across an UNI at the ATM layer. These ATM connections can be of different ATM service categories. Hence, the ATM layer offers a single cell stream as SDUs for the physical layer.

Cell rate decoupling   Since the rate of assigned ATM cells (i.e., cells with valid payload from higher layers) generated by the transmitting side of the UNI may be lower than the link rate capacity of the UNI (physical

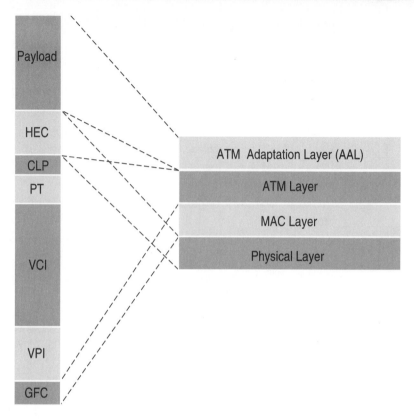

Figure 8–7 A mapping of the ATM cell format (UNI) to the ATM layered model

layer), additional cells may need to be inserted to the non-contiguous assigned cell stream to transform them into a continuous cell stream. The cell rate decoupling function is responsible for inserting unassigned cells at the transmitting side of the UNI and extracting them at the receiving end of the UNI. The cell rate decoupling function is not necessary for all physical layer interfaces. Cell rate decoupling only applies to physical layers that require continuous cell streams from the ATM layer, such as SONET, DS3 and 8B/10B block coded interfaces. It is not needed for those with asynchronous cell time slots such as 4B/5B block coded interfaces. Unassigned cells have a well-defined cell header formats (GFC, VPI, VCI and CLI all zeros, see Table 8-3). Note this cell rate decoupling at the ATM layer using unassigned cells is based on the The ATM Forum's UNI model. This is different from the ITU model, which achieves cell rate decoupling at the physical layer using the idle cells (which are physical layer cells and have no specific ATM cell header format).

Cell discrimination   The ATM cell header can be used to indicate different types of ATM cells using predefined VPI/VCI and PTI values, as shown in Table 8-3 and Table 8-4, respectively. The following VPI/VCI values are predefined for the following usages: unassigned ATM cells (VPI/VCI = 0/0), meta-signaling (VCI = 1), point-to-point signaling (VCI = 5) and ILMI (integrated local management interface) messages (VCI = 16). For meta-signaling, general broadcast signaling and ILMI messages, the VPI = 0 is the default value used for communication between the user and the directly connected ATM switch across the UNI, while other VPI values are reserved for other pairs of entities (such as other users or remote networks). Signaling and OAM protocols are discussed in more detail below and in the signaling chapter.

Cell header generation/extraction   Since the ATM layer is terminated at the user side of the UNI, the ATM cell header (the ATM layer protocol control information or PCI) is generated during cell transmission and extracted during cell reception.

Loss priority indication and selective cell discarding   As discussed above, this is achieved by the CLP bit on the ATM cell header.

Traffic shaping   This allows the user to control the cell generation process to meet the traffic contract agreed for the ATM connection. Traffic shaping involves a cell-pacing algorithm on a per virtual connection basis.

In addition to the UNI functions, the ATM layer also is responsible for VPI/VCI translation within the ATM switches. These ATM layer functions are summarized in Table 8-1.

8.2.4 ATM Adaptation Layer (AAL)

The AAL is the third layer of the ATM protocol model. While all information is carried by the same 48-octet payload of ATM cells across the ATM network, almost all information does not come in 48-octet size. Since it is a universal problem for ATM to adapt all information into the fixed size 48-octet payloads, ATM designers defined the common protocol layer for mapping different information types into the ATM layer. Hence, this is called the ATM adaptation layer (AAL).

The AAL consists of two sublayers: the segmentation and reassembly (SAR) sublayer and the convergence sublayer (CS). The CS, the higher sublayer, is responsible of encapsulating the PDU from the higher layer protocols above (which can be applications, services or protocol stacks) for carrying over the ATM network. In addition, it can provide error control and data delineation functions. The SAR sublayer, the lower sublayer, is responsible for segmentation of CS-PDU into 48-octet units for carriage as the ATM cell payload in the ATM layer. At the receiving end, the SAR sublayer performs the reverse operation, i.e., reassembly of the 48-octet payload from the ATM layer to the CS-PDU. Hence, the SAR is responsible for making the ATM layer application-independent by performing the mapping functions of application data of different lengths.

In addition, since different application classes have different networking requirements (such as error, delay and end-to-end timing), there is more than one type of AAL defined. Different types of AAL are defined to support different types of applications. The currently defined AAL types are: AAL 1, AAL 3/4 and AAL 5. AAL 5 is the most popular AAL type because it is used for ATM signaling protocols and data communications. AAL will be discussed in detail in the next chapter.

8.2.5 Higher Layer Protocols

Above the AAL is a collection of ATM protocols and non-ATM protocols, as well as applications. An important ATM protocol carried above the AAL is the ATM signaling protocol, which is responsible for connection setup and tear down. Many non-ATM protocols can be supported over AAL, such as TCP/IP. Applications can be carried directly over ATM without any intermediate protocol stack. For example, MPEG II protocol can be carried over AAL5.[8]

8.3 The Hourglass Model

As shown in the last section, the ATM layer protocol with a fixed size cell format has been designed to run on many different physical layer interfaces, such as copper, coaxial cable and fiber and even wireless environments. At the same time, the ATM layer is designed to support all types of applications using different AAL types. As discussed above, the TC sublayer is responsible for making the ATM layer physical medium independent, while the AAL is responsible for making ATM layer application independent. Hence, conceptually, we can represent the common ATM layer as hourglass model as shown in Figure 8-8. This is central to the ATM paradigm to have a unifying protocol to support all applications over different physical media (at different speeds).

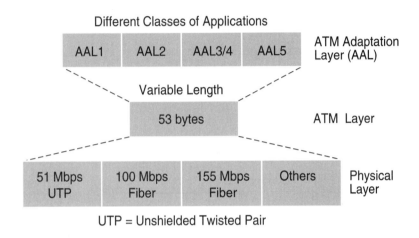

Figure 8–8   The ATM hourglass model

8.4 Multi-Plane Model

The OSI seven-layer model from the ISO was designed to provide an interoperability model between packet switched networks for *data* communications. As the ITU (previously known as the CCITT) tried to design the B-ISDN to support a variety of applications to carrying different information types (such as audio and video) in addition to only data, the OSI model became insufficient. Furthermore, the OSI model does not address the issue of connection-oriented services and connection control protocols to support them. (Note that although ITU had designed connection-oriented protocols such as X.25, there was no distinctive virtual connection to support connection control and user information.)

As part of designing the protocols to support B-ISDN, the ITU has defined the formal protocol reference model (PRM). Although there are similarities between the OSI and the formal PRM of B-ISDN in sharing the layered model concepts, the PRM has an added dimension – the plane concept (see Figure 8-9). In addition to the three basic layers discussed above, the ATM protocols also are organized into different protocol planes: user, control and management. They represent user data transfer protocols, signaling protocols for call/connection control and management protocols, respectively. It is important to note that though the OSI model does not have a separate plane for control information, it does require exchanging control information. It sends control information in the same way as it sends user information. In other words, signaling is in-band in the OSI model, while B-ISDN uses out-of-band signaling. (Note that the separation of user and control information occurred first in ISDN using B and D channels, respectively.)[9]

It is interesting to note that the partition of the user and control planes occurs at the AAL and above, but not at the ATM layer or physical layer. That is because the ATM layer does not care about the payload of the ATM cells, whether it is control or user cells. They are multiplexed at the ATM layer over different VCCs (using distinct VPI/VCI). The partition of the management plane to both user and control occurs at all layers because every layer requires management protocol support.

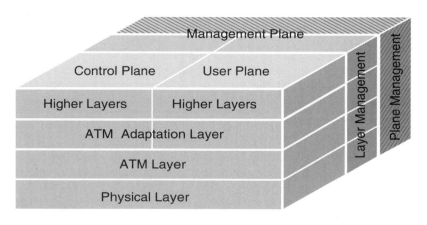

Figure 8–9   The B-ISDN ATM protocol reference model (PRM)[10]

8.4.1   User Plane

For the AAL and higher layers, the protocol functions are divided into the user and control planes. The user plane refers to the protocols for exchanging user data between ATM endpoints as well as switches. The user plane consists of the layered architecture discussed earlier. User plane protocols are carried only over pre-established virtual connections (VPCs and VCCs). The user plane also includes the various traffic management protocols such as congestion control and error recovery.

8.4.2 Control Plane

The control plane consists of protocols used for call and connection control—the signaling protocol. The signaling protocol is responsible for setting up and tearing down connections. It also includes adding parties to and dropping parties from a multiparty connection. These dynamic connections controlled by the signaling protocols are known as switched VCs (SVCs). Similar to the user plane, the control plane also consists of the basic layered architecture discussed above. In other words, the signaling protocols also run on the AAL transferred as ATM cells over the ATM network. The ATM signaling protocols are discussed in a later chapter.

8.4.3 Management Plane

The management plane in the PRM includes all the management protocols for ATM. In addition to classic network management functions, the management protocols also include connection control functions in a permanent virtual connection (PVC) environment. PVCs are set up and torn down by the management protocol, similar to the way the signaling protocol set up and tears down SVCs.

The management plane consists of two management aspects: layer management and plane management. Layer management consists of protocols for managing individual layers in the ATM layered architecture: physical layer, ATM layer and AAL. It handles operations, administration and maintenance (OAM) information flows specific to the particular layer. The ATM Forum UNI 3.1 (and 4.0) defines a set of management functions known as the interm (later renamed integrated) local management interface (ILMI) functions that specify a number of OAM flows, which are part of layer management for the ATM layer for the user plane. The meta-signaling protocol, a management plane protocol, is used to set up the signaling channel. Hence, meta-signaling protocols belong to the management plane, while the signaling protocols belong to the control plane.

Plane management consists of protocols for managing the various planes: user, control and management planes. In other words, plane management performs management functions for the entire ATM system as a whole and has no layered structure.

8.5 B-ISDN PRM and ISO OSI Reference Model

Given our understanding of the PRM of ATM protocols, how does this model relate to the famous ISO OSI seven-layer model? It is important to point out that there are still ongoing debate in the interpretation of such relationship. Nevertheless, in this section, we present an interpretation that is most logical to the author. Some of the ideas in this section are based on [11].

To understand the relationship between the PRM and the OSI model, it is important to keep the following two ideas in mind:

- The PRM is designed to support all types of (real-time and non-real-time) applications carrying all information types (time-based and non-time-based), while the OSI model was designed for data communications over a packet switched network only.
- The interpretation of the relationship between the B-ISDN PRM and OSI depends on the following two environments of the deploying ATM networks: homogeneous and heterogeneous. Homogeneous refers to deploying a pure ATM network, while heterogeneous refers to interconnecting an ATM network with other networking technologies. These two environments are discussed next.

8.5.1 Pure ATM Networks

Understanding the relationship between the PRM and OSI for the pure ATM network environment is important for designing the end-system software architecture to optimize the usage of ATM networks.

A logical interpretation of the relationship can be made by mapping the functions of the different layers of the PRM to the OSI model. This was observed by Staalhagen[11] and Table 8-5 shows an extension of his interpretation. The function-by-function mapping clearly indicates that the PRM physical layer, with lower PMD and high TC sublayer, actually map to both the physical layer and data link layer of the OSI model. The MAC layer of the PRM also maps to the datalink layer of OSI. The ATM layer maps to the OSI network layer (with the minor exception of the cell rate decoupling function under the ATM Forum model). This should not be surprising given that the ATM layer is responsible for cell switching and multiplexing/demultiplexing. To be exact, the OSI network layer consists of two sublayers: the lower subnetwork and higher internetwork sublayers. The subnetwork layer refers to the networking layer of a given networking technology, in this case the ATM layer of the BISDN. The internetwork sublayer applies to the internetworking (heterogeneous environment discussed below) of multiple networking technologies by a common internetworking layer, for which the Internet Protocol (IP)[12] is a prime example. In a pure ATM network environment, the OSI internetwork sublayer is null and there is only the subnetwork sublayer, which maps to the ATM layer.

The AAL maps to the transport layer of the OSI because AAL is processed only on an end-to-end basis. Furthermore, it includes the error control functions found in the transport layer.

8.5.2 Internetworking

Since the ATM technology is still in the early deployment stage, the majority of the environment for which ATM will be deployed requires internetworking with existing networking technologies. As a result, interoperability issues for ATM with other networking technologies are very critical for the successful deployment of any ATM network. This requires an understanding of the relationship between the PRM and OSI in the heterogeneous environment. We will discuss an important internetworking environment for deploying ATM with legacy LANs to support IP.

8.5.2.1   Internetworking with Legacy LANs using IP

IP is an internetworking technology that runs on different network technologies (link layer). IP is carried over different legacy networks such as Ethernet through a thin layer of ARP (address resolution protocol) that maps an IP address to the link layer address.[13] Figure 8-10 shows the networking topology for internetworking between ATM and legacy network to support IP end-to-end. One way of supporting IP across an ATM network is to treat the ATM network as a layer 2 technology similar to Ethernet from the IP point of view. Beneath the IP layer, there is an ARP layer for both legacy networks and ATM. For ATM, the ARP layer is also known as the "IP over ATM" layer.[14] Below the IP over ATM layer are AAL and ATM layers. There is more than one model to support IP over ATM networks. They include LAN Emulation (LANE),[15] and Multiprotocol over ATM (MPOA).[16] They are beyond the scope of this book. Readers are encouraged to consult the references listed.

Table 8–5 *A mapping of B-ISDN PRM to the ISO OSI seven-layer reference model.*

B-ISDN PRM	Sublayers	Functions	OSI Reference Model
Higher layers		Various services and applications	Session layer and higher
AAL	Service specific CS	Reliability with retransmission (SSCOP for signaling)	Transport layer
	Common part CS	Framing and end to end verification; Higher layer PDU delineation	Transport layer
	SAR	Segmentation and reassembly	Transport layer
		Multiplexing of CPCS connection in AAL3/4	Transport layer
ATM		Cell header generation/extraction	Network layer
		Cell switching	Network layer
		Cell multiplexing and demultiplexing	Network layer
		Cell VPI/VCI translation	Network layer
		Cell rate decoupling (ATM Forum model)	Data Link layer
MAC		Generic Flow Control	Data Link layer
Physical	TC	Cell rate decoupling (ITU model)	Data Link layer
		HEC generation/verification	Data Link layer
		Cell delineation	Data Link layer
		Transmission frame adaptation	Data Link layer
		Transmission frame generation/recovery	Data Link layer
	PMD	Bit timing	Physical layer
		Physical medium	Physical layer

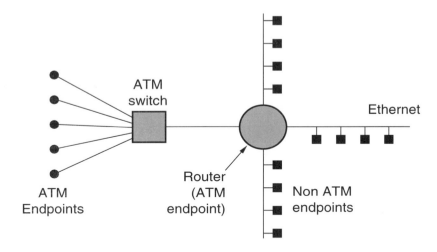

Figure 8–10   An internetwork consisting of both an ATM network and a non-ATM network connected by a router

8.6 Summary

In this chapter, we presented the layered protocol model of ATM. We gave an overview of the characteristics and functions of the different layers of the ATM protocol stack. Then, we discussed the protocol reference model of ATM defined by ITU. The PRM is very important for understanding how various ATM functions fit together in a framework. We also showed that ATM can be viewed as an hourglass model. Furthermore, we demonstrated how ATM can internetwork with other networking protocols by showing the relationship between the PRM and the OSI model.

8.7 References

[1]The ATM Forum Technical Committee, Physical Interface Specification for 25.6 Mb/s over Twisted Pair Cable, Nov.7, 1995.

[2]The ATM Forum, ATM 52 Mb/s Category 3 UTP.

[3]ANSI, T1.646.

[4]The ATM Forum, ATM User-Network Interface Specification, Version 3.1, Prentice Hall, 1995.

[5]The ATM Forum, ATM 155 Mb/s Category 5 UTP.

[6]The ATM Forum, DS1 PHY v1.0 Specification.

[7]The ATM Forum, 6,312 Kbps UNI v1.0 Specification.

[8]The ATM Forum, Audio Visual Multimedia Specification for Video on Demand, Version 1.0, 1996.

[9]ITU-T Recommendation I.320, ISDN Protocol Reference Model, 1988.

[10]ITU-T Recommendation I.321, B-ISDN Protocol Reference Model and its Applications, 1991.

[11]L. Staalhagen, "A Comparison between the OSI Reference Model and the B-ISDN Protocol Reference Model," *IEEE Network,* January/February 1996, pp. 24-33.

[12]RFC 791, "The Internet Protocol," *DARPA Internet Program Protocol Specification,* Sept. 1981.

[13]D. Comer, Internetworking with TCP/IP, Vol.1, Third Edition, Prentice Hall, 1996.

[14]M. Laubach, Classical IP over ATM and ARP, RFC 1577.

[15]The ATM Forum, LAN Emulation Specification, Version 1.0, 1995.

[16]The ATM Forum, Multi-Protocol over ATM Specification, Version 1.0, 1997.

Chapter 9

ATM Adaptation Layer

9.1 Introduction

The ATM protocols have been designed to support a wide range of applications with diverse communications requirements. The ATM network, or more specifically the ATM layer, uses fixed size protocol data units (PDUs), the 53-octet ATM cells, to carry all types of information (time-based or non-time-based) from any application (real-time or non-real-time). Since different applications (including protocols) generate different data block sizes, an adaptation function is required to convert different application data unit (ADU) sizes into the ATM cell formats. As this function is common to all applications, the ATM protocols specify a new layer of protocol above the ATM layer, the ATM Adaptation Layer (AAL) to support this function. As discussed in the last chapter, the AAL provides the key mechanism for ATM protocols to support a wide variety of applications using the same ATM cell structure across the network. The objective of this chapter is to discuss the AAL in detail.

169

In addition to the variations in ADU size, the traffic and QoS requirements of different applications vary significantly (as discussed in detail in Part I). Although ultimately it is the responsibility of the core ATM network (the set of ATM switches) to satisfy the communications requirements of an application, there are certain functions that can be provided by the AAL at the end-stations to alleviate these requirements for the network. There are different AAL types designed to address different requirements of applications, as shown in Figure 9-1. Since all ADUs will be segmented by any one of these AAL types into the same fixed size ATM cell service data unit, SDU (48 octets), for transmission over the ATM network, this allows a unified transport and switching mechanism to support all applications at the ATM layer.

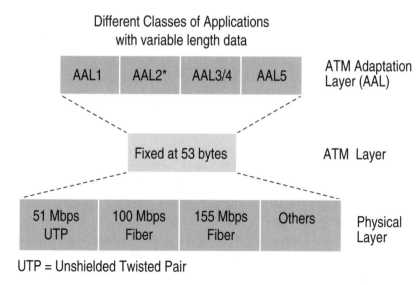

Figure 9–1   The basic ATM protocol stack

In this chapter, we first discuss the role of AAL in the end-to-end ATM protocol model. Then, we describe the major functions of AAL. After that, we explain the various AAL types in detail. Finally, we provide a summary to compare the different AAL types.

9.2 End-to-end ATM Protocol Model

Since the ATM protocols are based on the fast packet switching principle, unnecessary processing of user information is avoided within the

ATM network to improve switching performance. Furthermore, there is no need to interpret the user payload by the ATM switches, especially once the VC has been setup. Hence, the AAL processing for user information occurs only at the sending and receiving ATM endpoints and not within the ATM network (that is, not at the ATM switches). This allows the ATM switches to concentrate on cell switching and not AAL processing of user information. This is illustrated by the ATM end-to-end protocol reference model used to transfer user information in Figure 9-2. Otherwise, the AAL processing can significantly increase the network processing requirements and introduce bottlenecks, as it involves segmentation and reassembly of user data units to and from the ATM cell payload, respectively.

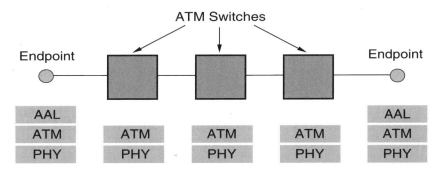

Figure 9–2   End-to-end ATM protocol model for user information transfer

In addition to the user plane information, both the control and management plane messages require AAL processing because they also are carried in ATM cells across the ATM network. Figure 9-3 shows the ATM protocol reference model discussed in the last chapter. The control and management plane information is communicated between ATM endpoints *and* the ATM network (the ATM switches) and also within the ATM network (among the ATM switches). In the other words, the ATM switches can send and receive these control and management messages. Hence, the ATM switches do need to process AAL functions for control plane and management plane messages, even though they do not process the AAL functions for the user plane. This is acceptable because control and management traffic constitutes a very small percentage (typically less than 1%) of the overall traffic. Hence, such AAL processing has a minimal impact on the performance of the ATM switches for fast cell switching. Furthermore, the termination of control and management messages and the corresponding AAL processing functions are typically implemented separate from the fast cell switching functions in the ATM switches. (Nevertheless, there is a potential performance issue in terms of call control performance such as call setup latency and number of calls per second, which can be limited by the processing power on the switch. In any case, this call control performance is not related to the AAL processing, because they are part of signaling protocol processing above the AAL.)

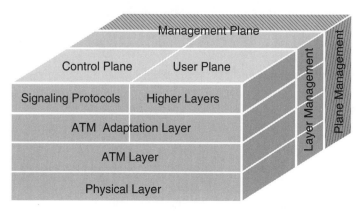

Figure 9–3   The ATM protocol reference model

Note that the switches cannot avoid interpreting the control messages because they are fundamental to setting up and managing a connection through the switches. Similarly, management messages are critical to the management of the ATM network.

9.3 AAL Functions

To support different classes of applications in the ATM network, the AAL provides a number of important functions to satisfy the diverse application requirements. In this section, we discuss the various functions that can be provided by the AAL. In general, only a subset of these functions is present in each AAL type, because each AAL type was designed for a specific set of application requirements.

9.3.1 Segmentation and Reassembly

Since most ADU and higher layer protocol data unit (PDU) lengths are not 48 octets long and many of them are larger, a segmentation function is provided by the AAL to convert them into 48-octet packets for transmission in the ATM cell payload. We refer to the data units offered to AAL (the ATM network) as the AAL-SDUs (service data units), while the control information added by the AAL is called the protocol control information (PCI). Conversely, at the receiving ATM endpoint, the AAL provides the inverse function to reassemble them back to their original sizes. This AAL function is known as the segmentation and reassembly (SAR). On the other hand, if these ADUs are fewer than 48 bytes less the AAL overhead (control headers and trailers), the AAL fills up the ATM cell payload with padding bytes (or combine multiple ADU/PDUs into a 48-byte payload).

In reality, there are limits to the size of AAL-SDUs that can be handled by the AAL. The AAL-PDU (AAL-SDU plus AAL-PCI) is the basic transmission or reception unit for an endpoint, as supported by the AAL. If the AAL-PDU is too long, then the probability of corruption (due to transmission bit errors, cell loss, or corruption) increases correspondingly. Note that the ATM layer does not provide a retransmission mechanism for individual ATM cells. Also, the larger the AAL-PDU, the more data will be lost when the entire AAL-PDU is dropped due to a detected error. (Although forward error correction, or FEC, can be implemented for data recovery, FEC is expensive and adds overhead to the AAL. Hence, FEC is only used for selected applications.) Even if the AAL-PDU can be retransmitted, a large amount of data needs to be retransmitted, wasting significant network bandwidth. Therefore, the SDU size is limited for AAL types by design, such as 64 Kbytes for both AAL 5 and AAL 3/4 PDUs. (Note that this limitation of AAL-SDU size is not unique to ATM networks; Ethernet limits its SDUs to about 1500 bytes long.)

For large data transfers, such as files or video delivery, each data is divided into multiple AAL-SDUs. This is the function of a higher layer protocol such as the IP layer in the TCP/IP protocol. The IP layer segments the blocks of data into less than 9188 Kbytes by default, in the case of using classical IP over ATM protocol.[1]

9.3.2 Reduction of CPU Processing Overhead

The AAL also serves the function of reducing CPU processing overhead to handle individual cell payloads of 48 octets. In a PC or a workstation, the general purpose CPU is accustomed to processing much larger

PDUs than 48 octets. The smaller the data unit, the larger the *number* of PDUs that require CPU processing (higher the frequency of arriving loads to the CPU), for the same amount of total data. If we require a general purpose CPU to process each ATM cell's payload, we have to increase the CPU protocol processing power requirement by up to 3 orders of magnitude.

By providing the SAR function and handling the individual cells directly, the AAL allows the CPU to handle a much larger PDU (as large as 10s Kbytes long) for transmission over the ATM network. This allows the CPU to be interrupted on the AAL-PDU basis and not on an ATM cell basis when communicating across the ATM network. Furthermore, cell-by-cell AAL processing can be achieved by specialized hardware, such as on an ATM network interface card (NIC) inserted to the PC.

9.3.3 Error Control Mechanisms

Errors in the ATM network can take the form of bit errors and cell losses. Bit errors are caused mainly by transmission errors on the links and, to a lesser extent, the processing errors at the ATM switches or endpoints. Bit errors can corrupt the cell header and the payload. Data corruption for the AAL-PDU can be caused not only by bit errors in the cell payload, but also by those in the cell header. If the bit error in the cell header is detected by the HEC field at an ATM switch, the cell will be dropped (unless a header bit error correction mechanism is provided by the switch). Cell dropping results in AAL PDU corruption. Undetected bit errors in the cell header at the switch can lead to misrouting of ATM cells to a different destination. This is equivalent to a cell loss for the VC, and hence AAL-PDU corruption. Furthermore, this in turn might also lead to a mistaken merging of this corrupted ATM cell with another active ATM cell stream of another VC, resulting in corrupting an AAL-PDU for that VC. Hence, in this case, a cell header corruption affects more than one VC.

Cell losses are caused by dropped or misrouted cells at the ATM switches. Since ATM is based on packet switching, the indeterministic cell arrivals may cause buffer overflows at the ATM switches during congestion or temporary overload. Cells also can be dropped even when there are buffers available because they may exceed the traffic contract and are dropped by the policing functions on the switch. Another cause of dropped cells is the detection of bit errors in the cell header by the ATM switches, which are checked at every ATM switch. It is an optional functionality for ATM switches to correct a single bit error in a cell header. As discussed above, cell misrouting is caused by undetected cell header corruption.

Hence, a key function of the AAL is to provide error control mechanisms for a wide variety of applications that require different levels of error protection. Since the ATM layer has error protection only for the cell header information (mandatory bit error detection and optional bit error correction), additional error protection for the cell payload (AAL-PDUs) caused by either cell losses or bit errors is required for many applications. Since different applications have different error constraints in terms of cell loss and bit errors, different AAL types can be designed to support different types of applications. Such error control mechanisms can use error detection or error correction on a combination of a per bit, per cell, or per AAL frame basis. The error control mechanisms for the AAL also can provide retransmission of corrupted AAL frames, such as the AAL used for signaling, to provide reliable data delivery.

9.3.4 Synchronization and Clock Recovery

The AAL also can provide timing information for synchronization. Timing information is critical for real-time streaming applications, such as video conferencing. Real-time streaming applications deliver data in a continuous fashion for a period of time. Since the receiver is expected to process the data continuously at the same rate, it must synchronize its local clock to the sender's clock. Otherwise, as data arrives, the differences between average cell arrival rate (on average equal to the average cell generation rate at the source) and the average receiver processing rate can lead to receiver buffer overflow or underflow over a period of time, leading to data loss. To ensure the sender's and receiver's rates are as close as possible, the sender and receiver must have synchronized clocks within sufficient accuracy that can be tolerated by the receiver.

One way of achieving clock synchronization is to send the source clock with the data stream. The AAL can insert timing information as part of the control information carried with the AAL-PDU to achieve clock recovery at the receiver. Hence, one of the AAL types defined below provides a time synchronization mechanism (as not all applications require the time synchronization function).

Note that another clock synchronization approach is to provide timing information at a higher layer. For example, in MPEG 2, there is a field called program clock reference (PCR) designed for this purpose, and is carried with the MPEG 2 stream. So, in this case, we do not need an AAL type that provides the timing information.

9.3.5 Maintenance of Traffic Patterns

For a circuit emulation application, a TDM-based bit stream such as the T1 transmission, which is typically carried over the TDM-based PSTN, is carried over the cell-based ATM network. The source traffic pattern is a CBR stream presented to the AAL at the sending ATM endpoint. At the receiver, a CBR stream should be delivered by the AAL to the higher layer (such as for forwarding to another TDM network).

For applications such as circuit emulation, the maintenance of a traffic pattern from the sender to the receiver is very important. This means that there is a constraint in cell delay variation (CDV) between the sender and the receiver. However, there are jitters in the ATM network due to queuing in ATM switches along the path (a result of packet switching), as well as endpoint processing (such as depacketization jitters). Such cell delay variations must be compensated to satisfy this circuit emulation requirement. This can be achieved by the receiving AAL using a buffer to filter out the jitters and recreating a CBR stream to the higher layer. The AAL buffer must be large enough to tolerate the expected CDV, or the CDV must be bounded (if possible) to avoid AAL buffer overflow or underflow.

9.3.6 Receive Buffer Allocation

Another function that can be provided by the AAL is to receive buffer allocation. By indicating the size of the AAL-PDU at the beginning of the AAL-PDU (the AAL header), the receiver can allocate the memory needed to receive the AAL-PDU. However, the effectiveness of this approach for receive buffer allocation was controversial in the computer industry. The reason is that such an AAL header can lead to misalignment of AAL-SDU boundaries for fast processing, resulting in additional processing overhead (see AAL 3/4 discussion later). Hence, this has not been used for AAL 5, the AAL type proposed by the computer industry for data communications, though this is used in AAL 3/4.

9.3.7 Multiplexing of Multiple Data Streams

Finally, the AAL can provide multiplexing of multiple data streams within a single VC. This is achieved by providing an identifier in the AAL-PDU to distinguish the different streams. For example, this allows multiplexing of different protocols (such as IP, IPX and Appletalk) into a single VC. This can be useful if the number of active VCs is a constraint. Alternatively, this multiplexing function can be provided by a higher layer protocol (above the AAL) using an encapsulation scheme (such as link layer multiplexing, LLC) to self identify each PDU for each protocol type. In this case, the protocol multiplexing over the same VC would be transparent to the AAL.

Another use of the AAL multiplexing function is to support multi-point-to-point VCs. A multipoint-to-point VC allows multiple senders sending to the same receiver over the same VC. This requires merging of the ATM cells from different sources towards the receiver, which sees cells from all the senders using the same VPI/VCI. However, this creates the problem of interleaving the cells of different AAL-PDUs from the different sources, because the receiver cannot distinguish the source of each cell to reassemble a complete AAL-PDU, due to identical VPI/VCI. A unique AAL identifier for cells from each source can allow the receiver to correctly demultiplex cells from different sources, as discussed in AAL 3/4 below.

9.4 AAL Service Classes and AAL Types

9.4.1 Origin of AAL Types

When ATM was adopted by the ITU as the solution to B-ISDN in the late 1980s, a model for supporting different classes of service for B-ISDN was also designed. Four classes of service (A, B, C, and D) were first defined to be supported by the AAL, based on the qualitative distinctions between different types of applications, as shown in Table 9-1. The intention was to define a specific AAL type to support each class of service. Hence, there was a one-to-one mapping of AAL service classes (A, B, C, D) to AAL types (1, 2, 3 and 4, respectively). Also, this class of service model is used in UNI 3.1 specification. These service classes are discussed in more detail next.

Table 9–1 *The original ITU model for classes of services and corresponding AAL types*

	AAL Service Classes			
Attributes	A	B	C	D
AAL Types	AAL 1	AAL 2	AAL 3	AAL 4
Bit Rate	CBR	VBR		
Timing Requirement	Required	Not Required		
Connection Mode	Connection-oriented			Connectionless

9.4.2 Attributes of AAL Service Classes

The AAL service classes are categorized according to three qualitative attributes: source traffic pattern, end-to-end timing relationship and connection mode.

9.4.2.1   Source Traffic Pattern

The service classes can be classified into supporting constant bit rate (CBR) versus variable bit rate (VBR) applications.

9.4.2.2   End-to-end Timing Relationship

For applications that deliver continuous streams, such as real-time streaming applications, stringent timing synchronization between the sender and the receiver is required to prevent overflow or underflow at the receiver buffer. The receiver must absorb (process) data at the same rate at which the sender transmits it. Hence, there is a strict timing synchronization between the source and receiver for these applications. On the other hand, for bursty traffic (even for real-time block transfer applications), there is no such timing requirement because such data is not sent in a continuous fashion. The key requirement for these bursty applications is to avoid buffer overflow, which can be solved by flow control, not clock synchronization.

9.4.2.3   Connection Mode

Applications can require either connection-oriented or connectionless service from the network. While real-time streaming applications expect a connection oriented service, most LAN traffic (layer two or three protocols, such as Ethernet and IP packets, respectively) expect connectionless service. Hence, the AAL must provide both connectionless and connection-oriented services.

9.4.3 AAL Service Classes: An Overview

Table 9-1 shows the four classes of AAL service based on these three service attributes and the AAL types envisioned by the ITU. In addition to the four classes of service originally specified by the ITU, another class of service has been specified in UNI 3.1, known as class X. They are explained next.

9.4.3.1 Class A

The class A service supports CBR applications that have strict timing relationships between the source and the receiver. Not only must an application generates a CBR stream to the sender's AAL, the AAL at the receiver must also guarantee a CBR stream delivered to the AAL-user (the application). The CDV in the ATM network must be controlled and the AAL at the receiver needs to remove the jitter by a smoothing buffer. Applications that can use class A service include circuit emulation and real-time CBR streaming video applications.

9.4.3.2 Class B

This class of service is similar to class A except that it supports VBR applications. Class B service can be used to support real-time streaming VBR compressed video application.

9.4.3.3 Class C

Class C service supports connection-oriented VBR applications. However, this class differs from class A and B in that there is no timing requirement between the sender and the receiver. Applications that can take advantage of class C service are legacy data communications, especially wide area data services connecting multiple corporate sites. One way to support this service is to have an ATM VC between each pair of corporate sites. This is similar to frame relay connection-oriented data service.

9.4.3.4 Class D

Class D service is similar to class C except that the former provides a connectionless service. Most of today's LAN applications, such as those running on IP (layer 3) or Ethernet (layer 2), expect a connectionless networking technology below to support it. Each packet can go to a different destination as indicated by the destination address on the packet header. To support these applications, a connectionless service must be provided on top of ATM that allows each packet to be carried across the ATM network to the right destination.

9.4.3.5   Class X

Class X is a raw ATM layer service that is an ATM only service. There is no higher layer (AAL service) support provided by the ATM network and so the network will not process the AAL parameters during the call setup process. Class X is a connection-oriented service for which the AAL type (may be proprietary), the traffic pattern (CBR or VBR), and the timing requirements between the sender and the receiver are all user-defined and transparent to the ATM network. The Class X user still specifies the bandwidth and QoS requirements, as these are ATM layer service requirements.

In the UNI 3.1 specification, only classes A, C, and X are supported.

Connectionless service over ATM   Since ATM is a connection-oriented protocol, how can it support connectionless service? There are two general approaches: permanent VC (PVC) and switched VC (SVC). PVCs are established between each ATM endpoint to all the potential destination endpoints of the connectionless service. There is a table at each ATM endpoint (that supports connectionless service) that maps the packet destination address to the PVC to which a packet should be forwarded. Alternatively, with SVC support, a new protocol can be designed to automatically trigger a new SVC setup to the right ATM destination endpoint to forward a new packet. This new protocol needs to convert the destination address on each packet to the corresponding destination ATM endpoint address. Then, a call setup using this destination ATM address is made to establish a new VC to which this packet is forwarded. If there is already a VC to the destination, the packet can be forwarded on the existing VC, instead of creating a new one.

While Class D service is not supported in UNI 3.1 specification, connectionless service is supported by the LAN Emulation[2] and Classical IP over ATM[1] specifications.

9.4.4 Service Model Evolution

However, the one-to-one between an AAL type and an AAL service class has been de-emphasized gradually since the early 1990s. One reason was that the AAL type 5 was proposed by the computer industry in the early 1990s for supporting class C and D services, while the AAL type 3/4 (a merged version of the original AAL type 3 and 4) was deemed inappropriate for data applications (discussed in more detail later). Since then there has been widespread deployment of ATM network interfaces that support only AAL type 5. As a result, the AAL type 5 has also been used to support class A and B service as well. All these events broke the notion of such one-to-one mapping and demanded rethinking of the purpose of AAL types in general. Recently, there has been consensus that AAL types should be decoupled from the AAL service classes.

Although the AAL service class model embodied in Table 9-1 gives us a *conceptual* understanding of different service classes to support different applications, it does not provide an operational model that both the ATM endpoints (the users) and the ATM network can use effectively for setting connections with specific bandwidth and QoS requirements. Hence, a new ATM service model has emerged to replace this model for UNI signaling and traffic management 4.0 specifications, which will be discussed in a later chapter on traffic management and ATM service categories.

9.5 AAL Types

In general, an AAL type consists of two parts or sublayers (see Figure 9-4): a common part (CP) and a service specific part (SSP). The CP is the lower sublayer. As the name suggests, the CP of an AAL type is used by all applications using the AAL type. The SSP is the higher sublayer and consists of specific functions that are service dependent. These functions may include additional reliability and timing information for the specific application requirements. If there is no need for any service specific function, the SSP becomes a null layer and applications can directly use the CP.

The AAL CP is further divided into two sublayers: the convergence sublayer (CS) and the segmentation and reassembly (SAR) sublayer (see Figure 9-4). They serve two sets of functions for the AAL. The CPCS is the higher sublayer responsible for functions related to the AAL-PDU as a whole and interacts closely with the AAL user (the application, or typi-

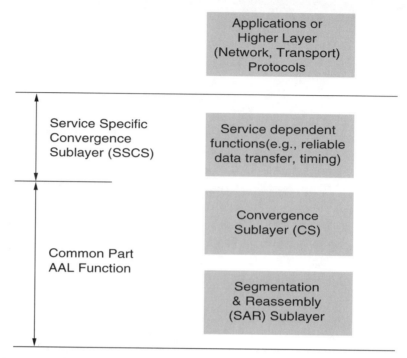

Figure 9-4   The protocol structure of the AAL

cally the next higher protocol layer such as IP), especially if the SSP is not used. The CPCS is responsible for encapsulating service data units (SDUs) from the application (or the higher layer protocol) into a framing structure, forming the CS-PDU (or the AAL-PDU). The basic function provided by the CPCS is to perform SDU delineation. Additional functions that the CS may perform include error protection mechanisms and data alignment on the AAL-PDU level. For example, the CS framing structure can include a CRC field for error detection (or correction) on a per CS-PDU basis. Different CS functions are designed for different AAL types.

The SAR sublayer is the lower sublayer of the AAL-CP, responsible for mapping the CS-PDU into the ATM layer. The SAR sublayer deals primarily with cell level issues, as opposed to AAL-PDU level issues for CPCS. The basic function of the SAR sublayer is segmentation on the transmitting endpoint and reassembly on the receiving endpoint of the CS-PDU. Additional functions that can be provided include data alignment and error control mechanisms on a per cell basis.

Although four types of AAL were originally conceived when the service classes A, B, C and D were designed, only 3 types of AAL have been defined:[3] AAL 1, AAL 3/4 (combined AAL 3 and AAL 4) and AAL 5, as shown in Table 9-2. AAL 5 was proposed to support data communications such as LAN traffic by the computer industry. Though not part of the original ITU AAL types, AAL 5 has become the most important AAL type because it is used to support ATM signaling protocols. This means all switches and end points that support SVCs must support AAL 5. Hence, there is a lot of interest, especially in the U.S., to use AAL 5 for a variety of applications, in addition to signaling and legacy LAN applications. In fact, AAL 5 has become the most widely deployed AAL type to date.

Table 9–2 *The current AAL types*

AAL Service Classes			
Attributes	A	B	C	D
AAL Types	AAL 1 AAL 5	AAL 2[*] AAL 5	AAL 3/4 AAL 5	AAL 3/4 AAL 5
Bit Rate	CBR	VBR		
Timing Requirement	Required	Not Required		
Connection Mode	Connection-oriented			Connec-tionless

* The AAL Type 2 is yet to be designed. Use of AAL 5 is under study.

Both AAL 1 and 5 can be used for class A service. The AAL type 2 for class B has yet to be specified. However, AAL 5 can be also be used for class B service and is under consideration at standards bodies. Both class C and D services can use AAL 3/4 or AAL 5. (There is also a new AAL type called AAL-CU, composite user, being defined for voice applications.) In general, the choice of an AAL type depends on the application requirements on error resiliency, packing efficiency, processing efficiency and timing synchronization. We discuss all the defined AAL types (1, 3/4 and 5) in detail next.

9.5.1   AAL 1

The key functions of AAL 1 are discussed first. Then, the CPCS and SAR sublayers of AAL 1 are explained in detail.

9.5.1.1   Functions

AAL 1 was designed to provide class A service, which is to support CBR applications with a timing requirement between sending and receiving ATM endpoints. The AAL 1 has a fixed size PDU that can be carried in exactly one cell. This implies that the SAR sublayer does not need to perform a segmentation or reassembly function, as the AAL 1 payload fits into one cell. There is no depacketization as with an AAL-PDU with multiple cells long.

However, AAL 1 also requires significantly more overhead for endpoints to process single cell PDUs (the CPU interrupt frequency discussed earlier). Hence, AAL 1 is mainly suitable for endpoints with dedicated hardware processing. Otherwise software processing would be limited to supporting low data rate applications.

Constant bit rate service   Providing class A service means that at the sending ATM endpoint, the AAL 1 service must accept data from the CBR application continuously at a constant rate because of the streaming traffic type. More importantly, at the receiving ATM endpoint, the AAL 1 service also must present the same bit stream at a constant rate to the AAL 1 user. Since there is jitter in the ATM network introduced by buffering and multiplexing at each ATM switch along the path, the AAL 1 at the receiver must perform jitter removal (by using a smoothing buffer, for example) to maintain a constant rate when presenting the stream to the AAL 1 user (the CBR application above). In the other words, from the time data is presented to the sending AAL 1 layer to the time the same data is presented by the AAL 1 service to the higher layer, a constant delay for all such data ideally should be incurred.

Furthermore, the constant rate at which the receiving AAL 1 presents to the higher layer must be the same as the data rate submitted to the AAL 1 service at the sending endpoint. Otherwise, the receiver buffer will overflow or underflow over a period of time. Rate mismatch or timing recovery between the sender and receiver is another reason (in addition to network jitter) for buffer overflow and underflow to carrying stream-type traffic. When the ATM cells are arriving too fast, the receiver buffer may overflow; the receiver side AAL 1 layer is then responsible for dropping the ATM cells with an indication to the AAL 1 user. Conversely, if there is buffer under-flow, AAL 1 is responsible for generating dummy cells to maintain a constant rate to the AAL 1 user. Timing recovery is discussed next.

Timing recovery The timing requirement between source and destination for class A service refers to the rate mismatch problem discussed above that can lead to the overflowing or underflowing of the receiving buffer. This is equivalent to the problem of recovering the clock of the source at the receiver, because the receiver can use the source clock to deduce the actual transmission rate or data arrival rate so as to process the incoming data (this also known as "locking to the source clock").

There are two general approaches for solving the clock recovery problem: synchronous and asynchronous. They are used by AAL 1 depending on the particular application supported.

Synchronous clock recovery The synchronous approach simply means that the local clocks of both the sender and the receiver are all synchronous (frequency locked) to a common network clock. This guarantees that the transmission rate of the sender can be derived accurately at the receiver because they have the same clock (to sufficient accuracy). Although this solves the clock recovery problems, this introduces the complexity of not only providing a common network clock, but also the synchronization requirement of the local clocks to the network clock. Other approaches must be provided environments that cannot have a network clock. Such environments require the asynchronous approach.

Asynchronous clock recovery: In the asynchronous approach, neither the sender's nor the receiver's clock is synchronized to a common network clock, whether available or not. In the other words, the source clock must be carried over the ATM network either explicitly or implicitly. Two methods are available: synchronous residual time stamp (SRTS) and adaptive clock recovery. SRTS requires the availability of a common network clock, while the other does not.

SRTS: SRTS assumes a common network clock available to both the sender and the receiver (such as the SONET clock from the physical layer). The SRTS takes advantage of this clock by having the source send its local time clock explicitly as a differential to this common network clock, which is referred to as the residual time stamp (RTS). Since the source clock should not be significantly different from the network clock, the RTS requires far fewer bits to encode than the complete source clock and is more efficient for transmission. The receiver then uses the RTS together with the network clock to recreate (or recover) the source clock. Note that even though this method assumes a common network clock is available, neither the source's nor the receiver's clock is synchronized to it.

Adaptive Clock Recovery: The adaptive clock recovery scheme neither requires a common network clock nor transmits the source clock explicitly. Instead, it relies on the arrival rate of the ATM cells at the receiving ATM endpoint to deduce the transmission rate from the source. It takes advantage of the fact that the average rate of arrival of the ATM cells at the receiver should be equal to the constant rate at which it is sent by the source (unless there is a significant cell loss, which is unlikely for class A service). The arriving ATM cells are stored at the receiver buffer temporarily and the buffer occupancy is used to adjust the output rate of the AAL 1 service. In the other words, the receiver buffer occupancy level is monitored, which drives the phase lock loop for the local receiver clock. The local receiver clock in turn drives the read rate for the buffer (to maintain the occupancy between a maximum and a minimum point).

However, there is network jitter in the ATM network and the receiver buffer is also responsible for removing the network jitter using the same process. Hence, the buffer occupancy is not entirely accurate and this affects the clock recovery. In other words, the adaptive clock recovery method will perform best (recover the clock more accurately and quickly) if there is no network jitter. Furthermore, the rate must be measured over a period of time (counting the number of cell arrivals over a period of time). The assumption that the arrival rate is equal to the transmission rate is only true when measured over a long enough period of time for the total number of arrived cells. The more jitter that is introduced in the network, the longer the period needed to estimate the source transmission rate by the receiver. This implies a larger receiving buffer is needed to account for both the instantaneous network jitter and the period of discrepancy between the estimated source clock at the receiver and the true source clock. Also, the adaptive clock recovery scheme has the limitation that it cannot compensate for all clock wanders (i.e., long term variation in clock rates) because it is limited by network jitter that might introduce a low frequency component.

Nevertheless, a major advantage of this scheme is that it does not require the presence of a common network clock, without which the other two schemes discussed above cannot function.

Error protection Since timing recovery is critical to class A service, the error protection mechanism of AAL 1 has been designed around this issue. Two types of errors in the delivery of ATM cells will affect timing recovery: cell loss or time stamp corruption. A sequence number is used on a per cell basis to not only detect for missing cells, but also to identify which particular cell is missing. In addition, there is an error detection and correction mechanism for a single bit error for both the sequence number and the time stamp. There is also optional forward error correction for the payload.

Unstructured and structured data transfer service AAL 1 can support both unstructured and structured data transfers. Unstructured data transfer (UDT) refers to carrying continuous bit streams that are not delineated into individual blocks. This can be used to emulate a point-to-point DS1 or E1 circuit. The service is defined as a clear channel pipe, which carries an arbitrary 1.544 Mbps or 2.048 kbps data stream. Both synchronous and asynchronous time recovery approaches can be used for UDT.

Structured data transfer (SDT) refers to the transfer of an octet stream that consists of fixed size blocks of repetitive structure. There is a pointer in AAL 1 to indicate the beginning of a block. The SDT is required for carrying Nx64 kbps service, such as fractional DS1 or E1 service. Each block consists of N octets, one from each 64 kbps channel for a 125 microsecond frame. This might involve more than 2 endpoints, such as demultiplexing of a DS1 from a source endpoint to multiple receiving endpoints (and multiplexing in the reverse direction). Since more than 2 clocks need to by synchronized, only the synchronous time recovery approach can be used for SDT. That is, all sending and receiving entities must be synchronized to a common primary clock.

9.5.1.2 Convergence Sublayer

The AAL 1 SDU size can be one bit long (for circuit emulation) or one octet long (for video and voice transport). The convergence sublayer for AAL 1 has two formats: non-P format and P-format. The P-format is designed for SDT to provide the pointer to indicate the block boundaries discussed before. The UDT uses only the non-P format. Both formats have a 47-octet CS-PDU structure. However, neither provides any error protection for the payload or the CS header. Both formats are shown in Figure 9-5.

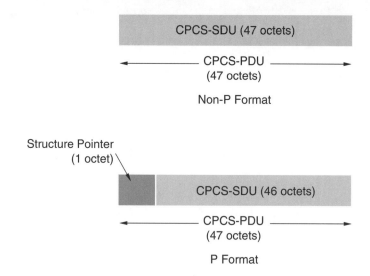

Figure 9–5   AAL 1 convergence sublayer (non-P and P formats)

CS-PDU non-P format   The CS-PDU non-P format consists of 47 octets of CS-SDU and no PCI present. In other words, the user of the AAL 1 non-P format presents a block of 47 octets to the CS. The CS in turn submits these 47 octets to the SAR sublayer. The UDT only uses non-P format because this provides a clear channel transmission of the unstructured data from the user. For UDT, the CS is a null layer. The SDT uses both non-P and P formats in alternate cells. The non-P format is always carried in an SAR-PDU with an odd sequence counter value, as discussed below.

CS-PDU P format   The CS-PDU P format also consists of 47 octets, but there is a 1-octet CS header (CS-PCI). In other words, the AAL-user information consists of only 46 octets. CS-PCI is a one-octet header called the structure pointer (SP). SP is used only in SDT and indicates the beginning of a block in the SDT. Again, the SDT uses non-P format and P format CS-PDUs in alternating CS-PDUs.

9.5.1.3   SAR Sublayer

The SAR-PDU consists of a 1-octet header and 47-octet payload. The latter is the CS-PDU, for both the P and non-P formats. The SAR header consists of two fields of 4 bits each: sequence number (SN) and sequence number protection (SNP), as shown in Figure 9-6.

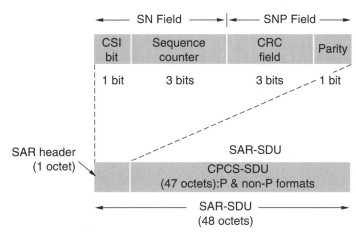

Figure 9–6   AAL 1 SAR sublayer

The SN field further consists of two subfields: a 1-bit convergence sublayer indication (CSI) and a 3-bit sequence counter (SC). The use of the CSI is optional. The CSI can provide three functions. First, the CSI can be used to carry one of the 4-bit residual time stamps (RTS) when SRST is used. The RTS is always carried in the SAR-PDU encapsulating a non-P format CS-PDU with an odd sequence counter value. Second, the CSI also can be used in the SDT mode (by setting to 1) to indicate that the P-format CS-PDU is used and an SP field is present. The SP indicates the offset in octets from the end of the pointer field to the first start of the next structured block of data. Note that the SP is carried in a SAR-PDU with an even sequence counter value. Hence, there is no conflict with the RTS transmission in odd sequence value cells. When not used, CSI has a value of 0. Third, the CSI can be used to indicate FEC is used.

The SNP field also consists of two subfields: 3-bit CRC and 1-bit Parity check, as shown in Figure 9-6. The SNP field is for detecting and possibly correcting bit errors in the SAR-PDU header. There is no error protection for the SAR payload by the SAR header.

Note that to reduce packetization delay for certain applications, such as voice transmission, the SAR payload may not be filled in its entirety. In this case, the number of leading octets used in each SAR-PDU payload is a constant (excluding the SP).

9.5.1.4   Applications

We now discuss two important applications that AAL 1 supports: circuit emulation and CBR video.

Circuit emulation   Many applications today are designed to be carried over the PSTN (POTS or ISDN), which is a circuit switched network (providing CBR service only). To avoid redesigning such applications for delivery over ATM networks, an adaptation function can be provided to emulate the same circuit-based service with fixed bit rates at both ends of the ATM network that interconnect two PSTNs. The goal of the ATM circuit emulation service is to provide this adaptation function. Circuit emulation can be achieved by using the AAL 1 to provide timing recovery, such as using the SRTS algorithm. In addition, both the UDT and SDT modes can be supported for circuit emulation. The UDT mode can be used to emulate DS-1 or E1 circuits, while the SDT mode can be used to emulate Nx64 kbps (fractional T1 service), allowing multiplexing and demultiplexing of individual 64 kbps channel.

CBR video   Another important application for AAL 1 is to support CBR streaming video applications. A CBR streaming video application requires constant bit rate delivery with source clock recovery. In the case of carrying MPEG 2 transport stream (TS) video, the incoming rate is constant at the MPEG 2 TS packet level, which means the MPEG 2 TS packets (fixed size at 188 octets) are presented to the AAL 1 at a CPR (constant packet rate). Since the MPEG 2 TS CPR delivery expects the underlying network to have little or no jitter, class A service provided by AAL 1 can help ensure both CBR delivery and clock synchronization. Nevertheless, the MPEG2 TS already has its own clock recovery mechanism in its bit stream. If the network jitter is insignificant, no additional clock synchronization is needed for AAL 1.

9.5.2   AAL 3/4

Originally, the AAL 3 and AAL 4 were designed for supporting class C and D services, respectively. This means they support VBR connection-oriented and connectionless data service without timing requirements, respectively. Later, they were combined into a single AAL type called AAL 3/4 to support both class C and class D services. Since both classes of service support data communications, error protection is a very important function for AAL 3/4. Different error protection mechanisms are provided by both CS and SAR sublayers in AAL 3/4. However, AAL 3/4 CP does not provide a retransmission mechanism when an error is detected. Retransmission (only in units of the AAL 3/4 SDUs) is the responsibility of a higher layer, or can be supported by defining an AAL 3/4 service specific convergence sublayer (SSCS) above. Corrupted AAL 3/4 frames are dropped.

9.5.2.1   CS Sublayer

The AAL 3/4 CS-PDU has a variable length, as opposed to the AAL 1. The length of the CS-PDU payload (or the CS-SDU) is AAL-user selectable up to 64 Kbytes (minus 1 byte, to be exact), as indicated by a two-octet length field. The CS-PCI consists of both a header and a trailer, each consisting of 4 octets, as shown in Figure 9-7. The header has three subfields: a 1-octet common part indicator (CPI), a 1-octet beginning tag (Btag) and a 2-octet buffer allocation size (BAsize). The trailer also consists of three subfields: a 1-octet alignment (AL), a 1-octet end tag (Etag) and a 2-octet Length of CPCS payload. The CPI specifies how the rest of the header and trailer should be interpreted. If the CPI equals zero, the BAsize contains an estimate of the size of the PDU in octets, while the Length indicates the exact size of the CS-SDU in octets. BAsize is used for hinting to the receiver to allocate sufficient buffer size to receive the incoming CS-PDU. The Btag and Etag are chosen by the AAL 3/4 at the source ATM endpoint to have equal value for each CS-PDU, such that the receiving AAL 3/4 can ensure data integrity. This is to detect and prevent the combining of two PDUs to become a new PDU. The Btag and Etag will change from PDU to PDU during the transmission of a particular connection. The AL subfield is used for aligning the trailer to be 32-bit aligned. In addition, the payload is 32-bit aligned by adding the PAD field at the end which can be 0 to 3 octets long.

The AAL 3/4 CS provides the following functions:

Error detection   Error detection is achieved in two ways for the AAL 3/4 CS. It detects cell losses and misinsertion by providing a length field to check the octet counts. It protects against two partial CS-PDUs combining to form a PDU with the length of the second PDU, thus escaping the length field check. This is achieved by checking matching Btag and Etag values. However, there is no bit error checking on the CS-PDU level,

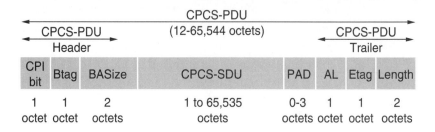

Figure 9–7   AAL 3/4 convergence sublayer

because it is provided in the AAL 3/4 SAR sublayer on a per cell basis (as discussed below).

Buffer allocation   AAL 3/4 CS provides an indication to the receiver through the BAsize field the required buffer size to receive the AAL 3/4 PDU. This field is included in the first cell of the CS-PDU. The fact that this is the first cell of the CS-PDU is indicated by the SAR layer information as described below. (However, the effectiveness of this buffer allocation mechanism has been controversial and deemed unnecessary for the computer industry. Hence, this function was not provided in the AAL 5 proposed by the computer industry.)

9.5.2.2   SAR Sublayer

As with other AAL SAR-PDUs, the AAL 3/4 SAR-PDU is 48-octets long. The SAR-PCI contains a header and a trailer, both 2-octet long (see Figure 9-8). The CS-PDU (that is, including the CS header and trailer) is segmented by the SAR into 44-octet segments. The last segments are padded to 44 octets.

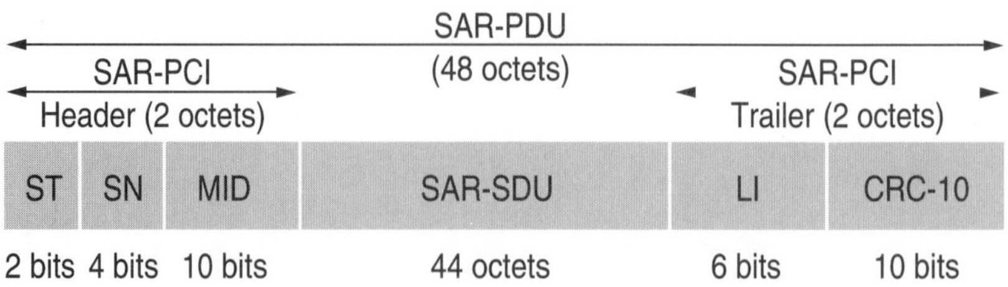

	SAR-PDU		
SAR-PCI Header (2 octets)	(48 octets)	SAR-PCI Trailer (2 octets)	

ST	SN	MID	SAR-SDU	LI	CRC-10
2 bits	4 bits	10 bits	44 octets	6 bits	10 bits

Figure 9–8   AAL 3/4 SAR sublayer

The header consists of three subfields: a 2-bit segment type (ST), a 4-bit sequence number (SN), and a 10-bit multiplexing identification (MID). ST indicates whether the payload of the SAR-PDU represents the beginning (BOM, beginning of message), the middle (COM, continuation of message), the last segment (EOM, end of message) of a CS-PDU, or a single segment CS-PDU (44 octets or less long). The SN represents the sequence number (modulo 16) of this segment in the CS-PDU. The MID field can be used for multiplexing different services (such as different applications or protocols) onto the same VC. The MID field of the cells from the same CS-PDU has the same value and is used for reassembly checking. If the multiplexing mechanism is not used, the MID field is set to all 0s.

The trailer consists of two subfields: a 6-bit length indication (LI) and a 10-bit CRC. The LI is used to indicate the length in octets of the SAR payload, which can be from 1 to 44 octets long. (The LI can also be used for additional error checking in case its value is outside this range.) The CRC provides bit error detection for the entire SAR-PDU.

The SAR sublayer provides the following functions:

Error protection   There are four error protection mechanisms in the SAR sublayer. The 10-bit CRC provides bit error protection over the entire SAR-PDU. This is very useful for locating errors within a particular cell for an AAL 3/4 PDU. This is particularly useful for applications that cannot have retransmission. However, for applications that provide retransmission by a higher layer, this can be overkill for an low error rate environment such as fiber. Second, the LI provides compatibility checking with the CS sublayer length field. Third, the reception of inconsistent ST fields (such as consecutive BOM cells, or the arrival of a COM or EOM cell without a BOM cell of the same MID being present) help detect cell losses. Finally, the MID field protects against cell misassembly due to VPI/VCI corruption.

Multiplexing   The MID field provides a mechanism for multiplexing different data streams onto the same VC. This can be used for sharing different protocols on the same VC and demultiplexing them at the end points. Also, this can be used to support multipoint-to-point and multipoint-to-multipoint types of VCs, because it allows demultiplexing of ATM cells with same the VPI/VCI value originating from different sources.

9.5.2.3   Message and Streaming Modes

The AAL 3/4 supports two modes of operation: message and streaming. They refer to the ability of AAL 3/4 to support blocking and pipelining functions during the transmission and reception processes. In the message mode, the SDU for AAL 3/4 is transferred from the AAL 3/4 user in exactly one unit (called the interface data unit, or AAL-IDU). AAL 3/4 has to wait for the entire AAL-SDU (the same as AAL-IDU) to be submitted by the AAL user before transmission of the AAL can occur. No pipelining is provided in the message mode. However, one can define a SSCS for AAL 3/4 (above the CPCS) to support an internal blocking/deblocking function by collecting multiple AAL-SDUs into a single SSCS-PDU (in the case of short fixed size AAL-SDUs). Also, the SSCS can support an internal segmentation and reassembly function (in addition to the SAR sublayer) by segmenting an AAL-SDU into multiple SSCS-PDUs (in the case of a variable size AAL-SDU).

The streaming mode at the AAL 3/4 sender supports pipelining by initiating the AAL-PDU transfer before all the payloads corresponding to a complete AAL 3/4 SDU are received from the AAL user. Supporting the streaming mode can reduce the packetization delay of AAL processing. Similarly, providing the streaming mode at the AAL 3/4 receiver allows pipelining and reduces depacketization delay and jitter. Each cell of an AAL 3/4 PDU can be delivered to the higher layer immediately on arrival after SAR processing, without waiting for the entire PDU to arrive. Since the AAL 3/4 SAR provides per cell CRC to check for data corruption, the AAL 3/4 can indicate immediately on a per cell basis whether a cell has been corrupted before it passes the cell to a higher layer. The per cell CRC is better than per CS-PDU CRC in supporting streaming mode because it does not need to retroactively indicate to the higher layer after the entire PDU has arrived that the PDU delivered earlier was in fact corrupted. Otherwise the higher layer mistakenly assumes such data was correct if only per CS-PDU CRC is provided at the end of the PDU.

9.5.3 AAL 5

Although the AAL 5 is the most recently standardized AAL type (compared to the other two above), it has become the most important AAL type because it must be supported by all ATM switches and endstations that implement switched VCs. The reason is that the ATM signaling protocols (UNI and NNI) have been standardized on using AAL 5.

The motivation for AAL 5 was to design a simple AAL type that is efficient both in terms of low processing overhead and transmission overhead, especially if the endstation is a PC or workstation, instead of some specialized hardware. In fact, the AAL 5 was known as Simple and Efficient Adaptation Layer, or SEAL. Although the AAL 3/4 had been defined to support the same two classes of service, the computer industry feels that the AAL 3/4 incurs too much protocol processing and transmission overhead for endstation devices that are workstations and PCs. Many of the AAL 3/4 functions such as multiplexing, per cell CRC, sequence numbering, and buffer allocation are eliminated for AAL 5.

We discuss the key functions and internal structure of AAL 5 next.

9.5.3.1 Functions

Error protection Since the AAL 5 was originally designed for data communications, error protection is an important function of the AAL 5. The AAL 5 assumes the data link is reasonably error free because fibers are expected to be heavily used in ATM networks. Instead of a per cell CRC check, AAL 5 provides a per AAL 5 PDU level CRC protection. A strong CRC, the 32-bit CRC used for Ethernet and FDDI frames, was adopted. It can be used for detection of bit errors, cell loss or cell gain (caused by misrouting of corrupted cells). In addition, the AAL 5 PDU maintains a length check per AAL 5-PDU to determine any cell loss or gain.

Data delineation Instead of a per cell indication of its position in the AAL5 PDU (such as using a sequence number or indicating whether it is the beginning, middle, or end of a packet), only the end of an AAL 5 PDU (the last cell) is indicated. AAL 5 takes advantage of the PTI field (payload indicator) in the ATM cell header to indicate whether the ATM cell is the last cell of an AAL 5 PDU. The fact that this is indicated in the ATM cell header means that certain advance congestion features can be implemented. For example, during congestion, it is more effective to drop cells that belong to a particular AAL 5 PDU or limited number of them, instead of randomly dropping ATM cells across many different PDUs. The reason is that, for data communications applications, a cell loss means that the entire PDU is useless and retransmission is needed. Minimizing the number of PDUs with cell losses means minimizing the number of retransmissions of PDUs across the congested ATM network.

The ATM switch can check the ATM cell headers in case it decides to drop all the cells belonging to an AAL 5 PDU, by dropping all the cells up to the last cell of the PDU that arrive at the switch. This will be discussed in more detail in a later chapter on traffic management.

9.5.3.2   CS Sublayer

As for any AAL type, the CS sublayer of AAL 5 consists of two parts: the common part and the service specific part. The service specific part layer is above the common part layer. The common part convergence sublayer (CPCS) is used by all AAL 5 users and is discussed next. Different service specific parts can be defined. An SSCS has been defined for signaling to provide reliable data transfer (discussed in the next chapter on signaling).

The AAL 5 CPCS PCI consists of an 8-octet trailer and no header, as shown in Figure 9-9. The trailer consists for three fields: a 2-octet reserved field, a 2-octet length field and a 4-octet 32-bit CRC. The reserved field is for control information: user-to-user indication (UU) and common part indication (CPI). The actual usage of the reserved field is to be determined. The length field indicates the length in octets of the AAL 5 CPCS SDU. To align the CPCS PDU to a multiple of 48 octets for submission to the SAR layer, a padding length from 0 to 47 octets is added after the CPCS payload, before the trailer. Similar to the AAL 3/4, the AAL 5 allows a maximum PDU size of 64 Kbytes (minus 1 byte).

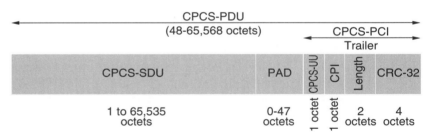

Figure 9–9   AAL 5 convergence sublayer

The 32-bit CRC at the end is for detection of bit errors and cell loss or cell gain (which is same CRC used for Ethernet and FDDI frames). It also can detect burst errors.[4] The per frame CRC is more resilient to burst error than the per cell CRC in AAL 3/4. It is less likely for undetected burst error in an AAL 5 frame than an AAL 3/4 frame because the latter has no CRC check on the frame level.[5]

9.5.3.3   SAR

Another major simplification in AAL 5 is the very simple SAR layer, as shown in Figure 9-10. It has almost no per cell SAR protocol processing. There is no trailer or header for the SAR-PDU. The SAR-PDU consists entirely of 48-octet SAR-SDUs from the CPCS sublayer. This simplifies the protocol processing significantly because there is no per cell protocol processing. The only major SAR layer function indicates the end of the PDU by setting the PTI field to 001 in the last ATM cell of the CPCS PDU's ATM header, while the rest of the cells' PTI field is set to 000.

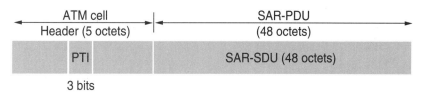

Figure 9–10   AAL 5 SAR sublayer

9.5.3.4   Comparison Between AAL 5 and AAL 3/4

The AAL 5 has three major advantages over AAL 3/4 for connection-oriented data communications. First, the AAL 5 has lower transmission overhead, only 8 octets per AAL 5 PDU, versus an additional 8-octet per cell for the AAL 3/4. Second, the AAL 5 has less processing overhead because it removes the need to process MID, SN, and per cell CRC in the SAR layer. Hence, the AAL 5 SAR layer function is almost null, except for the end of PDU indication. Similarly, the BAsize, Btag, and Etag in the CS layer are removed. AAL 5 shifts the multiplexing function to the higher layer. Third, the AAL 5 provides stronger error detection for burst errors (especially short bursts that hit only a cell payload) than the AAL 3/4, because the AAL 5 contains a per PDU CRC check.

However, the AAL 3/4 does have an advantage over the AAL 5 for certain applications that require the location of bit errors within a single cell, because the AAL 3/4 provides per cell CRC, while the AAL 5 uses per AAL5 PDU CRC, and cannot locate the errors within the PDU. A single bit error may result in an entire AAL 5 PDU being dropped. Also, the AAL 3/4 can be used to support multipoint-to-point and multipoint-to-multipoint type VCs, because it has the MID to allow demultiplexing at the receiver. This is not possible with the AAL 5, for which some other method must be designed to support these types of VCs.

9.5.4 Comparisons of AAL Types

Table 9-3 shows a comparison of the differences of AAL 1, AAL 3/4, AAL 5, and AAL 0. AAL 0 is also known as the null AAL, for which user data is directly mapped into the 48 octet payload of an ATM cell.

Table 9–3   *A comparison of different AAL types*

	AAL 1	**AAL 3/4**	**AAL 5**	**AAL0 (null)**
Overhead per CS-PDU	1 or no octet	8 octets	8 octets	None
Overhead per SAR PDU	1 octet	4 octets	None	None
Per CS-PDU error control	None	Length field, matching beginning and end tags	32-bit CRC PDU length	None
Per cell error control	4-bit (3-bit CRC plus parity bit) on SAR header only, not payload	10-bit CRC on entire SAR-PDU	None	None
Error protection for payload	(Optional FEC)	Only per cell 10-bit CRC	Only per CS-PDU 32-bit CRC	
Depacketization jitter	None	Reduced by streaming mode	Proportional to packet length	
Cell sequence number	3 bit	4 bit	None	None
Sender - receiver timing	optional SRTS, or adaptive clock recovery	optional adaptive clock recovery	optional adaptive clock recovery	

9.6 Summary

In this chapter, we discussed the role of AAL in the end-to-end ATM protocol model. We presented the original AAL service classes from ITU that motivates the different AAL types. Then, we described the major functions of the AAL. After that, we explained the various AAL types in detail. Finally, we provided a summary to compare the different AAL types.

9.7 References

[1] M. Laubach, "Classical IP over ATM," IETF RFC 1577.

[2] ATM Forum, LAN Emulation Version 1.0, 1995

[3] ITU-T Recommendation I.363, *B-ISDN ATM Adaptation Layer (AAL) Specification*, March, 1993.

[4] C. R. Kalmanek and W. T. Marshall, "Error Control in ATM Networks," *Second IEEE B-ISDN Workshop*, April, 1992.

[5] J. M. Simmons, R. G. Gallager, "Design of Error Detection Scheme for Class C Service in ATM," *IEEE/ACM Transactions on Networking*, Vol.2, No.1, Feb. 1994, pp. 80

Chapter 10

ATM Access (UNI) Signaling

10.1 Introduction

ATM is a connection-oriented protocol. A virtual connection (VC) must be established between the communication parties in the ATM network before an information transfer can take place. The ATM signaling protocols enable an end system application to set up a VC on demand across the ATM network.

The ATM signaling protocols define sets of procedures and signaling messages to set up and tear down different types of VCs for different applications. A key function of the signaling messages is to indicate the networking requirements of the connections, such as the traffic and QoS requirements, for network resource allocation. Another key function is to carry parameters for end-to-end compatibility checking. The signaling procedures specify how and which signaling messages are exchanged to establish, modify and tear down ATM connections. The ATM signaling protocol belongs to the control plane in the ATM Protocol Reference Model (PRM).

There are two classes of ATM signaling protocols: access and network. The ATM access signaling protocol specifies the interaction only between an ATM end system and its attached ATM switch. Since the access signaling protocol is used only at the UNI, it is also called the ATM UNI signaling protocol. The network signaling protocol specifies the interactions between two ATM switches and between two ATM networks. Hence, this is also called the network node interface (NNI) signaling, as this is communicated across the NNI. Therefore, access signaling protocol affects all ATM endpoints, while network signaling is transparent to the endpoints. Although network signaling protocols are beyond the scope of this book, the understanding of access signaling is critical to learning network signaling because network signaling protocols are based on the access signaling protocol.

In this chapter, we discuss the ATM access signaling protocol in detail. We first discuss the basic ATM signaling concepts, including switched versus permanent VCs, VPI versus VPCI, signaling AAL, ATM addressing, address registration and the anycast capability. Then we explain the different connection types used to support multi-party communications. Finally, we explore the ATM UNI signaling protocol for setting up point-to-point VCs in detail, which forms the foundation of setting up multi-point VCs. A key goal of this chapter is to provide the fundamentals on ATM signaling protocols. Also, it provides the concepts behind the ATM UNI signaling specifications (UNI 3.1[1] and 4.0[2]) that are important to understand for implementers.

10.2 ATM Signaling Concepts

10.2.1 Permanent and Switched VCs

ATM VCs can be classified into permanent and switched virtual connections (PVCs and SVCs), depending on how they are set up, modified and torn down. As discussed in an earlier chapter, PVCs are set up and torn down by management protocols; they are provisioned as part of the overall network management function (that is, the management plane of the ATM PRM). PVCs are tailored for subscription-based services and are typically maintained for a long period of time. For example, PVCs can be used to interconnect multiple corporate locations to create a virtual private network. PVCs should automatically be re-established after network failure, otherwise users cannot re-establish the PVCs themselves without a signaling mechanism. At the beginning of ATM network deployment, only PVCs can be supported because signaling is not available.

While PVCs are set up statically by the network management system, SVCs are set up and torn down dynamically by the ATM end systems using a UNI signaling protocol. SVCs are important for individual applications that require services on a demand basis. SVCs can remain active indefinitely, until they are explicitly torn down by the signaling protocol (on application request). SVCs can also be torn down due to network failure, but they would not automatically be re-established by signaling.

In general, for large scale ATM network deployments, supporting SVCs are very important because the management overhead for PVCs is not scalable. The reason is that to support a PVC, the end-to-end ATM elements (endpoints and switches along the path) must be configured with all the proper PVC parameters by centralized management (which can involve human intervention). The management overhead for building large PVC-based network can be prohibitively expensive. Furthermore, this may involve management of entities that belong to different authorities, such as the public ATM network serving businesses. On the other hand, in the SVC environment, such VC parameters along the path are configured automatically by the signaling protocols in a distributed fashion.

10.2.2 Signaling Virtual Channel

Since all information carried in the ATM network must be part of a VC and be identified by a unique VPI/VCI, signaling messages are no exception. They are carried in a separate VC, the signaling VC, as distinguished from the SVCs carrying user information for which the signaling messages are trying to set up. Hence, the ATM signaling protocol is an out-of-band signaling protocol. The signaling VC has a default VPI/VCI value of 0/5 across the UNI (for both UNI 3.1 and 4.0 specifications). Typically, a single dedicated signaling VC is shared by all signaling messages over the UNI. We discuss two exceptions to this later.

Since SVCs are set up by the signaling protocol, then the logical question is: Which protocol is responsible to set up the signaling VC? The signaling VC must be established *a priori* before any SVC can be set up by definition. The metasignaling protocol is responsible for setting up the UNI signaling VC as part of network configuration when the ATM end system is connected to the ATM network. Since the signaling VC must be available all the time for ATM endpoints to set up and torn down VCs by sending signaling messages over it, it is set up as a PVC and should be automatically reestablished upon any network failure. This implies that the metasignaling protocol is considered a management protocol (part of the management plane in the PRM), instead of a signaling protocol.

The UNI signaling VC is a PVC between an ATM endpoint and its attached ATM switch. Hence, while all ATM cells carrying user information (distinguished by VPI/VCI values) are forwarded to the switch output ports, the signaling VC is terminated at the ATM switch. The ATM switch terminates the signaling VC by reassembling the ATM cells to process the signaling messages.

Typically, the UNI signaling VC controls (manages the set up and tear down of) the virtual paths and virtual channels across the UNI. While only a single signaling channel across a UNI is supported by default (in the UNI 3.1[1]), more than one signaling VC can be established across the UNI. This means that signaling VCs with different VPI/VCI values not equal to the default value can be used provided there is agreement between the two sides of the UNI. In fact, even if there is only one signaling channel across the UNI, the metasignaling protocol can be used to set up a signaling VC that has a different VPI/VCI value from the default value of 0/5. The concept of multiple signaling channels across a physical link is related to the concepts of VPCI and VPI, which are discussed next.

10.2.3 VPI and VPCI

A UNI signaling message is made up of a set of parameters known as information elements (IEs). An IE called the connection identifier is used to uniquely identify the particular VC being set up or controlled by the signaling message. The connection identifier is a concatenation of two entities: the VPCI (virtual path connection identifier) and VCI, to represent the virtual path and virtual channel of the VC, respectively. The ATM switch on the network side of the UNI assigns the values to the VPCI and VCI during the connection set up. These values only have local significance on the UNI.

It is important to note that the signaling protocol represents the VP using the VPCI instead of the VPI (on the ATM cell header). The VPCI is 16-bit long, instead of the 8-bit for VPI at the UNI. The VPCI value of a VC is only of significance to the signaling channel controlling the VC.

In fact, the signaling protocol does not see the VPI value used on the ATM cells at all. Both the ATM end system and the switch must understand the relationship between VPCI and VPI for each virtual path. There is a local mapping table between the VPI and VPCI at both the ATM end system and the ATM switch. They are configured during service provisioning (by the management plane protocols). They perform a one-to-one mapping locally from the VPCI indicated by the signaling message at call setup for the new VC to the VPI used on the ATM cell header. Hence, the VPI and the mapping process are transparent to the signaling protocol.

By using the VPCI (16-bit), a signaling VC can control up to 64,000 VPs, much larger than the 256 values of the VPI (8-bit) space at the UNI (see Figure 10-1). In the default case, there is a single signaling VC that controls all the VPs on that UNI (between an ATM end system and an ATM switch). As such, the mapping between VPCI and VPI can be done in a straightforward fashion using an identity mapping, at both the ATM end system and the ATM switch. The 8-bit VPI value is mapped directly to the lower order 8 bits of the VPCI, with its high order 8-bit set to all 0s. In fact, this is the way specified in the ATM Forum UNI 3.1 specification.[1]

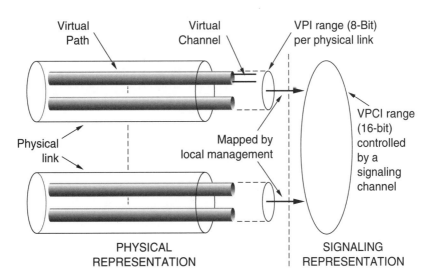

Figure 10–1 Relationship between the VPCI used by a signaling channel and the VPI assigned locally on each physical link for each virtual path.

The motivation for using the VPCI instead of the VPI for the signaling protocol is to decouple the control domain of signaling channel from the physical link on which it resides. More specifically, this allows the signaling VC on a physical link to control VPs on different physical links (different switch ports connecting ATM endpoints), because the local mapping tables map the VPI space on each physical link to a different VPCI space. The 16-bit VPCI space allows a signaling VC to control up to 256 physical links. The VPCI concept helps extend the signaling capabilities to support proxy signaling and virtual UNIs, as discussed next.

10.2.3.1 Proxy Signaling Capability

For ATM end systems that do not have signaling capability (not implemented UNI signaling), SVCs can still be supported for them using the proxy signaling mechanism. Proxy signaling uses a special ATM end system, called the proxy signaling agent (PSA), to control the VC setup of the nonsignaling ATM end systems. Figure 10-2 shows a proxy signaling configuration with an ATM switch connected to three nonsignaling ATM end systems and a PSA. Both the switch and the PSA supports UNI signaling. The PSA can take advantage of the larger VPCI field to control multiple VPI space (physical links). By mapping the VPI space of each nonsignaling ATM end system (UNI = A, B and C) to the VPCI space, the PSA can set up VCs for these nonsignaling ATM end systems as if they are VCs on the UNI of the PSA to the ATM switch. Again, the fact that these VPs are on different physical ports is transparent to the signaling protocol, because the mapping of the VPCI to VPI is done locally at the switch and the PSA. Figure 10-2 shows the VPCI-to-VPI mapping defined during provisioning. Proxy signaling is supported in UNI Signaling 4.0.[2] Proxy signaling also is referred to as the non-associated facility signaling protocol (a signaling VC controls VPs on a different facility or link).

The proxy signaling capability also is useful for a signaling ATM end system with multiple physical interfaces, such as a high-performance video server connected to an ATM switch. Only a single signaling channel is needed as all these different UNIs are connected between the same ATM end system and the same ATM switch. The mapping of VPCI to VPI occurs at both the ATM end system and ATM switch. Hence, proxy signaling allows high-end servers to support connections with aggregate bandwidth exceeding the line rate of any given interface.

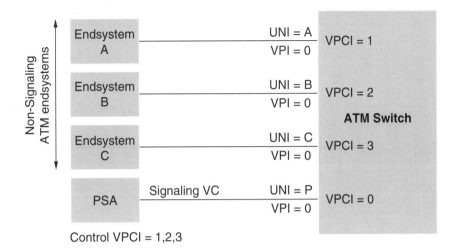

Control VPCI = 1,2,3

VPI	Interface	VPCI
0	A	1
0	B	2
0	C	3
0	P	0

©1996 The ATM Forum

Figure 10–2   Proxy Signaling Configuration and the provisioned VPCI-to-VPI mapping table

10.2.3.2 Virtual UNIs and ATM Multiplexer

While the proxy signaling uses a single signaling VC to control multiple physical interfaces (UNIs), we discuss the opposite variation (from the default case) to support multiple signaling VCs on the same physical link. Each signaling VC controls only one VP on that link; we can have as many as 256 signaling VCs on the physical link. This is useful for supporting a non-signaling ATM multiplexer (one that does not support signaling) that only supports the VP crossconnect function at an ATM access network, as shown in Figure 10-3.

The ATM multiplexer supports multiple ATM end systems and multiplexes all traffic to the attached ATM switch over a single physical link. The ATM multiplexer is used to reduce the number of physical links (interfaces) to the ATM switch (which are expensive resources in the public network) to support many ATM endpoints. The signaling VCs terminated at the end systems can all use VPCI/VCI = 0/5, as in the default case. However, at the ATM multiplexer, each signaling VC is translated into VPI/VCI = x/5 on the link to the ATM switch, where x can be 1 to *n* (*n* is the number of end systems). This VP crossconnect function avoids duplication of VPI/VCI values for all the signaling VCs (and user VCs) from the ATM end systems. While these signaling VCs terminated at the ATM switch use different VPI values, the signaling protocol running over these VCs all use the same default VPCI value of 0. This is possible because VPCI values only need to be unique within a signaling VC, not across multiple signaling VCs (even when they share the same physical link). Hence, the ATM end systems can still use the default mapping of VPI to VPCI. In other words, the ATM multiplexer is transparent to the ATM end system from a signaling point of view. This capability of supporting multiple signaling VCs over a single physical link is known as virtual UNIs.

Virtual UNIs was introduced in the UNI signaling 4.0 specification. Since virtual UNI is transparent to the ATM end systems, it allows backward compatibility to existing end systems that support only UNI 3.1 specification, while we enable virtual UNIs support at the ATM switch using UNI 4.0.

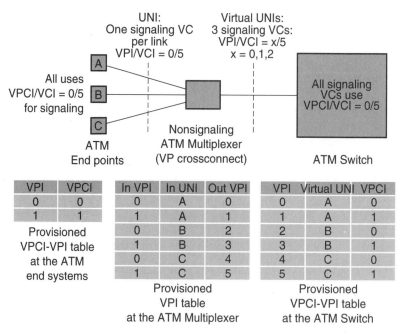

Figure 10–3   Supporting virtual UNIs with an ATM multiplexer

10.2.4 Signaling Protocol Model and SAAL

The ATM Forum UNI signaling protocol is based on the Q.2931 protocol from ITU-T. The signaling protocol layered model is shown in Figure 10-4. The Q.2931 protocol is supported over its own AAL, known as signaling AAL or SAAL. As in other AAL types, the SAAL is composed of two layers: common part and service specific part. The AAL 5 common part has been adopted as the SAAL common part. The AAL5 provides an unassured information transfer mode. It does not guarantee reliability of data delivery; it only provides a mechanism for detecting corruption in the payload (SDU). To provide recovery of corrupted SDUs, a reliable protocol is used in the service specific convergence sublayer (SSCS) of the SAAL; that is, above the AAL5 common part. The SSCS of SAAL also consists of two sublayers: Service Specific Connection Oriented Protocol (SSCOP) and Service Specific Coordination Function (SSCF). The SSCOP (the lower sublayer) is a reliable protocol that provides error recovery via retransmission, which is specified in ITU's Q.2110. The SSCF (the higher sublayer) maps the Q.2931 messages into the SSCOP and is specified in Q.2130.

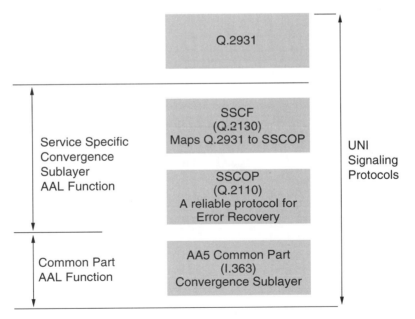

Figure 10–4   ATM UNI signaling protocol layer model

10.2.5 ATM Addressing

An ATM end system address (AESA) is used to identify one or more ATM end systems in the ATM network. There are two types of ATM addresses: individual and group. An ATM individual address identifies a single ATM end system, while an ATM group address identifies one or more ATM end systems.

For private ATM networks, ATM addressing uses the 20-octet ISO Network Service Access Point (NSAP) encoding format. However, private ATM addresses are not true NSAP addresses, even though they use the same format. An NSAP encoding format consists of three parts: Authority and Format Identifier (AFI), Initial Domain Identifier (IDI) and Domain Specific Part (DSP). The AFI specifies the format of the IDI and network addressing authority responsible for allocation of the values of the IDI. The IDI specifies the network addressing domain from which the values of the DSP are allocated and the network addressing authority responsible for allocating values of the DSP from that domain [2]. Hence, the AFI and IDI together uniquely specify an administrative authority that has responsibility for allocating and assigning the values of the DSP. The combination of the AFI and IDI fields is also known as the Initial Domain Part (IDP).

There are three different NSAP encoding formats defined for ATM as specified by three different AFI values: Data country code (DCC), International Code Designator (ICD) and E.164 formats (see Figure 10-5). They are distinguished by the first octet, the AFI, which identifies the authority allocating the DCC, ICD and E.164 numbers. The IDI for both DCC and ICD formats is allocated and assigned to individual countries, and not private organizations. The DCC values are allocated and assigned to each country's ISO National Member Body which allocates and assigns the Administrative Authority. The ICD values are allocated and assigned by the ISO 6523 registration authority. Both the ICD and DCC AESAs are used for organizations to establish private numbering plans. The IDI values for the E.164 format are assigned to public network operators worldwide. Private organizations can use the E.164 IDI format by obtaining a set of E.164 numbers from its public network operator(s). Such private E.164 format can be used to reach end system connected to public ATM network, as discussed later.

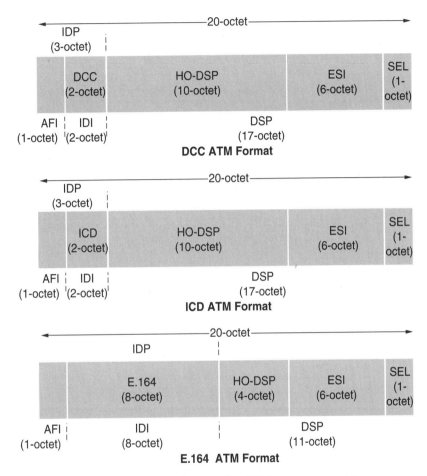

Figure 10–5   NSAP encoding formats for ATM end system addresses

The DSP consists of the higher order DSP, the end system identifier (ESI) and selector (SEL). The ESI is 6-octet long and can contain an IEEE 802 address. The 1-octet SEL is used for further demultiplexing within the end system. Both the ESI and the SEL are common for all formats.

For public ATM networks, the public UNI supports either the above NSAP address formats or the native E.164 addresses, or both. Native E.164 addresses can be up to 15 digits in length. They are specified by ITU recommendation E.164 and are administrated by public network operators. While each E.164 address uniquely identifies a public UNI, a public UNI can have multiple E.164 addresses.

According to UNI signaling 4.0,[2] if the public UNI only supports native E.164 address format, an endpoint on a private ATM network connected to such a UNI can be reached using the appropriate native E.164 address in the called party number IE and the private ATM address in the called party subaddress IE. If the public UNI supports the private ATM address format, the private ATM address will be carried in the called party number IE.

Since the private UNI only supports private ATM addresses, the issue arises as to what happens if an ATM end system connected to a private UNI wants to call another ATM end system connected to a public ATM network that only support native E.164 address formats. The solution is for the originating ATM end system to encode the destination E.164 address using the NSAP formatted E.164 private ATM address format, with the DSP field set to zero, into the calling party number IE.

10.2.6 Address Registration

Each UNI (public or private), or its corresponding ATM end system, is identified by an ATM address(es). An address registration procedure to dynamically assign an address to the UNI has been defined in UNI 3.1 using integrated local management interface (ILMI) protocol.[3] Address registration usually occurs at initialization when the ATM end system is connected to the ATM switch providing the UNI.

The address registration procedure depends on whether it is a private ATM address or a native E.164 address. For a private UNI, the AESA is divided into two parts: network prefix and user parts. The user part consists of the ESI and SEL fields, while the network prefix consists of the rest of the private ATM address. The SEL is ignored for the address registration process as the ESI uniquely identifies an ATM end system. The network prefix is supplied by the ATM switch, while the user part is supplied by the ATM end system. After exchanging the two parts between the network and user sides, the ATM address is registered at both sides as the combination of the two parts. For public UNIs, if a native E.164 address is used, the network side supplies the entire ATM address. The network prefix is the native E.164 address, while the user part must be null. For both private and public UNIs, multiple ATM addresses can be supported for a UNI by having the network side supply multiple network prefixes to the ATM end system.

10.2.7 Anycast and Group Address

The ATM anycast capability allows an ATM end system to make a point-to-point connection to a member of an ATM group. An ATM group is a set of ATM end systems which have registered to the same ATM group address. In this case, each group member typically has two ATM addresses: an individual and a group address (assuming they all belong to a single group). When the calling ATM end system make a point-to-point call using the ATM group address as the calling party number, the ATM network is responsible to route the call to one of the members of the ATM group. The selection of the member may depend on the proximity of the group member to the calling end system, as defined by a scope information.

The ATM anycast capability is very useful to support a network service by providing a well-known address (an ATM group address). A network service can be provided by a set of ATM end systems distributed across the ATM network. When a user makes an anycast call using the well-known address, a connection will be made to one of the end systems providing such a service. The selection or location of the network service is transparent to the calling user. Since the network service can be reached by a well-known address, it simplifies service provisioning and allows portability of client software for the network service. Anycast also provides redundancy for network services because multiple end systems can provide the same service transparently.

10.3 ATM Connection Types

The ITU-T has defined the following 4 connection types for ATM. In general, a single application can be supported by one or more connections of different types. Currently, only point-to-point and point-to-multipoint connections have been specified in UNI 3.1 and 4.0.

10.3.1 Type 1: Point-to-Point

The type 1 connection is a bi-directional, point-to-point connection between two parties. Bandwidth, QoS service class is independently specified in each direction, which means that asymmetric bandwidth can be supported. In fact, the unidirectional connection is the special case with zero bandwidth in one direction. The type 1 connection also specifies that the physical route taken by the connection in each direction must be identical. Also, to simplify VC table management, the VPI/VCI values chosen in both directions must be the same for each link along the path.

10.3.2 Type 2: Point-to-Multipoint

The type 2 connection is typically referred to as the point-to-multipoint connection. It is a multipoint connection involving three or more parties. It is initiated by an ATM end system, which is referred to as the root. All the other parties are called the leaves. The root can set up the connection either with a single leaf first and add new leaves later, or with all the leaves at once. A leaf can leave at any time during the connection. However, the root must be present during the entire duration of the connection. Otherwise, the connection is torn down when the root leaves.

The point-to-multipoint connection is a unidirectional connection for which the root is the only source. Hence, it does not make sense to have a point-to-multipoint connection without the root. The root only sends a single copy of its information over the connection and the network is responsible for replicating the copy to all the leaves.

In the basic type 2 connection, the root has full control over the connection. Only the root can add new parties (leaves) to the connection, although leaves can disconnect by themselves. This is supported in UNI 3.1. An extension to the basic type 2 connection allows a leaf to initiate joining the connection independently without the permission of the root. This is known as leaf-initiated join or network-controlled join point-to-multipoint connection in UNI 4.0. It is up to the root to specify, during the connection set up phase, whether it allows independent join for the leaves, and if allowed, whether the root should be notified of such requests.

The point-to-multipoint connection is important for supporting efficient distribution of information to multiple end systems in the ATM network. Since the network is responsible for the replication, the source ATM end system avoids sending multiple copies of the same information to different end systems. Its applications include broadcast TV and supporting LAN protocols that require an underlying broadcast mechanism.

The type 2 connection is also useful in supporting IP multicast over ATM networks. The current IP multicast over ATM IETF standard[4] specifies two approaches based on the type 2 connection. One way is to build a fully meshed set of type two connections, one for each source to all the multicast group members as leaves. The other way is to use a multicast server, which sets up a type 2 connection (hence is the root) to all the multicast group members (leaves). All multicast senders have a point-to-point connection to the multicast server. The multicast server is responsible to redirect the traffic from each source to all the multicast group members through the type 2 connection.

10.3.3 Type 3: Multipoint-to-Point

A type 3 connection is usually referred to as the multipoint-to-point connection. It is a unidirectional multipoint connection with multiple sources and a single receiver. This has the same logical configuration as the type 2 connection, except the information flow is reversed, from the leaves back to the root.

Although supporting this connection type is straightforward from the signaling standpoint (the same way as the type 2 connection above), it is nontrivial from a traffic management standpoint. The reason is that the type 3 connection introduces the cell interleaving problem. The cells from different sources (leaves) arrive at the destination (root) carrying the same VPI/VCI, as they belong to the same connection. Since these cells from different leaves are interleaved in general when they arrive at the root, the root cannot reassemble the AAL PDUs correctly. (Actually, the merging point can occur at any point along the path.) The only exception for which interleaving is not a problem is when only single-cell messages are sent. This cell interleaving problem is the main challenge for supporting the multipoint-to-point connection. The type 3 connection is still under study and has not yet been standardized.

One solution to the cell interleaving problem is to use the AAL 3/4 because it has the MID field that can be used for demultiplexing at the root. However, since AAL 3/4 is not widely deployed, we need another solution to support other AAL in general, especially for the much more popular AAL 5.

Another solution is to implement a serialization function at each ATM switch. Such a function resequences the arriving ATM cells from different input ports for the same type 3 connection such that after merging, consecutive cells are guaranteed to be from the same source until the end of the AAL-PDU. However, there are open issues with this approach. First, this introduces additional hardware complexity to the ATM switch design. Second, this requires all ATM switches in the network be upgraded with new hardware design to support type 3 connections for all endpoints, which can take a long time.

Third, this introduces a variable delay to the cells from the leaves. Once an ATM cell has been selected from one of the input sources, the switch has to finish transmission of all ATM cells that belong to the same PDU (from the same source). This means that all other ATM cells from other sources must incur a queuing delay during this period. If the switch forwards the ATM cells of a PDU before its entirety has been received at the switch, all other sources must be waiting until the rest of the PDU have arrived and transmitted again. The slower the speed of the arriving cells of PDU or the arriving link, the longer the queuing delay for other sources. Alternatively, to avoid this kind of delay, the switch only transmits an ATM cell if all the other cells of the same PDU have already arrived at the switch and buffered. However, this means all sources must incur a complete PDU transmission delay because of the stored-and-forward approach. Therefore, the QoS degradation effect needs further study.

Actually, this serialization function is also performed by the multicast server above. All the sources to a multicast group send their cells to the multicast server using point-to-point connections. The multicast server serializes them before resending it on the point-to-multipoint connection for the multicast group members.

A third solution is to restrict one leaf to send at a time and no other leaves can send until the active leaf has finished transmission of an integral number of AAL-PDUs. Such coordination can be achieved out-to-band (not using the signaling protocol) by the application. The problem with this approach is application specific (aware), because it requires an application to implement such coordination function. Another problem is scaling to large networks. It introduces high latency to coordinate leaves that are far apart.

The type 3 connection is important for many applications. One application is the live broadcast scenario with multiple cameras. It is very useful to have a multipoint-to-point connection from all these cameras to each viewer of interest. The reason is that at any one instant, there is only one camera active from the viewer's point-of-view, so the type 3 connection is efficient for this application. Otherwise, if a separate point-to-point connection is established from each camera to the viewers, only one of the connections is active at any one time, and the rest are wasted. The switching of the cameras in this application is controlled by the director; this can be achieved out-of-band by a third party that is not part of the type 3 connection.

10.3.4 Type 4: Multipoint-to-Multipoint

The type 4 connection is also called the multipoint-to-multipoint connection. It is a multipoint connection that allows any party to send to all other parties of the connection. This connection type faces the same challenge of cell interleaving as the type 3 connection, and hence may be solved with similar solutions.

Although the multipoint-to-multipoint connection seems to be similar to the IP multicast model, there is one important difference. The source of an IP multicast group does not need to be a member of the multicast group. In fact, the IP multicast group defines a set of receivers only, not senders. Any end system can be a sender to the multicast group, given the IP multicast address. On the other hand, the multipoint-to-multipoint connection defines both the sets of senders and receivers. All senders (and receivers) must be part of the connection to send to (and receive from) the connection. Hence, IP multicast cannot be supported simply by establishing a single multipoint-to-multipoint connection among all multicast group members. Otherwise, this would exclude sources outside of the IP multicast group, while providing send capability to endpoints that do not want to send to the multicast group. Exact mapping of IP multicast to the type 4 connection occurs only when all multicast group members are sources and there are no additional sources outside the multicast group.

The multipoint-to-multipoint connection is important for supporting group communication, such as multi-user games and multiparty multimedia conference calls, and for supporting LAN protocols. Unfortunately, the type 4 connection is still under study and not yet standardized. To support the equivalent function of a type 4 connection, one can combine a full mesh of type 2 connections, each rooted at a different party of the connection. Obviously, this does scale to large number of endpoints.

10.3.5 First Party Versus Third Party Control

We have assumed all the connection types discussed above use first party control. First party control connections are those that have one of the parties of the connection as the controlling end system. For multipoint connections, this controlling end system is also known as the root party. This is similar to the current telephony model of three-way calling for which one of the parties is responsible for adding other parties.

However, we can also have a third party control connection, for which the controlling end system is not one of the communicating parties of the connection. In this case, the controlling end system is also referred to as the third party controller. If the communicating parties do not support signaling, the third party controller is also called the proxy signaling agent. All of the above connection types can be implemented with a third party controller.

10.4 ATM UNI Signaling Protocol

The ATM UNI signaling protocol is used only at the source and destination UNIs. Hence, only two pairs of entities are exchanging the UNI signaling (for a point-to-point connection): between the calling party and its attached (originating) ATM switch, and between the called party and its attached (destination) ATM switch (see Figure 10-6).

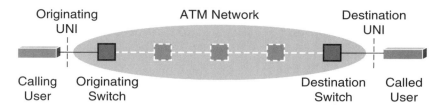

Figure 10–6   ATM UNI signaling model

Obviously, there needs to be other signaling protocols in the ATM network to complete the connection setup.[5] Between the private ATM switches or networks, the Private-Network Node Interface (P-NNI) signaling protocol is used. Between the public ATM switches or networks, the Broadband Inter-Carrier Interface (B-ICI) protocol is used.

The ATM UNI signaling protocol consists of the signaling procedures for exchanging signaling messages to accomplish call control such as setting up a connection. Both signaling messages and procedures are discussed in detail next.

10.4.1 Signaling Messages

A signaling message is made up of a number of information elements (IEs). Each message is designed for performing well-defined operations, as specified by the IE called message type. The message type IE is one of the four required IEs for all signaling messages, as shown in Table 10-1. These mandatory IEs are discussed next, while other conditional IEs (required for certain message types) are explained as we discuss the signaling procedures.

10.4.1.1 Protocol Discriminator (1 octet)

Signaling messages can be based on a protocol other than Q.2931. A protocol discriminator is used to indicate the type of protocol being used for signaling. These other signaling protocols can be Q.931, X.25 and others to be defined.

10.4.1.2 Call Reference (4 octets)

It is a local identifier (that is, no global significance) to identify a particular call of the UNI. For each call, there is a state machine maintained at both sides of each UNI. The call reference is used to uniquely identify the state machine of the call. During the call setup phase, the call reference of each UNI is assigned by the originating side of the UNIs. If there are multiple signaling channels across the UNI (such as one per VP), each signaling channel will have its own set of call references, which need to be unique per signaling channel only. For each signaling channel, there is also a global call reference defined to refer to all calls across all the VPs controlled by the signaling channel.

Note that there is a subtle difference between a call and a connection, which have been used interchangeably so far. In general, a call can support more than one connection. Hence, in the signaling protocol, they are identified by different IEs to allow such flexibility: the call reference IE identifies a call, and the connection identifier IE identifies a connection. Since we only consider single-connection per call scenarios in this book, a call is the same as a connection for our discussions.

10.4.1.3 Message Type (2 octets)

This identifies the type of message. The key message types defined at the UNI include SETUP, CALL PROCEEDING, CONNECT, CONNECT ACK, RELEASE and RELEASE COMPLETE. The set of message types for UNI signaling of point-to-point and point-to-multipoint connections are shown in Table 10-2 and Table 10-3, respectively. Table 10-4 shows the messages involving the global call reference. More detail explanation of their usage can by found in ATM Forum specifications.[1, 2]

10.4.1.4 Message Length (2 octets)

The Message Length IE indicates the number of octets for all the additional IEs following itself. This is zero if there are no more IEs other than these four mandatory IEs.

Table 10–1 *The IEs used by point-to-point and point-to-multipoint connection types for UNI 3.1[1] and UNI signaling 4.0*

Information Elements	Length (octets)	Purpose	Comments
4 Mandatory IEs			Required for all message types Occurred in the following order
Protocol Discriminator	1	Types of Protocol	Q.2931, X.25, etc.
Call Reference	4	Local identifier of the call (no global significance)	Assigned by calling endstation
Message Type	2	Type of Message	e.g., setup, connect, connect acknowledge
Message Length	2	Length of Message	Count bytes following this field only => = 0 if no more IE following
Conditional IEs			Required dependent on Message Type
AAL Parameters	4-21	AAL type and its parameters	SETUP (requested parameters) CONNECT (counter offered parameters) AAL3/4 & 5: F&B* SDU size (0 for unidirectional traffic; SSCS Type (null, SSCOP, Frame Relay); AAL1: source clock recovery mechanism, FEC, SDT, partially filled cell options
ATM Traffic Descriptor	12-30	Traffic Descriptor	F&B PCR (CLP=0); F&B PCR (CLP=0+1) F&B SCR (CLP=0); F&B SCR (CLP=0+1) F&B MaxBurstSize (CLP=0); F&B MaxBurstSize(CLP=0+1) Best Effort Indicator = QoS class0 or UBR F&B Tagging Option F&B parameters independently specified, except for Best Effort (both direction)
Broadband Bearer Capability	6-7	Class of Service Traffic Type Timing Requirements Clipping Susceptibility Connection Configuration	Bear Class: A, C, X UBR (no indication), CBR, VBR No indication, End-to-end requirements Yes or No Point-to-point, Point-to-Multipoint

Table 10–1 *The IEs used by point-to-point and point-to-multipoint connection types for UNI 3.1[1] and UNI signaling 4.0* continued

Information Elements	Length (octets)	Purpose	Comments
Broadband Higher Layer Information: B-HLI	4-13	Compatibility checking for Higher Layer Information	Transparent to the network Public network (Public-UNI) is optional (must be negotiated to carry B-HLI) Private Network is mandatory to carry
Broadband Lower Layer Information: B-LLI	4-17	Lower layer compatibility checking	Mandatory for network to support
Called Party Number	≤ 25	Destination address	Mandatory
Called Party Subaddress	4-25	Destination subaddress for private network	Mandatory for network to support, if sent by the setup message
Calling Party Number	4-26	Source address	
Calling Party Subaddress	4-25	Source address for private network	
Connection Identifier	9	Local ATM connection resource	Always assigned by network VPCI (2 bytes) &VCI (2 bytes) If signaling channel control single interface, VPCI = VPI. VPCI is significant to a particular signaling virtual channel
QoS Parameter	6	F&B QoS Class	Class 0 (unspecified) Class 1,2,3,4 If requested not available from the network, UBR is returned
Endpoint Reference	4-7	Identify a leaf	Used only for point-to-multipoint call, not point-to-point call = 0 for 1st party of PMP call nonzero for subsequent parties 15 bits Value => 32k leaves maximum
LIJ Call Identifier	4-9	LIJ call ID set by root LIJ call setup	Included only for Network Join option; Not included for Root Prompt LIJ Join; Unique among LIJ calls from same root; Used by Leaf to join this call

Table 10–1   *The IEs used by point-to-point and point-to-multipoint connection types for UNI 3.1[1] and UNI signaling 4.0* continued

Information Elements	Length (octets)	Purpose	Comments
LIJ Parameters	4-8	Root to indicate the LIJ options	When present, LIJ call ID and calling party no. Must also be included (i.e., support LIJ). Present implies this is a Network LIJ connection. Indicate a LIJ network join with or without root notification
Leaf Sequence Number	4-8	Leaf ID	Set by Leaf when sending join request

* F = Forward direction; B = Backward direction

Table 10–2   *ATM UNI signaling message types for point-to-point calls and their usage for UNI 3.1[1]*

Signaling Messages	Purpose	Senders	Mandatory IEs (plus 4 basic IEs)	Optional IEs
Call Establishment				
SETUP	setup a connection	Calling user → network; network → called user	ATM traffic descriptor; Broadband Bearer Capability; Called Party Number; Connection Identifier (n→u)* only; QoS Parameter	AAL Parameters; B-HLI B-LLI Broadband Repeat Indicator; Called Party Subaddress; Calling Party number and subaddress Endpoint Reference (pmp)
CALL PROCEEDING	(Optional) To reset the timer to a larger value	Called user → network; network → calling user		Connection Identifier (n→u); Endpoint reference (required if included in setup)

Table 10–2   *ATM UNI signaling message types for point-to-point calls and their usage for UNI 3.1*[1] *continued*

Signaling Messages	Purpose	Senders	Mandatory IEs (plus 4 basic IEs)	Optional IEs
CONNECT	Indicate call acceptance	Called user → network; network → calling user		AAL Parameters; B-LLI; Connection Identifier (n→u); Endpoint reference - required if included in set up
CONNECT ACKNOWL-EDGE	Indicate call awarded by network	Network →called user; calling user → network		
Call Clearing				
RELEASE	Terminate a call	By either user or network	Cause	
RELEASE COMPLETE	Must respond the release	By the receiving party/network		Cause
Miscellaneous				
STATUS ENQUIRY	Solicit status	By network or user		Endpoint reference (p-mp only)
STATUS	Report status	Respond status enquiry	Call State; Cause	Endpoint Ref. Endpoint state

*   Network to called user

Table 10–3   *ATM UNI signaling message types for point-to-multipoint calls and their usage*

Point-to-Multipoint Call/Connection	Purpose	Senders	Mandatory IEs	Optional IEs
Root Initiated Join				
ADD PARTY	Add to existing connection	Root → network; network → new leaf	Called party no.; Endpoint reference	AAL parameters; B-HLI; B-LLI; Called party sub-address; Calling party no. & subaddress
ADD PARTY ACKNOWL-EDGE	Indicate Add Party successful	Respond to Add Party	Endpoint reference - same as ADD PARTY	
ADD PARTY REJECT	Indicate Add Party unsuccessful	Respond to Add Party	Cause; Endpoint reference - same as ADD PARTY	
DROP PARTY	Clear a party	By root or that leaf party	Cause; Endpoint reference	
DROP PARTY ACKNOWL-EDGE	Indicate the party is dropped	Respond to drop party	Endpoint reference	Cause
Leaf Initiated Join				
SETUP (include with above)	Setup point-to-multipoint call with LIJ options	Root to network; network to first leaf	Same as original setup message above	Add the following LIJ call identifier LIJ parameters Leaf sequence no.-required if respond to leaf set up request

Table 10–3 *ATM UNI signaling message types for point-to-multipoint calls and their usage* continued

Point-to-Multipoint Call/Connection	Purpose	Senders	Mandatory IEs	Optional IEs
LEAF SETUP REQUEST	Leaf joining a point to multi-point call	Sent by a leaf to the network	Call reference must be a dummy; Calling party number; Called party number; LIJ call identifier; Leaf sequence number	
LEAF SETUP FAILURE	Indicate unsuccessful leaf initiate join	Root to network; network to the initiated leaf	Cause; Leaf sequence number	Called party no.; Called party sub-address; Transit network selection
NEW LEAF ANNOUNCE	Announce the addition of a new leaf to existing call	From the network to the root	Endpoint reference	Called party no.; Called party sub-address
NEW LEAF ANNOUNCE ACKNOWL-EDGE	Acknowledge receipt of NEW LEAF ANNOUNCE	From root to network	Endpoint reference	Called party no.; Called party sub-address

Table 10–4 *Signaling message types involving global call reference in UNI 3.1*[1]

Messages with Global Call Reference	Purpose	Senders	Mandatory IEs	Optional IEs
RESTART	Release one or all VCs controlled by the signaling VC	User to network; network to user	Restart indicator	Connection Identifier
RESTART ACKNOWL-EDGE	Acknowledge receipt of RESTART	User to network; network to user	Restart indicator	Connection Identifier

10.4.2 Signaling Procedures

To understand the signaling procedures and the usage of the signaling messages and IEs, we will walk through the procedure of setting up and releasing a (first-party) point-to-point connection below. The point-to-point call setup procedure forms the basis of connection set up procedure for all other more complex connection types.

10.4.2.1 Point-to-Point Connection

Call setup　The procedure for setting up a point-to-point type VC is straightforward. It is basically a three-way handshake procedure:

1. the caller sending a SETUP message;

2. the called user (and the network) responding with a CONNECT message (if the call is accepted); and

3. acknowledging the receipt of the CONNECT message with the CONNECT ACK message.

The detail of the procedure is shown in Figure 10-7, which is described in the following steps for UNI 3.1,[1] highlighted by communicating the following signaling messages:

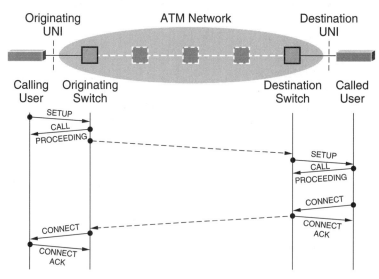

Figure 10–7　Signaling procedure for setting up a point-to-point connection

SETUP message from the calling party to the attached ATM switch: A point-to-point connection is initiated by one of the two end systems because this is a first party call control. The originating end system (the calling party) begins the call set up procedure by sending a SETUP message (indicated by message type IE as SETUP) to the ATM network over the originating UNI. The SETUP message indicates to the ATM network that the calling party wants to set up a point-to-point connection with another end system (the called party) on the ATM network. The SETUP message must include the class of service, the traffic and QoS parameters for each direction of the connection, and the destination party's ATM address. If there is enough resource in the network, the originating end system expects the network to forward the SETUP message to the destination end system to establish the connection.

Hence, in addition to the four mandatory IEs above, the SETUP message must carry the following mandatory IEs:

- ATM Traffic Descriptor: It specifies the forward and backward traffic parameters, which include the peak cell rate (PCR, the peak bandwidth measured in cell/sec), sustained cell rate (SCR, the average bandwidth) and maximum burst size for CLP = 0 only and CLP = 0+1. The forward and backward traffic parameters are independently specified. The tagging option can also be indicated. For Unspecified Bit Rate (UBR) class, none of these traffic parameters are specified. Instead, it includes the Best Effort Indicator to indicate the UBR service request UBR is discussed in the next chapter.
- Broadband Bearer Capability: It indicates the bearer service requested which can be one of the AAL classes of service (A, B, C, D and X). Currently only a subset of these AAL service classes (A, C and X) are specified in UNI 3.1. This IE also specifies the AAL service requirements (such as whether timing between source and receiver is required) and the connection type, which is point-to-point in this case. (Only point-to-point and point-to-multipoint are defined for UNI 3.1 and 4.0.)
- Called Party Number: This is the ATM end system address of the destination party, which can be either an E.164 number or a 20-octet NSAP encoding format address.
- Quality of Service Parameter: Contrary to the name of this IE, this specifies the forward and backward QoS class: Class 0, 1, 2, 3 and 4. QoS classes 1, 2, 3, 4 are supposed to meet the service class A, B, C,

D performance requirements, respectively. While the UNI 3.1 specification does not allow passing QoS parameters, they can be specified in UNI 4.0.

In addition to these required IEs, there are a number of optional IEs that can be included in the SETUP message, including the caller's own ATM address. Other optional IEs are higher layer parameters (above ATM layer) such as:

- AAL parameters: This IE indicates the requested AAL parameters. These include the type of AAL requested and the corresponding associated parameters. They have end-to-end significance (at both calling and called parties). The associated parameters include the CPCS-SDU size and SSCS type for the AAL 3/4 and AAL5 in each direction. For a unidirectional connection, the CPCS-SDU size is zero in the idle direction. Note also that the CPCS-SDU size in each direction must both be present or both absent. For the AAL 3/4, these also include the MID range. For the AAL 1, the IE includes the kind of source clock frequency recovery, error correction method, CBR rate, SDT Block size and partially filled cell method. Also, this IE indicates the kind of SSCS used (such as SSCOP and Frame Relay), if any.
- Broadband Higher Layer Information (B-HLI): This is transferred across the network for compatibility checking between ATM end systems, which can be inter-working units such as routers. It is carried transparently across the ATM network: The switches along the path do not interpret this IE. The B-HLI can be used as a service access point (SAP) within the end system to demultiplex an incoming call for a particular destination entity (software subsystem) within the end system. There are also code points within the B-HLI IE to define user specific information. Since this provides a way for user to pass information during the call set up process and can tear down the call without paying for it, the public network operators do not have to carry this IE. Hence, if this IE is present in the SETUP message, it is mandatory only for the private network to carry end-to-end to the destination.
- Broadband Lower Layer Information (B-LLI): This is also transferred across the network transparently for compatibility between end systems. This IE indicates the type of layer 2 and layer 3 protocols to be used

between the end systems. Layer 2 protocols are link layer protocols such as X.25 link layer, HDLC or LAN LLC, or user specified. Layer 3 protocols are network layer protocols such as X.25 network layer, OSI connectionless mode protocol, or user specified protocols. Since the B-LLI IE is specified for protocol compatibility use and not user-to-user information, both public and private networks are required to transfer this IE. Similar to the B-HLI, the B-LLI is also used as a SAP for demultiplexing incoming call at the ATM end system for the proper protocol stack to handle. The dedication of a VC for a single protocol is known as VC-based multiplexing for multiprotocol support (or null encapsulation).[6] Alternatively, the B-LLI can also allow an unspecified protocol stack so that multiple protocol stacks can share the connection. Instead of indicating the specific protocol in the SETUP message (control plane), the specific protocol stack can be specified in the user plane on a per PDU basis, each with a self-identifying header such as IEEE 802.1 SNAP identifier to indicate which protocol it is for. This is called the multiprotocol encapsulation scheme.

(Optional) CALL PROCEEDING message replied by the attached ATM switch: On receiving the SETUP message from the calling party, the first (originating) ATM switch processes this SETUP message to evaluate if there is sufficient resource locally. At the same time, the ATM switch can optionally reply to the calling party with the CALL PROCEEDING message to indicate that it has received the SETUP message successfully and is processing the message. This message is useful for large ATM networks for which the reply from the called party might take longer. In this case, the calling party might time out before it is necessary. The CALL PROCEEDING is sent to reset the timeout on the calling party to a longer time period to adjust for the expected delay.

Also, the CALL PROCEEDING message carries the connection identifier IE, which indicates VPCI/VCI to be used for the connection. (VPCI is translated to VPI locally at both sides of the interface for use on the ATM cell headers.) The connection identifier is always assigned by the network, but the user can also decline the call on the basis of VPCI/VCI incompatibility. Since the CALL PROCEEDING message is optional, the VPCI/VCI assignment also can occur later when the call is granted by the network through the CONNECT message.

If there are sufficient resources in this originating ATM switch to support the ATM Traffic Descriptor, the QoS parameters and the Broadband

Bearer Capability, then the switch will forward the call setup request across the ATM network over a path chosen by the ATM routing protocol (as part of the NNI signaling protocol, not the UNI signaling). However, if there are not sufficient resources from the network to support this call, this call will be rejected by responding to the calling user with the RELEASE COMPLETE message (including the reason for call rejection). Similarly, if there are not sufficient resources in the rest of network towards the destination party, it will also result in sending a RELEASE COMPLETE message back to the calling party.

SETUP message to the called party from the destination ATM switch: When this setup request arrives at the ATM switch connected to the called party (the destination ATM switch), the switch generates the same SETUP message with the additional connection identifier IE to indicate the VPCI/VCI to be used for this connection. Note that the both the connection identifier and call reference IEs at the destination UNI are different from the corresponding IEs at the originating UNI, because they are only of local significance. If the first SETUP from the calling party includes the end-to-end parameter IEs (such as AAL parameters, B-HLI and B-LLI), this SETUP from the destination switch to the called party must also carry these IEs (except it is optional to forward the B-HLI in the public network).

(Optional) CALL PROCEEDING message replied by the called party: On receiving the SETUP message from the destination ATM switch, the called party also can respond with the CALL PROCEEDING message to the switch while processing the SETUP message. Again, this message is optional, similar to the source UNI. There is less need for this to be implemented at the destination UNI because this is only a single-hop delay, in contrast to the entire network delay for the source UNI above.

CONNECT message replied by the called party: If the called party accepts the call, it responds with a CONNECT message to the destination ATM switch to indicate call acceptance. However, the user information transfer from the called party cannot begin until the called party receives the confirmation, which is the CONNECT ACKNOWLEDGE message below.

CONNECT ACKNOWLEDGE message by destination ATM switch: On receipt of the CONNECT message from the called party, the destination switch responds with a CONNECT ACKNOWLEDGE message to the called party to indicate it has received the CONNECT message.

CONNECT message sent to the calling party: When the destination ATM switch responds with the CONNECT ACKNOWLEDGE message to the called party, it also forwards the call acceptance message across the ATM network to the originating ATM switch. The originating ATM switch then sends a CONNECT message to the calling party to indicate that the call has been accepted and established. If the originating switch did not send the CALL PROCEEDING message earlier (which would include the VPCI/VCI assignment), this CONNECT message would include the VPCI/VCI assignment for this connection.

CONNECT ACKNOWLEDGE message replied by the calling party: On receipt of the CONNECT message from the originating ATM switch, the calling party responds with a CONNECT ACKNOWLEDGE message to the ATM switch to indicate it has received the CONNECT message. Then the call is fully established end-to-end and both parties can begin transferring user information.

AAL Parameter negotiation The CSCP-SDU size, carried in the AAL Parameter IE, can be negotiated by the called party to indicate a different set of AAL Parameters in the CONNECT message. The called party can only indicate a smaller CSCP-SDU size than the one in the SETUP message for each direction. If the called party does not include the AAL Parameter IE in the CONNECT message, the calling user shall assume the called user accepts the requested AAL parameters.

Connection negotiation In UNI 3.1, if the call setup parameters are not satisfied by either the network or the end user, the call set up will fail, even if the calling user can accept a different (lower) capability that could have been supported by the calling user. The only choice for the calling user is to initiate another call set up for a different parameter set up with lower requirements. Since the calling user has no clue about the available network resources, the user can only guess the proper parameters in each call set up.

One of the key capabilities introduced in UNI signaling 4.0 is connection negotiation. It allows the calling user to negotiate during the call set up in two ways. First, it allows PCR negotiation by specifying both the desired PCR and the minimum PCR acceptable. The call will become successful if the network has at least the minimum PCR available.

Extending the negotiation process to a set of IEs simultaneously must take into account that there might not be a strict order relationship between two sets of IEs. Hence, the UNI 4.0 supports such negotiation by having the SETUP message to include two sets of parameters: primary and alternate. The primary set is used for connection set up first. If successful, this becomes the parameter set for the connection. Otherwise, the network tries the alternate set. The call would still be successful if this alternate set is accepted by the network and the called user.

Premature data transfer problem and the NOTIFY message   If one examines this call set up procedure closely, one might realize a potential flaw. When the called party receives the CONNECT ACKNOWLEDGE from the network, it assumes the connection is open and can begin communication by starting to send user information. However, as shown in Figure 10-7, at this point there is no guarantee the calling party has already received the corresponding CONNECT message from the network to know the connection is established. This results in the called party premature data transfer problem.

To prevent the called party from beginning transmission until the calling party receives the CONNECT message, we need to allow the confirmation from the calling party to be transferred all the way back to the called party. Hence, a new message called NOTIFY has been introduced in UNI 4.0 to achieve exactly this purpose.

Call release   To tear down a point-to-point call is very simple. It can be initiated by sending the RELEASE message by either the network or one of two user parties across the UNI. On receiving a RELEASE message, the user party (or the network) should disconnect the virtual channel and then send a RELEASE COMPLETE message to the network (or the user) and release the call reference and the virtual channel (VPCI/VCI).

10.4.3 ATM Call States

For each call, as identified by the Call Reference at the UNI, there are call states associated for both the user side and the network side of the call. The call states at the user side is shown in Figure 10-8 and is explained below:

- Null state: no call exists
- Call Initiated state: a call SETUP message has been sent to the network
- Outgoing Call Proceeding state: after receiving the CALL PROCEEDING message
- Call Present state: a call SETUP has been received from the network

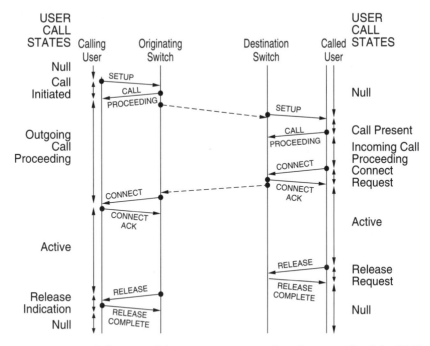

Figure 10–8   Call states of the point-to-point call at the user side of the UNI

- Connect Request state: when the called party answers the call and accepts the call by sending a CONNECT message, but is still waiting for the CONNECT ACK from the network
- Incoming Call Proceeding state: after the user responds to the SETUP message with the CALL PROCEEDING message
- Active state: the calling party (called party) has received the CON-NECT (CONNECT ACK) from the network to indicate the call has been awarded.
- Release Request state: when the user has requested the network to tear down the connection and waits for a response
- Release Indication state: on receiving the disconnect request from the network, as the network has disconnected the connection

10.4.4 Timers

Associated with each state are timers on the user and network sides of the UNI with specific timeout values. Each timer is associated with a particular call state. For example, timer T303 is started on the user side once the

SETUP message has been sent. In the other words, T303 runs in the Call Initiated state. It has a value of 4 sec. T303 can be stopped by receiving CONNECT, CALL PROCEEDING or RELEASE COMPLETE messages. If it expires (that is, none of these messages are received by the caller within 4 sec), it will retransmit the SETUP message. If it expires the second time, it will clear the internal connection. Readers should refer to the UNI 3.1[1] and UNI 4.0[2] for the complete list of timers. Note that UNI 4.0 has increased some timer values from UNI 3.1.

10.4.5 Point-to-Multipoint Connection Type

In general, the point-to-point call signaling protocol is used as a basis for more complicated connection types, such as type 2 connection. In the point-to-multipoint connection type, there is data from only from one party (the root) to all other parties (the leaves). All the information from the root is replicated by the ATM network through the copy function of the switches along the path. This is also known as point-to-multipoint with zero return bandwidth. There are two types of (first party) point-to-multipoint connection: root initiated or leaf-initiated. Here, we only give an overview. For detailed step-by-step set up procedures of this connection type, the reader should consult UNI 3.1 and 4.0 specifications.

10.4.5.1 Root Initiated

The point-to-multipoint connection is first defined as a root-initiated type and is specified in UNI 3.1. It is a very simple extension to the point-to-point connection set up protocol, by adding a new IE called Endpoint Reference and a new message called ADD PARTY. This is explained below.

To set up a root-initiated point-to-multipoint connection, the root first sends a SETUP message to the first leaf of the call as if it is establishing a point-to-point call. There are only two differences in the SETUP message from the point-to-point connection. First, the Broadband Bearer Capability IE indicates that this is a point-to-multipoint call instead of point-to-point call. Second, there is a new IE called endpoint reference in the SETUP message. The endpoint reference IE identifies the individual leaves in the point-to-multipoint call and is assigned by the root. It always has a value of 0 for the first leaf and a distinct nonzero value for each subsequent leaf added. Similar to the call reference IE that is used to identify a call at the UNI, the endpoint reference IE is used to identify a particular party of a point-to-multipoint call. The rest of the procedure for setting up the connection between the root and the first leaf party is similar to the point-to-point call setup procedure.

To add the second leaf to the point-to-multipoint call, the root sends a new message ADD PARTY with the ATM address of the second leaf as the calling party address. It must contain the same call reference of the first point-to-multipoint call set up to the first leaf party. It also must contain a new endpoint reference IE (nonzero value) for this second leaf party assigned by the root. Both the ATM address and the endpoint reference IE are mandatory for the ADD PARTY message.

Since the QoS parameters, the Broadband Bearer Capability and ATM Traffic Descriptor are identical to the first leaf, they are not included in the ADD PARTY message. Similar to the SETUP message, it is optional to include IEs for higher layers such as the AAL parameters, the B-HLI and the B-LLI IEs.

States: link and party In addition to the above states of a point-to-point call, there is a new set of states for describing individual parties in the point-to-multipoint call. The original call states are now called link states which specify the condition of the point-to-multipoint call on both sides of the UNI. The new states are called party states. They specify the UNI conditions of individual parties of the point-to-multipoint connection.

10.4.5.2   Leaf Initiated Join Call

In UNI 4.0, the original (root-initiated) point-to-multipoint connection has been extended to support leaf-initiated joining to the connection. There are two types of leaf-initiated join (LIJ) call: Network LIJ or Root LIJ. In both cases, a leaf joins a LIJ call by sending a LEAF SETUP REQUEST with the leaf sequence number (for reference of the request later), the called party address and the LIJ ID. The LIJ ID is known to the leaf from an out-of-band mechanism. The network uses the called party address and the LIJ ID to form the global call ID (GCID) to locate this call. If the leaf attempts to join an inactive call, the network always forwards the leaf join request to the root. The root has to decide whether to create such a call. In other words, the root is always the one responsible for setting up the first leaf.

The Network and Root LIJ differ by whether the LEAF SETUP REQEST message from the leaf are forwarded to the root, when there is an active point-to-multipoint connection. For Network NIJ, the network automatically adds the new leaf which has sent the LEAF SETUP REQEST to the active point-to-multipoint connection, provided there are sufficient network resources. For Root NIJ, such a request is forwarded to the Root and the root adds the leaf in a standard point-to-multipoint add leaf fashion, by sending the ADD message.

10.5 Summary

In this chapter, we discussed ATM access signaling in detail. We first discussed the basic ATM signaling concepts, including SVCs versus PVCs, VPI versus VPCI, signaling AAL, ATM addressing, address registration and the anycast capability. Then we explained the different connection types in the ATM network as defined by ITU: point-to-point, point-to-multipoint, multipoint-to-point and multipoint-to-multipoint. Currently, only the first two connection types have been defined and standardized. Next, we explored the ATM UNI signaling protocol for setting up point-to-point VCs in detail. The connection setup procedure is a three-way handshake procedure. The point-to-point connection set up procedure forms the basis of setting up other types of more complicated connections. Finally, we gave an overview of the point-to-multipoint connection setup procedure.

10.6 References

[1] The ATM Forum, *ATM User-Network Interface (UNI) Specification*, Version 3.1, Prentice Hall, 1995.

[2] The ATM Forum, *ATM User-Network Interface (UNI) Signaling Specification*, Version 4.0, 1996.

[3] The ATM Forum, *ATM Integrated Local Management Interface (ILMI) Specification*, Version 4.0, 1996.

[4] G. Armitage, "Support for Multicast over UNI 3.0/3.1 based ATM Networks," *IETF Request for Comments: 2022*, November 1996.

[5] G. Dobrowski, D. Minoli, *Principles of Signaling for Cell Relay and Frame Relay*, Artech House, 1995.

[6] J. Heinanen, "Multiprotocol Encapsulation over ATM Adaptation Layer 5," *IETF Request for Comments: 1483*, July 1993.

Chapter 11

Traffic Management and ATM Service Categories

11.1 Introduction

ATM traffic management is the cornerstone of ATM to effectively support applications with diverse traffic and QoS requirements. Traffic management and the associated ATM service categories are the focus of this chapter.

In this chapter, we first define traffic management and discuss the key ATM traffic management mechanisms. Then, the traffic contract and its traffic and QoS parameters are discussed in detail. Next, we present the five ATM service categories recently defined by The ATM Forum in its traffic management 4.0 (TM 4.0) specification.[1] TM 4.0 introduces an important new service category called the available bit rate (ABR) service, which also will be discussed.

11.2 Traffic Management

The classic packet switched network provides only one type of service, namely, best-effort service. The key network performance objective is to maximize network throughput. Since congestion leads to performance degradation in the form of reduced network throughput, the main focus of traffic control is to avoid and control congestion. Also, its traffic control does not provide any bandwidth or QoS guarantee for any applications. The amount of bandwidth available to an application depends on the load generated collectively by other applications sharing the path of the application. Furthermore, the traffic control does not guarantee each application gets an equal share of the bandwidth; a greedy application can get more than its fair share of the bandwidth. Since many data applications in the classic packet switched networks are non-real-time applications (such as email and file transfer), this traffic control paradigm has been sufficient for those applications. However, as real-time (streaming and block transfer) applications, such as live and stored video delivery, multimedia conferencing and Web browsing, have emerged to become very important, a new traffic control paradigm is required.

ATM represents a new paradigm of packet-switched networking because its fundamental requirement is to support real-time applications. Hence, additional traffic control measures must be taken to guarantee the QoS for real-time applications. The goals of ATM traffic control are not only to allocate sufficient resources to a real-time application to satisfy its traffic and QoS requirements, but also to prevent other applications from exceeding their legitimate traffic load, which could degrade the bandwidth and QoS for real-time applications. The mechanisms designed to achieve these goals are referred to as traffic management mechanisms.

Theoretically, if the network is over-provisioned such that there is sufficient bandwidth for all applications, there should be no need for traffic management. However, even with abundant bandwidth, QoS may not be always guaranteed for all applications, because queues can still build up at the switches, due to the statistical nature of packet switching. Hence, variable delay can still be incurred and QoS cannot be truly guaranteed. Also, as the network grows, the networking requirements becomes a moving target, today's over-provisioned network can become congested tomorrow. With rapid introduction of new applications (especially on the Internet), there is no guarantee that a new application will not overload the once over-provisioned network, unless traffic management mechanisms have already been in place.

ATM traffic management mechanisms[1] can be classified into two categories: connection-based or cell-by-cell-based. They manage the macroscopic and microscopic traffic behavior, respectively. Both are required in the ATM network to support the wide variety of applications.

11.2.1 Connection-based Traffic Management

Connection-based traffic management mechanisms are performed on a per-connection basis during the connection set-up phase. They are particularly effective for an application with a predictable traffic behavior, because its cell-by-cell behavior is well-defined by the traffic description communicated during the call set up. Since real-time streaming applications typically generate continuous traffic patterns, connection-based mechanisms are very appropriate for these applications. Nevertheless, cell-by-cell-based mechanisms are still required for real-time streaming applications, as discussed later. Connection-based mechanisms include both connection admission control and network resource management. They are discussed in more detail below.

11.2.1.1 Connection Admission Control

For each new connection request, a set of actions is taken by the ATM network to determine if the network has sufficient resources to support the application. This mechanism is called connection admission control (CAC). Only if CAC determines such resources are available does it accept the connection request. Otherwise, the request is rejected. If a connection request is accepted, a traffic contract is established between the network and the application's endpoints. To obtain the service (bandwidth and QoS) guarantees based on the connection request, the endpoints are required to honor the traffic behavior as specified by the connection request. Otherwise, no such guarantees are provided. Such traffic monitoring to ensure the contract is honored after the connection setup is the responsibility of the cell-by-cell traffic management mechanisms, as discussed later.

CAC is critical to avoid over-commitment of network resources and to guarantee the bandwidth and QoS of existing applications on the network. This is especially important for supporting real-time applications. Again, for real-time streaming applications, CAC is straightforward to perform because such applications have a predictable traffic pattern and can be described easily. However, for real-time block traffic applications, which have an unpredictable traffic pattern, it is more difficult to describe and CAC can only be performed in a statistical fashion. Nevertheless,

CAC is still required for real-time block transfer applications and non-real-time applications to avoid over-commitment for these applications.

11.2.1.2 Network Resource Management

There are two key sets of resources (among others) in the ATM network: bandwidth and buffers. Network resource management (NRM) allocates the bandwidth and buffers to an application during the connection setup phase according to its connection requests. In fact, CAC depends on NRM to report if resources are available for new connection requests. NRM manages the available bandwidth and buffer at each switch along the path so as not to over-commit the network resources to ensure the QoS of all admitted applications. For each new successful connection request, NRM assigns a share of network resources along the path of the connection. Additional NRM functions can include assigning applications belonging to the same class of service with the same VPI, which allows simplified of identification traffic with the similar traffic and QoS requirements.

11.2.2 Cell-by-Cell-Based Traffic Management

Although connection-based mechanisms are quite effective for real-time streaming applications, they must be augmented by cell-by-cell-based traffic management mechanisms for these and other applications. Cell-by-cell-based mechanisms are enforced after the connection set-up process and apply to each cell transmitted by the application. They are necessary for monitoring and controlling the cell-by-cell transmission behavior of each application, so as to guarantee the traffic contracts established are observed during the life of all connections. Hence, all applications can obtain an appropriate share of resources to guarantee their performance accordingly. The various cell-by-cell-based mechanisms are discussed in detail next.

11.2.2.1 Usage Parameter Control

As discussed above, once CAC has determined that there are sufficient resources to admit the application, a traffic contract is established between the network and the endpoints of the connection based on the connection setup information. The traffic contract specifies the traffic characteristics that are generated by the application and the QoS provided (if any) to the applications by the network. The endpoints of the connection are responsible to stay within the traffic characteristics. Otherwise, the network would not guarantee the QoS provided to the connection.

To ensure that the traffic contract is observed by the endpoints, the network needs to police the traffic generated by each connection. Otherwise, the misbehaving endpoints (unintentional or malicious) can affect the QoS provided to other applications. Usage parameter control (UPC) is the set of policing mechanisms implemented by the network at the UNI to monitor and control the traffic submitted by each endpoint. UPC can drop or tag (i.e., change the CLP bit on the ATM cell header to indicate low-priority) the cells that violate the contract. UPC can also be implemented within the network (between switches over the NNI), which is sometimes referred to as network parameter control (NPC).

11.2.2.2 Traffic Shaping

To prevent traffic generated by the application from exceeding its traffic contract, traffic shaping should be performed by the endpoints to schedule or space transmissions of ATM cells accordingly. Traffic shaping is required not only for real-time applications, but also for non-real-time applications. Otherwise, the excess traffic can be dropped by the network (UPC function) to prevent the degradation of the QoS for other applications. Hence, traffic shaping is a key mechanism to guarantee QoS in the ATM network. Traffic shaping parameters (such as peak bandwidth) also can be adjusted according to the feedback information from the network (such as loading) or the destination endpoints, if feedback control is implemented (to be discussed later).

Ideally, traffic shaping also should be performed within the network. The reason is that even with traffic shaping at the endpoints, the well-behaved traffic can be perturbed at the multiplexing points (the output ports of the ATM switches) along the path, resulting in the cell clumping effect. Cell clumping occurs when the spacing between cells of an ATM connection is decreased because of insertion of cells of other connections. This effect counteracts the traffic shaping done by source, which means that traffic submitted to successive switches along the path may exceed the traffic contract, resulting in similar QoS problems as if there were insufficient traffic shaping performed by the source.

11.2.2.3 Scheduling

NRM is a connection-based mechanism for managing bandwidth and buffers, which must be combined with its cell-by-cell-based counterpart mechanisms to be effective for supporting a wide variety of applications.

Scheduling is the bandwidth management mechanism responsible for allocating bandwidth to each connection on a cell-by-cell basis. A scheduling algorithm is typically achieved at the output ports of each ATM switch. The scheduling algorithm decides the allocation of cell transmission time slots to each active connection (arriving ATM cells) destined to that output port.

Scheduling is important not only for real-time applications, but also for non-real-time applications. For real-time applications, to guarantee bandwidth and QoS, their transmission bandwidth must be guaranteed on a cell-by-cell basis according to the traffic contract. For non-real-time applications, even though no bandwidth is reserved in advance, available bandwidth (if there is leftover bandwidth from the real-time applications) is still allocated on-demand to them as traffic being submitted by the non-real-time applications. The amount of available bandwidth that is allocated to each non-real-time application should be managed so as to avoid a greedy application hoarding all the available bandwidth. Hence, there also needs to be a fair allocation of available bandwidth to the set of non-real-time applications going through each ATM switch.

The simplest scheduling algorithm in packet switching is the first-in-first-out (FIFO) algorithm, which requires only a single-queue-buffer per output port. All cells destined to the same output port are transmitted on a first-come-first-serve basis. If the buffer has any cells waiting for transmission, any newly arrived cells are buffered on a FIFO basis. Because of the simplicity of the FIFO algorithm, packet switches in most classic packet switched networks are based on this algorithm. However, the FIFO algorithm has an important limitation – it can provide only a single class of service because it treats all cells equally. This means that there are no QoS guarantees to any application. Hence, these classic packet switched networks can only provide best-effort service.

To support QoS, a more sophisticated scheduling algorithm that organizes the traffic into multiple (logical) queues per output buffer is required. As such, traffic from different connections can be classified into different queues, each characterized by a different class of service. This means that there is one queue per class of service offered, though more queues can provide even more sophisticated bandwidth management within each class. The scheduling algorithm specifies how often and in what order each queue is served, which depends on a number of factors, such as the traffic contracts, the traffic patterns and the buffer occupancy of each queue.

For example, the two-queue priority-scheduling algorithm represents a significant improvement over the FIFO algorithm to provide QoS. It consists of two queues per output port: high and low-priority. The high-priority queue is always served first until it becomes empty. At that point, the low-priority queue is served until it becomes empty, assuming the high-priority queue remains empty during this period. Otherwise, the high-priority queue is served when any new cells have arrived for that queue, until it becomes empty again. 100% of the output port bandwidth is available to the connections assigned to the high-priority queue. The bandwidth available to the low-priority queue is the leftover bandwidth from the high-priority queue. Hence, the low-priority queue receives variable bandwidth as a function of the load on the high-priority queue. Since one queue always has higher priority over the other, this is called static priority scheduling.

The QoS guarantees achieved through static priority depends on whether proper CAC, NRM and UPC are implemented. Without CAC, NRM and UPC, over-commitment of bandwidth can occur even for the high-priority queue and connections for this queue have no QoS guarantees, not to mention those for the low-priority queue. Under overload conditions for the high-priority queue, no bandwidth would be available to the low-priority queue. On the other hand, NRM can limit the bandwidth allocated to the high-priority queue to a fraction of the total bandwidth. CAC will turn down any new requests that exceed that fraction. UPC guarantees no misbehaving applications will affect the QoS of other applications. The rest of the bandwidth can be shared by the applications assigned to the low-priority queue to provide best-effort service. These low-priority applications can be non-real-time applications and no bandwidth is allocated by the NRM. The two-queue priority-scheduling algorithm is sufficient for providing two classes of service: one with bandwidth guarantees (for real-time streaming), and the other with best-effort service (for non-real-time applications). Nevertheless, static priority scheduling is not appropriate to support two classes that have similar QoS requirements and require protection against greedy users from either class.

To support applications with similar bandwidth and QoS requirements, a round-robin scheduling algorithm can be used. The round-robin scheduling algorithm[2] is based on a multi-queue output buffer, each assigned to an application. Instead of applying static priority among the queues, the round-robin algorithm serves each queue in a cyclic order, with a single cell transmitted for each (non-empty) queue. This provides an equal share of bandwidth among active applications. Similarly, this can be generalized to support applications with different bandwidth guarantees. The weighted-round-robin scheduling algorithm serves each queue in cyclic order with a weighted frequency according to their relative bandwidth requirements.

The weighted fair queuing (WFQ) algorithm[3] represents a further generalization of this algorithm by providing a bit-by-bit weighted round-robin algorithm. Although WFQ provides good bandwidth sharing for packet switched networks that carry variable size packets, WFQ introduces significant complexity in its implementation.[4] Furthermore, since ATM uses fixed size packets, the performance of WFQ is very close to the weighted round-robin algorithm.

11.2.2.4 Buffer Management

Buffer management is the cell-by-cell-based traffic management mechanism for allocating buffers in the ATM switches. It specifies the queuing structure (such as single or multiple queues per output port) and allocates buffers to each connection according to a particular queuing algorithm. For example, FIFO scheduling is based on a single queue per output port using the first-come-first-buffered (FCFB) queuing algorithm. The FCFB algorithm queues all cells in the same queue in the order of arrivals, and the cells are transmitted in the same order (FIFO scheduling). If a cell arrives for an output port with a full buffer, the cell will be dropped. This applies to all connections because FCFB only provides a single class of service for all applications.

Although the FCFB mechanism is simple to implement, it has a significant disadvantage. It can lead to high packet loss rates for higher layer protocols (such as IP) in the ATM network. The reason is that to support IP service in the ATM network (or any higher layer protocols for that matter), IP packets are segmented into a number of ATM cells before sending over the ATM network (using AAL5). An ATM cell loss translates into an IP packet loss, because AAL5 does not provide cell loss recovery. The longer the IP packet, the higher the likelihood of a packet loss due to cell loss, because there are more cells constituting the IP packet. In fact, if P_c is the cell loss rate in the ATM network, it translates into a packet loss rate of $1 - (1 - P_c)^n$, where n is the number of ATM cells required to carry a single IP packet. For small P_c, the packet loss rate is close to $n P_c$. Hence, the packet loss rate is n times the cell loss rate and this leads to poor performance of carrying packet-based traffic over the ATM network.

Such higher packet loss rate than the cell loss rate is caused by the dropping of cells that are likely to belong to different packets during a buffer overflow. More specifically, consider a packet switch and an ATM switch with the same output buffer size under the same traffic overload conditions. If dropping a single IP packet worth of data is sufficient to control the congestion, the ATM switch has to drop n ATM cells with the same packet length. These n ATM cells can belong to n different packets. From the IP layer point of view, this has the effect of dropping n IP packets, even though the network has dropped a single packet worth of data to reduce congestion. This explains the factor of n higher in packet loss rate over cell loss rate. Hence, the approach of reducing the packet loss effect in the ATM network is to concentrate the cell dropping to the smallest number of packets possible. In other words, the cell dropping policy should be packet-based to be sensitive to the effect of packet loss rate for the higher layer protocols. Hence, more advanced buffering management schemes must be used in the ATM switch to support IP service to significantly reduce packet loss rates.

One such packet-based buffer management scheme is known as selective cell discarding.[5] The idea is very simple. Whenever the queue overflows and a cell is dropped for a particular packet, all the subsequent cells that belong to that packet also will be dropped. At first glance, this seems to violate the layering of the ATM models, because, in general, the ATM layer does not know the nature of the ATM cell payload to tell the boundary of IP packets. Fortunately, in the case of using AAL5 to carry IP packets, the AAL 5 uses the (last bit of the) PTI field in the ATM cell header to indicate the end of an AAL5 frame (IP packet). PTI is equal to 001 or 011 (depending on whether congestion is indicated) for the last cell of the AAL 5 frame, while PTI is equal to 000 or 010 for other cells of the frame. Hence, the ATM switch can be used to drop cells that belong to the same packet. It is also called partial packet discard (PPD) because cell dropping usually starts at a random position of the packet and lasts until the end of the packet. So typically, only partial packets are discarded.

However, the packet loss rate improvement of PPD has been limited because when an arriving cell is dropped during buffer overflow, many cells belonging to the same packet may have been buffered or transmitted earlier. Hence, PPD can waste both bandwidth and buffer space on the network. This lead to the idea of early packet discard (EPD),[6] which is to drop entire packets, instead of partial packets. To avoid searching for the beginning of a packet in the buffer, it needs to start dropping cells at the beginning of a packet as they arrive to the output queue. However, it is most likely too late to wait until the buffer is full before starting dropping the beginning cells of packets. The reason is that the arriving cells on average are not at the beginning of packets and we would be forced to drop cells that are not at the beginning of packets when the buffer is full. (Note that it is very difficult to search in the buffer to find existing packet beginnings and selectively drop them. Furthermore, it is likely that many beginning cells have been transmitted already, and dropping them would require coordination with other ATM switches downstream along the path. Hence, we need to focus on newly arrived beginning cells.) This implies that in order to drop entire packets, we need to begin dropping cells way before the buffer is full. A threshold on the buffer occupancy is established such that beyond which a newly arrived beginning cell and its following cells of the same packet are dropped until the end of that packet.

It has been shown that EPD is more effective in reducing packet loss rate than PPD.[6] In fact, TCP over ATM using EPD has very similar throughput to the packet network counterpart of TCP over IP routers. One key reason is that since EPD forces the packet drops to occur before actual buffer overflows (when the buffer threshold has been reached), it allows more reaction time for the TCP window mechanisms to slow down (as a result of packet loss) and avoids further overloading the network. The additional buffer between the threshold and the actual buffer size can be used to allow for the feedback delay for the TCP to slow down. There is additional complexity in implementing EPD in monitoring the buffer occupancy to see when the threshold has been reached, but is believed to be relatively inexpensive.[6] However, it is unclear that EPD has the same advantage over PPD for UDP traffic for the same buffer size, as UDP does not slow down like TCP to help reduce the load and hence the packet loss rate. Furthermore, the effective buffer size of EPD is reduced to the threshold buffer from the full buffer size of PPD, which has the effect of increased packet loss rates.

Similar to TCP over packet networks, there is no fairness guaranteed with EPD or PPD. Fairness may require per VC queuing and accounting, such as using WFQ, or the Fair Buffer Allocation (FBA). FBA uses per VC accounting on FIFO buffers.[7] The decision to drop a cell is based on the current usage of its VC on the current buffer. Those that exceed their fair share will be dropped first.

11.2.2.5 CLP Control

The CLP bit on the ATM cell header provides a simple indication of priority among cells within an ATM VC. CLP = 0 indicates normal priority, while CLP = 1 indicates low priority. The CLP value is assigned by the source on a cell-by-cell basis. Typically, all cells are indicated as CLP = 0 by default. When an ATM cell is assigned with CLP = 1, it means that such a cell can be dropped if the network experiences congestion.

It is important to note that all cells, regardless of CLP values, must be delivered in the same sequence as those sent by the source. This means that cells of the same VC with different CLP values should not be queued independently (such as in high- and low-priority queues) in an ATM switch, which can result in out-of-order transmission.

Another use for the CLP bit is for the UPC function. If the UPC determines that the source has exceeded the traffic contract, it can assign the violated cells with CLP = 1. This is known as cell tagging. These excess cells will be dropped first if any switch along the path experiences congestion.

11.2.2.6 Feedback Control

In the above traffic mechanisms, we have implicitly assumed that the rates (peak and average cell rates) at which an application transmits on the ATM connection is determined during connection setup and honored thereafter as part of the traffic contract. This paradigm is called open loop control[8] because there is no feedback mechanism (at the ATM layer) to indicate any change of rate by the network or the receiver as a result of the new traffic conditions in the network. Open loop control works well for predictable traffic such as real-time streaming applications, for which the network has reserved the required bandwidth to support such an application. As long as the application does not exceed those rates specified by the traffic contract, there is no need for any feedback to change the rate.

Unfortunately, many applications have unpredictable traffic characteristics, such as real-time block transfer and non-real-time applications. For such applications, the traffic contract established during call setup is only mildly useful and additional cell-by-cell-based traffic mechanisms must be used. This is especially important for non-real-time applications, for which no bandwidth has been reserved as part of the call setup process. Their performance depends not only on the amount of leftover bandwidth from the real-time applications, but also on the collective load of other non-real-time applications. The goal of supporting non-real-time applications is to balance the tradeoff of maximizing the utilization of leftover bandwidth while avoiding congestion. Since the available bandwidth changes constantly for each non-real-time application, the traffic load generated by the non-real-time applications should be controlled on-the-fly. This is achieved through feedback information from either the network or the receiver to the source to regulate its traffic submitted to the network in real-time. The use of feedback control mechanisms for these applications represents the closed loop traffic control paradigm, which forms the core of the new ABR service category. ABR service is discussed at the end of this chapter.

11.3 Traffic Contract

The traffic contract is a fundamental component of the ATM traffic management paradigm. The traffic contract between the user and network specifies the traffic characteristics of the source and the QoS requirements of the application at the ATM layer. More specifically, the ATM traffic contract of a connection is specified by the connection traffic descriptor and the set of QoS parameters for each direction, which are discussed in detail next.

11.3.1 ATM Traffic Parameters and Source Traffic Descriptor

The traffic characteristics of a source at the ATM layer are specified by the ATM traffic parameters. When an endpoint requests a connection setup over the ATM network, it specifies its traffic parameters in the call setup message. Once the connection is established, both the network and user are bound by the traffic contract based on these traffic parameters; the endpoint is responsible for not exceeding these traffic parameters. The conformance to these traffic parameters is policed at the UNI by the UPC of the network. This implicitly requires the endpoint to provide a traffic shaping mechanism to conform to these parameters. The traffic parameters communicated by UNI Signalling 4.0^9 are peak cell rate, sustained cell rate, maximum burst size and minimum cell rate. Collectively, this set of traffic parameters form the source traffic descriptor. These traffic parameters are discussed in more detail next.

11.3.1.1 Peak Cell Rate

Peak cell rate (PCR) specifies the peak bandwidth that can be sent by the source, measured in cells per second. As alluded to in Chapter 4, PCR cannot be simply defined as the reciprocal of inter-cell transmission time interval. Otherwise, such a definition fails to specify certain ranges of data rates. Since ATM is based on a fixed transmission time slot system, the inter-cell interval is an integral number of ATM cell time and cannot be a fraction of cell time. For example, the inter-cell arrival time of 1-cell and 2-cell intervals corresponds to a PCR value equal to 100% and 50% of link speed, respectively. Hence, it is impossible to specify a PCR between 50% and 100% of the link rate using this model, because the inter-cell arrival time cannot be any value between 1 and 2 cell times.

To specify and measure the conformance to a PCR of arbitrary values, the inter-cell arrival times have to be evaluated over a period of time which involves more than two cell transmissions. A continuous-state leaky bucket algorithm, also known as the generic cell rate algorithm (GCRA), has been defined to measure the PCR conformance in TM 4.0.[1] The leaky bucket algorithm is modeled after an imaginary bucket of a fixed size K that leaks at a rate of R. The traffic generated by a source is used to fill the leaky bucket (draining at rate R) starting with an empty bucket. An arriving cell from the source is conforming to a PCR = R if it does not cause an overflow. K is specified as a tolerance to amount of cell clumping allowed for the cell stream, as described in the cell delay variation tolerance parameter below. The GCRA can be represented by a flow chart to determine if each cell generated by the source is conforming to the contract. Detail discussion of the GCRA is beyond the scope of this book, but can be found in TM 4.0.

11.3.1.2 Sustainable Cell Rate

Conceptually, sustainable cell rate (SCR) specifies the average data rate (in cells per second) that can be sent by the source. Similarly, the SCR can be specified by the leaky bucket algorithm using the SCR parameter instead of PCR.[1]

11.3.1.3 Maximum Burst Size

Maximum burst size (MBS) roughly specifies the maximum number of cells that can be sent at the PCR rate and is proportional to the leaky bucket size associated with the SCR definition.

11.3.1.4 Minimum Cell Rate

Minimum cell rate (MCR) was introduced by the new ABR service category. It is the minimum bandwidth guaranteed for an ABR service connection. The MCR can be set to zero.

11.3.2 Connection Traffic Descriptor

The connection traffic descriptor[1] specifies the traffic characteristics of the ATM connection as a whole. Hence, it includes, in addition to the source traffic descriptor, the cell delay variation tolerance (CDVT) and the conformance definition for the UPC to specify the cell conformance test appropriately. They are discussed in more detail below.

11.3.2.1 Cell Delay Variation Tolerance

Conceptually, cell delay variation tolerance (CDVT) specifies the tolerance of an ATM network for incoming traffic that exceeds the PCR value. A nonzero CDVT must be allowed when evaluating conformance at the public UNI because there is cell clumping as the cells traverse through the private ATM network, even though the source might have shaped the peak rate correctly at PCR. In addition, there is randomness of cell inter-arrival time which can be caused by multiplexing with OAM cells of the same connection and transmission convergence sublayer overhead insertion. Both are beyond the control of the ATM source. The CDVT represents the amount of clumping allowed by the public UNI when checking conformance. For a large enough CDVT (depending on PCR and link rate), back to back cells can be transmitted and still be considered in agreement with the traffic contract. The CDVT is proportional to the leaky bucket size used to define PCR conformance.

11.3.2.2 Cell Conformance and Connection Compliance

For each connection, the network must decide if the traffic generated conforms to the traffic contract on a cell-by-cell basis (UPC). Again, a dual leaky bucket algorithm (two GCRAs) is used to determine cell conformance for PCR and SCR. However, the UPC function implemented at the UNI does not need to be restricted to the GCRA algorithm. Other equivalent algorithms can be used as long as they result in the same cells being conformed and thus the same cells to being non-conformed. In any case, UPC must preserve the QoS objectives of conforming cells.

A compliant connection does not imply all the cells are conforming, because even under ideal condition, some cells can be non-conforming. The network is required to honor the QoS objectives with respect to the traffic contract of all conforming cells of a compliant connection. On the other hand, a connection with all cells conforming is a compliant connection. For non-compliant connections, there is no need for the network to respect the agreed QoS objectives. However, it must not ignore the QoS objectives of a connection simply because not all the cells are conforming, because this can still be a compliant connection.

11.3.3 ATM QoS Parameters

The QoS requirements of an application are specified by the ATM QoS parameters at the ATM layer. When an endpoint requests a connection setup over the ATM network, it specifies its QoS parameters, together with traffic parameters, in the setup message. Once the connection is established, if the endpoint is conforming to the traffic contract, the network is required to guarantee the QoS (as specified by the QoS parameters) for the applications. The key QoS parameters are maximum cell transfer delay, cell delay variation and cell loss ratio, which are discussed below.

11.3.3.1 Maximum Cell Transfer Delay

Maximum cell transfer delay (CTD) specifies the time elapsed between when a cell of the connection exits the source UNI and when it exits the destination UNI. The maximum CTD specified for a connection is defined as a statistical guarantee using a probability parameter α, where α is a very small number, such as 10^{-6}. The network has to guarantee the maximum CTD to be met with a probability of $1 - \alpha$. For real-time streaming applications, there is a maximum end-to-end delay requirement beyond which those late ATM cells are treated as lost cells. If this end-to-end delay requirement is specified by the maximum CTD, α can be viewed as the probability of cell loss that can be tolerated by an application due to late arrivals.

11.3.3.2 Peak-to-Peak Cell Delay Variation

The cell delay variation (CDV) specifies the variation in delay incurred in the ATM network. This is formally defined as a peak-to-peak CDV, which is the maximum difference in CTD among all the cells of the connection. Since the CDV defined using two separate points in the network (source and destination UNIs), it is also called a two-point CDV. This is equivalent to the maximum CTD minus the minimum CTD. The minimum CTD is the fixed delay incurred by a cell for that connection if there is no queuing delay along the path, because it is the queuing delay that introduces the CDV. It is important to distinguish CDVT discussed above from CDV. CDVT is a traffic parameter that can be measured at the UNI to determine conformance as part of UPC, while CDV is a QoS parameter.

CDV is also defined as a statistical parameter that is satisfied by 1 - β of all the cells transferred in the connection. A real-time streaming application has a delay variation requirement beyond which the receiving buffer will either underflow or overflow. Hence, β is the cell loss probability due to receiving buffer overflow or underflow.

11.3.3.3 Cell Loss Ratio

Cell loss ratio (CLR) specifies the probability of cell loss during that connection. This is equal to the total number of lost cells divided by all transmitted cells over the duration of the connection.

11.4 ATM Service Categories

As discussed in the AAL chapter, a service model for B-ISDN was established by the ITU to classify services (or bearer capabilities) based on the qualitative distinction of different types of applications. Four classes of service (A, B, C, and D) were first defined. The original intention was to define a specific AAL type for each class of service. Although this AAL-based model gives us a *conceptual* understanding of different service classes, it does not provide an operational model that both the users and the ATM network can use effectively for call admission and resource allocation. More specifically, the qualitative attributes used, such as the connection mode, are not only irrelevant at the ATM layer, but also insufficient to describe a service model.

Hence, another service model has been proposed to address the limitations of the AAL-based service class model. This new model is a pure parameter-based approach and uses only a set of traffic and QoS parameters for establishing contracts between users and the network, without dividing services into application classes. By using only quantitative parameters to describe the entire application space, all applications are represented as part of a continuum range of possible combinations of values of all these parameters. However, there is also a big drawback to this pure parameter-based approach. It is very difficult to define a single set of TM mechanisms that can effectively support the entire application space because different application classes (real-streaming, real-time block transfer and non-real-time) require different combinations of TM mechanisms.

Hence, a refinement of this parameter-based approach is to classify services for all applications into a small number of ATM service categories such that the classification should lend itself to a unique set of TM mechanisms for application to each category. This refined approach has been adopted in TM 4.0. Each service category can share one set of TM mechanisms and can be specified by a particular set of traffic and QoS parameters. Applications supported within a service category differ only by the values of the corresponding set of traffic and QoS parameters. Again, the use of a specific AAL type has been decoupled from the specific service category, because an AAL type can support multiple service categories.

There are five ATM layer service categories defined, with distinct attributes in traffic and QoS parameters, as shown in Table 11-1 from TM 4.0. TM 4.0 classifies ATM service categories into real-time and non-real-time services depending on whether the QoS delay objectives (CTD and CDV) must be satisfied. CBR and real-time (rt)-VBR are real-time services, while non-real-time (nrt)-VBR, UBR, and ABR are non-real-time services. TM 4.0 defines real-time service as one that provides real-time delivery of time-based information such as video, audio, voice, or animation. Real-time service can be used to support real-time streaming applications. This can be a CBR or rt-VBR service, depending on whether the traffic is CBR or VBR, respectively. These five service categories are discussed below.

Table 11–1 *ATM service categories and attributes*

Attributes	ATM Layer Service Categories				
	CBR	rt-VBR	nrt-VBR	UBR	ABR
Traffic Parameters					
PCR, CDVT	specified			specified	specified
SCR, MBS, CDVT	N/A	specified		N/A	
MCR	N/A				specified
QoS Parameters					
Peak-to-peak CDV	specified		unspecified		
Max CTD	specified		unspecified		
CLR	specified			unspecified	
Other Attribute					
Feedback	unspecified				specified

11.4.1 CBR

Users of the ATM layer CBR service category are expected to send CBR traffic with a specified PCR (SCR is implicitly equal to PCR) and CDVT. The QoS requirements for CBR service include CDV, max CTD, and CLR. Hence, real-time streaming applications with CBR can use this service category. These include circuit emulation and real-time CBR video delivery.

11.4.2 rt-VBR

The rt-VBR service is very similar to the CBR service category above, except that it is for VBR instead of CBR applications. A user for rt-VBR is expected to send VBR traffic with specified peak (PCR) and average (SCR) bandwidth, and associated traffic parameters (CDVT and MBS). The specified QoS objectives are peak-to-peak CDV, maximum CTD and CLR. Real-time streaming applications that send at variable bit rate can use this service category.

11.4.3 nrt-VBR

A user of non-real-time VBR (nrt-VBR) service specifies the same traffic parameters as the rt-VBR service: PCR, SCR, CDVT and MBS. However, nrt-VBR is a non-real-time service for which neither max CTD nor CDV needs to be specified. nrt-VBR service provides bandwidth guarantee at a PCR, but no guarantee on delay bounds. Hence, real-time block transfer applications can be supported by this service category, because the PCR guaranteed by nrt-VBR is be used to satisfy the block transfer delay. (Note that the term "real-time" in TM 4.0 is reserved only for real-time delivery of time-based information, while "real-time" used in this book also includes real-time delivery of non-time-based information, which are the real-time block transfer applications.) CLR is still specified because this affects the integrity and ultimately the throughput of the data transfer.

11.4.4 UBR

Unspecified bit rate (UBR) service was proposed to support non-real-time applications that only need best-effort service. Hence, there are no QoS requirements or QoS objectives specified. Traffic parameters (such as

PCR and CDVT) can be specified for UBR service, but they are not required either. It is up to the network to decide whether the PCR is subject to traffic policing. The PCR also may be used to indicate the smallest bandwidth limitation along the path of the connection. However, the problem with using UBR is that there are no CLR guarantees for these applications, while on many of these non-real-time applications expect a packet loss rate similar to existing LANs. This is one of the key motivations of the ABR service.

11.4.5 ABR

Available bit rate (ABR) service is an improvement of the UBR service to not only reduce CLR to an acceptable level, but also to provide more efficient use of the available network resources. The ABR service attempts to dynamically share the available bandwidth among all ABR users in a fair manner. When the network has a low load, an ABR user should be able to send at the PCR and increase the efficiency of the network. The ABR service relies on a feedback control mechanism to throttle the source rate according to the current loading conditions of the network. The ABR user is expected to adapt the transmission rate according to this feedback and, as a result, should experience a low CLR and a fair share of the bandwidth. The CLR guarantees provided by the ABR service are based on this procedural commitment, instead of a quantitative one. If the ABR user does not behave according to the feedback mechanism and adjust for a lower cell rate during overload, the user can incur significant cell loss.

The traffic parameters specified by an ABR user are PCR, CDVT and MCR (minimum cell rate). The MCR is a new traffic parameter introduced by the ABR service category to indicate the minimum bandwidth the ABR service must support for the user. This means that the ABR user can always send at MCR and still complies with ABR traffic contract. If MCR is set to zero, there is no guarantee of any bandwidth for the ABR user. The ABR service and its feedback mechanism are discussed in detail in the next section.

11.5 ABR Service

The main objective of the ABR service is to support best-effort applications by fully utilizing the available bandwidth leftover by other services (especially those with bandwidth and QoS guarantees). The available bandwidth to an ABR user changes dynamically as a function of the load of other connections (using both ABR and non-ABR services) on the network. A feedback mechanism is used to dynamically adjust the rate of each ABR connection according to the current loading conditions of the network. The ABR flow control shares the available bandwidth with all the ABR users. Given the packet loss rate multiplying effect of cell loss rate in the ATM network discussed above, another important objective of ABR service is to ensure the cell loss rate is minimal, so as to provide a comparable or better packet loss rate as compared to the legacy network.

Before we explain the ABR flow control mechanisms, we first discuss feedback mechanisms in general, because they form the framework of these ABR mechanisms.

11.5.1 Feedback Mechanisms

Feedback mechanisms can be classified according to the amount of feedback information and the default behavior of the source during the intervals between receiving feedback information.[8] The amount of feedback information can range from implicit, binary, detail to explicit rate. Implicit feedback means that neither the network nor the receiver sends any feedback information to the source. To detect congestion, the source continuously measures the cell loss and cell delay for the connection, such as by using OAM cells and time-stamps. If the cell loss or delay exceeds a certain threshold, it assumes that there is congestion and reduces its rate accordingly. Although an implicit feedback mechanism is simple for the network to implement (in fact, nothing needs to be implemented), this introduces more complexity in the end system in determining the appropriate transmission rate. More importantly, implicit feedback has a slow response time because of the round-trip feedback delay incurred. Furthermore, it has to wait until the congested switch buffer overflows (which can be too late in the congestion phase), unless EPD is implemented.

Binary feedback provides explicit feedback (by the network or destination) to indicate whether the network is congested. This binary state can be communicated by the (second bit of the) PTI field in the ATM cell header. At the congested switch, the PTI field is modified to indicate congestion. The destination is required to return the congestion indication to the source. This is known as explicit forward congestion indication (EFCI). The source is supposed to reduce the rate accordingly. However, with such limited information, the binary feedback can only indicate the existence of congestion on the path, but cannot pinpoint the severity or location of the congestion. Furthermore, similar to implicit feedback, EFCI incurs an entire round-trip propagation delay (and the response time of the destination) for the source to respond to congestion. Nevertheless, this represents a simple network feedback mechanism. This round-trip delay can be reduced by having the congested switch immediately send the congestion indication using an extra cell directly (backward) to the source, at the expense of introducing additional traffic to the network and additional complexity at the switch. This is known is backward explicit congestion notification (BECN).[10]

More detailed information than the single bit information can be sent through special ATM cells known as resource management (RM) cells. Such RM cells can carry queue levels and cell loss rates at switches along the path. Finally, the RM cells can carry the rate at which the source should send at a given instant explicitly. Explicit rate reduces the complexity of the endpoints at the expense of additional complexity to the switches, because each switch needs to calculate the appropriate rate for each connection going through it that requires feedback information.

Feedback mechanisms also can be classified according to the default behavior of the traffic source in the interval between receiving feedback into positive, negative and explicit rate. With positive feedback, the source continues to decrease its transmission rate until it receives a positive feedback, which indicates that there is no congestion. At this point, the source increases its transmission rate to compensate for the amount of rate decrease in the last interval, plus an additional fixed amount. This is considered a pessimistic feedback mechanism. Positive feedback has the advantage of being loss-tolerant for feedback information, especially during congestion. Even if the feedback is lost during congestion (which is definitely possible), the source continues to decrease its rate in the absence of feedback, which is exactly the desired behavior.

With negative feedback, the source behaves the opposite way. The default source behavior between receiving feedback is to increase its transmission rate. Hence, this is an optimistic mechanism. It is vulnerable during congestion phases that result in losing the feedback, because the source will continue to increase the transmission rate and further aggravate the congestion situation in the network.

Finally, explicit feedback provides the exact rate at which the source needs to send at a given time. It is to maintain that rate until the next feedback is received. It avoids the oscillating behavior of either of the above feedback types. Furthermore, it allows the source to reach its desired rate quickly, instead of waiting for the oscillation period to converge to a particular rate. Again, the drawback is the additional complexity of the network to calculate the proper rate for the source.

11.5.2 ABR Flow Control

In ABR flow control, the source periodically sends RM cells to probe the network state (bandwidth availability, state of congestion, impending congestion). Such RM cells are inserted into the cell stream of the connection, with the same VPI/VCI value, and distinguished by the PTI value of 110. The RM cells can be sent as in-rate (with CLP = 0) cells, if their combined load with data cells are still below the PCR negotiated. Otherwise, the RM cells must be sent as out-of-rate (CLP = 1) cells. The forward RM cells (those sent by the source) are turned around by the destination. The RM cells sent by the destination to the source are known as backward RM cells. The switches along the path modify the RM cell payload as necessary to indicate congestion or the explicit rates for the connection. The source is required to adjust its rate accordingly.

The ABR flow control uses a positive feedback mechanism. By default, the source decreases its rate using a multiplicative decrease (MD) factor. If it receives a backward RM cell with a no-congestion indication (expressed in the CI, congestion indication, field in the RM cell payload), it increases its rate to compensate for the decrease since the receipt of the last RM cell plus a fixed additive increase (AI) amount. AI and MD are set during ABR connection setup. Not surprisingly, the values of AI and MD have significant effects on TCP performance over ABR connections.

There are two modes in ABR flow control defined in TM 4.0: the binary mode and the (optional) explicit rate mode. The binary mode supports forward and backward explicit congestion notification (FECN and BECN). The FECN scheme used in the binary mode is known as EFCI marking, for which the source sends all user cells with EFCI = 0 (that is, the second bit of the PTI field). It also sends forward RM cells periodically with CI field = 0. If there is congestion in a switch along the path, the switch will modify the EFCI to 1. Then, the destination will modify the forward RM cell to indicate CI = 1 and return them as the backward RM cells. An advantage of this FECN scheme is that it is compatible with existing ATM switches with such EFCI functions, because they do not need to process RM cells. The processing of RM cells occurs only at the end systems for the EFCI marking scheme.

The BECN scheme for the binary mode is called relative rate marking. In this case, the congested switch either marks the backward RM cells with CI = 1 or generates its own backward RM cell to indicate the congestion. Again, the BECN scheme reduces feedback delay at the expense of increased functionality of the switches, which need to process RM cells.

With the explicit rate mode, the switches must calculate the explicit rate (ER) of each ABR connection that passes through them by monitoring the load (buffer occupancy) and detecting any congestion. Then, the switch indicates the ER in the forward (or backward) RM cells. Again, this introduces significantly higher complexity for the switch. The ABR explicit rate mode performance depends largely on the switch algorithm used to calculate such explicit rates. Since the switch algorithms used do not affect interoperability, they are not standardized (and hence by definition proprietary).

Finally, the support of ABR flow control introduces higher complexities for the UPC function. Instead of setting the UPC parameters (such as PCR) only once during connection setup, it requires on-the-fly UPC adjustment according to the RM cells. For binary mode, it must emulate the ABR source behavior to appropriately police the source. For explicit rate mode, it can use the ER from the RM cells.

11.6 Summary

In this chapter, we gave an overview of the traffic management paradigm of ATM. This is central to support applications with diverse traffic and QoS requirements in an effective manner. We first defined the traffic management concept and discussed the key ATM traffic management mechanisms. These can be classified into connection-based and cell-by-cell-based mechanisms. The former includes connection admission control and network resource management, while the latter includes usage parameter control, traffic shaping, scheduling, buffer management, CLP control and feedback control.

Then, the traffic contract, including the traffic and QoS parameters, was discussed in detail. ATM traffic parameters include peak cell rate, sustained cell rate, maximum burst size and minimum cell rate. The key ATM QoS parameters include maximum cell transfer delay, peak-to-peak cell delay variation and cell loss ratio. The traffic contract specifies the traffic and QoS parameters, cell delay variation tolerance and cell conformance definition. After that, we presented the five ATM service categories recently defined by The ATM Forum in TM 4.0. They are CBR, rt-VBR, nrt-VBR, UBR and ABR. Finally, we discussed the ABR flow control mechanisms in detail.

11.7 References

[1] The ATM Forum, *The ATM Traffic Management Specification*, Version 4.0, Apr. 1996.

[2] L. Kleinrock, *Queuing Systems, Volume 1: Theory*, New York: Wiley-Interscience, 1975.

[3] A. Demers, S. Keshav, and S. Shenkar, "Analysis and Simulation of a Fair-Queuing Algorithm," *Proc. ACM SIGComm Symp.*, Austin, TX, Sept. 1989, pp. 1-12.

[4] M. Garrett, "A Service Architecture for ATM: From Applications to Scheduling," *IEEE Network Magazine*, May/June 1996, pp. 6-14.

[5] G. Armitage and K. Adams, "Packet reassembly during cell loss," *IEEE Network Magazine*, vol. 7, no. 5, Sept. 1993, pp. 26-34.

[6] A. Romanow, S. Floyd, "Dynamics of TCP Traffic over ATM networks," *IEEE Journal of Selected Areas in Communications*, Vol. 13, No. 4, May 1995, pp. 633-641.

[7] J. Heinanen and K. Kilkki, "A Fair Buffer Allocation Scheme," submitted for publication.

[8] T. Chen, S. Liu, V. Samalam, "The Available Bit Rate Service for Data in ATM Networks," *IEEE Communications Magazine*, May 1996, pp. 56-71.

[9] The ATM Forum, *The ATM UNI Signaling Specification*, Version 4.0, 1996.

[10] P. Newman, "Traffic Management for ATM Local Area Networks," *IEEE Communications Magazine*, vol. 32, Aug. 1994, pp. 44-50.

PART III

Residential Broadband Networks: ATM-to-the-Home

Chapter **12**

Residential Broadband Service and Network Architectures

12.1 Introduction

In the early 1990s, there was a major drive to deploy residential broadband networks by public network operators (telephone and cable companies) around the world. To prepare for the cross-industry competition between the telephone and cable industries that was expected to emerge from the deregulation of the telecommunications industry worldwide, these companies have strong incentives to expand their markets beyond the existing telephone and broadcast TV business. The shared vision of many public network operators was to deploy residential broadband networks to deliver interactive television (ITV) services to the home.[1]

However, by the mid-1990s, the ITV market had taken longer than expected to materialize. There was no obvious killer application. Even for the highly touted ITV application, video-on-demand, the projected revenues cannot justify the billions of dollars of investment. Moreover, the networking equipment for residential broadband networks has taken longer to develop and the task of integrating complex networking hardware and software for the first time turned out to be significantly more difficult than anticipated. Furthermore, it became clear that deployment of entirely new residential broadband infrastructures that require significant plant upgrades is impractical, as it will take years to complete and would not produce any return for many years.

Around 1995, while the ITV market was fading, the Internet "phenomenon" suddenly took many companies by surprise. Consumer interest in accessing the Internet for browsing the World Wide Web has exploded.[2] Web browsing has emerged as one of the most popular Internet applications, as verified by the traffic statistics of the NSF Backbone[3] (which was the Internet backbone until 1995). Web traffic, as measured by HTTP[4] (Hypertext Transfer Protocol, the client-server protocol for Web browsing) in terms of packet counts, had jumped from a mere 1.5 percent in January 1994 to 21.4 percent in April 1995. However, the current narrowband residential infrastructure using circuit-switched-based dial-up (either POTS or ISDN) for Internet access is too slow, which led to the term "World Wide Wait." Also, using a circuit-switched infrastructure to access the Internet (a packet switched network) is fundamentally broken. It can tie up the telephone circuits for hours, not atypical for today's online access duration of a subscriber. Bypassing this dial-up infrastructure can allow significant cost savings to the telephone companies because it avoids the need for upgrading their circuit-switching infrastructure to support online services.

Deploying residential broadband (RBB) network based on packet switching[1] for Internet access not only solves the bandwidth bottleneck problem at the residential access network, but also bypasses the dial-up infrastructure to avoid holding up telephone circuits. Since there is a clear pent-up demand for bandwidth to get much better user satisfaction, as opposed to the illusive ITV market, high-speed Internet access has been viewed as the new killer application for residential broadband networks. The key focus for public network operators now is to deploy residential broadband networks that require minimal physical plant upgrades and commercially available equipment.

The main objective of this chapter is to give an overview of residential broadband service requirements and network architectures based on ATM. We first give an overview of the existing residential network and Internet access architectures and their limitations. Then, we present the end-to-end residential broadband service requirements. Next, we describe the different networking components of residential broadband architecture based on the ATM-to-the-home architecture that can satisfy these requirements. Finally, since many homes (and small businesses) with online services have multiple PCs (and that ratio continues to increase), we explore in detail the in-home network architectures to support multiple PCs. This chapter provides the background for the discussions of residential broadband network architectures based on xDSL and cable modems in the following chapters.

12.2 Legacy Residential Networks and Internet Access

The telephone and the cable TV networks are the two main networks connected to residences today. The residential telephone network is a circuit switched network (see Part I). It provides a two-way, point-to-point communication between any two users on the network (see Figure 12-1).

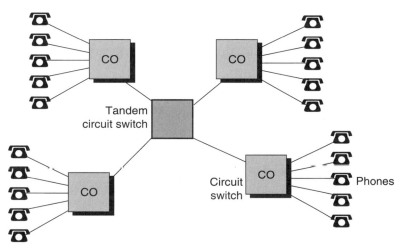

Figure 12–1 The telephone network architecture

In contrast, the cable TV system is a broadcast network. It provides a one-way, one-to-many distribution of information. As shown in Figure 12-2, the headend receives analog video signals and then broadcasts them through the tree-and-branch architecture of the coaxial cable distribution plant to the subscribers. Analog video signals are multiplexed using frequency division multiplexing. In the United States, each signal is carried over a 6 MHz frequency channel. The cable TV network architecture will be discussed in detail in a later chapter.

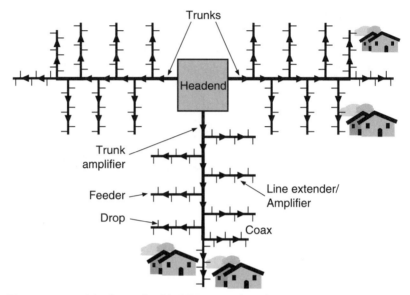

Figure 12–2   Traditional cable TV network architecture

However, neither the existing telephone network nor the cable TV network can support the envisioned two-way residential broadband services (see Table 12-1). The key value provided by today's telephone network is the ubiquitous communication between any two phones anywhere in the world. However, the bandwidth available to each home is not only very limited, typically 64 Kbps or less, but also suffering from the inefficiency and inflexibility of a circuit switched network.

On the other hand, the traditional cable network has the advantage of a broadband transmission medium to the home that can potentially (when digitized) deliver information at Gbps to each neighborhood (in a shared fashion). However, the cable TV network is currently still primarily a broadcast network and has no switching capability. Furthermore, the current cable TV network have very limited, if any, upstream transmission capabilities. Hence, it cannot support point-to-point switched connectivity or two-way interactive services.

Another problem is that the "cable network" actually consists of disjointed islands of local cable systems, because communications between

Table 12–1 *Comparison of traditional telephone and cable networks with the switched broadband residential network*

Attributes	Legacy Telephone Network	Legacy Cable Network	Switched Broadband Residential Network
Transmission	analog or digital (ISDN)	analog	digital (and analog for backward compatibility)
Information Type	voice, low-quality video, narrowband data	broadcast quality video	all information types
Connection Types	two-way point-to-point and multipoint-to-multipoint (by bridge)	one-way broadcast, not fully connected (islands of connectivity)	one-way or two-way; point-to-point, point-to-multipoint, multipoint-to-multipoint
Service	switched	broadcast	switched, multicast & broadcast
Data rate	low speed (at most on the order of 100 Kbps)	no data communications	~ Mbps to each home

these islands of cable networks has not been necessary for broadcast TV. The headends of cable systems are not connected, except they might share common sources of programming from the same national superheadend through satellite delivery. Hence, a regional broadband network to interconnect headends is required to provide end-to-end broadband connectivity between cable subscribers.

12.2.1 Dial-up Internet Access

Currently, residential customers access the Internet primarily using POTS (analog) or ISDN (digital) dial-up connections to the Internet service provider (ISP)'s points of presence (POPs). These connections have to go through the telephony switch at the central office (CO), as shown in Figure 12-3. The circuit switched connections are terminated at the dial-up terminal servers at ISP's POPs. The dial-up terminal provides modem banks for dial-up termination and IP services for connecting to the Internet.

Internet access over a dial-up connection primarily uses the point-to-point protocol (PPP).[5] After the dial-up connection is established, PPP is used to authenticate the user and assign the IP address to the user before IP protocols can be carried over the dial-up connection. In addition to providing IP packet encapsulation over the serial line, PPP can provide compression and encryption on the IP traffic.

The terminal server multiplexes traffic from the dial-up connections. It can be connected through an Ethernet switch to have an additional level of traffic concentration before connecting to the router responsible for providing connectivity to the Internet, as shown in Figure 12-3. (There can be two layers of routers that run different routing protocols: intra- and inter-domain routing for local and Internet backbone communications, respectively.) The router typically reaches the Internet connection through a network access point (NAP), where ISPs connect for exchanging Internet traffic. If the ISP is also an Internet backbone provider, the router can be connected to the ISP's own backbone IP network, which in turn has access to multiple NAPs across the country. In addition, the ISP POP contains a set of servers responsible to provide Internet services such as E-mail, chat and news applications.

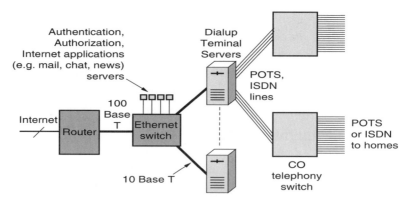

Figure 12–3   An example network configuration of a dial-up internet access through an ISP POP

Since the connection to the ISP's POP is through a circuit switched connection, and a typical online session can last over an hour or more, this introduces a serious problem for the telcos as this ties up their telephone switch circuits for a long time. In fact, this breaks the traffic-engineering model of telephone switch designed for an average 3 - 5 minutes holding time for voice conversations. As a result, the telephone switch capacity becomes grossly inadequate as more people use such online services. Furthermore, such additional traffic volume does not result in increase in revenue, because local calls typically have a flat fee structure. Hence, another model must be designed to bypass the telephone switch. This call-blocking problem can be solved by a packet switched access to the ISP instead such as one provided by a residential broadband network, as discuss later.

12.3 Residential Broadband Service Requirements

The residential broadband service requirements can be classified in two categories: connectivity and functional requirements.[6, 7] The former specifies the types of service providers to which connectivity are provided. Functional requirements are specific capabilities provided by the network to support applications.

12.3.1 Connectivity

In addition to providing a broadband access network, the public network operator must provide access to multiple networking services: the Internet, corporate networks, local content services and peer-to-peer communications as shown in Figure 12-4.

12.3.1.1 The Internet

Providing high-speed Internet access is a key value for both home users and small businesses. The Internet is accessed through one or more ISPs connected with high-speed connections from the COs or headends. These high-speed connections can be part of a regional broadband (ATM) network.

12.3.1.2 Corporate Networks

For telecommuting to be truly effective, the remote access connectivity must be high speed to provide an experience similar to the office environment. Hence, another key residential broadband service is to provide high-speed telecommuting service. There are two ways to access corporate networks. One is to use an IP tunneling mechanism through the Internet

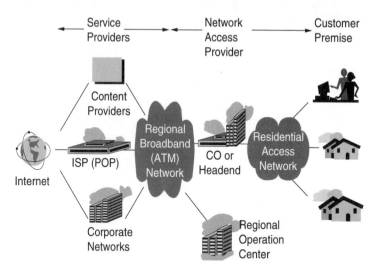

Figure 12–4   Access requirements: the internet, corporate networks, local content and peer-to-peer communications

(using PPTP, L2F, or L2TP) to reach the corporate network. This design obviates the need for dial-up modems at the corporation while leveraging the Internet as the virtual private network. This, however, also means the connectivity may be limited by the bandwidth of the Internet. A second method is to use the network operator's own regional broadband network, as shown in Figure 12-4, to provide direct high-speed connectivity to the corporate network. This has the advantages of not only higher speed, but also greater security.

12.3.1.3 Local Content

A key advantage of a residential broadband network is the ability to host local content and deliver it at high speed to the residence, without going through the Internet. Local content may be stored at the POPs (points of presence) of the ISPs, content providers, the COs, the headends and the regional operation centers (ROCs). Local content can be created locally (such as merchant services for retailing) or generated remotely (Web content from the Internet cached in local servers).

12.3.1.4 Peer-to-peer Communication

The ability to interconnect consumers at high speed enables high quality peer-to-peer communication applications such as video telephony or interactive gaming. Demand for this connectivity may ramp up more slowly than the services described above, but mass deployment of residential broadband networks.

12.3.2 Functional Requirements

In addition to the connectivity requirements, residential broadband services have the following functional requirements.

12.3.2.1 Easy Migration from Existing ISP Access Infrastructure

Since ISPs already have an infrastructure to support dial-up access based on PPP, any new broadband Internet access solution must take into account this architecture. Ideally, the broadband service model for accessing ISP service can re-use most of the networking, management and administration infrastructure (such as IP address and domain name administration) and will not require a paradigm shift for the ISP.

12.3.2.2 Simultaneous Connectivity: Internet and Corporate Network

A telecommuter working from home may need to access the Internet while connected to the corporate network. There are two ways to allow such simultaneous connectivity. One way is to access the Internet through the corporate network's own Internet gateway. The other way is to support a separate Internet connection simultaneously with the corporate connection. In many cases, the second way is more appropriate because it allows the telecommuter to access the Internet directly for non-work related reasons (such as entertainment) without using the corporate network resources. However, some corporations may not trust the simultaneous connections because this may open a back door to the corporate network from the Internet through the telecommuter's PC. In this case, such simultaneous connectivity should be restricted.

12.3.2.3 Multi-Protocol Support

Since not all corporations run IP exclusively, providing corporate connectivity requires interconnecting non-IP networks over the broadband access network. Hence, such connectivity involves protocol negotiation and address assignment.

12.3.2.4 Security

Telecommuters and branch offices must be able to communicate to the enterprise in a fashion that supports authentication, authorization and privacy. Security is also important for connecting to the Internet since the

ISP already authenticates all user access. The ISP must identify users and provide them with the contracted level of service.

12.3.2.5 Multicast

There has been an explosion of interest in IP multicast service. For example, during recent elections, most Internet sites carrying real-time results were jammed with users trying to log in. If it had been possible for this information to be pushed out using multicast, there would have been no congestion. Live events are now commonly offered in audio and video on the Internet, and multicast is the preferred delivery mechanism. A first-order requirement for the broadband access network is to deliver IP multicast service to homes and small businesses.

12.3.2.6 Multiple Service Class Support

It has become very clear that many services, including Internet access, cannot depend solely on a "one size fits all" paradigm. Different classes of service are required to satisfy the different needs of, for example, power users versus occasional users. Such differences in service class can be based on a variety of attributes, such as maximum, average or minimum bandwidth. In other words, multiple service classes can be provided even without QoS support in the network.

12.3.2.7 Quality of Service Support

Real-time streaming audio and video applications have become increasingly popular, especially over the Internet. These applications, and other real-time applications, require QoS guarantees to ensure their performance.[8] QoS guarantees also imply that the network can prevent aggressive or rogue users from consuming network bandwidth and degrading the performance of other users.

12.4 Residential Broadband Service Architecture

To design residential broadband (RBB) networks, we need to understand the end-to-end service architecture between the customer premise (home or small business) and the service provider networks and services. For discussion purposes, we assume the home device that is connected to the Internet is a PC, though there will be other intelligent devices in the future that can also be connected to the Internet, such as set-top boxes (with TV displays). The PC is the primary communications device at home for Internet access and it is in about forty percent of the homes in the United States.

A model of the end-to-end residential broadband service architecture is shown in Figure 12-5. There are four main subnetworks between a customer PC and the service provider network: the in-home network, the residential access network (RAN), the CO or headend network and the regional broadband network. Although the RBB network architecture chosen by a network operator involves mainly the RAN, there are ramifications to the CO/headend and in-home network because the RBB network is terminated by equipment in these two subnetworks.

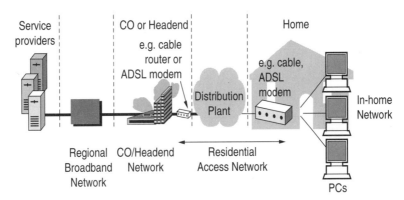

Figure 12–5   Residential Broadband Service Architecture

In this book, we focus on the end-to-end ATM architecture between the customer premise (terminated at a PC) and the service provider networks. This also implies it is an ATM-to-the-Home architecture because ATM cells are carried over the RAN.[1] The end-to-end ATM architecture enables of the benefits of ATM such as QoS support and scalability to higher bandwidth that matches the RAN bandwidth. This reference model can support IP end-to-end to enable Internet access, for which IP is terminated at a PC at the customer premise. IP packets are carried over an ATM VC to the ISP through the RBB network. Also, this model can support access to non-IP corporate network over ATM VCs, as discussed in the next chapter.

12.4.1 Residential Access Network

Existing telephone and cable networks can be upgraded to RBB networks using different RAN architectures such as various advanced digital subscriber line (xDSL)-based network, fiber-to-the-curb (FTTC) and fiber-to-the-home (FTTH) network architectures and the hybrid fiber coaxial (HFC) network architecture. The RANs chosen by the public network operators to provide residential broadband services differ significantly because of their different existing infrastructures. The telephone companies have extensive copper loops to the residence and can be upgraded by deploying high-speed modems (xDSL) alone, or fibers on the plant (FTTC and FTTH). The cable companies have their existing tree and branch coaxial cable architecture and can be upgraded to the HFC architecture by deploying fibers in their plant (as described later). Public network operators are deploying these RBB architectures at different pace and scale. In this book, we only focus on xDSL and cable modem (HFC)-based RBB networks because they are more mature and closest to large-scale deployment.

From an application or user point of view, the type of RAN chosen is not important, as long as it can support the desired applications with various traffic and quality of service requirements. In other words, applications developers and users are and should be network agnostics.

From the IP layer point of view, the RAN can be just another layer 2 subnetwork that carries IP packet, similar to Ethernet. Using the ATM-to-the-home architecture, the layer 2 protocol is ATM. The key issues for deploying the end-to-end ATM architecture are how to map the ATM protocols over the various RAN architectures and support various broadband services over ATM. They are discussed in detail in the next two chapters.

12.4.1.1 XDSL Modems

For the telephone companies, a leading architecture for residential broadband services is based on the high-speed modem technologies called the xDSL family. ADSL is the most popular member of the xDSL family used in current RBB trials. A key advantage of the ADSL technologies is that they can be implemented over the most existing copper loops without upgrades. The ADSL-based RBB network can be deployed by simply deploying a pair of ADSL modems on both ends of the copper loop (at home and at the CO or remote terminal). The main requirement is that the loop can meet the distance limitations. In particular, ADSL with 1.5 Mbps downstream and 64 Kbps upstream can be supported up to 18 Kft copper loops, which can be satisfied by approximately 75% of American homes.[9] The higher speed version of ADSL can support 6 to 8 Mbps downstream and 640kbps upstream up to 9-12 Kft (depending on the loop characteristics). A key characteristic of this architecture is that such bandwidth is dedicated to the pair of ADSL modems for each loop, instead of shared among many modems as for the cable modems discussed below.

Also, POTS can be supported simultaneously on the same copper loop because POTS and ADSL use different regions of the frequency spectrum. At the CO, the analog telephony signals from the loop are routed to the CO telephone switch, while the data signals are routed to an ATM network, as discussed below. A similar process takes place at home that splits the voice and data signals to the telephone and the PC, respectively.

12.4.1.2 Cable Modems

For cable companies, residential broadband services can be supported by upgrading their coaxial cable plant to the HFC architecture and enabling the return path (upstream from home to the headend) for two-way communications. (Note that the upgrade to HFC can be justified on other grounds, such as decreasing maintenance cost and supporting the emerging digital broadcast TV services.) The RBB network for the cable operators consists of three components: the HFC cable plant, cable modems at homes and cable switch/router(s) at the headend. We only provide an overview of the HFC-based RBB network here, because it will be discussed in a later chapter.

The HFC architecture is a modular architecture that divides the subscriber service area into neighborhood areas of about 500 (to 2000) homes passed. For each neighborhood area, there is a fiber from the headend extending to the area and terminating at a fiber node. From the fiber node, multiple coaxial cables extend to pass the homes in the area. The HFC architecture uses a passband transmission system, which divides the frequency spectrum into downstream (above 50 MHz) and upstream spectrums (5 to 42 MHz). The downstream spectrum, which is typically from 50 to 550 or 750 MHz, consists of 6 MHz wide channels. While the lower part of the downstream spectrum is reserved for current analog broadcast TV channels, the upper part of the downstream spectrum (such as 50 to 450 MHz) can be used for digital services. The typical bandwidth available for this architecture is about 27 Mbps downstream for each 6 MHz channel (using 64 QAM modulation) and about 2 Mbps upstream.[1] This means that over 1 Gbps downstream bandwidth is deployable over the HFC network to each area. Upstream bandwidth as high as 16 Mbps (using more frequency spectrum than the 2 Mbps version) is being considered by the IEEE 802.14 committee (a committee responsible for defining cable modem standards).

The HFC bandwidth in both directions is shared by all the homes served by the same fiber node, as opposed to the dedicated bandwidth available to the ADSL subscribers. The minimum average bandwidth available is equal to the capacity divided by peak number of simultaneously active cable modem users. For example, if the take rate (percentage of homes which subscribe to cable modem service) is 10% and at peak hours 50% of the subscribers are active, the average available downstream bandwidth (using a single 6 MHz channel) for a 500 home node is 1.1 Mbps. Note that the HFC architecture can scale as the bandwidth requirements increase. If the network is overloaded, more downstream and upstream spectrum (up to a limit) can be allocated to spread the load. This may be justified economically because of increased service demand.

12.4.2 CO and Headend Networks

Increasing the performance of Internet applications such as Web browsing cannot be solved by residential broadband networks alone, because the bandwidth bottleneck is not only at the access network (narrowband dial-up networks), but also at the Internet backbone. Although one can upgrade the capacity of the Internet backbone to match the load, this is expensive and takes time. Given the ad hoc nature of the operation and architecture of the Internet (being an interconnection of multiple networks belonging to different organizations), it is hard to justify economically for all the Internet service providers (regional and national) to increase network capacity fast enough to avoid such bottleneck, especially with the flat rate pricing structure. In addition, the explosive rate of traffic growth on the Internet makes it very difficult to keep up the pace of bandwidth growth.

The alternative solution is caching the content at the local headend or CO or at the ISP POPs, which allows high-speed delivery over the residential broadband network. (However, there are applications such as wide area real-time conferencing applications that cannot be solved by this approach, because they cannot be cached due to the real-time nature of the information.)

The CO/headend network has a number of important functions (see figure 12-6). First, it provides termination for the RAN. A cable access switch in the headend is used to terminate the HFC network to communicate with the cable modems at homes. A set of ADSL modems (or a DSL access multiplexer, DSLAM) at the CO terminates the copper loop to communicate with the corresponding ADSL modems at homes. Second, the CO/headend network provides a distribution function for the services and applications supported by the CO/headend servers, which include Web caching servers and local content servers.

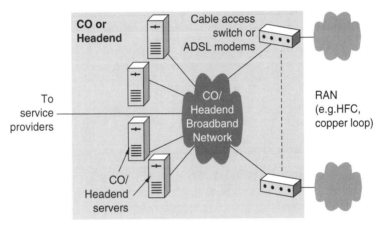

Figure 12–6 CO/headend network architecture

Third, the CO/headend network can provide connectivity to the Internet either directly (as an ISP pop itself) or indirectly through an Internet service provider (ISP). If the ISP is different from the cable or telephone company, then the responsibility of the CO or headend network is to provide high-speed IP connectivity (through the regional broadband network) to the ISP's POP. If the public network operator also acts as an ISP, then the CO or headend network will provide ISP services and applications (Internet mail, chat and news) by hosting such servers. Finally, the CO/headend network can provide direct connectivity to corporations through a regional ATM network, without going the Internet. This allows higher bandwidth and higher level of security.

12.4.3 Broadband Internet Access

With the RBB network, the subscribers are connected through a high-speed IP service over an end-to-end ATM network, instead of the dial-up circuit switched connection, as shown in Figure 12-7. This has a number of advantages. First, since this bypasses CO telephony switch, this avoids congesting the telephony switch by online subscribers. Second, the packet switched connection significantly increases bandwidth efficiency for Internet traffic. Third, it provides much higher speed access to the ISP. Fourth, the ISP can avoid dial-up modem banks, which are expensive and introduce additional blocking probability. Instead, a single ATM link from the CO or headend can directly terminate onto a router. Finally, this allows the home PC to be always connected to the Internet, instead of requiring dial-up delay incurred in the narrowband case. The PC can leave the VC up indefinitely because it can be an UBR or ABR service (as opposed to a circuit switched connection that ties up bandwidth and connectivity), for which no bandwidth are consumed when the PC is idle.

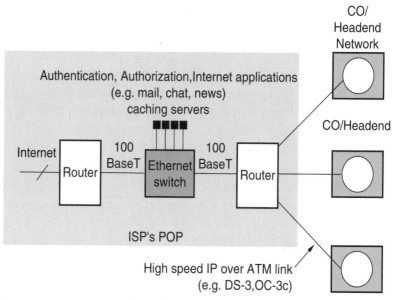

Figure 12–7   An example configuration of a broadband ISP POP

The POP can be connected to a WAN that is part of the ISP's national backbone network (such as an ATM network). In this case, not all the traffic needs to go to the Internet for access because the destination may be reachable directly through this backbone network. This is desirable not only because the Internet typically has lower throughput and higher latency, but also because the network operator can provide a value-added option of higher performance. Furthermore, such a nationwide broadband network can also provide direct connectivity to businesses. Hence, there is a synergy of providing broadband connectivity for both businesses and residences to allow high-speed telecommuting services through the same national broadband network infrastructure. Again, if the public network operator that runs the CO/headend is also responsible for providing ISP service, then the ISP POP can actually be part of the CO/headend network.

12.4.4 In-Home Network

The in-home network architecture is a very important consideration for designing RBB services, especially for homes with multiple PCs that need to communicate with the Internet. Different in-home network architectures are shown in Figure 12-8. They are distinguished by supporting one or more PCs, using internal (PC network interface cards, NICs) versus external modems and whether a separate home network is created to connect different home devices.

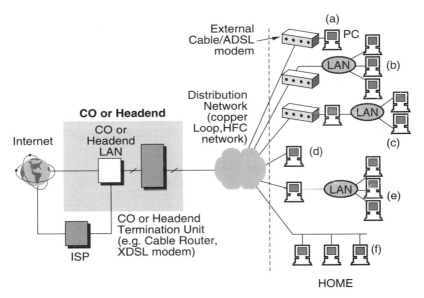

Figure 12–8   In-home network architectures

Many PC households have multiple PCs and they are growing rapidly. PCs are purchased for both adults for work at home and children for educational purposes. Also, people continue to get additional PCs that offer higher performance to run more current applications. Therefore, we consider the scenario of how an external or internal modem scenario can evolve from supporting a single to multiple PCs at home, and the issues surrounding them.

12.4.4.1 External Modem

Many cable and ADSL modems are currently designed as external modems, as shown in Figure 12-8(a). They are connected to the PC via an external connection or network for a variety of reasons. First, it is simpler to implement a standalone device than to fit it into the PC, for both hardware and software integration reasons. This allows faster time to market, which is critical, as this broadband modem market has become very competitive. However, this reason will be irrelevant as the modem technologies become mature. Second, an external modem allows easier demarcation points between the public network and the subscribers. This is an important consideration for support from network operators. If things go wrong with the PC, it is much clearer whose problem it is. Third, external modems avoid the need of the telephone or cable company's installation crew to open up a subscriber's PC as part of the installation process. This would require significant new training beyond the current responsibilities of their field crews. Fourth, in the HFC environment, the external modem configuration helps reduce the upstream noise that might be generated by the PC if it were implemented as an internal PC card. Nevertheless, this external PC approach implies higher cost because of the need of a network connection between the modem and the PC, as well as fewer integration opportunities than the internal PC options.

The external network connectivity between the PC and the modem can allow easier migration to support additional PCs, by connecting them to the same network. There are many different options to connect between the PC and the external modem. Due to the popularity of Ethernet and its low component costs, most external modems have an Ethernet (10baseT) interface. This also requires an additional PC network interface card (NIC), if it does not already have one for connecting to other devices such as printers. However, the 10baseT connection might limit the maximum downstream throughput to 10 Mbps, instead of the 27 Mbps available in the HFC-based network. Also, Ethernet does not provide quality of service guarantees. Nevertheless, initially the 10 Mbps bandwidth is probably sufficient as the number of home devices is typically small (this is not true in the corporate network case) and they may not be active simultaneously.

However, there are many problems with the Ethernet approach and an ATM link between the PC and the external modem may be more appropriate. The Ethernet approach requires termination of the ATM protocol at the external modem. This increases the cost of the external modem because it requires SAR hardware to reassemble the ATM cells and convert them to Ethernet frames. Also, an internetworking protocol (such as LAN Emulation, IP over ATM or Multi-protocol over ATM) must be implemented on the modem because the modem serves as an interworking unit between an ATM and a non-ATM network. This increases the complexity of external modem. On the other hand, if an ATM interface is used, it provides an end-to-end ATM connectivity to the PC to take advantage of the ATM benefits, such as QoS guarantees and the flexibility to signal directly for specific applications requirements. It significantly simplifies the external modem design as it reduces the modem to a layer 1 (and MAC protocol for HFC network) device. (There are other in-home networking options such as IEEE 1394 and wireless, but they are beyond the scope of this book.)

There are a number of ways for adding new PCs to the home that already has a PC with the external ADSL/cable modem connection. If the connection between the PC and the modem is an Ethernet, then additional PCs can be connected to the same Ethernet (such as by a shared hub). However, this might require multiple IP addresses supported per home (which can be a problem if real IP addresses are used because they are a scarce resource). This is shown in Figure 12-8 (b). If the connection is an ATM connection to the PC, then additional PCs can be supported by additional ATM interfaces on the modem. Since this might be expensive, a better approach is to support additional PCs via a separate Ethernet connected to the first PC (which is connected to a modem via an ATM interface), which acts as a dual-home host, as shown in Figure 12-8 (c). In this case, the first PC can act as a proxy server and a firewall for other PCs to protect them from Internet intruders. As more software functions (such as routing) are supported in today's PC operating systems, this becomes a very attractive approach because it avoids a separate router at home.

12.4.4.2 Internal PC Modems

An alternative to the external modem implementation is the PC NIC implementation of the equivalent modem, as shown in Figure 12-8 (d). In the long run, it should be a cheaper implementation from a modem cost point of view, because it allows tighter integration and avoids an additional network cost (no need for an additional NIC). Also this allows for direct access to the QoS functions on the ADSL link or the HFC link by the PC operating system. This avoids the need to provide QoS over the extra Ethernet link in the case of an external modem connected via Ethernet.

We discuss two ways to support multiple PCs in this environment. First, we can add a separate NIC (such as Ethernet) to the first PC that contains the internal modem, such as in Figure 12-8(e). Again, the first PC can act as either a router to forward IP traffic to the Internet, or as a proxy server to provide Internet access. This allows the gateway PC to negotiate quality of service on behalf of the rest of the PCs. This can take advantage of the routing and internetworking functions in today's PC operating systems.

Second, we can acquire a new internal modem for each new PC added (Figure 12-8 (f)). However, there are two drawbacks for this architecture. First, all communication between the PCs within the home must go through the headend (or CO), potentially wasting a lot of valuable bandwidth in the HFC RAN. This makes this architecture less of an in-home network, even though it appears this way physically. Second, it requires multiple ADSL or cable modems for each home, which is not cost effective. Hence, the first approach is more desirable.

12.4.5 End-to-end ATM Architecture

There are two approaches for supporting IP service in the residential broadband networks: connectionless or connection-oriented. In the connectionless approach, the CO/headend network architecture is similar to the legacy LAN architecture and connectionless packets are carried over the RAN, providing an Ethernet interface to the customer premise. Early implementation tends to be connectionless based. For example, each ADSL modem at the CO can have an Ethernet (10 Mbps) interface to connect to an Ethernet switch, which in turn connects to a core router in the CO. Similarly, the cable router or switch (which terminates many cable modems from homes) can have a fast Ethernet (100 Mbps) interface to the core headend network router. The key disadvantages of the connectionless approach are the lack of QoS and security because it is a legacy LAN architecture originally designed for internal corporate networks. Also, this requires routers at the CO or headend, which introduces a potential throughput bottleneck and increases maintenance expertise requirements for technical support of a router-based network.

More advanced implementation can be based on the connection-oriented architecture. This provides a virtual "dial-up" paradigm for Internet service to the ISPs. Instead of dial-up through the PSTN, it is using a virtual connection such as an ATM VC. The ATM end-to-end architecture is a connection-oriented architecture, for which ATM cells are carried all the way to the home over the RAN terminated at the PC. In this case, the CO/headend network is an ATM network, which is connected to the ISP POPs and corporate networks through the regional broadband ATM networks.

12.5 Summary

This chapter gave an overview of residential broadband service requirements and network architectures based on ATM. We first gave an overview of the existing residential network and Internet access architectures and their limitations. Then, we presented the end-to-end residential broadband service requirements such as providing connectivity to the Internet, corporate networks and local content and supporting peer-to-peer communications. Also, the RBB network should support simultaneous connections to multiple destinations, IP multicast, multiple service classes, QoS and security mechanisms, among other functions. Next, we described the different networking components of residential broadband architecture based on the ATM-to-the-home architecture that can satisfy these requirements. They include the in-home network, RAN, CO/headend network and regional broadband network. Finally, since many homes (and especially small businesses) have multiple PCs (and that ratio continues to increase), we explore in detail the customer premise network architectures to support multiple PCs, using both internal and external modems. This chapter provided the background for the discussions of residential broadband network architectures based on xDSL and cable modems in the following two chapters.

12.6 References

[1]T. Kwok, "A Vision for Residential Broadband Services: ATM-to-the-Home," *IEEE Network*, Sept./Oct, 1995, pp. 14-28.

[2]T. Berners-Lee et al., "The World-Wide Web," Commun. ACM, vol. 37, no. 8, Aug. 1994, pp. 76-82.

[3] W. R. Stevens, TCP/IP Illustrated, vol.3, Reading, MA: Addison-Wesley, 1996.

[4] T. Berners-Lee, R. Fielding, and H. Frystyk, "Hypertext Transfer Protocol – HTTP/1.0," IETF RFC 1945, May 1996.

[5] W. Simpson, "The Point-to-Point Protocol (PPP)," *IETF Request for Comments*: 1661, July 1994.

[6] T. Kwok, "Residential Broadband Internet Service Architectures based on xDSL Systems," presented at the ADSL Forum, www.adsl.com, Seattle, Dec., 1996.

[7] T. Kwok, I. Verbesselt, D. Veneski, P. Shieh, J. Loehndorf and R. Mwikalo, "An Interoperable End-to-End Broadband Service Architecture over ADSL Systems," white paper from Microsoft, Alcatel, Cisco Systems, FORE Systems, US Robotics and Westell, Version 1.0, http://www.microsoft.com/industry/telecom, June 1997.

[8] T. Kwok, "Residential Broadband Internet Services and Applications Requirements," *IEEE Commun. Mag.*, June 1997, pp. 76-83.

[9] D.L. Waring, J.W. Lechleider, T.R. Hsing, "Digital Subscriber Line Technology Facilitates a Graceful Transition from Copper to Fiber," *IEEE Commun. Mag.*, March 1991, pp. 96-104.

Chapter **13**

ATM Over xDSL Network Architecture

13.1 Introduction

The local copper loop has long been considered the key bottleneck to providing residential broadband services. Since the late 1980s, a lot of research has gone into enabling high-speed communications over the copper loop. This has resulted in a family of digital subscriber line (xDSL) transmission technologies that makes broadband services over most existing loop possible. x stands for different members of the DSL family: high speed, single line, asymmetric and very high speed (HDSL, SDSL, ADSL and VDSL, respectively). xDSL is basically a high-speed modem that significantly increases the bandwidth available over the local loop to the Mbps range using advance signaling processing technologies. It is about two orders of magnitude higher than current voice band analog modem (28.8 Kbps or less) in one or both directions.

285

13.1.1 Interactive TV Market

xDSL technologies were first introduced in the late 1980s by Bellcore researchers to exploit the existing copper loops to support high-speed digital services to homes. This is an alternative to massively upgrading the local loop infrastructure with fiber optics, which takes time and money. In the early 1990s, there was a tremendous momentum for public network operators (telephone and cable companies) to deploy interactive TV services. The telephone companies (telcos)' general approach was to upgrade or replace their distribution plant to a new residential broadband architecture based on either HFC or FTTC architectures. Although there were ADSL trials ongoing, ADSL technologies were not viewed as the real deployment for residential broadband architectures for ITV services. The main reason was its much higher cost per household (thousands of dollars) which meant it did not scale for massive deployment. Another reason was that xDSL does not support analog TV transmission, which was very important for the ITV market for backward compatibility with existing analog TV services.

In the mid-90s, it became clear that the ITV market was not being realized as fast as had been predicted. This is partly because networking vendors found it difficult to deliver working equipment for these architectures, and partly because of the complexity of integrating a variety of novel hardware and software from different vendors. Furthermore, it would take a lot longer to deploy and cost much more than anticipated, which broke the original business models of the public network operators for the ITV market. At the same time, pending telecommunications deregulation (which finally happened in 1996) in the U.S. also contributed to the shift of telco investments into markets with more immediate pay back, such as entering the long distance markets.

13.1.2 Internet Opportunity and Cable Modem Threat

At the same time, the Internet and World Wide Web phenomenon suddenly sprang into the horizon to everyone's surprise, even though the Internet itself has been growing ever since it started more than two decades earlier. The cable companies began to view providing high speed Internet access as the immediate opportunity to exploit the Internet market. A lot of momentum has been built up in the cable industry to deploy high-speed cable modems to enable broadband Internet access.

This prompted many telcos to evaluate their strategic plans to provide broadband Internet access to compete with the cable companies. It became obvious that upgrading the telco plants by building new infrastructure using either HFC or FTTC architecture would not only be a costly proposition, but more importantly, would be too time consuming to react to the threat of the cable operators. Hence, the only option that does not require massive rebuild of the loop plants to enable broadband services was to use xDSL technologies.

Fortunately, since the early 1990s, xDSL vendors have continued to improve their technologies and reduce their cost, which are projected to reach reasonable costs for deployment in the 1997-98 time frame. This cost reduction coupled with the new demand for high-speed Internet access makes the xDSL based solution a very attractive residential broadband architecture solution.

The exponential growth in demand for Internet access has resulted in unexpected problems with the telephone network. Residential Internet accesses are primarily through analog modems dialing to local ISPs, which go through the local CO (central office) phone switches. The much longer holding time (on the order of hours) for Internet access has broken the original traffic engineering design of such circuit switches for an average 3 to 5 minutes of holding time. Note that even ISDN has the same problem as POTS because they are both based on circuit switching. Furthermore, such heavy usage on local phone switches does not generate any additional revenue of the phone companies, as local calls are based on flat rate calling plans. As we describe the xDSL network architecture later, it provides an alternative access to the Internet bypassing the CO telephone switch.

The rest of this chapter is organized as follows. We first give an overview of the subscriber loop architecture. Then we discuss the history of deploying digital and high-speed digital technologies in the loop and the CSA (carrier serving area) concept. After that, we give an overview of xDSL technologies. Finally, we describe an ADSL-based broadband service architecture that uses the ATM-to-the-home paradigm.[1] Based on existing PPP and ATM standards, this architecture uses PPP over ATM protocol to provide end-to-end broadband services.

13.2 Subscriber Loop Architecture

13.2.1 Subscriber Loop

The subscriber loop, also known as the distribution plant of the telephone network, consists of three physical portions: feeder cable, distribution cable and the drop wire.[2] This is shown in Figure 13-1. From the CO, there are a number of feeder cables extending to different neighborhood areas. Each feeder cable typically terminates at a remote access node in a concentrated customer area. The remote access node acts as a concentration point for all copper loops serving homes in the neighborhood area. In other words, the feeder cables can share the cost connecting many homes in a concentrated customer area using the same conduit. Currently, many feeder cables are fibers, as discussed in more detail below.

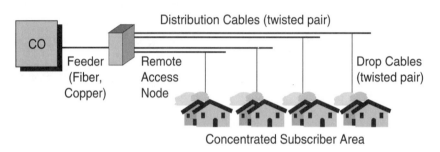

Figure 13–1   The subscriber loop architecture

The distribution cable connects the feeder to potential customer sites. Distribution cables are deployed even before customers move into the neighborhood. Unused distribution cables are terminated by bridged taps, which are open circuit pairs. When there are customers, their homes are connected from the distribution cables via drop wires.

A loop typically consists of different types of copper of different thickness (specified in terms of a gauge number) spliced together at different parts of the distribution plant. Thicker wires have lower resistance and are represented by smaller gauge numbers. According to Bellcore, an average U.S. subscriber loop is spliced 22 times.

To ensure a minimum signal quality, the loop distance is limited such that the loop resistance is less than about 1500 ohms. Increasing the loop distance beyond this limit has typically been achieved by installing loaded coils. Loaded coils are usually found in loop plants longer than 18 Kft. As we discuss below, such loaded coils make the loop unsuitable for deploying xDSL technologies to support high-speed digital services.

The loop length distributions vary significantly around the world. The same is true not only between cities in the U.S., but also within cities. About 75% of the loops in the U.S. are less than 18 Kft, while the rest typically have loaded coils. Also, since very few non-loaded plants exceed

18 Kft,[3] 18 Kft becomes a good working limit for designing residential broadband networks. The average lengths of non-loaded loops are about 7500-ft.[3] Figure 13-2 shows the subscriber loop architectures with different loop lengths.

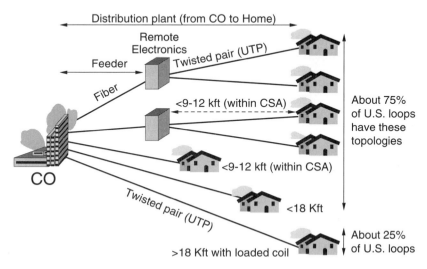

Figure 13–2 The subscriber loop architectures and CSA guidelines

13.2.2 Digital Transmissions in the Loop

We briefly discuss the history of deploying digital transmission technologies in the loop below, which form the precursor to xDSL technologies. They include the introductions of digital loop carrier systems, the CSA guideline and ISDN.

13.2.2.1 DLC Systems

Digital transmission technologies in the form of the T1 carrier (1.544 Mbps) over copper were first deployed between COs in the late 1960s. Each T1 link carries 24 voice channels. Many T1 lines between COs have been replaced by fibers since then. Deployment of digital transmission in the loop began in the 1970s.[4] Digital transmission in the loop first occurred in the feeder portion. It reduces the cost significantly by reducing copper lines dedicated to each home using shared T1 facilities that serve many homes. This is achieved by multiplexing many voice channels (multiples 24) on a single feeder cable using digital multiplexing technologies known as digital loop carrier (DLC). Another reason for the DLC systems is to reduce the distance between the remote access node and the subscribers, making it easier for the plant to provide future digital services to the homes.

The DLC systems are deployed from the CO to a concentrated customer area terminated by remote electronics located in the remote access nodes. Such an area serves between 1500 homes in suburban communities and 3000 homes in urban areas. Recent DLC systems typically use fibers, especially for longer loops, or copper using HDSL technologies (one of the xDSL technologies that support 1.5 Mbps in both directions). The deployment of DLC systems in the 1980s fueled a trend to deploy electronics in the loop, breaking the practice of having active electronics primarily in the CO. Such remote electronics require an environment enclosure (vault or cabinet) to get the same reliable protection as in the CO. From the remote electronics, the voice channels are delivered as analog signals toward the customer. The remote electronics performs digital to analog conversion for signals toward the subscribers and vice versa in the return direction. Hence, even with DLC systems, service to homes remains analog-based.

13.2.2.2   CSA Guidelines

To expedite the deployment of DLC systems in the loop and to position the loop for digital services in the future,[5] Bellcore established CSA (Carrier Serving Areas) guidelines for the loop architecture (see Figure 13-2).

The CSA guidelines are intended for performing upgrades to existing distribution plants or installation of new plants. These guidelines specify that the copper loop has a maximum distance of 9 Kft (for 26 gauge) to 12 Kft (for 24 gauge). The CSA guidelines eliminate the use of loaded coils for loop extensions. To support longer loops without loaded coils, DLC systems are used to carry signals from the CO to a remote access node that is located within the CSA guidelines on loop lengths. Therefore, by following the CSA guidelines, both long copper loops and loaded coils are eliminated, paving the way for delivering digital services in the loop. According to an estimate by the ADSL Forum, about 60% of the U.S. phone lines are within the CSA distance.[6]

13.2.2.3   ISDN: First Digital Service to the Home

The introduction of ISDN marked the first deployment of an end-to-end digital telephone network. Before ISDN, the digitalization only went halfway, from the core telephone network up to the COs or the remote access node (with DLC). With ISDN, digital services were introduced all the way to the homes for the first time.

In 1987, the basic rate interface (BRI) for ISDN was standardized to provide 160 Kbps digital service to the homes in both directions. BRI can be deployed for homes with loops up to 18 Kft long and without loaded coils. BRI includes two B channels of 64 Kbps each and a D channel of 16 Kbps. B channels can be used for voice, low bit rate video communications as well as data communications. The D channel is used for signaling in ISDN service as well as for additional data communications needs. In addition, there is a 16 Kbps channel for management functions.

ISDN was the first embodiment of the DSL technologies. To provide digital service to homes, DSL uses adaptive digital signal processing (DSP) for both pulse restoration and cancellation of transmit and receive echoes.[7] The DSL technologies used by ISDN are not particularly advanced, as the data rate supported is less than 200 Kbps.

Since loaded coils deployed in long loops preclude the use of self-adaptive transceivers, DSL technologies can only be deployed in unloaded loops. This is true not only for ISDN, but also for xDSL technologies discussed below. This limitation excludes about 25% of the 100 million subscriber loops in the United States. Nevertheless, there are about 75 million loops eligible for DSL technology of some form, which is still a huge potential market opportunity.

13.3 xDSL Technologies

Before we discuss xDSL technologies in detail, we first present a short history of xDSL technologies.[4] Then, we describe the common attributes of the xDSL family. With this background, we discuss the characteristics of each member of the xDSL family.

13.3.1 History

Since there are hundreds of millions of local loops around the world, representing billions of dollars of investment under the ground, it is extremely desirable to leverage this to support high-speed communications to homes. This can enable broadband services to homes immediately, without upgrading the distribution plants such as installing fibers close to homes. Hence, there has been active research to increase the bandwidth delivered over the copper loop since the 1980s. As discussed next, significant advances have been made especially over the past 10 years.

There are a lot of challenges to support high data rates over the copper loop. First, there is signal distortion due to attenuation and inter-symbol interference in the loop. Since such distortions increase with the frequency, they limit the maximum data rate that can be supported in the loop. In addition, there are other external interferences due to crosstalk and radio frequency. Hence, digital signals must be amplified and reshaped at the receiver to compensate for these distortions.

Second, such signal distortions are different for different loops, even for adjacent loops. As mentioned earlier, a typical loop consists of many twisted pairs of different gauges spliced together, and there may be bridged taps along the loops. Furthermore, loop plants are constantly under change as subscribers move in and out of the neighborhood, and detailed topological information is not easy to obtain. Hence, the amplification and reshaping of the digital signals must be adapted to each local loop pair.

Although the technology to overcome such transmission impairment has been available since the 1970s, the costs to add such electronics and to tune them to the unique loop characteristics have been prohibitively expensive. Hence, to enable high-speed communications over the copper loop, sophisticated self-adaptive transceivers must be developed to automatically optimize for transmitting signals over a particular loop.

Rapid advances in DSP technologies and microelectronics technologies in the 1980s provided new tools to solve these problems.[4] Self-adaptive transceiver technologies were developed to reshape signals unique to each loop and adapt in real time. Furthermore, as VSLI (very large scale integrated circuit) technologies became available at much lower cost in the 1980s, it became possible to produce devices that were highly sophisticated and practical in size and weight to implement these self adaptive transceiver technologies onto a small number of chips. This opened up a wide range of opportunities to develop different xDSL modem technologies since the late 1980s. Hence, as some xDSL proponents have said, "copper is buried, but not dead."

13.3.2 xDSL Characteristics

The xDSL-based residential access network has a number of characteristics that make them very suitable for providing residential broadband services. They are discussed below.

13.3.2.1 Bandwidth Improvement

The significant bandwidth improvement of xDSL technologies over voice band analog modems is made possible by three key factors. First, the xDSL technologies can use significantly wider frequency spectrum, on the order of MHz frequency bandwidth compared to about 4 kHz for analog modems. (Note that the 28.8 Kbps analog modem technologies have already achieved 10 bits/Hz encoding, approaching the theoretical bandwidth limit, excluding compression).[8] The reason is that the analog modem signals are carried end-to-end across the telephone network, which was designed with such frequency bandwidth limitation for each analog voice channel (see Figure 13-3). On the other hand, xDSL is designed to operate only between the CO (or remote access node or the curbside) and the customer, as shown in Figure 13-4. Second, the signal distortion (attenuation and interference) decreases with decreasing distance. Since xDSL technologies operate over significantly shorter distances, the transmission capacity of a xDSL system can be much higher. Third, xDSL uses more advanced DSP technologies made possible in VSLI technologies developed in the past 10 years.

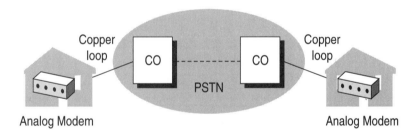

Figure 13–3　Analog modems are terminated at the destinations

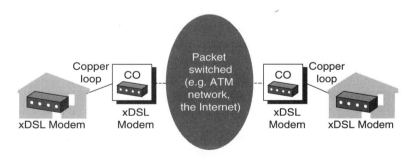

Figure 13–4　ADSL modems are terminated at the CO

13.3.2.2 Point-to-point

xDSL technologies such as ADSL and HDSL are point-to-point transmission technologies. They can be deployed on a per subscriber basis, significantly reducing the cost of entry for deployment. This means that the network operator can selectively deploy the xDSL technologies to the targeted subscribers in each neighborhood, instead of overbuilding to cover a large number of non-subscribers to incur the corresponding overhead costs. This allows xDSL architecture to scale gracefully from small deployment to large installation, as long as the CO xDSL termination equipment is designed to be scalable. An associated advantage of the point-to-point topology used in xDSL deployment is the dedicated bandwidth to each subscriber, unlike the HFC architecture used by cable modems (which requires bandwidth sharing with the neighbors).

13.3.2.3 Always "Connected"

The xDSL-based residential broadband network architecture can provide significant improvements over the current dial-up access architecture to the Internet. Since the analog modem operates on existing voice circuits, it is connected to the ISP's POP over a circuit switched connection through the CO switch. Hence, the analog modem requires explicit circuit set up before communications take place, which requires the subscriber to incur a long dial-up delay. More importantly, once connected, it ties up the phone line both on the subscriber loop and between the CO switch and the ISP.

On the other hand, the xDSL-based RBB network architecture can provide an "always connected" experience while avoiding tying up network resource by using a packet switched network architecture. The reason is that the xDSL modem pair is a physical layer technology that terminates at the CO (or a remote access node) and represents a dedicated bit pipe to each subscriber. The traffic beyond the CO termination do not pass through the circuit switched PSTN, but instead can go through a packet switched network. The packet switched architecture allows an "always connected" experience for not only connectionless layer 2 architecture (such as using a LAN-based architecture), but also connected-oriented layer 2 architecture. For example, if ATM is layered over the xDSL access network between the subscriber and the ISP's POP, an UBR VC can be maintained between the subscriber and the ISP, without consuming bandwidth when the user is idle. The ATM over xDSL architecture is discussed in more detail later.

13.3.2.4 Simultaneous POTS support

Most xDSL technologies such as ADSL can support the POTS simultaneously on the same twisted pair with high-speed data service. The reason is that the high-speed data delivered by the xDSL technologies are carried in the spectrum separate from the POTS voice band (0 – 4 KHz). Hence, they can coexist on the same twisted pair. Note that even ISDN connection requires a separate twisted pair to support the POTS, because ISDN uses the 0 - 80 KHz spectrum for data transmission, which overlaps with the POTS spectrum. Note that the analog modem modulates digital data directly into the POTS band, preventing the use of the phone while the analog modem is active. The ability to carry POTS simultaneously with ADSL is very advantageous from a deployment standpoint, because ADSL modems can be immediately installed to homes without adding additional phone lines.

13.3.2.5 Rate Adaptive

The xDSL technologies can be designed to provide the rate adaptive function. This means that the xDSL modem pair can adapt to given copper loop characteristics to provide the maximum bandwidth while maintaining a given bit error rate objective. This is achieved by a loop testing sequence at the beginning of the modem pair operation to find the maximum rate, similar to the analog modem operation today. In addition, since the loop characteristics may change over time as the environment changes, the rate adaptive function of the xDSL modem performs the test sequence periodically to find and maintain the maximum possible rate at that time. This rate adaptive function is important because the xDSL modem is expected to operate mostly in the "always connected" mode, making it necessary to perform periodical testing.

13.3.3 The xDSL Family

The xDSL family of high-speed digital technologies is summarized in Table 13-1. Most of these xDSL technologies use a single pair of copper lines, except one of the HDSL versions as indicated. Obviously, bandwidth can be increased with more than one pair of copper line.

The xDSL family of technologies differs by the following attributes. The first three attributes are all coupled:

Table 13–1   *The family of xDSL technologies and their key attributes.*

xDSL	Symmetry	Downstream bandwidth	Upstream bandwidth	Distance limit	POTS with lifeline
DSL (ISDN)	Symmetric	160 Kbps	160 Kbps	15-18 Kft	No (uses 0-80kHz)
ADSL	Asymmetric	1.5 Mbps	64 Kbps	15-18 Kft	Yes
ADSL	Asymmetric	6 Mbps (up to 8 Mbps)	640 Kbps (up to 1 Mbps)	9-12 Kft (CSA)	Yes
HDSL (2 pairs)	Symmetric	1.5 Mbps	1.5 Mbps	9-12 Kft (CSA)	No
HDSL (1 pair)	Symmetric	768 Kbps	768 Kbps	9-12 Kft (CSA)	No
SDSL	Symmetric	384 Kbps	384 Kbps	18 Kft	Most do
SDSL	Symmetric	1.5 Mbps	1.5 Mbps	10 Kft	Most do
VDSL	Asymmetric	12.96 Mbps	1.6-2.3 Mbps	4.5 Kft	Yes
VDSL	Asymmetric	25 Mbps	1.6-2.3 Mbps	3 Kft	Yes
VDSL	Asymmetric	52 Mbps	1.6-2.3 Mbps	1 Kft	Yes

13.3.3.1 Symmetry in Bi-directional Bandwidth

xDSL technologies can provide either the same or different upstream and downstream bandwidth. For example, ADSL and VDSL provide asymmetric bandwidth, while HDSL and SDSL provide symmetric bandwidth. In general, symmetric bandwidth tends to limit the loop distance as there are more crosstalk, as discussed later.

13.3.3.2 Bandwidth

The maximum bandwidth provided by each xDSL technology depends on the loop length and whether it provides symmetric bandwidth. In general, the longer the copper loop, the lower the maximum bandwidth.

13.3.3.3 Maximum Loop Distance

The different loop lengths supported by the different xDSL technologies are targeted for different deployment scenarios. The 18 Kft limit is targeted for households that generally have no loaded coils that prevent xDSL's operation. The 9-12 Kft limit is targeted to those homes which satisfy the CSA guidelines. The shorter loop lengths of 1 to 4 Kft require new fiber deployment deep into the neighborhood. This is mainly targeted for fiber-to-the-curb (FTTC) architecture. Hence, the xDSL family can be applied to different combination copper loop lengths and fiber lengths. Therefore, the xDSL-based systems are sometimes referred to as hybrid fiber *copper* (HFCu) systems. Furthermore, the xDSL based RBB architectures can be viewed as stepping stones to the evolution of fiber-to-the-home (FTTH) architectures.

13.3.3.4 Lifeline POTS Support

The POTS uses the 0 - 4 KHz spectrum to provide both power and voice communications for the lifeline service. If the xDSL technology does not use the 0–4 kHz spectrum, lifeline POTS can be provided simultaneously with the high-speed digital service. Otherwise, no lifeline POTS can be supported on the same twisted pair that supports xDSL. The reason is that powering of the xDSL modem would become the subscriber's responsibility as this can no longer be provided by the CO, even though voice communications can still be carried digitally in the xDSL spectrum.

We discuss the different xDSL technologies in more detail below. The DSL technology used in ISDN service is shown in Table 13-1 as a reference.

13.3.3.5 HDSL

HDSL[4] is the first high-speed DSL technology. HDSL was originally targeted for replacing the T1 carrier to support full duplex 1.5 Mbps between COs or providing T1 lines to businesses. It requires two pairs of copper. Each pair supports 784 Kbps and supports CSA guidelines of 9 - 12 Kft. Also, it uses the same spectrum as POTS service.

Although HDSL provides much higher speed than ISDN, there are three problems that make HDSL less desirable for providing high-speed services to homes. First, it requires an additional copper pair to support HDSL service. Second, it only reaches 9 - 12 Kft, while there are many homes that are up to 18 Kft from the CO. The distance is primarily limited by near-end crosstalk (NEXT) because of the symmetric bandwidth requirement. Third, since it uses the POTS spectrum, it cannot provide POTS simultaneously. It requires either a third pair of copper to support voice services, or analog/digital conversions at both ends of the HDSL modem pair. As a result, ADSL was designed to address all three of these problems to provide high-speed data service to homes.

13.3.3.6 ADSL

The ADSL technology can be deployed with the longest loop distance of the xDSL family. It has a maximum loop length of 15-18 Kft (depending on the gauge) and can be deployed immediately in existing loop majority of the plants without any fiber installation in the loop. It supports 1.5 Mbps downstream and 64 Kbps upstream at that distance. By reducing the loop limit to 9 -12 Kft (CSA guideline), the ADSL technology can support 6.3 Mbps (or even 8 Mbps) downstream and 640 Kbps (or even 1 Mbps) upstream.

The asymmetric bandwidth with higher bandwidth downstream is suitable for many emerging applications that provide rich multimedia content to the subscriber, but only require minimal upstream traffic mainly for commands. This matches the asymmetry of ADSL and allows multimedia delivered at high speed to the subscribers. Such applications include as Web browsing and video-on-demand.

Figure 13-5 shows an example of the spectrum utilization of ADSL modems of the two distance limits (maximum and CSA). Since ADSL does not use the POTS band of 0 - 4 kHz, ADSL signals can coexist with POTS. Hence, both the lifeline service and high-speed data service can share the same copper pair. This is an important advantage of ADSL because the subscriber does not need to get a new copper line to support lifeline service (as opposed to ISDN, HDSL or analog modems).

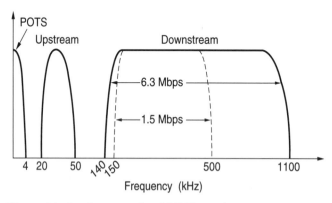

Figure 13–5   An example of ADSL modem spectrum usage

Figure 13-5 shows that both ADSL technologies (of two distance limitations) use only the spectrum above 20 kHz for digital communications. A POTS splitter is used at each ADSL modem (exact configuration to be discussed later) for frequency multiplexing and demultiplexing of both ADSL and POTS signals with a guard band between 4–20 kHz. The digital signals are further separated into upstream and downstream communications, which use different frequency bands. Both ADSL technologies use 20–50KHz for upstream transmission. For downstream communications, 150–500 KHz and 140 KHz - 1.1 MHz bands are used for the 1.5 Mbps and 6.3 Mbps ADSL modem, respectively.

There are two key modulation technologies used by the ADSL technologies: Carrierless Amplitude Phase (CAP) and Discrete Multi-Tone (DMT). CAP was used for the first generation ADSL modems and has become more mature in terms of commercialization and cost reduction. Hence, most of the ADSL modems deployed in trials today are CAP based. However, DMT is the technology that has been adopted by ANSI T1E1 as the ADSL standard and is expected to follow the CAP cost curves soon.

The ADSL technologies support forward error correction (FEC). There are two FEC modes: with and without interleaving. With interleaving, burst errors are transformed into bit errors, which significantly increases the probability of error correction and hence lower the resulting error probability. However, the disadvantage of interleaving is increased latency because this requires prebuffering of data for interleaving. The latency with and without interleaving is about 20 ms and 2 ms, respectively. Such latency from interleaving may exceed the delay requirements of some applications, such as voice communications without echo control mechanisms. ADSL modems can be designed to support both latency options (also referred to as dual latency), or even a continuous range of latency values by varying the interleaving depth of the FEC algorithm.

13.3.3.7 SDSL

SDSL (Single-line DSL) is the single copper loop pair version of HDSL technologies. Hence, SDSL has an important advantage over HDSL; it avoids an additional copper pair to each home. Of course, this comes at the price of reducing the data rate to 384 Kbps in both directions at 18 Kft. Some SDSL versions use spectrum above the POTS frequency and so allows simultaneous POTS support, another improvement over HDSL.

13.3.3.8 VDSL

At the other end of the xDSL family is the VDSL (very high speed DSL) technology. The VDSL technology can be deployed with the highest speed but with the smallest loop limit of the xDSL family. It requires fibers to be deployed from the CO to within about 4.5 Kft to even 1 Kft to homes to achieve 13 - 52 Mbps downstream to the home over that last stretch of copper. In fact, at 1Kft or less from the home, we are reaching the realm of FTTC. FTTC has a fiber from the CO deployed all the way to the curb terminated by the optical network unit (ONU), which serves 8 to 32 homes. The VDSL technology can be used over either copper or coaxial cable to the home to support 52 Mbps to the home. FTTC involves quite different architecture from other xDSL-based access network discussed above. FTTC supports multiple modems in a home sharing the same copper pair (or coaxial cable), which means it also supports a MAC protocol for upstream in this case. Finally, in the extreme case where a pure fiber loop is deployed to the home, we have FTTH architecture.

13.4 ADSL-based Broadband Service Architecture

In this section, we describe an ADSL-based residential broadband service architecture. The RBB network based on other xDSL technologies can be extended from this architecture. Figure 13-6 shows the ADSL network architecture, which consists of the access network, the regional broadband network and the home network.

The ADSL-based access network consists of an access node and a pair of ADSL modems, one at the CO (or remote access node) and one at the customer premise (such as at home). The ADSL modems at the CO and the residence are called the ATU-C (access termination unit) and the ATU-R, respectively. The ATU-R can be either a standalone external modem or an internal modem in a PC in the form of a NIC (network interface card). Also, the POTS splitter function can provided either by an external POTS splitter (shown in Figure 13-6) or by the ADSL modem (as an internal function). The access node is a multiplexer (at the CO or the remote node) that concentrates the upstream data from multiple ATU-Cs towards the regional broadband network, typically over a single physical link. Conversely, the access node also is a demultiplexer that distributes downstream data to the proper ATU-C(s). The regional broadband network (such as an ATM network) provides connectivity to various services such as Internet access and corporate network access.

With the external POTS splitter configuration, the ADSL modem only has two interfaces: the ADSL line interface and a network interface. The ADSL line interface is connected to the loop plant through the POTS splitters (at both ends) for communication between the pair of

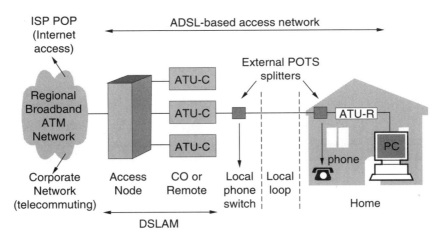

Figure 13–6   ADSL-based residential broadband network architecture

ADSL modems. The network interface for the ATU-R and ATU-C is to connect to the PC (or customer premise network) and the access node, respectively. For an external ATU-R, the network interface can be connected to the PC using an Ethernet, ATM (25 Mbps), P1394 or any other interface. For an internal ATU-R, the network interface can be a PCI bus interface inside the PC. Similarly, the ATU-C at the CO can also have different interfaces such as Ethernet and ATM, depending on the end-to-end network architecture.

The external POTS splitter has three interfaces: loop, ADSL and POTS interfaces. It can be placed outside the house. This simplifies home wiring as it allows direct connection from the POTS splitter's POTS interface to the entry point of the home telephony wiring system. A twisted pair connected to the ADSL interface of the POTS splitter (which delivers the higher spectrum that carries the ADSL signals) can be brought into the house to connect to the ATU-R. Note that the ATU-R must be powered separately inside the house. For regulatory purpose, the external POTS splitter can serve as the demarcation point and the ADSL modem becomes customer premise equipment (CPE).

If an ADSL modem provides the POTS splitting function internally, it will have an additional POTS interface. The ATU-C's POTS interface is connected to the CO telephone switch, while that of the ATU-R is connected to the home phone system. Since the ATU-R is located inside the house (for powering), this might require extra wiring from the ATU-R back to the side of the house where it enters the residential phone wiring system.

13.5 ADSL-based ATM-to-the-Home Architecture

To provide broadband services using ADSL, we need to design an end-to-end broadband service architecture in which the ADSL-based access network is only a subnetwork. Since ADSL is typically a telco deployment, they are required by regulations to provide connectivity to multiple service providers (such as ISPs and content providers). Hence, we need to distinguish between an access network provider (the telco providing ADSL service) and a service provider in the end-to-end service interoperability model. .

In this section, we discuss an ATM-to-the-home architecture over ADSL access network by designing an ATM architecture between the customer premise (terminating at home PCs) and the service networks (which also include corporate networks) to create an end-to-end broadband service architecture. This allows a virtual dial-up model based on ATM VCs instead of circuit switched connections (which lead to call blocking and inefficient bandwidth utilization). In addition to providing QoS, the ATM-based architecture can scale to different (asymmetric) rates to fully utilize the rate adaptive nature of ADSL. This also means that this architecture can evolve to support other xDSL technologies. Furthermore, it can support multiple layer 3 protocols (IP, IPX, etc.) using PPP over ATM architecture, as discussed below.

13.5.1 Architecture

To support ATM over ADSL is straightforward because ADSL is a physical layer technology using point-to-point transmission. Hence, supporting ATM over ADSL is very similar to supporting ATM over other standard physical layer technologies (such as SONET). We only need to define the transmission convergence sublayer for the ADSL technology, which has been recently specified by the ADSL Forum.[9]

13.5.1.1 DSLAM

In this ATM-to-the-home architecture, the access node is a multiplexer of ATM cells (an ATM layer device), while the ATU-Cs terminate the physical layer (ADSL). The access node can be combined with the attached ATU-Cs to form an ATM multiplexer with ATM ports terminating both physical and ATM layers. This combined device is called the digital subscriber line access multiplexer (DSLAM). The DSLAM multiplexes ATM

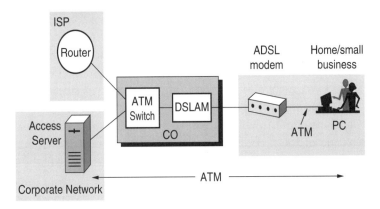

Figure 13–7   ATM over ADSL architecture

cells from the ADSL lines to the ATM access switch (typically over a single physical link) and demultiplexes cells in the reverse direction. The ATM access switch is a standard ATM switch that serves as the access switch to the regional broadband network. In addition, the ATM access switch might support additional functions to support certain DSLAM designs (to be discussed below). Figure 13-7 shows a simple configuration of the ATM over ADSL architecture, with the regional broadband network reduced to point-to-point ATM links to an ISP and a corporate network.

In the ATM-to-the-home architecture, a customer premise device terminates the ATM protocol with an UNI; each ADSL subscriber represents a UNI towards the DSLAM. However, this does not necessarily mean that the DSLAM terminates the UNI. In fact, there are different DSLAM designs that provide various levels of ATM functions. They represent different functional tradeoffs between the ATM access switch and the DSLAM.

A simple DSLAM design can provide only the virtual path crossconnect function without supporting any signaling protocols. A permanent VP can be assigned between each subscriber and the ATM access switch across the DSLAM. UNI signaling is transparent to the DSLAM and is terminated at the ATM access switch. Since there are multiple signaling channels from the UNIs of different ADSL subscribers, multiple signaling channels must be terminated at the ATM access switch over a single port. This DSLAM design implies that the ATM access switch supports the virtual UNI concept (as discussed in the signaling chapter) to provide SVCs between the customer premise and the destination networks.

Even with this simple DSLAM design (without signaling support), in many cases, SVCs can be supported with guaranteed QoS on an end-to-end basis (between the subscribers and the service providers). This applies to both downstream and upstream communications. Since downstream traffic to each DSLAM port originate from a single interface (from the ATM access switch), there is no output contention for downstream traffic at the DSLAM. This implies that downstream QoS can be guaranteed by virtue of the QoS guarantees provided by the ATM access switch to this output port. More specifically, for each connection request with a particular bandwidth requirement, the ATM access switch (which terminates UNI) ensures that the downstream bandwidth to individual ADSL subscriber does not exceed their ADSL link bandwidth. This is made possible by allocating a downstream peak bandwidth equal to the ADSL line rate (or lower by contract policy) to the VP for each subscriber and traffic shaping on a per VP basis at the access switch to DSLAM link. On the other hand, upstream traffic arrives on multiple ATU-C interfaces resulting in output contention similar to that of an ATM switch. Fortunately, the load of the ADSL subscribers are asymmetric with lower aggregate upstream rate, it is relatively easier to over-provision in the upstream direction so as to avoid dynamic bandwidth managing through signaling. However, if the DSLAM is designed to have such high concentration that there is no over-provisioning for upstream bandwidth, upstream QoS will not be guaranteed.

Nevertheless, there are two limitations to this simple DSLAM design. First, it introduces significant complexity to the ATM access switch because of the virtual UNI support. The reason is that the DSLAM can support hundreds of ADSL modem subscribers, which translates into hundreds of signaling channels terminating on the same port at the ATM access switch. Since ATM access switch is most likely based on a standard ATM switch, which has not been designed to support that many signaling channels per port. In addition, the ATM access switch needs to provide per VP based traffic shaping, which might not be widely available yet. Second, the virtual UNI approach has a limit of 256 signaling channels, because there are only 256 VPs available at the UNI. This limits the DSLAM to support at most 256 subscribers.

These limitations can be addressed by enhancing the DSLAM with UNI signaling capability. This means that the DSLAM can terminate the UNI signaling directly, instead of using either VP crossconnect or virtual UNI. Since there is usually a single port to the ATM access switch, the interface to the ATM access switch can be a UNI instead of the more complicated NNI. This means that a standard ATM switch can be used for the ATM access switch, because the latter only needs to support standard UNI (one signaling VC per port). The disadvantage of this approach is the increased complexity of the DSLAM to support UNI signaling. This can be avoided by off loading the signaling to an adjunct workstation that implements third party call control.

Note that for both DSLAM designs (VP crossconnect or with UNI signaling support), the customer premise sees an end-to-end ATM network connecting to the service providers. The DSLAM design choice is transparent to the ATM endpoints, because they are only functionality tradeoffs within the ATM network.

13.5.1.2 Customer Premise

In the ATM-to-the-home architecture, ATM is terminated at a PC at customer premise. This implies that either an external ATU-R has a standard ATM interface (such as ATM 25 Mbps) for connecting to the PC with the (same) standard ATM NIC, or the PC has an internal ATU-R implemented as an ATM-over-ADSL NIC. The latter means that the NIC terminates both ATM and ADSL protocols. With the external ATU-R, the ATM NIC must support traffic shaping on the aggregate upstream traffic to avoid overloading the upstream ADSL link.

13.5.2 Broadband Internet and Telecommuting Services

Point-to-point protocol (PPP)[10] is the primary protocol used for Internet access over PSTN dial-up connections. After the dial-up connection is set up to the ISP's terminal server, a PPP session is initiated to provide a wide range of functions required for Internet access, which include authentication, authorization, IP address and domain name assignment, encryption, compression and protocol negotiation (selecting IP among other layer 3 protocols). After the PPP process, the PC will have an IP address and can communicate as if it is on the Internet. As ISPs have invested heavily in this architecture, it is desirable to support a similar model when the connectivity is through an ATM network instead.

This leads to the approach of carrying PPP over ATM connections (using AAL 5)[11] for supporting broadband Internet access. Instead of a PSTN connection, we establish an ATM VC from the subscriber to the ISP, over which the PPP session is supported. The ATM connection can be terminated at a router at the ISP that has an ATM interface (instead of a dial-up modem bank). Initially, this can be either a UBR or ABR connection, if QoS is not required. Later, CBR and rt-VBR services can be added to support QoS, which requires bandwidth and QoS to be specified (implicitly or explicitly from the user point of view). This means that user can access the Internet by dialing an E.164 phone number (an ATM address format) similar to the PSTN dial-up access. Hence, the PPP over ATM approach adheres to the narrowband Internet service model currently driving the ISP business and provides a similar dial-up user interface.

Similarly, current remote access to corporate networks for telecommuting also uses the PPP over PSTN dial-up approach. The key potential difference from Internet access is that the layer 3 protocol used can be non-IP protocols (such as IPX or Appletalk), which is negotiated during the PPP setup. Hence, the PPP over ATM solution also applies to broadband telecommuting services. Furthermore, this model supports multiple ATM VCs carrying independent PPP sessions to both the ISP and the corporate network, allowing support of Internet access and telecommuting services simultaneously.

Although Internet access through an ATM network can be viewed as an internetworking problem between ATM and non-ATM networks, the internetworking protocols designed for campus networks such as LAN emulation,[12] classical IP over ATM (RFC 1577)[13] and multi-protocol over ATM (MPOA)[14] are not suitable. The reason is that they lack the security, session, and autoconfiguration functions required to support a public access network.

13.5.2.1 Null Encapsulation and VC Multiplexing of PPP over ATM

There are different ways of carrying PPP over AAL5, that is, different encapsulation schemes. From the end-to-end ATM architecture standpoint, PPP should be carried over AAL5 using VC multiplexing[15] (or null encapsulation). This means that there is no multiplexing with other protocols in parallel with PPP on the same VC. If protocol multiplexing is required, it can be supported by PPP because protocol multiplexing is a function of PPP. QoS can be guaranteed for each PPP session by specifying such requirements on the underlying ATM VC. Also, the security of the ATM connection is provided by the PPP security mechanisms, as all the data carried over the ATM VC are encapsulated within the PPP payload. Furthermore, this scheme avoids the overhead (both processing and transmission) associated with adding a multiplexing header to distinguish different protocols for each AAL5 frame.

The use of PPP over AAL5 based on null encapsulation can be specified during the UNI 3.1 call set up using the B-LLI information element's user information layer 3 protocol field. ISO/IEC TR 9577[16] already specified PPP with an IPI value of 0xCF in the extension octets.

13.6 Summary

In this chapter, we discussed the xDSL technology family in detail and explained how it can be used to enable residential broadband services. The xDSL family provides high-speed transmission over the copper loop. Also, an ATM end-to-end architecture over the xDSL-based network was discussed. We described how broadband Internet access and telecommuting can be simultaneously provided over this architecture.

13.7 References

[1]T. Kwok, "A Vision for Residential Broadband Services: ATM-to-the-Home," *IEEE Network Magazine,* Sept./Oct, 1995, pp. 14-28.

[2]W.Y. Chen and D. L. Waring, "Applicability of ADSL to Support Video Dial Tone in the Copper Loop," *IEEE Communications Magazine,* May 1994, pp. 102-109.

[3]D.L. Waring, J.W. Lechleider, T.R. Hsing, "Digital Subscriber Line Technology Facilitates a Graceful Transition from Copper to Fiber," *IEEE Communications Magazine,* March 1991, pp. 96-104.

[4]T.R. Hsing, J.W. Lechleider, D. L. Waring, "HDSL and ADSL: Giving new life to copper," *Bellcore EXCHANGE*, Bellcore, March/April, 1992, pp.3-7.

[5]P. J. Kyees, R. C. McConnell, K. Sistanizadeh, "ADSL: A New Twisted-Pair Access to the Information Highway," *IEEE Communications Magazine,* April 1995, pp. 52-60.

[6]The ADSL Forum, www.adsl.com.

[7]T. R. Hsing, C. T. Chen, J. A. Bellisio, "Video Communications and Services in the Copper Loop," *IEEE Communications Magazine,* Jan 1993, pp. 62-68.

[8]J. M. Cioffi, "Asymmetric Digital Subscriber Lines," Draft chapter from the CRC Handbook of Communications.

[9]The ADSL Forum, "ATM over ADSL Recommendations," TR-002, March 1997.

[10]W. Simpson, "The Point-to-Point Protocol (PPP)," *IETF Request for Comments: 1661*, July 1994.

[11]T. Kwok, I. Verbesselt, D. Veneski, P. Shieh, J. Loehndorf and R. Mwikalo, "An Interoperable End-to-End Broadband Service Architecture over ADSL Systems," white paper from Microsoft, Alcatel, Cisco Systems, FORE Systems, US Robotics and Westell, June 1997.

[12]The ATM Forum, LAN Emulation over ATM 1.0, af-lane-0021.000, Jan. 1995.

[13]M. Laubach, "Classical IP and ARP over ATM," *IETF Request for Comments: 1577*, Jan. 1994.

[14]The ATM Forum, MPOA 1.0, July 1997.

[15]J. Heinanen, "Multiprotocol Encapsulation over ATM Adaptation Layer 5," *IETF Request for Comments: 1483*, July 1993.

[16]ISO/IEC TR 9577:1990(E), "Information technology - Telecommunications and Information exchange between systems - Protocol Identification in the network layer," 1990-10-15.

Chapter **14**

Hybrid Fiber/Coax Network Architecture

14.1 Introduction

In the last chapter, we discussed a telco-based residential broadband network architecture. In this chapter, we discuss the cable-based residential broadband network in detail. We first give an overview of the legacy cable network architecture. It was originally designed to support only one-way analog TV broadcast service and has a tree-and-branch broadcast architecture. However, this architecture has many problems not only for supporting broadcast TV, but also for supporting new two-way interactive services such as broadband Internet access.

We discuss the emerging cable network architecture known as the hybrid fiber coaxial (HFC) network architecture. The HFC architecture not only solves the legacy cable network problems, but also can support two-way interactive services. We then show how a switched broadband cable network architecture can be achieved by designing an end-to-end ATM architecture. This is an ATM-to-the-home (ATTH) architecture because ATM cells are carried all the way to the home and terminated at the user terminals (set-top boxes or PCs).

14.2 Legacy Cable Network Architecture

The legacy cable network architecture is a broadcast network with a tree-and-branch topology (more detail below). It was originally designed for a one-way, one-to-many distribution of analog TV signals from the cable headend (the root). It was not until almost 1990 that the cable networks were seriously considered for two-way communications and interactive applications. In this section, we give an overview on current cable networks in the United States, which has a very extensive cable network infrastructure that passes 95% of the households. About two thirds of U.S. households subscribed to cable TV service in 1995.

14.2.1 History

The cable network was originally designed in the late 1940s to deliver broadcast TV signals to areas where antenna reception was unacceptable, such as rural areas or crowded urban areas with lots of high rise buildings making reception difficult. Each local community got its signals through a common antenna, which were then distributed through the coaxial tree and branch cable network architecture. Hence, the legacy cable television network has been called a community antenna television (CATV) system.

After the cable networks had saturated the areas with poor TV reception, the growth of cable network penetration became flat in the 1960s.[1] The arrival of satellite in the mid-1970s marked a significant turning point for the cable industry. Satellite provides each cable television network with additional TV channels that are not available through local TV broadcast. This made the cable networks much more than a CATV network for areas with poor reception. This additional content generates significant attractions for new subscribers even in areas that have good reception. Hence, this has substantially increased the penetration ever since, covering almost the entire population of the United States.

14.2.2 Topology

The legacy cable television network is a local video distribution system that serves a particular community. Each network can support from fewer than 100 subscribers (rural areas) to about a million subscribers (metropolitan areas). The cable network has a tree-and-branch topology that extends coaxial cables from the headend to the homes in its serving areas as shown in Figure 14-1. At the root of the tree is the cable headend, the information source of the network.

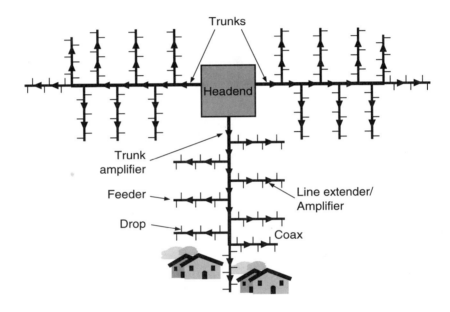

Figure 14–1   Legacy broadcast cable television system

The main purpose of the legacy cable network is to distribute video signals from its headend to the households within its serving areas. In general, each cable television system is operated independently with its own headend (partially because different cable television systems have different owners). Since the cable television networks were not designed for general communications networks between different communities, there is typically no connectivity between different cable television networks. Hence, the cable networks in the U.S. can be described as islands of disjoint local information distribution systems. For example, cable networks in San Francisco are not connected to those in Los Angeles.

The tree-and-branch cable network architecture consists of three parts: trunks, distribution plant and subscriber drops. A trunk is a point-to-point link that connects the headend to a neighboring area and is typically between 10 and 15 miles long. The trunks from the headend fan out in a star configuration to the neighborhood areas. Legacy trunks are primarily coaxial cables (see Figure 14-1). The advantage of coaxial cable is its ability to shield the transmission from off-air interference, allowing frequency reuse for each coaxial cable (similar to cellular telephony concept). However, the disadvantage of using coaxial cable is the high signal loss, which can be as much as 1 dB per 100 feet.[1] Hence, a coaxial trunk requires amplifiers installed every 2000 ft.; this results in about 30 or more amplifiers per trunk.[2]

Since a cable network may cover a large geographic area, multiple remote headends (hubs) may be used for distribution to individual local distribution plants, while all get their signals from a central headend. The connection between the central headend and the hubs can be coaxial cable, microwave links, or fibers.

Signals travel down a trunk and are broadcast to the distribution plant, the second part of the cable network. The trunk forms the backbone of the distribution plant in each neighborhood. The distribution plant consists of a number of rigid coaxial feeders connected to the trunk by bridge amplifiers. Each feeder has a maximum length of about a mile and a half, with one or two line extender amplifiers. Hence, both the trunk and the distribution plant are active (with amplifiers) requiring powering.

The subscriber drop cables, the third part of the tree and branch architecture, represent the final link to the subscribers. They also comprise 50% of the cable mileage of the cable networks, as compared to 12% for trunks and 38% for the distribution plants.[1] Subscriber drops are flexible, passive (no amplifiers) coaxial drop cables connected to each feeder by passive taps. This means that the subscriber drops are the only passive part of the cable network. Each coaxial drop cable is typically 150-200 feet long, but generally less than 400 feet.

14.2.3 Network Architecture: Passband and Broadcast

The legacy cable television network uses a passband transmission system to deliver video content in the downstream direction (from headend to subscribers). This means that it uses frequency division multiplexing (FDM) to carry multiple analog video signals over the cable network. In the United States, each analog video signal occupies a 6 MHz bandwidth (while some European countries use 8 MHz).

To support the passband distribution architecture, the headend consists of three key components: analog modulators, frequency translators and signal combiners. They are shown in Figure 14-2. Each analog modulator transmits TV signals onto a 6 MHz channel. Each 6 MHz-wide signal is frequency shifted to its corresponding 6 MHz frequency band by the frequency translator. Finally, the combiner multiplexes all these signals together (with non-overlapping frequency) onto the cable trunk for broadcast distribution.

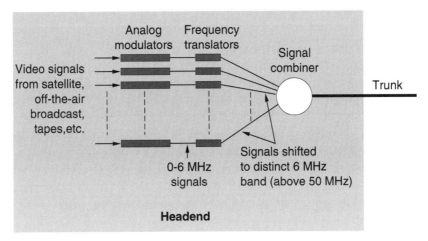

Figure 14–2   Legacy cable headend architecture

The legacy cable network has a one-way broadcast network architecture. All subscribers on the network share the same tree-and-branch network and the broadcast spectrum. Subscribers can receive any of the channels, provided they are authorized, by tuning to the desired channel with a tuner. There is no limit to the number of subscribers on the network that can receive the same channel or any combination of different channels. In other words, the cable network guarantees non-blocking for receiving broadcast signals for all subscribers. Therefore, the cable network architecture, though simple and without using any active switching equipment, can effectively support its main application – broadcast TV. However, the fact that the cable television network architecture has been optimized for broadcast applications makes it more difficult to support interactive applications that require switching functions in the network.

The cable headend is the source of information in the legacy cable network. The headend receives two types of content for the legacy cable networks: local and national. Live local content typically comes from local TV stations through off-air broadcast or microwave links. There is also content generated by a studio adjacent to the headend. In addition, there is recorded content such as local advertisements stored in tapes at the headend. The headend contains advertisement insertion equipment to interleave taped advertisement with the live local and national content. National content originates from one or more national centers and is sent to the headend via satellite.

14.2.4 Spectrum Allocation

The spectrum on the legacy cable network is divided into two parts: downstream transmission to and upstream transmission from the subscribers. The majority of the cable systems in the United States use a sub-split spectrum allocation scheme, which allocates the majority of the spectrum to downstream transmission. The sub-split system allocates frequency above 50 MHz for downstream transmission, while below 50 MHz (5 to 42 MHz or a subset of this range) is reserved for upstream transmission. We assume a sub-split cable network in the following discussion.

Cable networks in the United States can be classified according to the amount of frequency available for downstream transmission into three types: small, medium and large capacity.[1] Small capacity networks operate from 50 MHz to between 220 and 270 MHz, which can carry up to 30 channels. These networks are mainly old systems and account for less than 10% of total plant mileage in the U.S. Medium capacity networks operate from 50 MHz to between 330 and 400 MHz, which can carry between 40 to 52 channels. These cable networks account for 75% of the total plant mileage in U.S. and serve a wide range of communities. Large capacity cable networks operate from 50 MHz to between 450 to 750 MHz, carrying between 60 to 110 channels. These are mainly new plants or recently upgraded plants. Although they only account for about 15% of the cable plant mileage in the United States, increasing numbers of large capacity cable networks are expected as the cable industry expands its service to more than analog broadcast services.

Many cable plants, however, do not have the return amplifiers installed or activated (even if installed) to allow upstream transmission in part of or the entire upstream spectrum. Currently, less than 10% of the cable plants in the U.S. are two-way capable or active.[3] Hence, even though the cable television system is *potentially* two-way capable, a majority of the legacy cable television networks are one-way (downstream) broadcast networks only. Nevertheless, many urban cable systems are being rapidly upgraded to support high-speed cable data service,[4] such as broadband Internet access. This is discussed in more detail later.

14.3 The Hybrid Fiber Coax Network Architecture

14.3.1 Legacy Cable Network Problems

Although the legacy cable network architecture seems to be sufficient for delivering TV signals, it has problems in reliability, signal quality and return path communications.

14.3.1.1 Reliability

As discussed above, there are a large number of active elements (such as amplifiers) in the legacy cable television network, especially along the trunks. The failure of any amplifier can terminate the signals to all the subscribers downstream of that amplifier. Studies have shown that more than 50 percent of the outages are due to power surges, utility network outages, and blown out failures of active elements.[5] Hence, reducing the number of amplifiers in the cable plant can increase its reliability and reduce maintenance cost.

14.3.1.2 Signal Quality

Another problem is the quality degradation of the analog video received by the subscribers. This arises from the large number of amplifiers on the signal paths (each introduces distortion into the video signal), the gradual degradation in the quality of the coaxial cable and ingress noise. Signal quality is important not only because of customer satisfaction, but also because the FCC has specified a minimum signal quality in the early 1990s.

14.3.1.3 Return Path

There is also the problem of supporting upstream communications in the legacy cable network. This is critical for supporting two-way interactive applications and Internet access. To enable upstream data transmission, it requires more than just making the return path active with the return amplifiers and diplex filters. There are many problems in return transmissions.

There is a fundamental capacity limitation in the cable television network for upstream communications. Since the cable network is a shared medium, all subscribers on the cable network have to share the upstream spectrum for communications. As there are potentially thousands or tens of thousands of subscribers sharing the 37 MHz bandwidth (5 – 42 MHz) available, the average bandwidth available to each subscriber is very limited.

Another set of problems for upstream transmission in the legacy cable network has to do with the quality of such transmission. The noise in the upstream direction is significantly worse than that in the downstream direction due to the noise funneling effect.[6] Since the noise in the upstream direction from each subscriber (can be thousands) all get merged as they travel upstream to the headend, the noise aggregation in the return direction can be very serious. Another upstream transmission problem arises from mis-aligned return amplifiers, as a result of loose engineering practices over the years.

There are a number of noise sources in the return path. First, there is broadband impulse noise that come from both man made (engine ignition, motors, computers) and natural (such as lightning) sources. Second, there are a variety of noises that are generated within the subscriber's home. This is caused by home devices that are closed to the coaxial cable connectors (especially loose or open connectors). In-house noise management is a challenge because it is typically inaccessible and uncontrollable by the cable operators.[7] Third, there is the recurring narrowband ingress noise from such sources such as AM short-wave radio in the atmosphere in the 5-30 MHz spectrum. Such noise can enter the cable network through the distribution plant and the subscriber's in-house wiring. However, recent studies indicate that narrowband ingress noise is much less severe than the other two sources, contrary to earlier understanding.

All these problems with the legacy cable network architecture have led to the search for a better cable network architecture for the future. The hybrid fiber-coax (HFC) architecture has emerged to be the target network architecture for the cable industry. This is discussed in detail next.

14.3.2 The HFC Network Architecture

In the late 1980s, the hybrid fiber coaxial (HFC) cable network architecture was proposed.[8] The HFC architecture not only addresses the above cable network problems for supporting legacy TV broadcast applications, but also enables two-way switched broadband communications to support a wide range of residential broadband applications. Since the HFC architecture is critical for the cable industry to move beyond their mature cable TV businesses, it has become the target cable network architecture to introduce residential broadband services.

The HFC network architecture takes of advantage fiber optics transmissions and uses a new topology to significantly increase the bandwidth available per household. Also, it uses digital transmission and sophisticated modulation techniques to significantly increase downstream and upstream capacity. Furthermore, by enabling the return path and providing switching functions at the headend, the HFC provides two-way switched broadband communications. These key elements of the HFC architecture are discussed in detail next.

14.3.2.1 Fiber Optics

Since the early 1980s, the cable industry has been deploying fiber optics to replace coaxial cable-based trunks and the associated amplifiers. Fiber optics transmission systems have very low signal loss even over long distance. This significantly decreases the number of amplifiers from the headend to each home, from over 30 to as few as three only needed for the feeder portion. With fewer points of failure, this increases the cable plant reliability and reduces maintenance costs. Also, with fewer active elements, there is less cable plant power consumption, which results in lower operation costs. Furthermore, since fibers are much more immune to external noise than coaxial cable, they can preserve the picture quality delivered and help meet the corresponding FCC regulations.

Last but not the least, the much higher transmission bandwidth available on fiber opens the door of future growth in capacity of the cable network. Fiber provides a scalable path for deploying future multimedia applications that require high bandwidth. The HFC architecture takes advantage of these superior characteristics of fibers optics to support the envisioned residential broadband applications.

14.3.2.2 The HFC Topology: Node Architecture

The HFC architecture is not just the replacement of the coaxial cable trunks with fiber optics link, but also the introduction of the node concept. The node architecture divides all homes passed by the cable network into small neighborhood areas of about 500 (generally less than 2000). There is a dedicated fiber trunk from the headend extending to each neighborhood area to terminate at a fiber node, as shown in Figure 14-3. A fiber node typically has 3 to 4 coaxial feeders fanning out within the neighborhood area.[2] The main function of the fiber node is electro-optic conversion of signals between the fiber trunk and coaxial cables. As in the legacy cable distribution plant, each feeder is connected to a set of subscriber drop coaxial cables, each is connected to a house. The typical distance between the headend and a fiber node is about 25 km[4] while the distance between the fiber node and a house is typically less than 2 km.

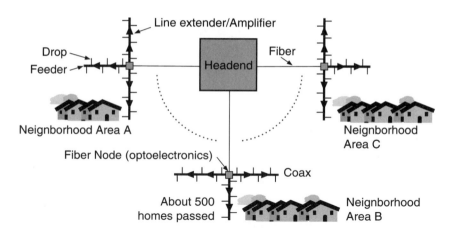

Figure 14–3 Hybrid fiber coaxial network architecture

The combination of using fibers and coaxial cable gives rise to the name **hybrid fiber/coax** network architecture (see Figure 14-3). The HFC topology has a star configuration with the headend as the center and a fiber extended to each neighborhood terminated at the fiber node. A mini tree-and-branch coaxial cable configuration extends from each fiber node to cover around 500 homes.

The node architecture has the advantages of increased reliability and upstream transmission capacity. The division of the entire service area into small neighborhood areas of about 500 homes makes each area independent of other neighborhood areas. This compares to the fiber trunk serving from 2000 to 5000 a few years ago[1] and is much smaller than the 10,000 to 15,000 homes passed per area a decade ago. This implies that the failure at any points in the cable plant, such as a fiber trunk or feeder cable, only affects a particular neighborhood area (or subset thereof), instead of the entire service area. This significantly increases the reliability of the network, which is in addition to the increased reliability achieved using fibers instead of coaxial cable and reducing the number of amplifiers. Some study have shown that the HFC architecture has increased availability from 99.97% to 99.995%; unavailability has improved from 2.5 hours to 25 min per year. The maintenance cost has also decreased with fewer failures and reduced power consumption by as much as 12%.[2]

Since the node architecture is very similar to the cellular network concept of frequency reuse, the HFC architecture allows sharing of downstream and upstream bandwidth among much fewer homes, about 500 as compared to 1000s or 10,000s in the legacy network. This significantly increases the bandwidth that can be provided to each subscriber. Furthermore, fewer homes sharing an upstream channel also implies fewer noise sources that contribute to the noise aggregation effect in the return direction.

14.3.2.3 Digital Transmission

In the early 1990s, the era of digital broadcast has also arrived with the promise of much larger capacity for more channels, and hence the notion of the "500 channels" cable network was proposed. This is possible because of advances in high-order digital modulation technologies and the arrival of standards-based video compression technologies such as MPEG-2.

To support digital broadcast services over the cable network, digital modulation on the cable plant is required. A key downstream modulation technique for HFC is QAM (quadrature amplitude modulation).[9] 64 QAM modulation carries about 27 Mbps of user data (after forward error correction, FEC, which is required due to the noise in the cable network) over a 6 MHz channel, while the emerging 256 QAM technology can support about 36 Mbps of user data after FEC. A competing modulation technique is VSB (vestigial side band).[10] The 16 VSB modulation supports about 38 Mbps of user data, which is roughly equivalent to the 256 QAM technology.

Also, MPEG-2 compressed movies require as low as 3 Mbps. Hence, each 6 MHz channel can support about 9 digital movies instead of only one analog movie using 64 QAM technology. With 60 channels between 50–450 MHz, potentially more than 500 channels can be supported. In practice, the number of channels that will be dedicated for digital transmission is primarily a business decision.

So far we have discussed a basic usage of the HFC architecture that primarily provides broadcast service, which still assumes a one-way passband transmission system that is very similar to the legacy tree-and-branch architecture (albeit much higher capacity). However, the power of the HFC is not only to deliver 500 broadcast digital channels, but also to enable two-way switched broadband communications. The latter requires enabling the return channel and providing switching functions in the headend, as discussed next.

14.3.2.4 Upstream Transmission

Activating the return path in the cable plants typically means providing the capability of upstream transmission in the range of 5 to 42 MHz. With the HFC architecture, the noise in the return direction has been significantly reduced due to the alleviated noise funnel effect, as there are much fewer homes sharing the same return fiber. Nevertheless, this still requires the following criteria being satisfied.

First, there must be return amplifiers that operate in that upstream spectrum on the coaxial portion of the cable plant. Second, there must be diplex filters to ensure only signals within the spectrum between 5–42 MHz get transmitted upstream, while signals above 50 MHz get transmitted downstream. Third, there are lasers that operate in 5–42 MHz spectrum in the return direction on the fiber trunks in the HFC architecture. Fourth, the coaxial distribution plant is carefully tightened up (especially at connection points) to ensure that there are no significant noise sources that contribute to a lot of the interference in the return path. Most of the noises come from the drop cable portion and in-home coaxial distribution.

Cable plants that are not currently return path active (more than 90% of cable plants in the United States as of 1996) can be in a number of different conditions. Some have no return amplifier at all as they were not designed to support upstream transmission. Some have return amplifiers but they were never turned on because they were never used. Also, even if they have amplifiers, they may be the older generations that operate only in the 5–30 MHz range and hence need to be upgraded to support 5–42 MHz. More importantly, since most of these plants have never been used for upstream transmission, the amount of noise in the upstream spectrum varies significantly. It is not uncommon to find a plant that has a lot of noise in the return path because this spectrum was never used before and so was never tested for ingress noise. Hence, potentially a lot of effort is required to clean up the plant (such as tightening the cable connectors) to ensure that there are no significant noise sources to affect upstream communications.

Since the upstream bandwidth in the HFC architecture is shared (similar to the legacy cable network), a medium access control (MAC) protocol is required to provide coordinated transmissions for the subscribers in each neighborhood area. This is to avoid contention of the upstream transmission. The choice of the MAC protocol is critical in optimizing the usage of the upstream bandwidth, providing upstream quality of service and supporting multicast capability. An ATM-based MAC protocol is being standardized by the IEEE 802.14 committee that provides QoS guarantees.

14.3.2.5 Switched Two-Way HFC Architecture

The HFC architecture segments the serving population into many independent neighborhood areas, each served by an individual fiber trunk extending to a fiber node. This modular architecture lends itself easily to providing switched services to each neighborhood area.

The HFC architecture can be extended from a broadcast to a switched network architecture by providing switching functions at the headend (assuming there is upstream communications capability). A switch or switched network (such as an ATM) in the headend is required to switch individual information streams to different homes, as opposed to broadcasting the same information for all homes (see Figure 14-4). The switch function is also required for upstream communications from the home devices (such as PCs and set-top boxes) to the headend servers, or external networks such as the Internet. Furthermore, the switched network allows both the servers and the home devices to communicate with external networks. The details of switching functions and configuration are discussed in the next section.

Hence, the switched HFC network architecture provides each subscriber with two-way interactive capabilities, allowing access to personalized information and interacting with the network service in an individual manner.

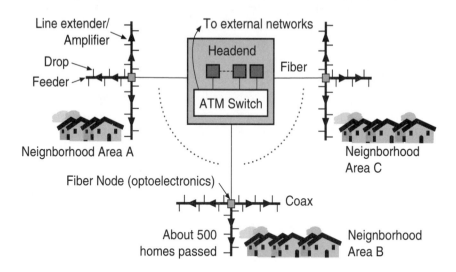

Figure 14–4 Switched broadband cable TV architecture

14.4 ATM-to-the-Home over HFC Network

In this section, we discuss how to design an ATM architecture over the HFC to enable a two-way switched broadband cable network. The ATM protocols are operating end-to-end from the customer premise devices to the destination networks (such as the Internet or corporate networks), making it an ATM-to-the-home architecture.

14.4.1 Interactive TV and the Internet

As discussed earlier, the key focus on residential broadband services has been changed from enabling interactive TV services to providing residential broadband Internet access. With ITV services, the home termination unit of the HFC network is typically a set-top box connecting to a TV as the display. On the other hand, with high-speed Internet access, the customer premise has a cable modem connecting to a PC. At the headend, it changes from an ATM node switch (discussed below) to the cable data modem termination system (CDMTS) (see Figure 14-5), which differs mainly by reducing the number of 6 MHz channels supported. Even though both the home devices and headend networking components are different for the ITV services and the broadband Internet services, they represent a very similar architecture from supporting ATM point of view. In fact, enabling broadband Internet access can be viewed as an intermediate step towards providing full blown interactive TV services.

14.4.2 ATM-to-the-Home Architecture

With an end-to-end ATM network between the home devices and the destination networks and services over the HFC network, the home devices view the HFC network as a standard ATM network. However, emulating an ATM network over the HFC system is less straightforward than over ADSL network, because the HFC network (unlike ADSL) is not a point-to-point network.

The HFC network is an asymmetric shared medium type network. All the homes supported by a neighborhood node share the HFC network for upstream transmission, with the headend terminal as the sole recipient. On the other hand, only the headend can transmit on the downstream direction and it performs one-to-many broadcast to all the homes. Furthermore, since the HFC system is a passband system, the home termination unit (set-top box or cable modem) must tune to the right upstream and downstream channels to communicate with the headend. Hence, depending on the pair of channels that the home unit tunes to, it can share the channels with a different set of home devices.

The challenge of designing the ATTH over HFC network is to emulate a point-to-point network to support ATM protocols. This is achieved by the combination of the headend termination unit (the ATM node switch or CDMTS) and the home termination unit to provide a layer of protocol that emulates a point-to-point network to ATM protocols. In addition, the ATTH architecture also provides connectivity to both external networks (such as the Internet or a third party content provider's network).

14.4.2.1 ATM Node Switch

The ATM node switch is a fundamental building block of the ATM-based HFC network, as shown in Figure 14-5. It interfaces the HFC's passband transmission systems at the headend and provides a standard baseband interface (such as an OC-3c ATM interface) to the other headend components or external networks. As such, it helps emulate a point-to-point link to each home termination unit on the rest of the network.

The ATM node switch is the basic unit of replication of the HFC architecture. Each ATM node switch is responsible for supporting a sepa-

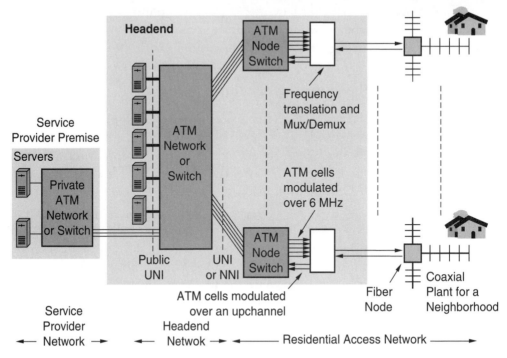

Figure 14–5 An ATM-to-the home over HFC architecture

rate neighborhood area (see Figure 14-5). (However, this ATM node switch model is only for the functional model. For actual implementation, an ATM node switch can support multiple nodes, especially if each node only has a single active downstream channel for interactive digital services.) Hence, the ATM node switch enables the modularity of the ATTH HFC design.

Figure 14-6 shows the functional components of the ATM node switch. Its implementation may involve multiple network devices internally. The ATM node switch provides a standard ATM interfaces (such as OC-3c) to the headend ATM network and UNI signaling can be supported on that link. In a smaller configuration where the ATM network and the ATM node switch are combined into a single ATM switch, UNI interfaces are provided to connect directly to the servers in the headend or the service provider networks.

To support the passband, asymmetric and shared HFC architecture, the ATM node switch is enhanced from a standard ATM switch in a number of ways. First, there are cable interfaces to the HFC access network. These cable interfaces are unidirectional interfaces for downstream and upstream communications over the HFC architecture. Each downstream interface carries ATM cells modulated using a digital modulation technique such as 64 QAM within 6 MHz. Each upstream interface demodulates upstream signals, followed by an inverse FEC if needed. It also provides a MAC protocol function to support upstream sharing of each upstream channel.

In the cable industry, since modulation equipment has not been standardized, the corresponding modulation and demodulation technologies in the home termination unit and the headend must currently be provided by the same vendor or close partners to ensure interoperability. This ATTH architecture limits the nonstandard components to the cable transmission's physical and MAC layer only, which is unavoidable until standards-based equipment becomes widely available. Hence, we can define the rest of the architecture with standard ATM interfaces to expedite interoperability. In the future, we expect standards and specifications from organizations such as IEEE 802.14 for the MAC and The ATM Forum for the ATTH over HFC.

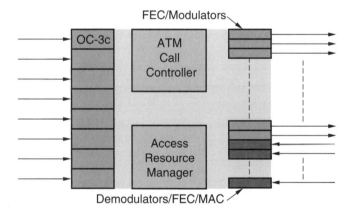

Figure 14–6   Conceptual components of an ATM node switch

The ATM node switch also differs from the current ATM switch in that the cable interfaces have separate upstream and downstream (unidirectional) ports, while standard ATM interfaces have bi-directional ports. Furthermore, the number of upstream and downstream interfaces is typically different. Since current ATM signaling only supports bi-directional ports, the signaling protocol needs to be extended to support this configuration.

The access resource manager (ARM) is responsible for bandwidth allocation and load balancing among multiple upstream and downstream ports. The bandwidth allocation and path selection is similar to the NNI functions of an ATM switch.

Hence, the ATM node switch serves the key functions of the ATTH architecture: enables modularity, emulates an ATM network, provides bandwidth management (and QoS guarantees) and provides standard interfaces. By combining the ATM functionality and cable components, it allows specifications of the standard external interfaces to expedite deployment.

The CDMTS is basically a scaled down version of the ATM node switch for supporting cable modems at home to enable broadband Internet services. It has one or a very small number of downstream ports and one upstream port, because supporting Internet access is much less bandwidth demanding than video or demand (which requires sustained high bandwidth).

14.4.2.2   Home Termination Unit

The home termination unit (HTU) is the home device that terminates the HFC network to process the physical, MAC layer and probably the ATM protocol. The HTU may or may not be the actual subscriber terminal for which the application information is finally processed and displayed. For example, for ITV services, the HTU is typically a set-top box and displayed through a TV, while for Internet service, the HTU is a cable modem and connects to a PC (externally or internally) for application processing and display.

The HTU is the counterpart to the ATM node switch in the headend. Together they help emulate a point-to-point link to support ATM protocols above. Reciprocal functions of the ATM node switch are provided at the HTU for modulation and demodulation of upstream and downstream signals, respectively. Hence, the HTU includes a downstream demodulator, upstream modulator and corresponding tuners.

In the ATTH architecture, the subscriber terminals (PC or set-top box) terminate the ATM protocols. This means that both the PC and the set-top box process the ATM layer protocols. If the HTU is not the subscriber terminal, another connection (ATM) is required for communication between the HTU and the subscriber terminal.

14.4.2.3 Headend Network

As discussed before, the headend network is responsible for providing the core switching capability for each home to access different services provided by the headend servers and external networks such as the Internet. For the ATTH architecture, the headend network can be a public or private ATM network (may consist of a single switch initially) that interconnects external networks to the HFC subscribers, through the ATM node switch or CDMTS.

14.4.2.4 Headend Servers

For ITV services, the headend servers are responsible for providing key residential broadband services offered by the cable operators to the subscribers. These servers include, but are not limited to, applications servers, billing servers, financial transaction servers, movie servers and authentication servers. Note the implementation of these broadband services can range from a single physical server providing multiple services, to multiple physical servers, each providing a single service to satisfy loading, response time and reliability requirements.

When a subscriber wants to access a service, he or she needs to communicate with a set of servers that provide the service. For example, if the subscriber wants to watch a movie, communications must be provided not only to the movie server to get the movie, but also to a financial transaction server to pay for the movie and an authentication server to make sure the person is authenticated.

For broadband Internet services, the headend servers can include Web-caching servers to provide high-speed access to popular Web pages and Web-hosting servers for local content. Alternatively, Web caching and hosting servers can be consolidated at the regional headend, instead of replicated at all the local headends. Such tradeoff depends on the cable plant configuration, subscriber population and communication costs.

14.4.3 Operation

Each downstream port on the ATM node switch is connected to a 6 MHz downstream channel of the cable plant. To receive ATM cells, the HTU must first tune to the right downstream channel before decoding the information. Each HTU can set up its virtual channels (VCs) within its 6 MHz downchannel. In other words, each HTU has a virtual link (carrying multiple VCs) between the home and the headend. This emulates a point-to-point link to support ATM protocols; the difference is that the link is virtual and has variable bandwidth. Each downchannel also is shared by multiple home devices to reduce cost (and increase efficiency). Each HTU receives its information by demultiplexing ATM cells based on a VPI/VCI that has been preallocated for its communications.

The return channel is used in a similar fashion to multiplex the return data from each home device, except that a MAC protocol is required to share the bandwidth in the upstream direction. Either the VC space is partitioned to share among the HTUs in same area, or an additional header is added to encapsulate the ATM cells to distinguish ATM cells from different HTUs.

14.4.4 End-to-end Protocol Architecture

Figure 14-7 shows the end-to-end layered protocol model for the switched broadband cable network architecture based on the ATTH architecture. All (non-signaling message) data from the headend servers or HTUs are encapsulated in IP packets before converting to ATM cells (by the AAL). The main reason for using IP over ATM is to provide a common internetworking layer so that the servers and set-top boxes can communicate to entities outside the cable system (which may not be on an ATM network). Furthermore, the software and applications developed for this ATM architecture can be reused on other networking architectures because they are shielded by the common IP layer.

To access the Internet or corporate networks, the PPP over ATM model discussed in the last chapter can also apply here to support security, layer 3 protocol negotiation, IP address assignment, among other functions. Hence, the above layered model needs to be amended by adding the PPP layer between the IP and ATM layers, as shown in Figure 14-8.

From the protocol layering point of view, the major difference between the upstream and downstream model is the addition of the MAC layer below the ATM layer for the upstream direction. This is necessary because the return spectrum is shared among all set-top boxes belonging to the same node. This MAC layer includes the use of FDM to support multiple upstream channels, and is responsible for coordinating access to these upstream channels.

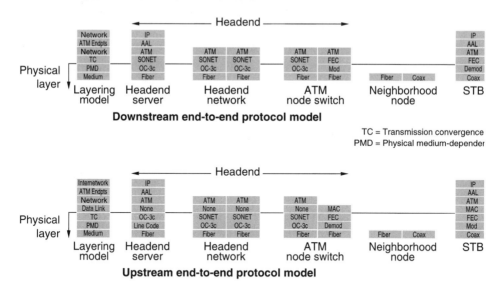

Figure 14–7 End-to-end protocol model of ATM-to-the-home HFC network architecture

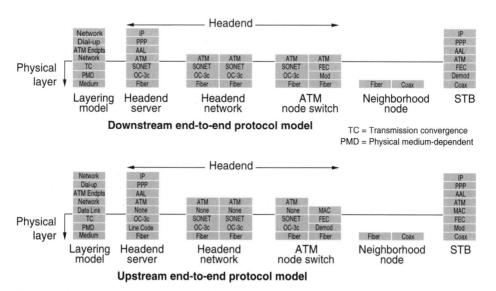

Figure 14–8 PPP over ATM model for the ATM-to-the-home HFC network architecture

14.4.5 Hybrid Cable Modem: Analog Modem Dial-up Return

Recently, a hybrid form of cable modem has been introduced for use only on the high-speed downstream channel of the cable network, while using another analog modem for return over the PSTN. The motivation of this type of hybrid modem is to deploy such modems in cable plants that have not been upgraded with return capability.

Although this hybrid approach helps expedite the deployment of high speed Internet access through the cable network, using an analog modem over the PSTN as the return channel introduces a number of problems to the Internet access architecture. First, it reintroduces the disadvantages of the narrowband dial-up Internet access, such as blocking probability in the network and tying up the phone line. Second, it complicates IP address assignment because this might require more than one IP address to be supported separately for the upstream and downstream communications. In general, the PC's protocol stacks need to be modified to support this scenario. Third, it introduces a complexity for coordinating the upstream and downstream as they are probably terminated at different locations in the network: upstream at the ISP, downstream at the headend. Fourth, using the analog return channel increases the asymmetry of the bandwidth and might introduce a downstream throughput limit because of limited upstream bandwidth. The reason for this is that many protocols (such as TCP) require two way communications that are dependent on each other; reducing the capacity in one direction can restrict the throughput in the opposite direction.

14.5 Summary

In this chapter, we discussed the cable-based residential broadband network in detail. We first gave an overview of the legacy cable network architecture. It was originally designed to only support one-way analog TV broadcast service and has a tree-and-branch broadcast architecture. However, this architecture has many problems not only for supporting broadcast TV, but also is not suitable for supporting new two-way interactive services such as broadband Internet access.

Next, we discussed the emerging cable network architecture known as the HFC network architecture. The HFC architecture not only solves the legacy cable network problems, but also can support two-way interactive services. We then showed how a two-way switched broadband cable network architecture can be achieved by designing an end-to-end ATM architecture. This is an ATM-to-the-home architecture because ATM cells are carried over the HFC network and terminated at the user terminals (set-top boxes or PCs) at the customer premise.

14.6 References

[1]W. Ciciora, "Cable Television in the United States – An overview," CableLabs, 2nd Edition, 1995.

[2]D. Hammer, "The major difference between HFC and FTTC," *Cable World,* Jan. 30, 1995, pp. 25.

[3]R. Brown, "The return path: Open for business?" *Communications Engineering & Design,* Dec. 1994, pp. 40-43.

[4]M. P. Vecchi, "TimeWarner's RoadRunner

' Service," *SCTE 1997 Conference on Emerging Technologies,* Jan 8-10, 1997, Nashville, Tennessee, pp. 203-211.

[5]R. Pinkham, "Combining Apples and Oranges: The modern fiber/coax network," *Telephony,* Feb. 7, 1994, pp. 28-32.

[6]C. Eldering, N. Himayat, F. Gardner, "CATV return path characterization for reliable communications," *IEEE Communications Magazine,* Aug. 1995, pp. 62-69.

[7]B. Bauer, "In-home cabling for digital: Future-proofing signal quality and minimizing signal outages," *Communications Technology,* April, 1995, pp. 60-68.

[8]J. Chiddix and D. Pangrac, "Fiber Backbone: A proposal fro an evolutionary CATV network architecture," *NCTA '88 Technical Papers,* 1988.

[9]B. Bauer, "Drop system and Component Performance: Emerging Requirements in a high bandwidth 64 QAM digital world," *NCTA Technical Papers,* 1993, pp. 244-270.

[10]R. Cita, R. Lee, "Practical Implementation of a 43 Mbit/sec (8bit/Hz) digital modem for cable television," *NCTA Technical Papers,* 1993, pp. 271-279.

Index

A

AAL 1, 183, 184–90
    applications, 190
        CBR video, 190
        circuit emulation, 190
    asynchronous clock recovery, 185–86
        adaptive clock recovery, 186
        synchronous residual time stamp
            (SRTS), 185–86
    convergence sublayer, 187–88
        CS-PDU non-P format, 188
        CS-PDU P format, 188
    functions, 184–87
        constant bit rate service, 184–85
        error protection, 187

        timing recovery, 185–86
        unstructured/structured data
            transfer service, 187
    SAR sublayer, 188–89
        sequence number (SN) field, 189
        sequence number (SNP) field, 189
    synchronous clock recovery, 185
AAL 2, 183
AAL 3/4, 183, 190–94
    compared to AAL 5, 197
    CS sublayer, 191–92
        buffer allocation, 192
        error detection, 191–92
    message and streaming modes, 194
    SAR sublayer, 192–93
        error protection, 193

multiplexing, 193
AAL 5, 183, 194–98
   compared to AAL 3/4, 197
   CS sublayer, 196
   functions, 195–97
      data delineation, 195–96
      error protection, 195
   SAR sublayer, 197
AAL-CU, 183
AAL-PDU, 172–78, 182, 184
ABR service, 255–59
   ABR flow control, 258–59
   feedback mechanisms, 256–58
   main objective of, 255–56
Absolute delay requirements, 86–90
   real-time block transfer applications,
      89–90
   real-time streaming applications, 87–
      89
      telephony, 87–89
ADD PARTY ACKNOWLEDGE mes-
   sage, 224
ADD PARTY message, 224, 234–35
ADD PARTY REJECT message, 224
Address registration, 212
Admission control, 117–18
ADSL-based ATM-to-the-home archi-
   tecture, 302–7
   broadband Internet and telecommut-
      ing services, 305–7
      null encapsulation/VC multiplex-
         ing of PPP over ATM, 306–7
   customer premise termination, 305
   digital subscriber line access multi-
      plexer (DSLAM), 302–5
ADSL-based broadband service architec-
   ture, 300–301
ADSL technology, 298–99

ADU loss ratio, 95
ADUs, *See* Application data units
   (ADUs)
Advertising industry, and ATM net-
   works, 7
"Always connected," 76, 294
Anycast capability, 213
Application classification, 41–58
   communication applications, 42–50
      definition, 42
      delivery requirements, 43–44
      human vs. non-human, 49–50
      information types, 42–43
      mobility, 48–49
      networking attributes of applica-
         tions, 42–50
      number of parties, 46–47
      symmetry, 44–46
      wired/wireless access, 47–48
   non-real-time applications, 56–57
   real-time block transfer applications,
      52–56
      bandwidth- vs. latency-limited
         applications, 55–56
      Internet applications, 53
      Web browsing, 53–55
   real-time streaming applications, 50–
      52
Application data units (ADUs), 42, 52–
   53, 61–63, 74–75, 89
Application QoS requirements, *See* Quality of service (QoS) requirements
Applications, networking attributes of,
   42–50
Application sharing, 54
Application traffic requirements, 59–78
   applications requirements, 60–61
      traffic and QoS requirements, 61

bandwidth, 70–77
    average bandwidth, 71–72
    peak bandwidth, 70–71
    real-time block transfer applica-
        tions, 73–75
    real-time streaming applications,
        72–73
    time-based information delivery
        requirements, 75–76
    traffic generation patterns, 61–70
        adaptive applications, 69
        ADU length distribution, 62–63
        CBR vs. VBR, 66–67
        continuous vs. bursty traffic, 62
        packet length distribution, 63–66
        self-similarity traffic, 66
        traffic asymmetry, 69–70
        traffic shaping, 67–68
    user level behavior, 76–77
ARPANET, 108
Asynchronous clock recovery, 185–86
    adaptive clock recovery, 186
    synchronous residual time stamp
        (SRTS), 185–86
Asynchronous time division (ATD) mul-
    tiplexing, 118 19
Asynchronous transfer mode, See ATM
ATM, 4–5
    admission control, 117–18
    advantages of, 119–23
        strategic, 122–23
        technical, 119–22
    and Broadband Integrated Service
        Digital Network (B-ISDN), 105
    asynchronous time division multiplex-
        ing, 118–19
    connectionless service over, 180
    definition of, 4–5

design, 4–5, 6
    key goal of, 5
fast packet switching, 109–17
goal of, 60
and the Internet, 5–8
and Intranets, 8
layered protocol, 129–30
NSAP encoding formats, 210–12
packet switching, 108–9
principles of, 105–24
Protocol Reference Model (PRM),
    143–68
and residential broadband networks,
    8–9
resource reservation and admission
    control, 117–18
scalability, 121–22
    bandwidth, 121
    geography, 121
    number of endpoints, 121
    physical media, 121
strategic advantages, 122–23
    compatible architectures, 123
    multi-vendor support, 123
    one networking architecture, 122–
        23
switched point-to-point architecture,
    107–8
technical advantages of, 119–22
    efficiency, 122
    flexibility, 120
    high bandwidth, 119–20
    integration, 120–21
    operations, 122
    quality of service guarantee, 120
    scalability, 121–22

xDSL network architecture vs.,
285–308
ATM access signaling, 201–36
ATM addressing, 210–12
ATM UNI signaling protocol, 218–36
call states, 232–33
connection types, 213–17
first party vs. third party control,
217–18
multipoint-to-multipoint connection, 217
multipoint-to-point connection,
215–16
point-to-multipoint connection,
214–15
point-to-point connection, 213–
14, 234–36
permanent and switched VCs, 202–3
SAAL, 209
signaling protocol model, 209
signaling virtual channel, 203–4
VPI and VPCI, 204–8
proxy signaling capability, 206–7
virtual UNIs and ATM multiplexer, 207–8
See also ATM UNI signaling protocol
ATM adaptation layer (AAL), 159–60,
169–99
comparison of types, 198
end-to-end ATM protocol model,
170–72
functions, 172–77
error control mechanisms, 174–75
multiplexing of multiple data
streams, 177
receive buffer allocation, 176
reduction of CPU processing overhead, 173–74

segmentation/reassembly, 172–73
synchronization and clock recovery, 175–76
traffic pattern maintenance, 176
service class attributes, 178–79
connection mode, 178–79
end-to-end timing relationship,
178
source traffic pattern, 178
service classes, 177–81
class A service, 179, 183
class B service, 179, 183
class C service, 179, 183
class D service, 179–80, 183
class X service, 180
service model evolution, 181
types, 181–98
AAL 1, 183, 184–90
AAL 2, 183
AAL 3/4, 183, 190–94
AAL 5, 183, 194–98
AAL-CU, 183
common part (CP), 181–82
comparisons of, 198
convergence sublayer (CS), 181–
82
origin of, 177–78
segmentation and reassembly
(SAR) sublayer, 181–82
service specific part (SSP), 181–82
See also AAL 1; AAL 3/4; AAL 5
ATM addressing, 210–12
address registration, 212
anycast capability, 213
group address, 213
ATM anycast capability, 213
ATM cell format:
8-bit VPI field in UNI format, 154

GFC field in UNI format, 154
16-bit VCI field in UNI format, 154
12-bit VPI field in NNI format, 154
ATM endpoints, 126–27
   negotiation between, 133
ATM end system address (AESA), 210,
   212
ATM Forum, 105–6
   UNI signaling protocol, 209
ATM group address, 213
ATM interfaces, 127–29
ATM layer, 152–59
   ATM cell format, 153–57
   ATM layer functions at the UNI,
      157–59
      cell discrimination, 159
      cell header generation/extraction,
         159
      cell rate decoupling, 157–59
      loss priority indication/selective
         cell discarding, 159
      multiplexing ATM connections,
         157
      traffic shaping, 159
   hourglass model, 160–61
   sublayers, 155–56
ATM layered protocol, 129–30
ATM networks:
   basic elements of, 125–27
   basic operations, 130–32
      call establishment, 130–31
      cell sequencing and VC routes,
         132
   call negotiation/renegotiation, 132–33
   connecting, 127
   standard interfaces, 127–29
   VC number:
      assigning, 133–34

      and translation, 134–35
virtual channel connection (VCC),
   136, 138–41
   multiple VCCs for an application,
      140
   one VCC for each application,
      139–40
   one VCC for multiple applica-
      tions, 139
   one VCC per pair of locations,
      141
virtual path connection (VPC), 136–
   38, 140–41
   one VPC per application, 140
   one VPC per component, 140
   one VPC per pair of locations,
      141
ATM QoS parameters, 251–52
   cell loss ratio (CLR), 252
   maximum cell transfer delay (CTD),
      251
   peak-to-peak cell delay variation
      (CDV), 251–52
ATM service categories, 252–55
   ABR service, 255
   attributes, 253
   CBR service, 254
   nrt-VBR service, 254
   rt-VBR service, 254
   UBR service, 254–55
ATM switches, 126
   serialization function at, implementa-
      tion of, 215–16
ATM-to-the-home architecture, 9, 273,
   309–10
   ADSL-based, 302–7
   analog model dial-up return, 330
   ATM node switch, 323–26

end-to-end protocol architecture,
  328–29
headend network, 327
headend servers, 327
home termination unit, 326
operation, 327–28
over HFC network, 322–30
ATM UNI signaling protocol, 218–36
  AAL parameter negotiation, 231
  ATM call states, 232–33
  connection negotiation, 231–32
  point-to-multipoint connection, 234–
    36
    leaf initiated join call, 235–36
    root initiated, 234–35
  signaling messages, 218–25
    call reference, 219
    message length, 219
    message type, 218, 219
    protocol discriminator, 219
  signaling procedures, 226–32
    AAL parameter negotiation, 231
    CALL PROCEEDING message,
      229–30, 233
    call release, 232
    call setup, 226–31
    CONNECT ACKNOWLEDGE
      message, 230, 232, 233
    connection negotiation, 231–32
    CONNECT message, 226, 230–
      33
    NOTIFY message, 232
    point-to-point connection, 226–32
    premature data transfer problem,
      232
    RELEASE COMPLETE mes-
      sage, 232

RELEASE message, 232
    SETUP message, 226, 227–29,
      230, 233
    timers, 233–34
    See also SETUP message
ATU-C, 300–301
ATU-R, 300–301
Authority and Format Identifier (AFI),
  210
Available bit rate (ABR) service, See ABR
  service
Average bandwidth, 71–72

B

Backbone switching, trunking connec-
  tions to simplify, 137
Bandwidth, 70–77
  average, 71–72
  peak, 70–71
  real-time block transfer applications,
    73–75
  real-time streaming applications, 72–73
Bandwidth- vs. latency-limited real-time
  block transfer applications, 55–56
BECN scheme, 258–59
BER, See Bit error ratio (BER)
Best-effort service, 37–38, 57
B-frames, 62
B-ICI (Broadband Inter-Carrier Inter-
  face), 129
Bi-directional applications, 44–45
B-ISDN, 105–11
  and ATM, 105–6
B-ISDN PRM:
  and ISO OSI Reference Model, 164–
    67
    internetworking, 165–67
    pure ATM networks, 164–65

Bit error ratio (BER), 64, 95–96

Bridges, 35, 39

Broadband Higher Layer Information (B-HLI), 228

Broadband Integrated Service Digital Network (B-ISDN), 105–11
    and ATM, 105–6

Broadband Inter-Carrier Interface (B-ICI) protocol, 218

Broadband Lower Layer Information (B-LLI), 228–29

Broadcast networks, 27–29
    circuit switching on shared medium, 28
    defined, 28
    one-way broadcast, 27–28
    packet switching on shared medium, 29
    two-way communications, 28

Buffer management, 244–46

Bursty traffic, 62

C

Cable data modem termination system (CDMTS), 322

Cable TV networks:
    classification of, 314
    as one-way broadcast type networks, 45
    topology of, 46

Call admission control (CAC), 117–18

Call establishment, 130–31

Call negotiation/renegotiation, 132–33

CALL PROCEEDING message, 222, 229–30, 233, 234

Call states, 232–33

CBR service, 254

CBR streaming video applications, 190

CBR vs. VBR, 66–67

Cell-by-cell-based traffic management, 240–48
    buffer management, 244–46
    CLP control, 247
    feedback control, 247–48
    scheduling, 241–44
    traffic shaping, 241
    usage parameter control, 240–41

Cell clumping, 241

Cell conformance and cell compliance, 250–51

Cell delay variation (CDV), 176, 179, 251–52

Cell delay variation tolerance (CDVT), 250

Cell dropping, 174–75

Cell losses, causes of, 174

Cell Loss Priority (CLP), 156–57

Cell loss ratio (CLR), 252

Cell rate decoupling, 157–59

Cell sequencing and VC routes, 132

Chat, 62–63

Circuit switching, 19–22, 25
    advantage of, 20
    multiplexing mechanisms, 21–22
    on shared medium, 28

Class A service, 179, 183

Class B service, 179, 183

Class C service, 179, 183

Class D service, 179–80, 183

Classic packet switching, problems of, 109–11

Class X service, 180

Clock synchronization, 175–76

CLP control, 247

Collaboration, 50, 54

Communication applications:

definition, 42

delivery requirements, 43–44

human vs. non-human users, 49–50

information types, 42–43

mobility, 48–49

networking attributes of applications, 42–50

number of parties, 46–47

symmetry, 44–46

wired/wireless access, 47–48

Community antenna television (CATV) system, 310

CONNECT ACK message, 226

CONNECT ACKNOWLEDGE message, 223, 230, 232, 233

Connection admission control (CAC), 239–40

Connection-based traffic management, 239–40

    connection admission control (CAC), 239–40

    network resource management (NRM), 240

Connection identifier, 204

Connectionless packet switched networks, 26, 115

Connection-oriented packet switching, 26–27, 113–16

Connection traffic descriptor, 250–51

    cell conformance and cell compliance, 250–51

    cell delay variation tolerance (CDVT), 250

CONNECT message, 223, 226, 230–33, 234

    replied by the called party, 230

    sent to the calling party, 231

Constant bit rate (CBR), 66–67, 178

Constant bit rate service, AAL 1, 184–85

Continuous traffic patterns, 62

    at network layer, 68

Continuous vs. bursty traffic, 62

Control plane, multi-plane model, 163

Control plane application requirements, 60

Convergence sublayer:

    AAL 1, 187–88

        CS-PDU non-P format, 188

        CS-PDU P format, 188

Corporate offices, and ATM networks, 7

CPCS PDU, 196

CPU processing overhead, reduction of, 173–74

CSMA/CD, 34, 36, 37

CS-PCI, 191

CS-PDU, 191–92, 194

CS sublayer:

    AAL 3/4, 191–92

        buffer allocation, 192

        error detection, 191–92

    AAL 5, 196

D

Data country code (DCC), 210

Data delineation, AAL 5, 195–96

Datagram model, 115

Default packet size limit, 64–65

Delay requirements, 81–92

    absolute, 86–90

        real-time block transfer applications, 89–90

        real-time streaming applications, 87–89

    delay components, 81–86

        packetization delay, 82

        processing delay, 85–86

propagation delay, 84
    queuing delay, 85
    transmission delay, 82–84
  delay distribution, 81
Delay variation (jitters) requirements, 90–92
Delivery requirements:
  information, 43–44
  and information type, 43–44
Dial-up:
  analog model dial-up return, 330
  Internet access, 267–69
Digital subscriber line access multiplexer (DSLAM), 302–5
Digital video encyclopedias, 6
Distance, ideal communications network, 9
DNS (domain name service), 65
Domain Specific Part (DSP), 210–11
DROP PARTY ACKNOWLEDGE message, 224
DROP PARTY message, 224

E

E.164 format, 210
Education, and ATM-based Internet, 6
8-bit VPI field in UNI format, 154
Electronic mail, 10, 44
Electronic yellow pages, 9
E-mail, 10, 44
End system identifier (ESI), DSP, 211
End-to-end ATM architecture, 282–83
End-to-end ATM protocol model, 170–72
End-to-end timing relationship, 178
Engineers, and ATM networks, 7
Error concealment, 100
Error control mechanisms, 174–75

Error protection:
  AAL 1, 187
  AAL 3/4, 193
  AAL 5, 195
Error requirements, 92–100
  error characterization, 95–96
    application layer, 95
    network layer, 95
    physical layer, 95–96
  error tolerances, 93–94
    components, 94
    compression ratio, 94
    information types, 93–94
    usage, 94
  for non-real-time applications, 100
  for real-time block transfer applications, 100
  for real-time streaming applications, 96–100
ESI field, 212
Ethernet, 5, 28, 33, 57, 107, 120, 280
  Fast, 38, 40, 123
  Gigabit, 37, 38, 40
  switched, 36–37, 123
  10-baseT, 36, 84

F

Fair Buffer Allocation (FBA), 246
Fast Ethernet, 38, 40, 123
Fast packet switching, 109–17
  techniques of, 111–17
    connection-oriented packet switching, 113–16
    hardware-based design, 111–12
    no link-by-link error control on payload, 116–17
    parallel processing, 111–12

short fixed size packet, 112–13

FDDI, 33

FECN scheme, 258–59

Feedback control, 247–48

Fiber optics, 317

File transfer applications, 55

First-in-first-out (FIFO) algorithm, and packet switching, 242

First party vs. third party control, 217–18

Frequency division multiplexing (FDM), 21, 312

Fully connected point-to-point networks, 16–18

G

G.723.1 audio codec, 72

Generic cell rate algorithm (GCRA), 249

GFC field in UNI format, 154

Gigabit Ethernet, 37, 38, 40

Graphics, as non-time-based information, 42–43

Group address, 213

H

H.263 video codec, 72

HDSL technology, 297

Headend network, 327

Headend servers, 327

Header error check (HEC), 147

Health care industry, and ATM-based Internet, 6

Hierarchical encoding, 100

Higher layer protocols, 160

Hospitals, and ATM networks, 7

Hotels, and ATM networks, 7

Hourglass model, 160–61

HTTP (hypertext transfer protocol), 6, 53, 264

Hub-based LANS, 36

Hybrid conversion point, 88

Hybrid fiber/coax network architecture, 309–31

ATM-to-the-home over, 322–30

digital transmission, 319–20

fiber optics, 317

legacy cable network architecture, 310–15

broadcast network architecture, 312–14

history of, 310

passband transmission system, 312–14

spectrum allocation, 314–15

topology of, 310–12

legacy cable network problems, 315–22

reliability, 315

return path, 315–16

signal quality, 315

node architecture, 318–19

switched two-way HFC architecture, 321–22

upstream transmission, 320–21

Hybrid fiber copper (HFCu) systems, 297

I

Ideal communications network, 9–12

distance, 9

location, 9–10

media, 10–11

time, 10

IEEE LLC/SNAP mechanism, 139

I-frames, 62

Image browsing applications, 44

Individual users, and ATM networks, 7

Information elements (IEs), 204, 218–19
    mandatory, SETUP message, 227–28

Information types, 42–43
    and delivery requirements, 43–44

Initial Domain Part (IDP), 210

Instantaneous overload, packet switching, 24

Integrated local management interface
(ILMI) protocol, 212

Integrated Service Digital Network
(ISDN), 8, 106
    POTS vs., 106

Interactive multimedia applications, 3–9
    ATM, 4–5
        and the Internet, 5–8
        and Intranets, 8
        and residential broadband networks, 8–9

Interactive television (ITV), 8, 263–65
    and the Internet, 322–23

International Code Designator (ICD),
210

Internet, 108, 271
    and ATM, 5–8
    characteristics of, 32–33
    and interactive TV, 322–23
    IP (Internet Protocol) packet, 32–33
    limitations of, 37–39
        best-effort service, 37–38
        broadcast shared medium architecture, 38
        internetworking, 39
    upgrading to an ATM backbone, 6

Internet applications, 53
    classification of, 51

Internet Engineering Task Force (IETF),
38, 39

Internet Protocol (IP), 165

Internet Service Providers (ISPs), points
of presence (POPs), 267–70, 276–79,
294

Internetworking, 35–36, 165–67
    with legacy LANs using IP, 165–67

Intranets:
    and ATM, 8
    characteristics of, 33
    hub-based LANS, 36
    internetworking, 35–36
    limitations of, 37–39
        best-effort service, 37–38
        broadcast shared medium architecture, 38
        internetworking, 39
        100 Mbps Ethernet, 37
        shared medium LANs, 33–35
        switching hubs, 36–37

Invalid ATM cells, 147–48

IP (Internet Protocol) packet, 32–33

ISSLL (Integrated Services over Specific
Link Layers), 38

ITU-T H.325 videoconferencing standard, 72

ITV, *See* Interactive television (ITV)

J

Jitters, 176, 186
    requirements, 90–92

L

LAN Emulation (LANE), 165

Large capacity cable networks, 314

Leaf-initiated join (LIJ) call, 235–36

LEAF SETUP FAILURE message, 225
LEAF SETUP REQUEST message, 225, 235
Leaky bucket model, 71, 249, 250
Legacy cable network architecture, 310–15
    broadcast network architecture, 312–14
    history of, 310
    passband transmission system, 312–14
    spectrum allocation, 314–15
    topology of, 310–12
Legacy cable network problems, 315–22
    reliability, 315
    return path, 315–16
    signal quality, 315
Link-by-link flow control, 109–10
Local area networks (LANs), 5, 8, 27, 33, 121–22
    shared medium LANs, 33–35, 37–38
Location, ideal communications network, 9–10
Locking to the source clock, 185
Loss packets, 65–66

M

MAC layer, 150–52
MAC (medium access control) protocol, 29, 34, 37, 64, 281, 321
Management plane, multi-plane model, 163
Management plane application requirements, 60
Maximum burst size (MBS), 249
Maximum cell transfer delay (CTD), 251
Maximum transfer unit (MTU), 64, 70
Media, ideal communications network, 10–11

Medium capacity cable networks, 314
Message and streaming modes, AAL 3/4, 194
Metropolitan area networks (MANs), 84
Minimum cell rate (MCR), 249
Mobility, 48–49
    types of, 49
Movie downloads, 44
MPE decoder, 85–86
MPEG-2 compression, 320
MPEG compression, 62
MTU size of link layer, 64
Multimedia applications:
    ideal communications network, 9–12
        distance, 9
        location, 9–10
        media, 10–11
        time, 10
    interactive, 3–9
Multimedia conferencing, 54
Multi-plane model, 161–63
    control plane, 163
    management plane, 163
    user plane, 162–63
Multiplexing methodology, for packet switching, 25
Multiplexing of multiple data streams, 177
Multipoint applications, 46–47
Multipoint-to-multipoint connection, 217
Multipoint-to-point connection, 215–16
Multiprotocol over ATM (MPOA), 163

N

Negotiation, calls, 132–33
Network access point (NAP), 268
Network architectures, 15–40

broadcast networks, 27–29
circuit switching on shared medium, 28
one-way broadcast, 27–28
packet switching on shared medium, 29
two-way communications, 28
fully connected point-to-point networks, 16–18
switched point-to-point networks, 18–27
circuit switching, 19–22
packet switching, 22–27
Network infrastructures, limitations of, 30–39
Networking attributes of applications, 42–50
Networking functions, categories of, 60
Network interface card (NIC), 174, 280–82
Network layer addresses, 35
Network multi-player games, 54–55
Network-node interfaces (NNI), 128–29
Private NNI, 129
Network resource management (NRM), 240, 241–43
Network Service Access Point (NSAP) encoding format, 210
NEW LEAF ANNOUNCE ACKNOWLEDGE message, 225
NEW LEAF ANNOUNCE message, 225
Non-real-time applications, 43, 56–57
Non-real-time VBR service, 254
Non-time-based information, 42
NOTIFY message, 232
nrt-VBR service, 254
NSF Backbone, 264

NSFnet, 65

O

100 Mbps Ethernet, 37
One-way broadcast, 27–28
One-way communication, 44–46
Open loop control, 247

P

Packet header, 23–24
Packetization delay, 65, 82
Packet length distribution, 63–66
default packet size limit, 64–65
effects of loss packets, 65–66
MTU size of link layer, 64
packetization delay, 65
packet loss probability, 64
transmission delay, 65
Packet loss probability, 64
Packet misrouting ratio, 95
Packet routing, 23
Packet switching, 22–27, 39, 108–9
and broadcast shared media, 25–26
connectionless/connection-oriented, 26–27
efficiency of, 25
and first-in-first-out (FIFO) algorithm, 242
instantaneous overload for, 24
multiplexing methodology for, 25
packet header, 23–24
packet switches:
functions of, 24
routing tables in, 24
problems of, 109–11
on shared medium, 29
PDU loss ratio, 95

Peak bandwidth, 70–71
Peak cell rate (PCR), 248–49
Peak-to-peak cell delay variation (CDV), 251–52
Permanent virtual connections (PVCs), 202–3
Personal mobility, 49
P-frames, 62
Physical layer, ATM, 146–50
Physical media dependent (PMD) layer, 146–47
Points of presence (POPs), ISPs, 267–70, 276–79, 294
Point-to-multipoint connection, 214–15, 234–36
    leaf initiated join call, 235–36
    root initiated, 234–35
Point-to-point applications, 46–47
Point-to-point connection, 213–14, 226–32, 234–36
    leaf initiated join call, 235–36
    root initiated, 234–35
Point-to-point networks:
    fully connected, 16–18
    switched, 18–27
        circuit switching, 19–22
        packet switching, 22–27
        permanent connections, 27
Point-to-point protocol (PPP), 305–7
Private-Network Node Interface (P-NNI), 129, 218
Private UNI, 129
PRM, *See* Protocol Reference Model (PRM)
Processing delay, 85–86
Program clock reference, 176
Propagation delay, 84
Protocol control information (PCI), 173

Protocol data units (PDUs), 172–74
Protocol Reference Model (PRM), 143–68
    layered architecture, 144–60
        ATM adaptation layer (AAL), 159–60
        ATM layer, 152–59
        higher layer protocols, 160
        MAC layer, 150–52
        physical layer, 146–50
Proxy signaling capability, 206–7
PSTN, *See* Public switched telephone network (PSTN)
Public switched telephone network (PSTN), 12, 15–16, 20, 30–32, 39, 59, 283
    advantages of, 30–31
    characteristics of, 30–31
    limitations of, 31–32
        bandwidth, 32
        inefficiency, 31–32
        inflexibility, 31

Q

QAM (quadrature amplitude modulation), 319
QoS requirements, *See* Quality of service (QoS) requirements
Quality of service (QoS) requirements, 79–102
    delay requirements, 81–92
        delay components, 81–86
        delay distribution, 81
        delay variation (jitters) requirements, 90–92
    error requirements, 92–100
        error characterization, 95–96
        error tolerances, 93–94

for non-real-time applications,
  100
for real-time block transfer applications, 100
for real-time streaming
  applications, 96–100
Queuing delay, 85

R

RBB networks, *See* Residential broad-
  band (RBB) networks
Real estate industry, and ATM networks,
  7, 8
Real-time applications, 43
Real-time block transfer applications,
  52–56
  bandwidth requirements, 73–75
  bandwidth- vs. latency-limited appli-
    cations, 55–56
  Internet applications, 53
  Web browsing, 53–55
Real-time streaming applications, 50–52,
  69, 178
  bandwidth requirements, 72–73
  two-way, 51
Real-time VBR service, 254
Receive buffer allocation, 176
Regional operation centers (ROCs), 270
RELEASE COMPLETE message, 223,
  232, 234
RELEASE message, 223, 232
Remote offices, and ATM networks, 7
Renegotiation, calls, 132–33
Residential access network (RAN), 273–
  74
Residential broadband (RBB) networks,
  263–84
  and ATM, 8–9

connectivity, 269–71
  corporate networks, 269–70
  Internet, 269
  local content, 270
  peer-to-peer communication,
    270–71
dial-up Internet access, 267–69
functional requirements, 271–72
  easy migration from existing ISP
    access infrastructure, 271
  multicast, 272
  multiple service class support, 272
  multi-protocol support, 271
  quality of service support, 272
  security, 271–72
  simultaneous connectivity, 271
legacy residential networks and Internet access, 265–67
service architecture, 272–83
  broadband (RBB) Internet access,
    277–79
  cable modems, 275–76
  CO and headend networks, 276–
    77
  end-to-end ATM architecture,
    282–83
  external modems, 280–81
  in-home network architecture,
    279–82
  internal PC modems, 281–82
  residential access network, 273–76
  xDSL modems, 274–75
service requirements, 269–72
Residential Internet accesses, 287
Resource reservation, 117–18
RESTART ACKNOWLEDGE message,
  225
RESTART message, 225

Routers, 32, 35, 39
RSVP (Resource ReSerVation Protocol), 39
rt-VBR service, 254

S

SAR-PCI, 192
SAR-PDU, 188–90, 192–93, 197
SAR-SDUs, 197
SAR sublayer:
    AAL 1, 188–89
        sequence number (SN) field, 189
        sequence number (SNP) field, 189
    AAL 3/4, 192–93
        error protection, 193
        multiplexing, 193
    AAL 5, 197
Scalability, 121–22
    bandwidth, 121
    geography, 121
    number of endpoints, 121
    physical media, 121
Scheduling, 241–44
    for real-time/non-real-time applications, 242
SDSL (single-line DSL) technology, 299
Selector (SEL), DSP, 211
SEL fields, 212
Self-similarity traffic, 66
Service class attributes, 178–79
    connection mode, 178–79
    end-to-end timing relationship, 178
    source traffic pattern, 178
Service classes:
    ATM adaptation layer (AAL), 177–81
    class A service, 179, 183
    class B service, 179, 183
    class C service, 179, 183

    class D service, 179–80, 183
    class X service, 180
Service Data Units (SDUs), 147
Service mobility, 49
Service model evolution, ATM adaptation layer (AAL), 181
Service Specific Connection Oriented Protocol (SSCOP), 209
Service Specific Coordination Function (SSCF), 209
SETUP message, 222, 224, 226, 227–29, 230, 233, 234
    from calling party to attached ATM switch, 227–29
    mandatory IEs, 227–28
        ATM traffic descriptor, 227
        broadband bearer capability, 227
        called party number, 227
        quality of service parameter, 227–28
    optional IEs, 228–29
        AAL parameters, 228
        Broadband Higher Layer Information (B-HLI), 228
        Broadband Lower Layer Information (B-LLI), 228–29
    to called party from destination ATM switch, 230
Shared medium LANs, 33–35, 37–38
Shared white board, 54
Side-tone echo, 88
Signaling messages, 131, 218–25
    call reference, 219
    message length, 219
    message type, 218, 219
    protocol discriminator, 219
Signaling procedures, 226–32
    AAL parameter negotiation, 231

CALL PROCEEDING message, 229–30, 233
call release, 232
call setup, 226–31
CONNECT ACKNOWLEDGE message, 230, 232, 233
connection negotiation, 231–32
CONNECT message, 226, 230–33
NOTIFY message, 232
point-to-point connection, 226–32
premature data transfer problem, 232
RELEASE COMPLETE message, 232
RELEASE message, 232
SETUP message, 226, 227–29, 230, 233
Signaling protocol, 27
Simple and Efficient Adaptation Layer (SEAL), *See* AAL 5
16-bit VCI field in UNI format, 154
Small capacity cable networks, 314
Small office/home office (SOHO), 5
SONET, 148, 185
Source traffic descriptor, 248–49
Space division multiplexing (SDM), 21
Speech activity detector (SAD), 92
SSCS-PDU, 194
STATUS ENQUIRY message, 223
STATUS message, 223
Stock brokers, and ATM networks, 7
Structured data transfer (SDT), 187
Subscriber drop cables, 312
Subscriber loop architecture, 287–91
    CSA guidelines, 290
    digital transmissions in the loop, 289–90
    ISDN, 290–12
    subscriber loop, 287–89

Sustainable cell rate (SCR), 249
Switched Ethernet, 36–37, 123
Switched point-to-point architecture, 107–8
Switched point-to-point networks, 18–27
    circuit switching, 19–22
        multiplexing mechanisms, 21–22
    packet switching, 22–27
        connectionless/connection-oriented, 26–27
        multiplexing methodology for, 25
        packet header, 23–24
        packet switch functions, 24
    permanent connections, 27
Switched two-way HFC architecture, 321–22
Switched virtual connections (SVCs), 202–3
Switching hubs, 36–37
Symmetry:
    applications, 44–46
    in bi-directional bandwidth, 296
    communication applications, 44–46
    traffic, 69–70
Synchronous clock recovery, AAL 1, 185
Synchronous residual time stamp (SRTS), 185–86
Synchronous transfer mode (STM), 118

T

T1 lines, 289–90
TCP/IP protocol suite, 32, 34, 69
Telephone networks, 30–32
    characteristics of, 30–31
    topology of, 46
Telephony, 51, 65

absolute delay requirements for supporting, 87–89
  echo constraints, 88–89
  pure delay constraints, 87–88
ADU for, 92
and circuit switching, 20–21
delay variation (jitters) requirements, 92
error requirements for, 96–99
  network layer, 96–98
  optimal packet class, 98–99
10-baseT Ethernet, 36, 84
Terminal mobility, 49
Text, as non-time-based information, 42–43
Time, ideal communications network, 10
Time-based information, 42, 50–51
  defined, 50
  real-time delivery of, 51
Time-based information delivery requirements, 75–76
Time division multiplexed (TDM) data stream, 42
Time division multiplexing (TDM), 21–22
Timers, 233–34
Timing recovery, AAL 1, 185–86
Token Ring, 33, 57
Traffic asymmetry, 69–70
Traffic contract, 248–52
  ATM QoS parameters, 251–52
  ATM traffic parameters, 248–49
    maximum burst size (MBS), 249
    minimum cell rate (MCR), 249
    peak cell rate (PCR), 248–49
    sustainable cell rate (SCR), 249
  connection traffic descriptor, 250–51

cell conformance and cell compliance, 250–51
cell delay variation tolerance (CDVT), 250
source traffic descriptor, 248–49
Traffic generation patterns, 61–70
  adaptive applications, 69
  ADU length distribution, 62–63
  CBR vs. VBR, 66–67
  continuous vs. bursty traffic, 62
  packet length distribution, 63–66
    default packet size limit, 64–65
    effects of loss packets, 65–66
    MTU size of link layer, 64
    packetization delay, 65
    packet loss probability, 64
    transmission delay, 65
  self-similarity traffic, 66
  traffic asymmetry, 69–70
  traffic shaping, 67–68
Traffic management, 237–48, 252–55
  cell-by-cell-based, 240–48
  connection-based, 239–40
  See also ATM service categories
Traffic pattern maintenance, 176
Traffic requirements, See Application traffic requirements
Traffic shaping, 67–68, 241
Transmission convergence (TC) sublayer, 146–47
Transmission delay, 65, 82–84
Tree-and-branch cable network architecture, 311–12
12-bit VPI field in NNI format, 154
Two-point CDV, 251
Two-way communications, 28

U

UBR service, 254–55
UNI Signalling 4.0, 248
Universities/schools, and ATM networks, 6, 7
Unspecified bit rate (UBR) service, 254–55
Unstructured data transfer (SDT), 187
Usage parameter control, 240–41
User-network interfaces (UNI), 128–29
    Private UNI, 129
User plane, multi-plane model, 162–63
User plane application requirements, 60

V

Valid ATM cells, 147
Variable bit rate (VBR), 66–67, 178
VCC, See Virtual channel connection (VCC)
VC number:
    assigning, 133–34
    and translation, 134–35
VDSL (very high speed DSL) technology, 299–300
Video, 38
    error effects on, 99–100
        error concealment, 100
        hierarchical encoding, 100
    as time-based information, 42
Video compression standards, 38
Videoconferencing, 10, 12, 43–44
    ITU-T H.325 videoconferencing standard, 72
Video mail, 8
Video-on-demand, 9, 12
Video phone, 12
Virtual channel connection (VCC), 136, 138–41

multiple VCCs for an application, 140
one VCC for each application, 139–40
one VCC for multiple applications, 139
one VCC per pair of locations, 141
usage in ATM networks, 138–41
Virtual channel identifier (VCI), 136
Virtual connections (VCs), ATM networks, 114
Virtual path connection identifier (VPCI), 204–8
Virtual path connection (VPC), 136–38, 140–41
    one VPC per application, 140
    one VPC per component, 140
    one VPC per pair of locations, 141
    usage in ATM networks, 138–41
Virtual path identifier (VPI), 138, 204–8
Virtual UNIs, 208
Voice mail, 10
VPC, See Virtual path connection (VPC)
VP switch, 138

W

Web browsing, 5, 41, 43, 44, 53–55, 89, 264
    file transfer applications, 55
    multimedia conferencing, 54
    network multi-player games, 54–55
Weighted fair queuing (WFQ) algorithm, 244
Wide area networks (WANs), 5, 27, 121–22
Wired/wireless access, 47–48
    base stations, 48
World Wide Web (WWW), 5–6, 8–10, 76

X

X.25, 27, 108, 116
xDSL family, 8, 295–300
    ADSL technology, 298–99
    bandwidth, 296
    bi-directional bandwidth, symmetry
        in, 296
    HDSL technology, 297
    lifeline POTS support, 297
    maximum loop distance, 296–97
    SDSL technology, 299
    VDSL technology, 299–300
xDSL modems, 274–75
xDSL network architecture:
ATM vs., 285–308
cable modem threat, 286–87
interactive TV market, 286
Internet opportunity, 286
introduction of, 286
subscriber loop architecture, 287–91
xDSL technologies, 291–95
    history of, 291–92
    xDSL characteristics, 292–95
        "always connected," 294
        bandwidth improvement, 292–95
        point-to-point, 294
        rate adaptive, 295
        simultaneous POTS support, 295